Of Men and Mountains

/\

by

WILLIAM O. DOUGLAS

1914

Contents

	Foreword	ix
I.	The Cascades	1
II.	Yakima	19
III.	Infantile Paralysis	30
IV.	Sagebrush and Lava Rock	36
V.	Ahtanum	51
VI.	Indian Flat—25 Miles	63
VII.	Naches—40 Miles	85
VIII.	Deep Water	100
IX.	Fear Walks the Woods	109
X.	The Campfire	124
XI.	Indian Philosopher	132
XII.	Sheepherders	144
XIII.	Trout	162
XIV.	Fly vs. Bait	168
XV.	A Full Heart	186
XVI.	Goat Rocks	199
XVII.	Jack Nelson	213
XVIII.	Roy Schaeffer	230
XIX.	Food	255
XX.	Snow Hole	274
XXI.	Klickitat	292
XXII.	Kloochman	314
	Glossary	330

Foreword

THE mountains of the Pacific Northwest are tangled, wild, remote, and high. They have the roar of torrents and avalanches in their throats.

Rock cliffs such as Kloochman rise as straight in the air as the Washington Monument and two or three times as high. Snow-capped peaks with aprons of eternal glaciers command the skyline—giant sentinels 11,000, 12,000, 14,000 feet high, such as Hood, Adams, and Rainier.

There are no slow-moving, sluggish rivers in these mountains. The streams run clear, cold, and fast.

There are remote valleys and canyons where man has never been. The meadows and lakes are not placid, idyllic spots. The sternness of the mountains has been imparted to them.

There are cougar to scout the camp at night. Deer and elk bed down in stands of mountain ash, snowbrush, and mountain-mahogany. Bears patrol streams looking for salmon. Mountain goat work their way along cliffs at dizzy heights, searching for moss and lichens.

Trails may climb 4,000 feet or more in two miles. In twenty miles of travel one may gain, then lose, then gain and lose once more, several thousand feet of elevation.

The blights of forest fires, overgrazing, avalanches, and excessive lumbering have touched parts of this vast domain. But civilization has left the total scene in strange degree alone.

These tangled masses of thickets, ridges, cliffs, and peaks are a vast wilderness area. Here man can find deep solitude, and under conditions of grandeur that are startling he can come to know both himself and God.

This book is about such discoveries. In this case they are discoveries that I made; so in a limited sense the book is autobiographical.

I learned early that the richness of life is found in adventure. Adventure calls on all the faculties of mind and spirit. It develops self-reliance and independence. Life then teems with excitement. But man is not ready for adventure unless he is rid of fear. For fear confines him and limits his scope. He stays tethered by strings of doubt and indecision and has only a small and narrow world to explore.

This book may help others to use the mountains to prepare for adventure.

They—if they are among the uninitiated—may be inspired to search out the high alpine basins and fragile flowers that flourish there. They may come to know the exhilaration of wind blowing through them on rocky pinnacles. They may recognize the music of the conifers when it comes both in whispered melodies and in the fullness of the wind instruments. They may discover the glory of a blade of grass and find their own relationship to the universe in the song of the willow thrush at dusk. They may learn to worship God where pointed spires of balsam fir turn a mountain meadow into a cathedral.

Discovery is adventure. There is an eagerness, touched at times with tenseness, as man moves ahead into the unknown. Walking the wilderness is indeed like living. The horizon drops away, bringing new sights, sounds, and smells from the earth. When one moves through the forests, his sense of discovery is quickened. Man is back in the environment from which he emerged to build factories, churches, and schools. He is primitive again, matching his wits against the earth and sky. He is free of the restraints of society and free of its safeguards too.

Boys, perhaps more deeply than men, know this experience. Eleanor Chaffee has expressed that concept poignantly:

Who but a boy would wander into the night
Against the sensible advice of those much older,
Where silent shadows cut the moon's thin light
And only maples lean to touch his shoulder?
What does he hope to find, what fever stirs
His blood and guides his feet to walk alone?

He will return, his sweater stuck with burrs
And in his hand a useless, shapeless stone,
But something in his face, secret, withdrawn
Will go with him upstairs, and to his sleep.
He is as furtive now as a young wild fawn:
His eyes are darker now, and large and deep.
Who but a boy can find such subtle magic
In the world his elders find so grave, so tragic?

These pages contain what I, as a boy, saw, felt, smelled, tasted, and heard in the mountains of the Pacific Northwest. At least the record I have written is as accurate as memory permits. Those who walked the trails with me as a boy—Bradley Emery, Douglas Corpron, Elon Gilbert, Arthur F. Douglas—are happily all alive. So they have let me draw upon their memories too and make many demands on their time and energies in the preparation of these chronicles.

The boy makes a deep imprint on the man. My young experiences in the high Cascades have placed the heavy mark of the mountains on me. And so the excitement that alpine meadows and high peaks created in me comes flooding back to make each adult trip an adventure. As the years have passed I have found in these experiences a spiritual significance that I could not fully sense before. That is why the book, though about a boy, is in total effect an adult version.

Many have assisted me in this task. It was the quiet encouragement of Phil Parrish and Stanley and Nancy Young that led me to finish the book. And it was the hard-edged mind of Phil Parrish that helped me put the text in final form. Many others have given me aid along the way. Lyle F. Watts, Walt Dutton, Lloyd Swift, H. J. Andrews, Fred Kennedy, Joseph F. Pechanec, Glenn Mitchell, Charles Rector, Chester Bennett, and Wade Hall of the Forest Service; Stanley Jewett, Elmo Adams, and John Scharff of the Fish and Wild Life Service; Ira Gabrielson, formerly chief of that service—these men have ridden the trails with me and helped me see and understand the beauties of the mountains. They also assisted me in analyzing a mass of scientific material bearing on the conservation of wildlife and water and topsoil that my mountain expeditions produced. That material was originally intended for this book; but in view of its

nature and volume it has been saved for later publication. William
A. Dayton, Donald C. Peattie, and Melvin Burke have been my patient instructors in botany. None could ask for better ones. Dean
Guie of Yakima, Palmer Hoyt of Denver, Saul Haas of Seattle, Rich-
ard L. Neuberger of Portland, Robert W. Sawyer of Bend, Alba Showaway of Parker, Mrs. George W. McCredy of Bickleton, John P.
Buwalda of Pasadena, and all those who walk through these pages,
particularly Jack Nelson, Roy Schaeffer, and the late Clarence Truitt
granted me assistance along the way. Walt Dutton, Josephine Wag-
gaman, James Powell, and Rudolph A. Wendelin produced the maps
that appear as end papers in this volume. Edith Allen and Gladys
Giese carried the burden of the typing.   .
    I must add a special word about two of the characters. Elon Gilbert
almost gave. his life for the book. When field studies were being
made in 1948, he was in a truck loaded with horses that rolled into
a canyon on the eastern slopes of Darling Mountain. It was he who
scaled the cliffs on Goat Rocks to drop a rope to me that I might
climb in safety. He also carried much of the burden of the field
research that went into this work. We shared together, as boys and
men, the adventure of this story.
    Doug Corpron was one of the doctors who attended me after the
horseback accident in October, 1949 that almost proved fatal. During
the first few days in the hospital it seemed that whenever I opened
my eyes—night or day—Doug was by my bedside. Then one day he
stood over me with a grin on his face. There was a note of bravado
in his voice as he said, "That was another tough climb we had together. But we made it, just as we once conquered Kloochman."
    That was a freakish accident in which Elon Gilbert and Billy
McGuffie were also involved.
    Billy McGuffie was at Tipsoo Lake on the morning of October 2,
1949, as Elon Gilbert and I started on horseback up Crystal Mountain on the expedition that almost proved fatal to me. He hailed me,
and I stopped briefly to talk with him before I took to the trail.
Rainier stood naked in all its grandeur across from us. Billy was
lighthearted as he pointed out all of the meadows and basins on its

slopes where he had once herded sheep. How Billy happened to be at Tipsoo this morning I do not know. "Providence sent him," Jack Nelson whispered to me a few days later in a Yakima hospital.

I had recently been into that country on skis and snowshoes when it was under thirty feet of snow. But there was much of it I had not seen in summer or fall for over thirty years.

This would be the ideal day to see it. There was not a cloud as far as the eye could see. The Oregon grape had turned to a deep port, the huckleberry to blood red, the mountain ash to a rich cranberry. The willow, maple, and tamarack were golden splashes across dark slopes of evergreens and basalt. As we skirted a steep and rugged shoulder of rock, I sensed a quiet air of waiting. It was as if the mountain were gathering itself together for the winter's assault.

Then the accident happened. I had ridden my horse Kendall hundreds of miles in the mountains and found him trustworthy on any terrain. But this morning he almost refused, as Elon led the way up a steep 60 degree grade. Knowing my saddle was loose, I dismounted and tightened the cinch. Then I chose a more conservative path up the mountain. Keeping it on my left, I followed an old deer run that circled the hillside at an easy 10 degree grade. We had gone only a hundred yards or so when Kendall (for a reason which will never be known) reared and whirled, his front feet pawing the steep slope. I dismounted by slipping off his tail. I landed in shale rock, lost my footing and rolled some thirty yards. I ended on a narrow ledge lying on my stomach, uninjured. I started to rise. I glanced up. I looked into the face of an avalanche. Kendall had slipped, and fallen, too. He had come rolling down over the same thirty precipitous yards I had traversed. There was no possibility of escape. Kendall was right on me. I had only time to duck my head. The great horse hit me. Sixteen hundred pounds of solid horseflesh rolled me flat. I could hear my own bones break in a sickening crescendo. Then Kendall dropped over the ledge and rolled heavily down the mountain to end up without a scratch. I lay paralyzed with pain—twenty-three of twenty-four ribs broken.

I could not move or shout. Would Elon ever find me in the brush where I lay concealed? He did—in twenty minutes that seemed like a century. Then, marking the spot where I lay, he raced down the mountain to see if he could find help. Again it seemed an endless wait, but in less than an hour there were sounds of men thrashing through brush—the rescue party that Billy McGuffie had organized. Soon there were strong arms lifting me gently onto a litter. Then a warm, rough hand slipped into mine, as I heard these whispered words: "This is Wullie McGuffie, my laddie; noo ever'thing will be a' richt."

Chapter I   *The Cascades*

MOST lawsuits, when viewed from the bench, are fundamentally fascinating. But there are dull moments even for a judge. There are interludes when the advocate is fumbling among his papers or having a whispered consultation with his associate. There is the occasional lawyer who drones on with accumulating monotony. I particularly recall one such time when, for a few minutes, I left the courtroom.

It was a day in late spring, when I stepped into the Big Klickitat. The water was high, so I pulled my waders snug to the armpits. They were stocking-foot waders. The shoes I wore had felt soles, fair footing for the black, lava rock bottom of the Klickitat. The chill of the water at once struck through waders and wool underwear.

"I must keep moving," I thought, "or I'll freeze."

I waded to midstream. The water of the Klickitat was around my waist. The whole weight of the river rushed against me. While it was a friendly push, it warned me to be careful of my footing. I leaned against it slightly, felt firm gravel under my feet, and started the slow ascent of the stream.

I was fishing a dry fly. I found some long floats with a May fly in the flat water below a spot of riffles. But I had no strike. I changed to a caddis bucktail and then to a coachman bucktail. Still no strike. I pushed on upstream. There on the left bank was a stretch of fast, flat water under overhanging branches of willow. The only way I could get a float beneath the willows was to cast across the stream at an angle. I crossed to the righthand bank, and was able to quarter it as I cast up to the base of the riffle.

I opened a fly box to make a new selection. After a moment of indecision I chose a Hallock killer. My first cast reached the base of the riffle. The current carried the fly a foot from the bank and down it drifted sitting high on the water like some new hybrid form of caddis that had dropped from a willow tree. Down it came—10 feet,

1

12 feet, 15 feet, 20 feet. There was a swirl under the fly. I lifted the tip of my rod to set the hook. My timing was poor. The fish turned over but I had not touched him. So he might come again.

I waited a few minutes. Once more I quartered the river, casting upstream to the base of the riffle. Again the Hallock killer swung toward the bank and came drifting down under the willows. It had moved about as far as before, when the trout—the same, I believe— struck again. This time I had him. I knew he was a rainbow because he broke water at once. All told, he jumped eight times. He stood on his tail, shaking his head to get rid of the hook. He rushed toward me, leaving the water in a graceful arc, eager for slack line so as to shake the hook loose. Downstream we went until we came to a small pool. There I held him until, in a few minutes, I brought him gently to the net. He was sleek and fat—14 inches long and a pound and three-quarters in weight.

I went back upstream and fished a few pools above the willow bank. I took one more trout—a 12-inch rainbow. But that was the only strike I had in 30 minutes on the Hallock killer.

"Time for a change," I thought, selecting a gray hackle, a No. 12 with a yellow body and red wings. "Maybe that's what they want." I tied it on and continued upstream to a big pool I had seen. This was at least fifty feet long. It was filled with white water at its head. The lower part was calm, and at least six or eight feet deep. I puzzled over the best way to fish it. If I cast upstream to the base of the white water at the head of the pool, the line would stretch across the calm water and disturb the trout. So I decided the best spot for the first cast was the lower end. Here the water picked up speed as it rushed for the exit, which was between two logs lying close and forming a sort of sluice gate. I dropped my gray hackle 20 feet above the sluice gate of the pool. It had gone scarcely a foot when it was sucked under in a swirl. I set my hook and knew by the feel that I had the champion.

Just then I heard the marshal's gavel. I came to. The court was rising. It was 4:30 P.M. The argument was over and another session of court at an end.

When I got to my chambers, I found my old friend Saul Haas waiting to see me. He had been in the courtroom during the latter part of the case. "Were you asleep in court this afternoon?" he accused.

I told him I had not been asleep; that when I became a judge I swore I would never doze on the bench, and my record so far was unsullied. Then I asked why he thought I had been sleeping.

"Well," he said, "you were off gathering wool."

I confessed I had been fishing.

"Fishing?" he queried. "For trout?"

I told him I had been after trout in the Big Klickitat of the Cascade Mountains in eastern Washington.

"Any luck?" he asked. I assured him I had had wonderful luck.

"You know," he said, "I'll bet you had better luck fishing this afternoon than you usually have." I inquired why.

"Well," he said, "I'll tell you. The loveliest, most beautiful women are those we meet in our dreams. And I figure that fishing is the same."

It was March, and there was only a touch of spring along the banks of the Potomac. The sun had not yet awakened the Japanese cherry trees. Neither the violets nor the dogwood had blossomed. The trees, though expectant, were still naked. Summer pressed harder each day. But winter hung on and kept its chill in the air.

There were robins everywhere. A meadow lark sang from a field by the river. A cloud of redwings swept across the sky, headed downstream for marshlands. A heron flapped lazily along the Virginia side of the river. And I saw on the edge of the path the year's first lily of the valley.

I stooped to pick it; and as I rose, I noticed a burst of yellow against a stand of dry and brittle weeds a hundred yards or so into the barren woods. After a long absence, the forsythia had returned overnight. The brilliance of its color against the drab shrubs and trees made it seem that the woods had been filled with the great rush of spring. The endless cycle persisted. There had been apparent atrophy and death. Now the floodtime of life was near. There would soon be a mysterious awakening of grass and trees. Melodious invaders from the Caribbean would drop from the sky. A reviving south wind would touch the land with wet wings.

Since the previous fall, I had hardly had time to look for a cardinal in Rock Creek Park or for a flight of geese or redheads over the Potomac. Indeed, I had been in the woods only a few times all winter. Like others in the nation's capital I had been caught fast in official and social duties.

The events of the winter had made me wonder at times, "Whither man?" I recalled an evening's conversation with a group of young folks. They deplored the fact that man was being more and more regarded only as a biological or economic being. He was put into tables and polls and considered as fungible as wheat or corn. One of them made the point that there was a diminishing recognition of the spiritual qualities—of the importance of quickening man's conscience and asking him to search his soul as well as his mind for answers to the perplexing problems of the day.

Perhaps man was losing his freedom in a subtle manner. He was becoming more and more dependent on other men. Part of that dependency was necessary, since man had to look to others for his food and fuel and essential services. But he had also become dependent on others for his entertainment and for his ideas. He looked to people rather than to himself and to the earth for his salvation. He fixed his expectations on the frowns or smiles or words of men, not on the strength of his own soul, or the sunrise, or the warming south wind, or the song of the warbler.

Once man leaned that heavily on people he was not wholly free to live. Then he became moody rather than self-reliant. He was filled with tensions and doubts. He walked in an unreal world, for he did not know the earth from which he came and to which he would return. He became a captive of civilization rather than an adventurer who topped each hill ahead for the thrill of discovering a new world. He lost the feel of his own strength, the power of his own soul to master any adversity.

The forsythia and its brilliant color stirred in me the memory of this after-dinner conversation. As I stood there with those ideas swirling in my head, I felt refreshed. My heart was relieved. I was excited by the very thought of being alive. The golden gleam of forsythia in bleak woods had given me a new hold on freedom.

I felt an almost irresistible urge to go West. It was the call of the Cascade Mountains. The sight of the forsythia this March day along the Potomac tripped the mechanism that flooded my mind with memories of the challenge of those mountains. The same has happened again and again in other circumstances.

Packed tight in a New York City subway, I have closed my eyes and imagined I was walking the ridge high above Cougar Lake. That ridge has the majesty of a cathedral. The Pacific Crest Trail winds along it under great cliffs that suggest walls and spires yet unfinished. At points along the trail are meadows no bigger than a city lot, from whose edge the mountain drops off a thousand feet or more. Here one stands on a dais looking directly down on the tips of pine and hemlock. At other points there are small pockets or basins set like alcoves off the trail and lined with balsam (alpine) fir in colonnade effect. Sharp, jagged shafts of basalt rock often tower over these alcoves. And at various angles they give impressions of roughly hewn church steeples.

When I am on that ridge at daybreak on an August or September day I feel like holding my breath so as not to break the solitude. The heartbeat sounds like a muffled drum. There is dew on the bunchgrass and the low-bush huckleberries. The air is crisp and cool. There is not a breath of wind. I find myself walking softly, almost on tiptoe, careful to avoid twigs and to keep my feet on the grass or the soft pine needles. For it pays to be noiseless when one moves along the ridge at that hour. It is the time of day when deer and elk are on the move.

There is no one within miles. A squirrel sounds an alarm from the top of a western hemlock. A chipmunk scuttles across the trail and, before disappearing into his hole, peers around the trunk of a white fir. There is an impish way about him. This is the first man he has ever seen, and he is full of indecision whether or not to explore the possibilities of friendship. Then he is gone with a flick of his tail. Overhead a hawk circles round and round, catching some current of air that even the tips of the fir and hemlock and cedar do not feel, as it glides gracefully along the contours of the ridge.

There is always a quick excitement, a tingling sensation up the spine, as I turn a bend in the trail and see a doe feeding. Her sensitive antennae detect my presence before I can inhale a breath. She turns her head to face me, her ears spread wide, her nostrils distended, her eyes fixed. In a split second her radar transforms the image into the symbol for an ancient enemy. She clears a patch of hellebore in a bound and disappears with nervous jumps into a stand of mountain ash. Within 50 or 100 feet even the white tail is blended in the woods and lost to sight.

In life the scene is almost as unreal as the memory of it is on a crowded subway. For the escape of the doe above Cougar Lake is as silent as her exit from a dream. She seldom cracks a twig as she goes bounding through brush and trees.

Long stretches of hard work often rob the night of sleep. There was one period when night after night I would be held at the office until two or three or four o'clock in the morning and then be back at my desk at nine. I would be dog-weary when I reached home, but wide-awake when I got to bed. And so I would roll and toss, unable to sleep. Some people count sheep; others play their golf courses hole by hole.

I would revisit in memory the Cascades and push up the Ahtanum over Darling Mountain and down into the Klickitat Meadows. I would catch cutthroat trout in the Little Klickitat and roast them on a stick over a willow fire.

I would push on to Conrad Meadows; lie on the bank of the South Fork of the Tieton; and watch white clouds in the west build patterns in the sky behind Gilbert Peak of the magnificent Goat Rocks.

I would go up to Goat Rocks on the Conrad Creek Trail; skirt

the base of Devils Horns and Tieton Peak; come to the basin below
Meade Glacier; cross the glacier and snow fields above it; and finally
sit in the rocky crow's-nest at the top of Gilbert Peak, with the vast
panorama of the Cascades spread out below me.

Or I would climb Hogback Mountain; drop to Shoe Lake; take the
up-and-down washboard trail to McCall Basin; climb Old Snowy of
the Goat Rocks, stand atop it, and feel the wind blowing through me.

I never got farther along those old trails before I was asleep. So
the memories of my early trips were relaxing influences better than
any chemical sedative.

Mount Adams has always had a special lure for me. Its memory
has been the most haunting of all. Adams is more intimate than
Rainier. Its lines are softer; it is more accessible. It has always been
my favorite snow-capped mountain. My long ambition was to climb
it. It was a mountain of mystery. It had been at one time, as I shall
relate, a brave Indian chief named Klickitat. It had exhibited recent
volcanic activity. High on its shoulders are crevasses that spout sulfur
fumes. The Indians would not go up to its glaciers. There in the fast-
ness of the mountain lived the Tomanows, the spirit chiefs of the
Indians.

This mountain was so legendary I might not have believed it
existed had I not lived in its shadow and seen it in sun and storm
for twenty years. The vision of it would come back to me in dusty
law libraries as I searched for the elusive thing called the law. High
in an office building on New York's Wall Street I would be lost in
the maze of a legal problem, forgetful of my bearings, and then
suddenly look from the window to the west, thinking for a second
that I might see Mount Adams, somber in its purplish snow at sunset. I have done the same thing while sitting deep in meditation
in a canoe on a Maine lake or in a boat in Florida's Everglades.

After a long absence from my old home town of Yakima, Washington, I have fairly raced by car down from Ellensburg or up from
Pasco to see Mount Adams before night dropped the curtain around
it. At such a time my heart has leaped at the first sight of it. Getting

out of the car I have stood in a field, thrilled at the sight as if it were my first. At those moments my spine has always tingled. There is a feeling of respect and admiration and pride. One has the sensation of being part of something much bigger than himself, something great and majestic and wholesome.

The Cascades have been particularly undeniable when I have lain in sickbed. In days of fever and sickness I have climbed Mount Adams, retraced every step from Cold Springs to the top, recrossed its snow fields, stood in a 50-mile icy wind at its highest point, and there recaptured the feel of adventure and conquest and the sensation of being back millions of years at the time of the Creation.

During hospital days I have explored many streams of the Cascades, looking for the delicate periwinkle. I have cast a fly on dozens of their lakes, and searched the pools of the Big Klickitat, the South Fork of the Tieton, Bumping River, and the Naches for rainbow trout. I have sat on the crags of Goat Rocks, 500 or 1000 feet below the summit, waiting for a mountain goat to appear in silhouette against the skyline. I have seen lively bug hatches on Fish and Swamp lakes. I have heard the noise of elk in the thickets along Petross Sidehill.

These have been haunting memories that in illness returned me to the world of reality even when it seemed I might be close to the other side of the river.

But the most vivid recollections have reached me in environments that have been bleak and dreary and oppressive. I remember a room in New York City on West 120th Street that overlooked an air well.

The sun reached that room but a scant two hours a day. There was no other outlook. The whole view was a dull brick wall, pierced by dingy panes of glass. In one of these windows some poor soul had set a tiny, scrawny geranium. There were lively zoological specimens around—such as cockroaches. But the only botanical specimen in sight was the geranium. I would see it in the morning when I arose and on rainy Sundays when I stayed indoors. In the poverty of that view the memories of the Cascades would come flooding back.

Lush bottom lands along the upper Naches, where grass grows stirrup high—succulent grass that will hold a horse all night.

A deer orchid deep in the brush off the American River Trail.

A common rock wren singing its heart out on a rock slide above Bumping Lake.

Clusters of the spring beauty in the damp creek beds along the eastern slopes of Hogback Mountain.

The smell of wood smoke, bacon, and onions at a camp below Meade Glacier.

Indian paintbrush and phlox on the high shoulders of Goat Rocks.

The roar of the northwesters in the treetops in Tieton Basin.

Clumps of balsam fir pointed like spires to the sky in Blankenship Meadows.

The cry of a loon through the mist of Bumping Lake.

A clump of whitebark pine atop Darling Mountain—gnarled and tough, beaten by a thousand gales.

A black, red-crested woodpecker attacking in machine-gun style a tree at Goose Prairie.

The scrawny geranium across the rooming house court in New York City brought back these nostalgic memories and many more. The glories of the Cascades grew and grew in the desolation of the bleak view from my window. New York City became almost unbearable. I was suffocated and depressed. I wanted to flee the great city with its scrawny geraniums and bleak courtyards. The longing for the silences of the Cascades, the smell of fir boughs at night, the touch of the chinook as it blew over the ridges—these longings were almost irresistible in the oppressiveness of my New York City rooming house.

I had had a similar experience on my way east to law school. I had left on a freight train from Wenatchee, Washington with 2000 sheep. That was in September, 1922. We had only reached Idaho when a railroad strike stopped the wheels. We had the sheep to feed and to water. Regular feeding points had been scheduled, but we did not reach them because of the strike. So we took the sheep out of the cars and herded them while we waited for an engine. In this way we spent eleven days moving by slow stages across Montana and North Dakota. Then came a wire from the owner to turn the sheep over to a buyer in western Minnesota. This we did. My companion returned to Yakima, and I caught the first freight to Chicago.

I knew the freight trains well. Hitchhikers of the period prior to the First World War chose them as a matter of necessity, because the great flow of highway traffic had nòt yet started. Like many others, I had ridden the rods up and down the Yakima Valley and to points east, to work in the hay- and wheatfields and in the orchards.

A literal riding of the rods is seldom done. This ordinarily means to ride under boxcars or passenger cars on a small platform of boards laid across rods that run lengthwise beneath some cars. It is a cramped space at best. It is frightfully dusty down there, the motion of the train whirling dirt and cinders its whole length. You lie on your stomach with your eyes closed, grimy and miserable. I hated that place. The open boxcars were more comfortable. But in them you might meet a fellow traveler who would not hesitate to toss you off the moving train after taking your money. Yet if you rode on top of cars you were subject to two other risks.

The first was the freight yard police, whom we called yard bulls. They were armed; and I was in mortal fear of them. They were not men of discretion or manners. Their technique was to beat you up first and then arrest you. The other risk was the train crew. More often than not they were friendly, but occasionally a brakeman would try to collect fares from the hitchhikers. A dollar or perhaps fifty cents would be enough; but unless payment were made, the passenger might be handed over to the yard bulls at the next station. This was the shakedown, but the immunity it purchased often seemed worth the price.

On this trip through Minnesota I paid toll to the crew of the freight train—fifty cents apiece, as I recall. When we came to a new division point, I discovered that the new crew was also collecting fares. I was easy prey, for I was on a flatcar—the only available space, except the rods and the top of the boxcars. This was a loaded and sealed train, carrying for the most part fruit in refrigerator cars. When the new brakeman came along he asked for a dollar and I paid him. Nothing more happened for a long time. Then along came the conductor. We were on the outskirts of Chicago. It was three or four o'clock in the morning on a clear, cold night. The conductor asked for a dollar; he said there were yard bulls ahead, he did not want me to get into trouble, and he would see that the yard bulls did not arrest me. It was the same old story.

I was silent for a while, trying to figure how I could afford to part with another dollar. I had only a few left. I had not had a hot meal for seven days; I had not been to bed for thirteen nights; I was filthy and without a change of clothes. I needed a bath and a shave and food; above all else I needed sleep. Even flophouses cost money. And the oatmeal, hot cakes, ham and eggs and coffee—which I wanted desperately—would cost fifty or seventy-five cents.

"Why should I pay this guy and become a panhandler in Chicago?" I asked myself.

He shook me by the shoulder and said, "Come on, buddy. Do you want to get tossed off the train?"

"I'm broke," I said.

"Broke?" he retorted. "You paid the brakeman and you can pay me."

"Have a heart," I said. "I bet you were broke some time. Give a guy a break."

He roared at me to get off or he would turn me over to the bulls. I was silent.

"Well, jump off or I'll run you in."

I watched the lights of Chicago come nearer. We were entering a maze of tracks. There were switches and sidetracks, boxcars on sidings, occasional loading platforms. And once in a while we roared over a short highway bridge. It was dark and the train was going about thirty miles an hour. The terrain looked treacherous. A jump might be disastrous. But I decided to husband my two or three remaining dollars. I stood poised on the edge of the flatcar, searching the area immediately ahead for a place to jump.

Suddenly in my ear came the command, "Jump!" I jumped.

Something brushed my left sleeve. It was the arm of a switch. Then I fell clear, hitting a cinder bank. I lost my footing, slid on my hands and knees for a dozen feet down the bank, and rolled to the bottom.

I got slowly to my feet as the last cars of the freight roared by and disappeared with a twinkling of lights into the east. My palms were bleeding and full of cinders. My knees were skinned. I was dirty and hungry and aching. I sat on a pile of ties by the track, nursing my wounds.

A form came out of the darkness. It proved to be an old man who also rode the rods. He put his hand on my shoulder and said, "I saw you jump, buddy. Are you hurt?"

"No, thank you," I replied. "Not much. Just scratched."

"Ever been to Chicago?"

"No."

"Well," he said, "don't stay here. It's a city that's hard on fellows like us."

"You mean the bulls?"

"Yes, they are tough," he said. "Maybe they have to be. But it's not only that. Do you smell the stockyards?"

I had not identified the odor, but I had smelled it even before I jumped.

"So that's it?"

"Yeah. I've worked there. The pay ain't so bad. But you go home at night to a room on an alley. There's not a tree. There's no grass. No birds. No mountains."

"What do you know of mountains?" I ventured.

It led to his story. He had come, to begin with, from northern California. He had worked in the harvests, and as he worked he could look up and see the mountains. Before him was Mount Shasta. He could put his bedroll on the ground and fall asleep under the pines. There was dust in the fields of northern California, but it was good clean dirt. People were not packed together like sardines. They had elbow room. A man need not sit on a Sunday looking out on a bleak alley. He could have a piece of ground, plant a garden, and work it. He might even catch a trout, or shoot a grouse or pheasant, or perhaps kill a deer.

I listened for about an hour as he praised the glories of the mountains of the West and related his experiences in them. Dawn was coming, and as it came I could see the smoke and some of the squalor of which my friend spoke.

I asked what brought him to the freight yards at this hour of the morning. He said he came to catch a west-bound freight—back to God's own land, back to the mountains. Lonesomeness swept over me. I never had loved the Cascades as much as I did that early morning in the stockyards of Chicago. Never had I missed a snow-capped peak as much. Never had I longed more to see a mountain meadow filled with heather and lupine and paintbrush. As dawn broke I could see smokestacks everywhere, and in the distance to the east the vague outlines of tall buildings. But there lay before me nothing higher, no ridge or hill or meadow—only a great monotony of cinders, smoke, and dingy factories with chimneys pouring out a thick haze over the landscape.

The old man and I sat in silence a few moments. He said, "Do you know your Bible, son?"

"Pretty well."

"Then you will remember what the psalmist said about the mountains."

I racked my brain. "No, I don't recall."

Then the old man said with intonations worthy of the clergy, "I will lift up mine eyes unto the hills from whence cometh my help. My help cometh from the Lord who made heaven and earth."

There was a whistle in the east. A quarter-mile down the track a freight was pulling onto the main line.

"That's my train," he said. "That train takes me to the mountains." He took my hand. "Good luck, son. Better come back with me. Chicago's not for us."

I shook my head and said good-by with sadness. He smiled. "Stay clear of the flophouses. They'll roll you when you're asleep. Go to the Y.M.C.A. It's cheap and clean and they're on the level."

The engine went by. The passing train was picking up speed. The old man was more agile than he looked. He trotted easily along the track, grabbed a handhold, and stepped lightly aboard on the bottom rung of the ladder. Climbing to the top of the boxcar, he took off his hat, and waved until he was out of sight.

I watched the freight disappear into the West. That old man had moved me deeply. I recognized his type from the hobo jungles I had visited between Yakima and Chicago. In Yakima the jungles were usually under or near one of the Northern Pacific bridges across the Yakima River. There hoboes met, contributed food to the pot, and cooked their meals. Not once was I allowed to go hungry in a jungle. I was always invited to share in whatever meal was cooking. Sometimes I could contribute to the pot, other times I could not; but that made no difference. There was companionship and friendship in the jungle.

I felt the jungle companionship in this old man of the stockyards. He was only a vagabond. But he was not a bum. I later realized that he had been a greater credit to his country than many of the more elite. He had made me see, in the dreary stockyards of America, some of the country's greatness—kindness, sympathy, selflessness, understanding.

I sat in the stockyards, watching the sun rise through the smoke and haze. There was a smell in the air that even the touch of the sun would not cleanse. There was not a tree or shrub or blade of grass in view. The Chicago I saw that morning was not the gracious, warmhearted city I later came to know. Nor was it the Chicago that Carl Sandburg painted:

> Hog butcher for the world,
> Toolmaker, stacker of wheat,
> Player with railroads and the nation's freight handler;
> Stormy, husky, brawling,
> City of big shoulders.

That morning I had only a distorted and jaundiced view. I was hungry, dead tired, homesick, broke, and bruised. And my welcome had not been cordial.

It seemed that man had built a place of desolation and had corrupted the earth in so doing. In corrupting the earth he had corrupted himself also, and built out of soot and dirt a malodorous place of foul air and grimy landscape in which to live and work and die. Here there were no green meadows wet with morning dew to examine for tracks of deer; no forest that a boy could explore to discover for himself the various species of wild flowers, shrubs, and trees; no shoulder of granite pushing against fleecy clouds and standing as a reminder to man of his puny character, of his inadequacies; no trace of the odor of pine or fir in the air.

I had a great impulse to follow my vagabond friend to the West, to settle down in the valley below Mount Adams and to live under its influence. Most of my friends and all the roots I had in life were in the Yakima Valley. There would be a job and a home awaiting me, and fishing trips and mountain climbs and nights on the high shoulders of Goat Rocks. It was a friendly place, not hard and cruel like these freight yards. People in the West were warmhearted and open-faced like my hobo friend. I would be content and happy there.

Then why this compulsion to leave the valley? Why this drive, this impulse, to leave the scenes I loved? To reach for unknown stars, to seek adventure, to abandon the convenience of home? And what of pride? What would I say if I returned? That I didn't have the guts to work my way east, to work my way through law school, to live the hard way?

These were my thoughts as the freight carried my vagabond friend into the West. Law school would open in a week. There was challenge ahead. New horizons would be opened, offering still untested opportunities.

My decision was spiritual. It was too late to go back. I would sleep the clock around and then return to the freight yards to catch a ride to New York City and Columbia Law School. I turned my face to the East—to my convictions—and walked along the railroad track, headed for the Y.M.C.A. as my friend had recommended.

Since that time I have often wondered whatever happened to the agile old man who befriended me in Chicago. I knew nothing much about him. But at least I have known that the mountains were important in shaping his kindness when he came to me through the night.

Mountains have a decent influence on men. I have never met along the trails of the high mountains a mean man, a man who would cheat and steal. Certainly most men who are raised there or who work there are as wholesome as the mountains themselves. Those who explore them on foot or horseback usually are open, friendly men. At least that has been my experience.

I saw the CCC camps in the early thirties work miracles with men. I remember a chap from Brooklyn whom I picked up out of La Grande, Oregon. We drove to Portland together. During the six or seven hours with him I learned something of his transformation. By his own admission he had been a pretty tough, mean character when he arrived in Oregon for work in the woods. He carried a chip on his shoulder. He was itching to punch "any bird" that pushed him around. And he did. One of them was the supervisor—an army officer, I believe—of the camp. He had found the world hard and cruel. There was always some guy to trim you, to do you in. You had to take care of yourself with your fists. He had learned the art on the streets of Brooklyn. When he punched the supervisor, he was given punishment—what, I do not recall. That did not soften him. It was the two years in the woods that changed his character.

He poured out his story on this long automobile ride. Things were different in the woods: "No use getting sore at a tree." There was nothing in the woods to hurt you—"but the mountains can give you quite a beating if you're careless." The air up there is "sure pure. Can't smell no garbage." It was kind of lonesome back in the woods: "No dames. And say, mister, I sure miss those Dodgers." But it was nice to have it quiet. "No radio blaring at you across the alley." The nights in the woods got to be pretty nice: "There's a kind of music in the pine trees at night when the wind blows."

This chap was mellow. Now he had no chip on his shoulder. He was considerate. He was a tough guy transformed into a philosopher. He had found how great and good his country was. He was going to try to repay it for what it had done for him.

The CCC had paid great dividends in citizenship of that character. His was not an isolated case. I heard the same story repeated again and again by supervisors of CCC camps. Jack Nelson, woodsman and philosopher (whose story I will later tell), bears witness to the miracles that happened.

I had puzzled many times over the reason for such a transformation of man by the mountains. A few summers ago an old friend, Dr. George Draper of New York City—father of psychosomatic medicine in this country—was spending a month with me at my cabin in the high Wallowas of Oregon. One night before the fire I put the question to him.

He thought a while and then said, "Man is at his worst when he is pitted against his fellow man. He is at his best when pitted against nature."

He was silent for a few moments. The tamarack log in the fireplace popped and threw sparks and coals against the screen as the fire roared up the chimney. The memory of my vagabond friend in the stockyards of Chicago came back to me as the doctor spoke. For the doctor too recited the words of the psalmist: "I will lift up mine eyes unto the hills from whence cometh my help. My help cometh from the Lord who made heaven and earth."

The doctor paused and then went on to say, "By 'help' the psalmist meant strength. By strength he meant spiritual vitality that comes from faith—faith in a universe of which he is a part, faith in a universe in which he has a place."

We sat for half an hour or so in silence. Mountains can transform men, I thought. Their lofty peaks, soft shoulders, and deep ravines have some special value to man, even though he does no more than view them from a distance. Those operating underground in the

French Resistance during Nazi occupation often took a mountain as their code name. For mountains symbolize the indomitable will, an unbending resolution, a loyalty that is eternal, and character that is unimpeachable.

There are other ways too in which mountains have spiritual values. When man ventures into the wilderness, climbs the ridges, and sleeps in the forest, he comes in close communion with his Creator. When man pits himself against the mountain, he taps inner springs of his strength. He comes to know himself. He becomes meek and humble before the Lord that made heaven and earth. For he realizes how small a part of the universe he actually is, how great are the forces that oppose him.

Maybe all this is meant by West Virginia's motto, *Montani Semper Liberi:* mountaineers are always free men.

Those were the thoughts that went through my mind after the doctor gave his answer to my question. Finally he turned to me and said, "You should write a book some day about the influence of mountains on men. If man could only get to know the mountains better, and let them become a part of him, he would lose much of his aggression. The struggle of man against man produces jealousy, deceit, frustration, bitterness, hate. The struggle of man against the mountains is different. Man then bows before Something that is bigger than he. When he does that, he finds serenity and humility, and dignity too."

Chapter II   *Yakima*

THE night was pitch-black. A soft, warm southwest wind was blowing over the ridges of the Cascades. Spring was coming to the Yakima Valley. I felt it in the air. It was after midnight. The houses of Yakima were dark. Only the flickering street lights marked the way. We had just arrived by train from California. Father was up ahead with the suitcases, walking with giant strides. Mother came next, with a lad of a few months in her arms. My sister and I brought up the rear.

There were strange noises among the occasional trees and shrubs that we passed. There were creepy sounds coming from the grass and from the irrigation ditch that ran along the sidewalk. I wondered if they were from snakes or lizards or the dread tarantula that I had been taught to fear in California! Maybe snakes were sticking out their forked tongues as they used to do under the steps of the house in Estrella! Maybe a tarantula would lie in wait and drop off a tree and get me when I passed! Maybe lizards in Yakima were giant lizards! And then there were the dread rattlesnakes that Mother spoke of with fear and trembling. Did they gulp young boys alive, like the snakes in the picture book that could swallow a whole sheep? Was the rustle in the grass the rustle of a rattler? These were alarming thoughts to a boy of five.

I looked anxiously over my shoulder. The trees and bushes with the strange noises in them seemed to take the form of monsters with long arms. I ran to catch up. Then, by the time I had once more looked furtively over my shoulder at the shapeless pursuing forms of the darkness, I discovered that I was far behind again. Why did Father walk so fast? I ran again to catch up. And so, block after block, I alternately lagged behind and ran, fearful of being lost and swallowed up in the night or grabbed by some demon of the dark.

Father walked west from the Northern Pacific railroad station up Yakima Avenue. At Fifth Avenue he turned north, looking in the darkness for the house where our relatives, the Pettits, lived. He apparently did not have their exact address, or having it, was not able to read the house numbers in the dark. He stopped several times to arouse a household, only to find he had picked the wrong place.

At one house he had hardly entered the yard before two great dogs came racing around opposite sides of the house, barking and snarling. I was frozen with fear. But Father did not hesitate or pause. He continued on his way, speaking to the dogs in a voice that was firm and that to the dogs as well as to me seemed to have the authority of the highest law behind it. The dogs became silent and trotted out to investigate us. They circled and sniffed me, putting their noses right into my face. I can still feel their hot, stinking breath. To me they seemed to be real demons of the darkness that had come to hold me for ransom. I wanted to scream. But the crisis was quickly passed. Father was soon back. He dismissed the dogs with ease, resumed his search, and presently found the house we wanted. A friendly door soon closed on all the strange noises and on the dangers of the outer darkness.

This was in 1904. Father, a minister, had moved up from California for his health. We had lived at Estrella, California, which is near Paso Robles, in the hot, arid interior. The doctors recommended a cooler climate for him, so he had accepted a call to Cleveland, Washington. We were en route to Cleveland when we made this first visit to Yakima.

Cleveland lies in Wood Gulch on the southern edge of the Simcoe Mountains, about 50 miles southwest of Yakima. In 1904, when we lived there, it was a lively village of a hundred or more inhabitants. There was a church and school, a post office, stores, and boarding houses. A half-dozen miles to the south was a small settlement appropriately called Dot. To the east three miles was Bickleton. Father had the pastorate at each of the three places, preaching three sermons on Sunday.

Stretches of the Columbia, some 30 miles to the south, could be seen from the fields around Cleveland. At that point the river runs through a valley of volcanic ash, sand, and sagebrush—the brush that decorates all the plains of eastern Washington and Oregon and is the state flower of Nevada. For 200 miles or more the Columbia flows noiselessly through parched land, with only an occasional glimpse of green to break the desert monotony. This is the portion of the river that I first saw. It was springtime, I believe, and we were crossing on the ferry at Roosevelt, Washington. I remember an endless supply of water, moving swiftly but silently. The river was slightly murky; but from a distance it was aquamarine and sparkling. It was filled with mystery for me, because on these first crossings I saw strange flashes below its surface—quick movements of salmon or steelhead or sturgeon that excited me.

Cleveland was a healthy place. It afforded relief from the heat of interior California, since the altitude was 3,000 feet above sea level. This plateau, stretching to the east, south, and west from Cleveland, was practically treeless. But there was a fine stand of ponderosa pine in Wood Gulch, and sprinklings of oak, willow, cottonwood, aspen, juniper, and black pine along the southern edges of the Simcoe Mountains. It was cool and relaxing in their shade. And there was a strong, bracing wind that blew from the west, carrying the coolness of Mount Adams on its wings.

Mother always felt that Cleveland was a healthy place in other ways too. The people were the most hospitable she and Father had known. They were wheat farmers and cattlemen. Their farms were large units, running from 600 to 6000 acres. Though the people were scattered over many square miles, they formed in spirit a compact community. They were neighborly folks. Perhaps that was because of their isolation and remoteness, in those horse and buggy days, from the Yakima Valley and from Goldendale, the county seat of Klickitat County, 30 miles to the west. Perhaps it was the character of the people. Whatever the reason, they were friendly and cooperative. In time of need they came in from all points to lend a hand, whether to raise a church or a barn, move a house, put out a fire, or dig a grave.

Some of them were small and selfish men. But Mother said that most of them were God-fearing folks—honest, warmhearted, humble, and dignified. These were the McCredys, Courtneys, Faulkners, Colemans, Talberts, Rossiers, Trenners, Mittys, Lingos, and Varners. This was good, solid American stock of the kind that has made the country great.

Father liked Cleveland and enjoyed ministering to its ⟨...⟩s. He was in his forties and seemed to have a useful life ahe⟨...⟩ ⟨...⟩ut before the year 1904 was out, he was carried to ⟨...⟩n for an emergency operation. He never returned. ⟨...⟩ one day and then he was gone—forever. There w⟨...⟩ another to lift me high in the air, to squeeze my ha⟨...⟩ ⟨...⟩ masculine praise. There were no longer any pocke⟨...⟩ ⟨...⟩h for nuggets of maple sugar. The step in the hallw⟨...⟩ ⟨...⟩ne jingle of coins in the pockets—these had gone as s⟨...⟩ ⟨...⟩ waters of the great Columbia. He never would return. At ⟨...⟩ was not sure it was so complete. Later I was gradually convinced.

When Father died we moved to Yakima, where Mother built a house for a few hundred dollars at 111 North Fifth Avenue. There we really settled down and lived for over 20 years.

Yakima is located in south-central Washington. It lies in a semi-arid valley 1065 feet above sea level. There is little rainfall; the long-term average for the valley is about eight inches annually. The Cascade Mountains on the west send numerous clear, cold streams tumbling down from their snow fields, the main one being the Yakima. To the east is a vast desert plateau (much of which will be irrigated by Grand Coulee Dam) extending almost 200 miles to the western foothills of the Bitterroot Mountains in Idaho.

The town of Yakima is rimmed by foothills, rising about 500 feet above the valley. The valley where the town is located is, indeed, a huge saucepan, somewhat narrower north-to-south than east-to-west. The Yakima River comes down from the north and enters the valley through Selah Gap—a pass through the hills worn down by centuries of erosion. It leaves the valley through Union Gap on the south, and from there runs 80 miles to the Columbia. This great expanse of land below Union Gap, some 20 miles wide and 80 miles long, is known as the Lower Valley. Both below and above Union Gap the orchards and alfalfa fields extend far to the west, until they meet the pine and fir straggling down the slopes of the Cascades. Whichever way one looks there is some reclamation project that has transformed desert land into green fields and orchards. Through the gap to the north of Yakima is the rich Selah Valley; and to the northwest through Naches Gap are the valleys of the Naches and the Tieton, which played an especially important part in my early life.

Father had ridden through the Yakima Valley one summer in the early nineties. It was then largely a wasteland of sagebrush, jack rabbits, and rattlesnakes. There were patches of alfalfa and some fields of hops in the bottom lands; and arms of orchards were beginning to extend out from the river. There were the white or Garry oak, cottonwood, willow, and sumac along the banks of the Yakima. But only those touches of green on the dusty sagebrush background were inviting to the eye of a Nova Scotian used to green hills and lush meadows.

The Cascades, some forty miles west as the crow flies, were dark blue in the afternoon sun. Their shade and the eternal snows of Mount Adams and Mount Rainier were tempting invitation to those who crossed the hot, parched valley on a summer day. To the uninitiated the barren foothills, which leave the cool timber to join the hot desert, were uninviting. We who lived among them and tramped them and discovered their secrets came to love them. But like the valley they encircled, those barren hills at first blush had little to offer the early traveler or settler.

The valley, however, was rich in feed for cattle and sheep, even before irrigation came. There was knee-high grass in the Cascades. And the dreary foothills also had food for stock. The famous bluebunch wheatgrass of the West (*Agropyron spicatum*) grows there; it is a species of bunchgrass that cures on the stalk and forms a superior feed for livestock through the whole of the year, as Lewis and Clark first observed. And in the spring there are fresh shoots of wild flowers, of tender grasses, of wild onions and cows, and a new growth of tender leaves of the sage.

Cattle were the first stock in the valley. Sheep followed; but cattle have always had a more prominent place in the economy.

The soil of the valley is volcanic ash. It was first irrigated in the seventies, when ditches were dug to bring water to the hay and grain fields of cattlemen. It was soon learned that almost any produce will grow there if water is on the land. Clear skies during two-thirds or more of the growing season mean more than twice as much effective sunshine as New York enjoys. Thus, when the United States Reclamation Service brought water down from the mountains, a desert became a garden. What was offered my father at a price as low as 50 cents an acre became worth many hundred times that amount, within a decade or so.

This is now a famous fruit country—apples, cherries, prunes, apricots, peaches, plums, and pears. At one time the balance of the economy was in apples, some orchards having been planted as early as 1870. Lessons learned from depressions brought more diversification. Sugar beets, sweet corn, asparagus, grapes, and tree fruits other than apples now assume a larger proportion. Hops have always been an important product of the valley. There are still cattle and sheep. But when Washington was admitted into the Union in 1889, fruit and other direct produce of the soil began to take the lead. And so it has remained ever since.

Thus the valley has had special attraction for those who love the soil. Its great productivity drew men like a magnet. In later years I saw sturdy Norsemen, refugees from the Dust Bowl where they had sweated and slaved and seen their crops parch and blow away, put their spades into the rich volcanic ash of Yakima, reach down and scoop both hands full, and stand with tears streaming down their faces, as the soft loamy soil ran through their fingers. This is a place where man will never starve, where he can build a home and raise strong sons. The snow of the Cascades will never fail to bring life to the desert and quench its thirst and the thirst of those who toil there.

This valley was the ancestral home of the Yakima Indians. Along with the other Indians in the Western Hemisphere, they presumably came from Asia by way of the Bering Strait. Collier in *The Indians of the Americas* estimates that this migration took place around 13,000 B.C. or 18,000 B.C. This was in the late Pleistocene era, when the central plain of Alaska was free of ice. The giant beaver, the mammoth, the camel, the dire wolf, and the four-horned antelope roamed the land; some of these have come down in the legends of the Indians.

The land in the Lower Valley west of the Yakima river is in large part within the eastern edge of their reservation. This reservation, a million and a quarter acres in size, was created by the Treaty of 1855.

Marcus Whitman had been murdered by the Cayuse in 1847 near Walla Walla at his Waiilatpu Mission, the mission that was the seedling of sturdy Whitman College. The westward push was on. Settlers had already poured into the Willamette Valley in Oregon. They were beginning to turn north through the Yakima Valley and cross the Cascades by old Indian routes to Puget Sound. There was uneasiness in the air. Conflict between the settlers and the Indians was imminent. The Treaty of 1855 was designed to ease the strain and avoid clashes.

In the four years it took for ratification of the treaty, war broke out. The Yakimas, seeing their land opened to setttlement before the treaty was ratified, went on the warpath, killing and raiding. Three years of warfare followed, the United States Army in 1858 finally crushing the military might of the Yakimas and their Indian allies to the east.

Then the first permanent settlers began to move in. Much later, in 1877 and 1878, the Yakimas were once more stirring uneasily;

there were more killings of white men. But that was the end of Indian violence. In 1880 the Federal government opened a land office in the valley and homestead filings began.

Today the Yakimas still own miles and miles of the rich bottom lands in the Lower Valley. They seldom operate or manage them; they are landlords, and lease to many different interests, including a cannery. There are rich ranges for stock in the mountain section of the reservation, which lies at the foot of Mount Adams. Large herds of cattle graze there. Each member of the tribe has grazing rights for 100 head of cattle, with the privilege of almost limitless additional grazing at the low cost of $2.50 per head. In the reservation is a primeval stand of virgin timber, made up principally of ponderosa pine but including Douglas fir, larch, white fir, and other conifers that total in the aggregate about four billion board feet.

We who were raised in Yakima did not know the Indians well. Some of them lived in town, but most of them held to the reservation. And most of the Indian children attended the public schools in the Lower valley. Not living with them or playing with them, we felt them strangers. We only saw them on the streets and in the stores and restaurants. Yakima Susie, for years said to be 110 years old, was usually on a street corner in Yakima, begging money. I remember her best on the northwest corner of First Street and Yakima Avenue, sitting on the sidewalk with high moccasins, beaded headband or scarf, and a light blanket over her shoulders. On Saturday afternoons we children would glue pennies to strings and drag them across the walk in front of her. She would shake her fist at us or come at us fiercely, screeching horrid-sounding Indian words.

Saturday nights the Indians would come into the stores for shopping. They had some amusing habits. They never would place their whole order at once. They would bargain for a single article at a time, and when the bargain for that article was completed they would pay the price and leave. They would be back in a jiffy, having left the purchased article outside. Then the negotiation for the next article on their list would start. And so the process continued until all purchases were made.

For the most part they spoke good English; and a few were well educated. I remember one storekeeper of a Saturday night going up to a squaw, dressed in moccasins and a buckskin shirt, and saying condescendingly, "Squaw catchum glove?" There was no response for a minute and then the squaw said in a tone and voice worthy of a graduate of an Eastern finishing school, "No, thank you. I am just waiting for my sister."

Occasionally a Yakima would fill himself with firewater and go on a spree. Sometimes we'd see a few in flashy cars visiting the town on a Saturday splurge. But these were the exceptions. By and large the Indians would come to town on Saturday night, mingle peacefully with the whites in stores, restaurants, and theaters, and then melt away into the night, back to their reservation. Their citizenship compared favorably with that of the rest of the people.

For a youngster the Indians added a touch of mystery and enchantment to the valley. Their folklore and legends gave a distinct flavor to the region. But the Indians were far in the background.

In the foreground were the mountains. All those who lived in the valley looked to the Cascades for health and sustenance. The mountains furnished water, and water was more precious than gold. Hence we were utterly dependent on the snow-capped ridges that lay against the western horizon. They became the symbols of our hopes and aspirations.

Over the years, Adams and Rainier in particular became personal friends of mine. I could see them from our front porch. Our home in Yakima was on what was then the western outskirts of the town. There were no trees to obstruct our view of Adams and Rainier. The locust and maple by the sidewalk had just been planted from nursery stock. The city officials, with a discerning look into the future, had brought irrigation water to each city lot, so that trees and grass could be grown. But the avenues of trees that now give shade to that lovely oasis were then only seedlings. So I saw from my home thousands of sunsets over Adams and Rainier, their glaciers tinged with red

or gold as if some artist of Paul Bunyan proporti⟨…⟩ing their
ice fields as his canvas.

On hot summer days I often looked longingl⟨…⟩ow-capped
peaks, imagining they were great chocolate⟨…⟩It took no
imagination to believe that the vast tongu⟨…⟩that poured
down from their snowy crests were cream⟨…⟩flowing over
ice cream. The idea caught my fancy. ⟨…⟩giant ice-cream
sundaes, made by Paul Bunyan who h⟨…⟩to this country
from Minnesota. Then as now, Paul Bu⟨…⟩were part of the
folklore of the region. Certainly a man whose ⟨…⟩ox measured forty
ax handles (plus the width of a tobacco can) between the eyes would
not be satisfied with sundaes of smaller proportions!

Mount Adams had the greater hold on me. In the dusk I had
often seen it cold and forbidding. When the moon and sky were
bright, its vague outline was visible from the valley, over which it
seemed to stand as a lonely sentinel. It rose in all its glory when on
a cloudless morning the rays of the sun first hit its icy sides. Then it
was truly resplendent, as a giant warrior in white armor tinged with
gold.

It was at Father's funeral that Mount Adams made its deepest
early impression on me. Indeed, that day it became a symbol of great
importance. The service was held in Yakima. Inside the church it
was dark and cool; and the minister's voice rolled around like an
echo in a cavern. It was for me meaningless and melancholy. I longed
to escape. I remember the relief I felt in walking out onto a dusty
street in bright sunlight. There were horses and carriages; and then
a long, slow trek to the cemetery. Dust, the smell of the horses, and
more dust, filled my nostrils.

It was a young cemetery. The trees were saplings. There was but
little green grass. Dust seemed to be everywhere. I heard hard, dry
lumps of dirt strike the casket. The cemetery became at once a place
of desolation that I shunned for years. As I stood by the edge of the
grave a wave of lonesomeness swept over me. Then in my lonesomeness I became afraid—afraid of being left alone, afraid because the
grave held my defender and protector. These feelings were deepened

by the realization that Mother was afraid and lonesome too. My throat choked up, and I started to cry. I remembered the words of the minister who had said to me, "You must now be a man, sonny." I tried to steel myself and control my emotions.

Then I happened to see Mount Adams, towering over us on the west. It was dark purple and white in the August day. Its shoulders of basalt were heavy with glacial snow. It was a giant whose head touched the sky.

As I looked, I stopped sobbing. My eyes dried. Adams stood cool and calm, unperturbed by an event that had stirred us so deeply that Mother was crushed for years. Adams suddenly seemed to be a friend. Adams subtly became a force for me to tie to, a symbol of stability and strength.

Chapter III   Infantile Paralysis

THERE was a driving force that took me first to the foothills and then to the mountains, though I myself did not recognize it for what it was until years later. From the time I was about twelve years old I took every occasion to slip out of town for hikes into the foothills. The occasions were not frequent, for each day after school I delivered newspapers and on Saturdays I worked in stores, creameries, and cold storage plants. In the summer months I worked in the packing houses and orchards at all the jobs that were available—thinning of fruit, spraying, irrigating, picking, making boxes, packing fruit, icing and loading refrigerator cars. There was a regular sequence of fruit during the summer—cherries, apricots, peaches, pears, and apples. But there were gaps between the crops. And in the fall, winter, and spring, there were Sunday afternoons, holidays, and occasional evenings when a few hours would be free. On these occasions I explored the foothills.

I would leave the town and head toward Selah Gap, the point of the foothills nearest my home on North Fifth Avenue. There I would test my legs and lungs against the hillside. It was hard work: two miles at the fast pace of perhaps five or six miles an hour; the climb of a hillside 500 feet or more in elevation; then a return to home and bed, dead tired, every muscle of my legs aching. Time and again I followed this routine, turning my back on more pleasant diversions that Yakima offered.

A friend who preferred the shade of the locust trees in the city, the movies, and the reading room of the Y.M.C.A. would taunt me about these trips. He conceded that it took something special to climb the monotonous foothills over and again. But he added, "Being a fool don't hurt any either."

It was, however, infantile paralysis that drove me to the outdoors. I had had it when I was a small child. I ran a high fever for several weeks. All but the country doctor despaired of my life, and he had only a slightly more optimistic view. He finally confided in Mother and gave her his candid opinion: There was a good chance that I would lose the use of my legs; even if I did not, I would not live long—probably not beyond forty. He had no remedy for the short life. He did, however, have a prescription for the legs—a prescription that the medical profession forty years later had hardly improved upon. His prescription was frequent massage in salt water, a fifteen-minute massage every two hours every day for weeks.

Mother kept a vigil. She soaked my legs in warm salt water and rubbed it into my pores, massaging each leg muscle every two hours, day after day, night after night. She did not go to bed for six weeks. The fever passed; but the massages continued for weeks thereafter.

I vaguely recall the ordeal. I lay in bed too weak to move. My legs felt like pipestems; they seemed almost detached, the property of someone else. They were so small and thin that Mother's hands could go clear around them. She would knead them like bread; she would push her hands up them and then down, up and down, up and down, until my skin was red and raw. But she would not stop because of that. She said she wanted me to be strong, to be able to run. She told me that when she was a girl she could run like the wind; no one could catch her. She wondered if I would ever be able to do so. And then she'd laugh and rub my legs—rub and rub and rub—and two hours later, rub some more.

One day the doctor came and I sat on the edge of the bed. I could not stand alone. I reached for Mother's hand, pulled myself up, and stood there weak and unsteady. I tried to walk but could not. I saw tears in Mother's eyes, and she and the doctor went away to have a whispered conversation.

The massages were continued. I lay in bed most of the time. Each day I tried to walk a bit. The weakness in my legs gradually disappeared. My feet would flop a bit; the muscles of my knees would twitch; curious numb sensations would come and go. But before many months I relearned to walk, and the frailty which the disease had caused seemed to pass. Someone said that the salt water and massages had effected wonders. Mother was silent awhile and then said, "So did my prayers."

But the ordeal had left its scars. Mother believed the doctor implicitly, and was convinced that the sand would fast run out of my glass. So she set about to guard my health, to protect me against physical strains, to do all sorts of favors designed to save my energy. I was waited on, hand and foot. Worse than that, I began to hear what Mother was saying to others: "He's not as strong as other boys; he has to be careful what he does—you know, his legs were almost paralyzed."

This solicitousness set up a severe reaction. It seemed to me I was being publicly recognized as a puny person—a weakling. Thus there began to grow in me a great rebellion. I protested against Mother's descriptions of me. But I believe my rebellion was not so much against her as it was against the kind of person I thought I was coming to be.

The crisis in my attitude was reached when I was around thirteen years old. I wore knee breeches, knickerbocker style. Black cotton stockings covered my legs. I was spindly. Concentrated exercise, like sprinting or wrestling, made me feel faint; and sometimes I'd be sick at my stomach or get a severe headache. I was deeply sensitive about my condition and used many a stratagem to conceal my physical weakness.

One day I was walking to school, carrying a pile of books under one arm. I heard a group of boys coming behind. They were older boys in the same public school, but strangers to me. As they caught up, one said, "Look at that kid's skinny legs. Aren't they something? Did you ever see anything as funny?"

The others laughed; then another one said, "Sure would cover them up if they were mine."

The words were a lash across my face. The laughter burned like an iron on my neck. I was humiliated and ashamed. I wanted to retort. But I trembled and my throat became dry so I could not answer. Then, as quickly as a flash flood, came tears.

I could not face up to the boys because of the tears. I had to turn away. It seemed that by crying I had not only confirmed but had proved the charge twice over. I stood condemned in the public eye— a weakling.

A great depression swept over me and lingered for months. I didn't want to go to school. I wanted to hide. I wanted long trousers —an idea that Mother pooh-poohed. I wanted to stay indoors. I felt ashamed of my appearance. I became self-conscious and shy. I was irritable and sensitive to criticism.

I imagined I saw in the appraising eyes of everyone who looked at me the thought, "Yes, he's a weakling." The idea festered. As I look back on those early years, I think I became a rebel with a cause. My cause was the disproof of the charge of inferiority that had been leveled by the jury of my contemporaries. There was no one in whom I could confide; no one to whom I could express my inner turmoil and tension. So the revolt grew and grew in my heart.

My first resolve, I think, was to prove my superiority by achievement in a field that was open even to a boy with weak and puny legs. That field was the schoolroom.

"I can get good grades, if I work," I said. "I can get better grades than any strong-legged boy in school. I can get 100 in every course."

No one could get higher grades than that. I'd prove I was not a weakling. So I threw myself into that endeavor. I poured every ounce of energy I could muster into my studies and came close to making the scholastic record I had set for myself.

But my scholastic achievements did not solve my difficulties. There was the haunting thought that infantile paralysis had left me a weakling, that I was indeed a cripple, unable to compete with other boys in the physical world. And the physical world loomed large in my mind. I read what happened to cripples in the wilds. They were the weak strain that nature did not protect. They were cast aside, discarded for hardier types. The coyote got the deer or fawn that was too weak to keep up with the others. The crippled bird did not have much chance to survive the cats and hawks and other enemies that roamed the countryside. Man was the same, I thought. Only strong men can do the work of the world—operating trains, felling trees, digging ditches, managing farms. Only robust men can be heroes of a war.

During my school studies I had read of the Spartans of ancient Greece. They were rugged and hardy people, the kind that I aspired to be. So I searched out the literature that described their habits and capacities to see if I could get some clue to their toughness. My research brought to light various staggering bits of information. I found in Plato's *Republic* a passage that shattered my morale. Plato talked of the dangers to the race through propagation of the "inferior" type of person. By the "inferior" he meant those who were physical weaklings. There was no doubt about it, because he described what should be done with children of that character,

The proper officers will take the offspring of the good parents to the pen or fold, and there they will deposit them with certain nurses who dwell in a separate quarter, but the offspring of the inferior, or of the better when they chance to be deformed, will be put away in some mysterious, unknown place, as they should be.

These were ideas that I struggled against. It was oppressive to think that I would have been destroyed by the Spartans to make room for some hardier boy. By boyhood standards I was a failure. If I were to have happiness and success, I must get strong. And so I searched for ways and means to do it.

One day I met another boy, whom I had known at Sunday school, coming in on a fast walk from the country. He was a husky, long-legged chap, to me a perfect physical specimen. I asked him where he'd been, and he replied that he had been climbing the foothills north of town. I asked him why he did it. He told me that his doctor had advised it; that he was trying to correct certain difficulties following an illness. He was climbing the foothills every day to develop his lungs and legs.

An overwhelming light swept me. My resolution was instantaneous. I would do the same. I would make my legs strong on the foothills.

Thus I started my treks, and used the foothills as one uses weights or bars in a gymnasium. First I tried to go up the hills without stopping. When I conquered that, I tried to go up without change of pace. When that was achieved, I practiced going up not only without a change of pace but whistling as I went.

That fall and winter the foothills began to work a transformation in me. By the time the next spring arrived, I had found new confidence in myself. My legs were filling out. They were getting stronger. I could go the two miles to Selah Gap at a fast pace and often reach the top of the ridge without losing a step or reducing my speed. Following these hikes the muscles of my knees would twitch and make it difficult for me to sleep at night. But I felt an increasing flow of health in my legs, and a growing sense of contentment in my heart.

Chapter IV *Sagebrush and Lava Rock*

THESE early hikes put me on intimate terms with the hills. I learned something of their geology and botany. I came to know the Indian legends associated with them. I discovered many of their secrets. I learned that they were always clothed in garments of delicate hues, though they seemed to be barren. I discovered that though they looked dead and monotonous, they teemed with life and had many moods.

There is a Russian saying that every devil praises the marshes where he was born. Early associations control the nostalgic urges of every person. For Holmes it was granite rocks and barberry bushes. For others it may be lilacs, sycamores, willows, the checkerboard of wheat lands, or rolling hills. My love is for what many would put down as the dreariest aspects of the dry foothills of the West—sagebrush and lava rock.

This sagebrush (*Artemisia tridentata Nutt.*) is found throughout the West. It is as American as the New England twang, the Southern drawl, the "You bet" of the West, or "Youse guys" from Brooklyn. It covers the foothills around Yakima. It grows at 8000 feet on Hart Mountain in southern Oregon. It holds the soil in place throughout the western belt from Canada to Mexico. It is the bush that Lewis and Clark called "southern wood." It commonly grows only a foot and a half or two feet high. But in gullies and ravines and other spots that collect water for part of the year, it may grow as high as a man's head. John Scharff, superintendent of the Malheur Bird Refuge in southern Oregon, bragged of the Steens Mountain sagebrush, "It's real timber, boys. This fall my first job is to run some lines and cruise and scale it."

It's tough and wiry; and it makes a quick, hot, pungent fire. In the springtime its tender new leaves make browse for antelope and sheep. Bunchgrass that cures on the stalk, and provides year-round food for stock, grows in its shade. It also furnishes protection and moisture for the myriad of wild flowers that in springtime briefly paint light streaks of blue and yellow and white on desert slopes. And it is in its full glory when spring rains fall.

That's the way I first remember it on the foothills of Yakima at night. A light, warm rain was falling. The air was permeated with the smell of freshly dampened dust and with the pungent but delicate odor of sage.

The lava rock is part of the great Columbia lava or basalt, which includes some andesite. Layer upon layer of it underlies eastern Washington and Oregon. During the Tertiary period it boiled up from the bowels of the earth. The period of its greatest activity was the Miocene, some 30 million years ago. There were at times centuries between the various flows. This molten rock poured largely out of great fissures, not from volcanoes. It flooded the entire Yakima country, which then was largely a lowland, and covered most of what is now the Cascades. There were at least 28 layers of the hot, liquid rock poured over this country. Their aggregate thickness is over 5000 feet. The magnitude of the Columbia lava as a geological phenomenon has never been surpassed and has been equalled only by the great Deccan basalts in India. The Deccan trap covers about 200,000 square miles on the west side of the peninsula of India. In the vicinity of Bombay it is about 6000 feet thick. The Deccan trap is older than the Columbia lava for it belongs to the Cretaceous rather than the Tertiary period. It is largely horizontal and has suffered greater decay than ours.

In the late Miocene there was great volcanic activity in the Cascades. Streams flowing eastward deposited light-colored sandstones and gravels (known as the Ellensburg Formation) on top of the basalt. Near Yakima are clay deposits covered by a lava flow a hundred feet thick. So it must be that a huge wave of molten rock once overran a large lake, obliterating it with a hissing of steam and filling the sky with clouds of smoke from the trees and shrubs that were ignited in the process. We know that this was long before the glacial period. The lava surfaces have been polished by thick tongues of ice that moved down from the north in the Pleistocene age, a million and a half years or more ago. A glacier indeed moved to the edge of the Yakima Valley and lay there on the lava for tens of thousands of years.

The Columbia River, eating its way through the Cascades as it pours its water toward the Pacific, has revealed many of these layers. The Snake River, when it carved Hell's Canyon between Oregon and Idaho and dug down 7900 feet to make the deepest hole on the continent, disclosed even more. That canyon reveals dozens of layers of the black lava, each 20 or 30 feet thick. They look at a distance like layers of rich chocolate in a Paul Bunyan cake.

A whole hillside 3,000 to 4,000 feet high is carved into a series of plateaus shaped like huge steps. Vast fields of bunchgrass run down hill between these outcroppings. Each field ends at the edge of a cliff of rimrock. Thus in this region it is not unusual during slippery weather to have cattle literally fall out of pasture and be killed.

Out of Yakima, along the Naches and especially the Tieton, the lava takes bizarre and startling forms. It may lie in sheets that appear as thin as flakes of chocolate candy. It often stands like cordwood on end, or rises like giant pillars against a hillside. Huge corners of it will form the shoulder of a ridge or a spire above the crest. And the discoloration caused by the lichens and moss that often grow on its exposed surfaces suggests the unfinished work of unseen artists.

This rock retains the heat of the sun throughout the night. For that reason the orchards of Yakima that are surrounded by outcroppings of it are quite free from frosts that kill fruit less favorably located. For that reason also, rattlesnakes are sometimes found curled on lava rock, warming their bellies.

Once a rattler, so positioned, struck at me. I was standing on a steep hillside, shoulder high to a ledge of rimrock. I heard the rattle, and from the corner of my eye I saw him coiled and ready to strike, not more than two feet from my cheek. As he struck I jumped, lost

my footing, and rolled 40 or 50 feet down the ravine. Remembering,
I still seem to feel his hissing breath near my ear.

That was carelessness. For we who were raised in the environment
of the Columbia lava know the risks of the rattler. All up and down
the Ahtanum, Tieton, and Naches were stories of fishermen who
were bitten on the fingers or face when they grasped lava ledges
above them without first exploring the top. One moves warily through
this lava rock country.

The rattlesnake—Wak-puch—is not entirely evil. Unlike other
poisonous snakes, he is sufficiently friendly to speak before he strikes,
to give notice of his plans. And he much prefers to escape man than
to attack him. His attack is only to repel a trespass. This is his
domain, his ancestral home. He was here long before man. Hence
there is reason why he can speak with authority. Moreover, according
to the lore of the Yakimas, he has magical powers. He hears what
people say and can avenge insults. To this day the Yakimas are super-
stitious about killing him. Thus on these earlier explorations of the
foothills the rattler added mystery, suspense, and magic to the land of
lava rock and sagebrush.

When I walked the foothills of Yakima on wintry nights I would
often build a bonfire of sagebrush at the base of an outcropping of
rimrock. There I would sit, my back to the rock, protected from the
wind, hoping the warmth of the fire would not awaken a den of
rattlers with the false message that an early spring had arrived.

I discovered on my early hikes that the moods of the foothills are
as variable as the seasons of the year or the hours of the day. In the
spring they have a light green tinge. Later they turn to yellows and
browns when the cheatgrass (Bromus tectorum) becomes a dry husk
and when the bunchgrass cures on the stalk. One who sees them
casually from a Pullman car would rate them dreary and dull.
Theodore Winthrop, the first white man to cross over the Washington Cascades from the west, described these foothills in Canoe and
Saddle in 1853 as a "large monotony." But they have great charm
for those who come to know them.

In the afternoon sun they can appear as soft and smooth as a lady's velvet gown. In the gathering haze of a storm they can be a bluish-green in the distance, somber and threatening. At sunrise after a storm they often glisten like a hillside of ripe grain. In the fall they take on a mustardy yellow hue.

Clouds can transform them from a drab to a warm, colorful backdrop for the valley. And the transformation can come as fast as the conception of life itself. A setting sun can turn their dull brown to red, orange, or blue. Those who were raised under the spell of the Green Mountains, the Berkshires, or the White Mountains would have difficulty in accommodating themselves to the poverty of our barren foothills. But one who watches them closely for an hour on a summer evening will see as many different moods as man himself has in a day.

It was a real ordeal for me to walk them in the dead of summer. Then they were parched and dry. They offered no shade from the hot sun and no springs or creeks where thirst could be quenched. Then the rattlesnake seemed to thrive. But in the spring, fall, and winter the foothills were interesting places to explore; my exercises on their slopes were then more fun than ordeal.

In the spring the tender leaves of the sage appeared. Blossoms of the bitterbrush painted streaks of yellow through the sage. In the draws and ravines the western ryegrass sent up new shoots. The earliest of the wild flowers was the pepper-and-salt, the diminutive member of the Lomatiums. It often flowered under the snow as the trailing arbutus does in New England. A soft carpet of violets, buttercups, yellow bells, and eye grasses would appear. But these were fragile flowers that hardly had a chance to taste the sweetness of life before they died. Then came the dwarf phlox and the delicate shooting stars. The lupine, dwarf sunflowers, sage pinks, and blue bells were hardier specimens and lingered longer. But they too were usually gone by June, leaving some relics behind. The relics were the pods of lupine that were poisonous to stock, and the dry leaves of the sunflower plant that rustled and rattled when I walked through them.

That sound always startled me with the thought that I had disturbed a snake.

Yet the disappearance of these flowers did not mark the passage of all color that transformed this parched land into a colorful garden. Later came the purple and white asters; the ever present yarrow; the sedum with its starry flowers of bright yellow; the wild onion, one of the loveliest of all the filigrees of nature, its six petals of deep purple set off by anthers of pale yellow; and the exquisite bitterroot. In some ravines, especially those out Cowiche way, came scatterings of wild rose, elderberry, chokecherry, and mockorange.

I do not envy those whose introduction to nature was lush meadows, lakes, and swamps where life abounds. The desert hills of Yakima had a poverty that sharpened perception. Even a minute violet quickens the heart when one has walked far or climbed high to find it. Where nature is more bountiful, even the tender bitterroot might go unnoticed. Yet when a lone plant is seen in bloom on scabland between batches of bunchgrass and sage, it can transform the spot as completely as only a whole bank of flowers could do in a more lush environment. It is the old relationship between scarcity and value.

These are botanical lessons of the desert which the foothills of Yakima taught me.

In the early spring, when the soft chinooks came up from the southwest, I especially loved to leave the city and take to the foothills. Chinook is the name of Indians who lived on the west side of the Cascades. Early settlers on the reaches of the Columbia called warm, damp winds by the name chinook because such winds ordinarily came from the direction where these Indians lived. Gradually the name was attached to the equatorial trade winds that sweep the north Pacific coast from the southwest. It was the wind I first felt on my cheeks the night Father brought us to Yakima. It was a beneficent wind. And because it sang softly on the ridges and stirred the whole valley to life, it seemed full of romance and enchantment.

The Yakimas have a legend about this wind that centers around the coyote. Coyote (Speel-yi) had a unique symbolic significance among the Yakimas and other tribes that inhabited the Columbia River Valley and the eastern slopes of the Cascades. He was the agent through which the Spirit Chief worked his will. Coyote had supernatural powers. He had only to give the command and a salmon would jump out of the river into his arms. He could change himself into a man, a dish, a board, or any other object. He could also transform others by his magic. Thus the water snipe and the kildee had been women who had rejected his overtures and scorned him, and whom he therefore had decreed should always live near the river and eat fish.

Coyote could be killed and yet return to life in his old form or in a new one. He was wily and smart, with keen insight into human motivations. Compared to him the fox was slow-witted. And though Coyote was crafty and selfish, his main concern was for the welfare of the people.

In each tribe there were a few elderly Indians who could understand the meaning of the howls of the coyote. In this manner the death of some important man in a far-off community was predicted by listening to the changing howls of the coyote. In addition to forecasting future events, these coyote howls were a method of communication between tribes. Thus Alba Showaway, son of Alex, chief of the Yakimas, told me that the death of a leading Indian in Warm Springs, Oregon, hundreds of miles away, was relayed by coyotes the very next day to the medicine men of the Yakimas.

Even today some of the Yakimas will not kill a coyote. Though many of them have discarded their old superstitions because of the bounty and the value of the pelts, a residue of the old attitude persists. Only recently Alba Showaway accidentally killed a coyote. He directed that the hide be removed and the carcass buried deep down in the ground. The next morning he discovered that his dog had dug up the body and was eating it. Shortly thereafter the dog had four puppies, which, according to Alba, died one after the other because the mother had partaken of the flesh of the coyote.

It has been thought that the deification of Coyote was due to the

fact that Tyhee, the Spirit Chief of the Indians of the Pacific Northwest, was a revengeful not a beneficent diety. He had no kindness or
compassion in his heart. The Indians observed that in the woods the
weaker animals survived only by cunning. That was therefore the
only route by which they could escape the vengeance of their god.
So they deified the weakest and craftiest of all major animals, the
coyote, to help them in their struggle for survival.

The legend of the chinook wind runs as follows: The Chinook
brothers caused the warm wind to blow from the southwest. The
Walla Walla brothers caused a cold wind to blow from the northeast.
These two groups were always fighting. The Walla Walla brothers
would freeze rivers; the Chinook brothers would thaw them. There
would be floods and the people would suffer.

Coyote finally refereed between these warring factors. Every time
a contestant fell down, Coyote would cut off his head. At last there
were only two left, and Coyote let each live. But Coyote told the
Walla Walla that he must blow lightly and never again freeze the
people. Coyote told the Chinook that he was the warm breath to
melt the winter's snow but that he should blow hardest only at night
and that he should always warn the people by blowing first on the
ridges of the mountains. Thus Coyote brought a mild climate to the
people.

The chinook wind did in fact seem to blow hardest at night. Then
it was exhilarating to be abroad. That was one reason why I liked to
start for the near-by foothills at dusk, have a light supper at the top
of a ridge before a sagebrush fire, and take off into the west.

The outdoors always seemed to come to life at night. These barren
windswept ridges, which seemed so dead and dull and listless under
the high sun, would fairly murmur in the darkness. When I stood
still and listened I could hear the chinook wind rustle the sage and
set up in the cheatgrass a faint vibration.

If I stretched out on the ground and listened, I could indeed hear
the cheatgrass singing softly in the wind. The sage, too, would join
the symphony. It was Peattie who said that the sage lets the wind go
softly and tirelessly through its fingers (*The Road of a Naturalist*).

But the legend is that, as it does so, it sings in memory of the Idaho Indians whose plains it covered as far as the eye could see and whose mountains it decorated far above the deep-snow line. And the verse of its song is always the same, "Shoshone, Shoshone."

A startled jack rabbit would stomp and give the alarm and make off through the sage. A mouse would scurry for his hole. An owl, interrupted in his prowl, would screech his disapproval of the intrusion and, flapping coarsely, make off into the night. In the early evening I would often see silhouetted against the skyline a coyote standing on some ledge or point of rock. Almost invariably, if I were out for a few hours, his plaintive cry would come floating down to me on the wind from a distant rimrock. And when I disturbed the desert life by putting a dog out in front, the noise was for a place of desolation a veritable commotion.

The air was fragrant with the delicate odor of sage. The chinook always carried, as it swept across this desert area, the distinctively refreshing smell of dusty earth freshly dampened. The chinook was soft and balmy and brought rain to the dry interior of Washington which had become parched when the Cascades rose to such heights that they cut off the moisture from the ocean.

When I tramped the foothills in dead of winter, the pulse of life on the ridges was slow. The wind swept down from Mount Adams and Mount Rainier, cold and piercing. When I bent forward walking into it, I soon would be looking for some black rimrock where I could find protection from the wind and where I could build a sagebrush fire. When I turned around and started home, the strong wind at my back made me feel as if the strength of giants was in me. I strode along the barren ridge in ease, commanding the city that lay at my feet.

Once the valleys hemmed in by these foothills were lakes. Beyond the gap to the north in the Kittitas Valley, there had been a lake. There had also been one in the Selah Valley to the northwest, in the Naches to the northwest, in the Ahtanum to the west, in the Moxee to the east, and in the Lower Valley south of Union Gap. The Indians had first arrived in the valley by boat. They came in the fashion of Noah, bringing with them various types of animals. That was the legend, and A. J. Splawn, early settler and noted authority on the Yakimas, marked the spot where they landed. It was north of the Yakima River on the side of the foothills where there is an oval-shaped spur resembling an inverted canoe.

The Indians lived on the ridges surrounding those lakes. They had difficulty with their food supply. Wishpoosh, a giant beaver, was abroad in the land. He took possession of the lakes north of Yakima. He was a vicious monster. He molested and devoured every living thing that passed his way. He was so dangerous that the people could not fish the lakes.

When Coyote came to this region he found the people in the midst of plenty of uncaught fish and on the verge of famine. So he decided to help them by destroying Wishpoosh. He took a strong spear and lashed it on his arm. He then went hunting for Wishpoosh. He found him asleep by the shore of the lake north of Yakima and at once drove the spear deep into his body. Wishpoosh, enraged, dived into the lake and went to the bottom, taking Coyote with him. There began a struggle for life or death between these powerful gods.

They plunged through the lake, tearing a gap in the foothills to the south. They went from lake to lake, crashing against ridge after ridge. Through the gaps they created, the whole region was drained of water.

There are geologic facts that may be the roots from which some of these legends have stemmed. The first land of the Far West was the Blue Mountains of eastern Oregon and the Siskiyous of southern Oregon and northern California. They started to emerge during the long Cretaceous period, from about 60 million to 70 million years ago, when most of Europe was still under the sea. Then came the Rockies and the Cascades. Before the end of the Cretaceous period the Cascades had become a dike, shutting out the ocean and creating a great inland sea that washed the western slopes of the Rockies and later was divided into a series of vast lakes. By the beginning of the

Tertiary period, the Cascades had not reached an elevation sufficient to exclude the warm, moist air from the Pacific. The Gulf of Mexico reached far to the north. Moreover, much of Alaska was probably then under water, making it possible for the Japanese current to flow northeast to Greenland and eliminate all snow and ice between the Pacific Northwest and the Arctic Ocean. These great inland areas were thus subtropical. There the palm tree and sequoia flourished; there the rhinoceros and saber-toothed tiger roamed.

But the Cascades did not remain a dike. They continued to emerge from the sea, casting off the sand and mud of the ocean bed, and reached an elevation that cut off the moisture of the ocean from the interior. The Alaska range pushed its backbone above the waters and shut off the Japanese current from the northern reaches of the continent. The interior country changed in climate, fauna, and flora. As folds of the earth rose and tilted, lakes were tipped like huge saucepans and emptied of their waters. Hot, molten lava overran others and destroyed them. Then came a new series of lakes. This was in Pleistocene time, about a million and a half years ago. For some reason not fully understood, water backed up along the Columbia and its tributaries and formed large fresh-water lakes. Water rose to about 1250 feet above sea level.

Probably the greatest of these was Lewis Lake, which lay in the Yakima Valley and reached far to the south and west. Icebergs that floated on it carried a cargo of boulders of granite, gneiss, and basalt and dropped them hither and yon across the valley. The herds of horses and camels that had inhabited the area were driven south by the cold. The mastodon, mammoth, mylodon, and broad-faced ox appeared. When the glaciers receded, great floods occurred. These floods followed the channels that had been dug in preglacial days and accelerated the creation of the drainage system of the Columbia. The vast region drained by the Columbia was spotted with a whole series of lakes, rimmed by foothills and ridges like those surrounding Yakima. These lakes became connected by drainage links from one to another, until they all finally linked up into one continuous stream that wore its way to the ocean through all barriers, including the Cascades. Thus was the mighty Columbia River created.

The Yakima had the same kind of origin, though it grew on a lesser scale. It, too, wore through ridges separating various lakes and linked them into one drainage system. Most rivers run around mountains or follow the contours of their base. But the Yakima was unorthodox—like the Columbia, it went cross-country, cutting through at least seven ridges or foothills as it reached out serpentine fashion to join the Columbia at Pasco.

The reason for this, geologists say, is that the surface movements of the hills, beginning in Pliocene time, and the erosive action of the water apparently were closely synchronized. The uplift of the ridges was so slow that the water was able to keep its spillways open and wear away the rock as fast as it rose in the channels.

When the region was drained, the hot, dry breath of the desert touched the land and parched it. The sagebrush appeared, perhaps from some airway of the world, and covered the land in a gray-green blanket. Wind and water and frost began a process of erosion that exposed the dark lava. It broke through the garment of topsoil that had covered it and disclosed patches of its black body throughout the farthest reaches of this desert land.

There are two early trips to the foothills that stand out specially in my memory. One was in early spring. I had left town before dusk and climbed the barren ridge west of Selah Gap. On the way up I had crossed a draw and caught the sweet odor of the mockorange. The species around Yakima is *Philadelphus lewisii*, discovered in 1806 by Lewis and Clark and named in honor of Lewis. It is the state flower of Idaho. It has four or five cream-white petals with a golden center of bright yellow stamens. Elk and deer browse it. The Indians used its slender shoots for arrow shafts, hence its other name, Indian arrowwood. In the darkness I could vaguely see the lone shrub that filled this draw with the fragrance of orange blossoms. It stood six feet high and in this barren ravine seemed strangely out of place because of the delicacy of its fragrance.

The night was clear and the moon had just reached the horizon. Mount Adams loomed in the west, "high-humped," as Lewis and Clark aptly described it when they saw it on April 2, 1806. Along the ridge of the Cascades to the north was Mount Rainier, cold, aloof, and forbidding. Below at my feet the lights of the town had come on, blinking like stars of a minor firmament. A faint streak of light, sparkling in the moonlight, marked the course of the Yakima as it wound its way across the valley, through dark splotches of sumac, cottonwood, and willow.

Above the dark rim of the foothills were the stars of the universe. They were the same stars that saw these valleys and hills and mountains rise from the murk of the ocean, reaching for the sun. They saw the Columbia lava, hot and steaming, pour in molten form across this land again and again, scorching to cinders everything it touched, burying great ponderosa pine four and five feet thick under its deep folds, and filling the sky with smoke that finally drew a curtain over the sun. They saw a subtropical land touched by the chill of the Arctic and rimmed with ice and snow. They saw the mighty Columbia and the Yakima grow from driblets to minor drainage canals to great rivers. They saw the glaciers recede and floods come. After the floods they saw the emergence of a desert that some unseen hand had sown with fragrant sage and populated with coyotes, rabbits, kangaroo rats, sage hens, sage sparrows, desert sparrows, bluebirds, and doves. They saw the Indians first appear on the horizon to the north, spreading out to all parts of the continent in their long trek from Asia. And thousands of years later they saw some newcomers arrive, the ones that fought, quarreled, and loved, the ones that built houses and roads and planted orchards, the ones that erected spires and lifted their eyes to the sky in prayer.

On the foothills that night I think I got my first sense of Time. I began to appreciate some of the lessons that geology taught. In the great parade of events that this region unfolded, man was indeed insignificant. He appeared under this firmament only briefly and then disappeared. His transit was indeed too short for geological time to measure.

As I walked the ridge that evening, I could hear the chinook on distant ridges before it reached me. Then it touched the sage at my feet and made it sing. It brushed my cheeks, warm and soft. It ran its fingers through my hair and rippled away in the darkness. It was a friendly wind, friendly to man throughout time. It was beneficent, carrying rain to the desert. It was soft, bringing warmth to the body. It had almost magical qualities, for it need only lightly touch the snow to melt it.

It became for me that night a measure of the kindliness of the universe to man, a token of the hospitality that awaits man when he puts foot on this earth. It became for me a promise of the fullness of life to him who, instead of shaking his fist at the sky, looks to it for health and strength and courage.

That night I felt at peace. I felt that I was a part of the universe, a companion to the friendly chinook that brought the promise of life and adventure. That night, I think, there first came to me the germ of a philosophy of life: that man's best measure of the universe is in his hopes and his dreams, not his fears; that man is a part of a plan, only a fraction of which he, perhaps, can ever comprehend.

The other trip was in April when I walked the ridge north of Yakima on a Sunday afternoon. Below me the Yakima Valley was a vast garden in bloom. The peach and cherry blossoms were out in all their glory. The valley resembled a giant bowl of short-stemmed flowers. The pink and white blossoms covered the bottom and sent traces of their fragrance even to the ridges. It was a delicately perfumed scene. Nature had brought a whole valley to life in a rush, changing its color, filling it with the hope of things to come, making it pregnant with the bloom of a new crop.

I looked down, and there in the sage at my feet was a scattering of the bitterroot or rockrose. It is a gentle membrane that the Creator has fashioned out of dust and made to decorate even places of desolation. It is a low plant with waxy flowers, delicate pink with a rib of darker hue. It has a translucent quality that makes it look fragile to the touch, as fragile as the gossamer wings of some tropical butterfly. It is the state flower of Montana. It was collected by Lewis at the mouth of the Lou Lou Fork of the Bitterroot River in Montana. Its roots are the spatlum known to Indians, explorers, and early settlers as valued food. They do indeed contain a rich supply of starch, and when eaten (dried and raw) have that taste. But it is a taste that is slightly bitter; hence its name. Its leaves dry up and vanish when the flowers appear. And the blossoms open with the sun and close with darkness. I never see the bitterroot blooming among the sage without feeling that I should take off my hat and stand in adoration at the wondrous skill of the Creator. I'll always remember the words of the artist who said, "I have grown to feel that there is nothing more amazing about a personal God than there is about the blossoming of the gorgeous little bitterroot."

A strong wind suddenly came up from the south. It brought the dust of Pasco and Prosser on its wings, and produced small flurries of petals from the fruit blossoms as it swept across the orchards. Behind the wind came dark clouds splattering rain on the Lower Valley. With the rain there were forked tongues of lightning that played along the ridges across the valley from me; then there was thunder that rolled endlessly as it echoed off the hills of the Ahtanum and Naches. In a little while the storm veered, turned east over Moxee, and slowly melted away on the eastern horizon. The sun appeared and the flowering basin of the valley once more lay in splendor below me.

To the west Adams and Rainier stood forth in power and beauty—monarchs of every peak in their range. The backbone of the Cascades was clear against the western sky, its slopes and ravines dark blue in the afternoon sun. The distant ridges and canyons seemed soft and friendly. They appeared to hold untold mysteries and to contain solitude many times more profound than that of the barren ridge on which I stood. They offered streams and valleys and peaks to explore, snow fields and glaciers to conquer, wild animals to know. That afternoon I felt that they extended me an invitation—an invitation to get acquainted with them, an invitation to tramp their trails and sleep in their high basins.

My heart filled with joy, for I knew I could accept the invitation. I would have legs and lungs equal to it.

Chapter V   *Ahtanum*

DURING the summer months of the following ten years I made many trips into the Washington Cascades. These treks into the mountains usually were no mere overnight or week-end jaunts; often they would last a week or two or even longer. On these trips I almost always had companions: Bradley Emery, Elon Gilbert, Douglas Corpron, or my brother Arthur. We usually went by foot, carrying our supplies on our backs.

In this fashion I hiked through much of the wild country between Mount Adams and Mount Rainier on the eastern slopes of the Cascades. I walked most of the trails in that region, climbed most of the peaks, explored many of the ridges, fished or looked down into practically all of the numerous lakes, camped in dozens of the meadows, and sampled the trout in almost every stream in that vast watershed. But for infantile paralysis I might not have done so.

Though I usually went by foot with a pack on my back, one of the earliest trips—and my first one into the beautiful Klickitat Meadows was at the same time both more luxurious and more painful.

One June, Elon and Horace Gilbert and their cousin Gilbert Peck were leaving early in the week by horseback for the Klickitat Meadows. I had a job picking cherries and could not afford to leave until Saturday. So we arranged that they would take the camp outfit, including my bedroll, in by pack train and meet me by midafternoon on Saturday near the top of Darling Mountain.

Klickitat means "galloping horse," and if the word is repeated rapidly, it is easy to see why. Its meaning has special significance to me because of the experience of this first trip of mine into the Klickitat Meadows.

The shortest route from Yakima is through the Ahtanum. That valley has a fast, clear-water stream by the same name, a stream that is rich in Indian lore. The Indians had frequented the Ahtanum more than they had the Tieton and Naches, for it was closer to the center of their ancestral home in the Lower Valley. Here they had fished for salmon and entered the Cascades in search of deer. They also had scattered their sweat lodges (We-ach) along the banks of the Ahtanum.

Dean Guie in *The Tribal Days of the Yakimas* calls these sweat lodges the most sacred and important of the Yakimas' ancient institutions. They were dome-shaped huts, three to five feet high, placed close to the water. Usually they were big enough to accommodate two sitters. The sweat lodges of men and women ordinarily were separate. Hot rocks were placed inside them, the door covered with a blanket, and water poured on the hot rocks. The person inside would be steamed.

Sweat lodges were common among the various tribes in the basins of the Columbia and the Snake. Lewis and Clark recorded that the Indians in the Snake River basin, the Nez Perce, made "great use of Swetting" with hot and cold baths. They described one underground sweat lodge that had a hole in the top through which hot stones would be dropped. Those on the inside "threw on as much water as to create the temperature of heat they wished." The Indians along the Columbia used the sweat baths frequently, both in sickness and in health and at all seasons of the year. They were particularly helpful in treatment of rheumatism, which was prevalent among these Indians.

The legend was that such sweat lodges were decreed by the Spirit Chief who, acting through Coyote, showed the Yakimas how to use them. They were places to bathe; but they were more than that. They were also places of prayer, for those who were sick and for those whose dreams had not come true. Medicine men renewed their "medicine" inside these huts; when one died, his sweat lodge was burned. Here evil spells were banished, aching limbs relieved, and illness cured. After each bath the bather usually would run to the river and jump in. The treatment was said to be particularly good for pneumonia.

But according to A. J. Splawn, famous authority on the Yakimas, the sweat lodge was no cure when the terrible scourge of smallpox swept through the tribe in 1836.

I, like most of the other youngsters, stayed clear of the sweat lodges. They were places so involved in magic and mystery as to be avoided. I thought that harm might come to one who molested them; perhaps he would run the risk of a curse. Moreover, it was legendary that Indians and fleas were closely associated. The talk was that the Indians moved their fishing camps along the Columbia to rid themselves of fleas. Lewis and Clark had, indeed, been plagued with fleas from eastern Oregon to Astoria. Every Indian visiting them had left fleas behind. Hours would be spent by the members of that expedition trying to pick fleas out of their clothes. The history of the region was full of this talk. The sweat lodge, being a place where fleas were deposited, was a place to avoid. But the fact that the sweat lodges were untouchable added mystery to the Ahtanum, where they were numerous.

The Ahtanum was an historic area in other respects also. On a green meadow on the banks of the river stands St. Joseph's Mission. This was established by the Oblate Fathers in October, 1847. It was burned in 1855 and rebuilt in 1867. It is made of logs, hand-hewn by skilled and faithful hands. It stands on the edge of an apple orchard planted in 1849, whose trees were still bearing fruit in 1949.

The Fathers who established the mission were the first white men to settle in the valley. They raised the Cross in what was then one of the most remote parts of the country. There was little to relieve the monotony and dreariness of the spot. There were, to be sure, scrub oak, cottonwood, and willow along the banks of the Ahtanum, bunchgrass in the valley, and the dark green of the Cascades to the west. But on three sides there were dusty hills covered with sagebrush and a vast expanse of desert. Yet here on the edge of an empty, barren land they built a temple of "adobe clay plastered upon a frame of sticks," as Theodore Winthrop described it in *Canoe and Saddle*. He visited it in 1853 when he crossed the Cascades from the west, traversed the western edge of the Yakima Valley, and then returned to the Old Oregon Trail at The Dalles.

He came up to it at sunset and found a service being held. Though the chapel was only a rude one of clay, it had about it "a sense of the Divine presence," a presence "not less than in many dim old cathedrals, far away, where earlier sunset had called worshippers of other race and tongue to breathe the same thanksgiving and the same heartfelt prayer." No service ever seemed more beautiful and moving to him. He wrote, "never in any temple of that ancient faith, where prayer has made its home for centuries, has prayer seemed so mighty, worship so near the ear of God, as vespers here at this rough shrine in the lonely Valley of the Atinam."

The road up the Ahtanum leading to the trails that crossed over Darling Mountain went by this mission. I never passed it without a feeling of respect and reverence for the men who came to that remote spot in order to bring the message of their faith to the Yakimas.

I wished that I could have known the men who picked this lonely place for their temple. I often wondered what their experiences with the Indians had been, and how big the salmon and trout were when they lived there. And in later years I wondered if they too had come to love the sagebrush and lava rock. I wondered if they too had been thrilled by the touch of the chinook on their cheeks. I wondered if that wind had helped relieve them of the lonesomeness of this desolate place.

On this Saturday in June when I went to meet Elon on Darling Mountain, I left Yakima in the early morning. I went by stage through Wiley City to Tampico twenty miles up the Ahtanum. Great fields of hops and grain lay on each side of the road as we left Wiley City. We went by the mission on our left and then on our right passed under a cliff that lies close to the river. It's called the Narrows and is a wall of basalt formed of large columns standing on end.

Tampico, with its general store, is a trading center for a vast cattle country. Some seven miles west of Tampico is Soda Springs, where my trail began. A dirt road leads there. On other trips I would often catch a ride out of Tampico. This day I had to walk.

I was without a pack to carry, so I settled down to four or five miles an hour. It was good to take long steps and feel the stretching of muscles at the back of my knees. It was good to keep the rhythm of the walk, never losing for a second the cadence of the swinging pace.

There were fields of blue chickory and asters in the vicinity of Tampico. Here were scatterings of *Pteryxia Californica*, with its dusty yellow flowers arranged in flat-topped clusters. And on every hand along the road was the ever present yarrow. Some Indians placed this plant inside salmon to promote the curing process while the fish were being dried. Folklore has given it dozens of uses, from the making of beer to the curing of toothaches. It bears the name of Achilles, who used it to cure the wounds of his soldiers at the siege of Troy. It has been generously scattered all over the eastern slopes of the Cascades.

Not far from Tampico were scatterings of the ponderosa pine, the big yellow pine that grows to tremendous heights on the lower reaches of the eastern slopes of the Cascades, the pine that lumbermen like. Soon the ponderosa pine began to be more abundant, thinning out the white oak and cottonwood, until higher in the canyon it finally left them behind.

In less than two hours I came to Soda Springs. Here in a grove of pine and green grass is a bubbling soda spring. I had associated soda water with drugstore counters where sweet, cold drinks could be had. So I made at once for the spring in the grove. I found an old tin cup on the grass, dipped myself a full measure of the water, and started to gulp it down. It was bitter, sulfurous water which I spit out at once. "Medicine," I muttered in disgust, as it brought back unpleasant memories of the sulfur compound Mother concocted each spring.

I did not tarry long in the cool ponderosa grove. The easy part of the hike was behind me. I had about ten miles to go before I met Elon. That distance was by a trail that climbed a few thousand feet.

The North Fork of the Ahtanum splits off at Tampico. I had followed it to Soda Springs. Beyond Soda Springs a mile or so, the

Middle Fork branches off to the south, dividing the North Fork. It was that fork that the old trail, like the present road, followed.

When I left the road at Soda Springs, I was at once in a deep forest that no ax had ever touched. Great yellow pine reached to the sky one hundred, two hundred feet. This was the dry, eastern slope of the Cascades. There was little underbrush; the woods were open, not dense. The sun came streaming in, as if it were pouring through long narrow windows high in a cathedral. The soft notes of some bird —a thrush, I believe—came floating down from the treetops. As I listened it was as though the music came from another world.

I had not gone a quarter-mile until I felt the solitude of the mountains. I had been in them before; but this was the first time I had been alone. This was the first time I had felt the full impact of their quietness.

It was so silent I could almost hear my heart beat. No moving thing was in sight. The quiet was so deep that the breaking of a twig underfoot was startling. I was alone, yet I felt that dozens of animals must be aware of my presence and watching me—hawks, flycatchers, hummingbirds, camp robbers, bear, cougar, deer, porcupine, squirrels. But when I looked I could see nothing but trees and sky.

Then I became aware of the fragrance of the trees. The ponderosa pine towered over all the others. But I began to see the scatterings of other conifers: black pine and whitebark pine, white and red fir, and the tamarack or larch. I stopped, looked up, and breathed deep. Then I realized I was experiencing a great healing.

In Yakima I had been suffering from hay fever. Now it was gone. My nose wasn't stuffy. My eyes were clearing. I breathed deeply of the fragrant air again and again, as I lifted my face to the treetops. And I realized what had happened. I had lost my allergy.

I had been hurrying, tense and strained. I was alone and on my own in unexplored land. I was conscious of being exposed to all the dangers of the woods, a prey for any predator hunting man. But now, strangely, that apprehension fell from me like ashes touched by a wind. I suddenly felt that these pine and fir that greeted the Fathers of the Ahtanum Mission in 1847 were here to welcome me, too. These trees were friends—silent, dignified, and beneficent friends. They were kindly like the chinook. They promised as much help and solace to me as had the sagebrush and lava rock.

I felt a warm glow of peace spread over me. I was at ease in this unknown wilderness. I, who had never set foot on this particular trail, who had never crossed the high ridge where I was headed, felt at home. One who is among friends, I thought, has no need to be afraid.

Then there was a roar—subdued and muffled at first, and then as loud as a great cataract. A wind had sprung up from the northwest. It swept the mountainside and set up a steady vibration in the tree-tops. I saw great pine and fir bowing before their master, swaying in the high wind. And as they swayed, their groans and creaks swelled into violence. A tremendous symphony had broken the quiet of the forest. I leaned against the trunk of a yellow pine that reached 150 or 200 feet into the sky. It towered over all the trees in the canyon. As I watched its top weaving back and forth in the gale that swept off Darling Mountain, it seemed to be a graceful partner of the wind. Had not the pine in fact been mistress of Boreas the wind from ancient days? The symphony that was being played was indeed the first music of the universe. It had been carried on the wings of this wind long before the Indians arrived from Asia, long before man walked the earth. The music of the wind in the trees brought messages floating down millions of years of time. It sang of the eternity of the universe, of the transient nature of man.

It was about nine miles to Cultus Hole; the trail had an easy grade; and I do not think I took three hours to reach it. Cultus Hole is a basin carved out of the mountainside just below the eastern shoulder of Darling Mountain. I stopped here for rest about noon and ate the sandwiches Mother had made for me that morning. The meadow of Cultus Hole was ablaze with blue lupine. There was also rich paint-brush that had been dipped in some lively pot of cerise or terra cotta. And there were splotches of blue and yellow of flowers with which I had not yet become acquainted. I lay down on my stomach and drank deep of cold water running from unseen snowbanks in ravines somewhere above me. For two hours or so I had been in the deep woods, unable to see any horizon. Now I could tell where I was. Below me to the east the Ahtanum was beginning to drop away fast. The contour of an opposite ridge was starting to take shape. Ahead of me was a pitch of hillside that promised a stiff climb to the top.

The trail rose sharply in a series of short cutbacks. It weaved around giant tamaracks that were standing on this ridge even before the First Congress met. Here were whitebark pine that knew America long before Jefferson and Lewis and Clark.

This was hard going and I took my time, stopping every dozen steps or so. It was perhaps a mile to the top, which I covered in about 30 minutes. I was ahead of time for the rendezvous with Elon.

This saddle on Darling is partially open, with scattered clumps of trees. As a result Mount Adams loomed up right in front of me before I had gone far in a westerly direction. To its left was Mount Hood; to its right was Mount St. Helens. Stretching away to the northwest were the rugged Goat Rocks, their dark basalt cliffs streaked with snow. One comes upon this view so suddenly that it is breathtaking no matter how often he walks the trail. These snow-capped peaks are so close it seems they can be touched. They rise so abruptly, tower so high, and are so majestic that they appear to belong to another world.

This day I sat down on a rock to wait for Elon. Before me were Hood, Adams, and St. Helens—mountains that once had been people, according to Indian legend. Adams had been Klickitat, a chief who ruled north of the Columbia. Wyeast, a younger brother, ruled to the south. They had quarreled over Loowit, the immortal and beautiful vestal virgin who kept the fire going on the Bridge of the Gods—a natural bridge that once stood a short distance upstream from where Bonneville Dam now stands. Tyhee, the Great Father, tired of the quarreling, and to settle it took drastic measures. He turned Klickitat into Adams and Wyeast into Hood. He put Loowit north of the Columbia and west of Adams and turned her into St. Helens.

This fantasy of the Indian legend occupied me until I was aroused by the pounding of hoofs. My three friends appeared in a rush, with whoops and hollers, on horseback and leading a horse for me. There were shouts of greetings, a short account of my trip, a description of plans that had been arranged, and then we were off.

I had driven horses in the orchards, and I had ridden workhorses bareback from field to barn; but I had never been in the saddle. I hardly had my feet in the stirrups and the reins in my hand before my young friends were headed for camp four miles distant on the Klickitat Meadows.

They rode like uncivilized Indians—on the dead run. There was no more holding my horse than turning the tide. He was not to be denied the companionship of the other horses or the prospect of early grazing in the lush Klickitat Meadows. The first half-mile led through willow and aspen and low-hanging fir. I lost my hat and almost my neck from overhanging branches.

On a swerve in the trail on a downhill pitch, I lost my stirrups. I regained them only to lose them again and again. But I never let go the reins or the horn. I "pulled leather" all the way. I had no control whatever of the horse.

It was a gentle downhill slope, which my horse took on a dead run. As he raced on and on in his mad way, I bounced to the rhythm of his pounding hoofs. He raced like a demon through a stand of giant tamarack and into a sizable grove of aspen. The leaves of the aspen trembled and shook as if they were cymbals in the hands of some weird dancer. Those who had preceded us in earlier years had carved their initials and the dates of their journeys into the white bark of these trees. Those cuts had healed leaving dark scars. Those scars combined with the natural dark splotches on the trunks of the aspens took fantastic forms. They formed faces—grotesque and distorted. "They are leering at me," I thought. "They are laughing—laughing at my bouncing." And as I raced by, bouncing in the saddle, the quivering of the leaves of the aspen, the laughter of their scarred trunks made it seem as if the trees themselves were twisting and weaving in some strange dance of a dervish.

I beat the saddle incessantly as I bounced up and down. I bounced so hard I jarred my teeth. I bounced so hard I was constantly winded.

I could not have yelled a command to the fleeing Indians had I been in earshot and had my life depended on it.

And then there was the pain in my legs. The legs that I had thought were getting strong and hardy had collapsed on me. Sick and puny? Legs like pipestems? Not as strong as other boys? Those were questions that pounded in my head. This was prophecy come true. The shooting pain in my legs was not imagination. No one was shouting at me derisively about them. Now my weakness appeared in a tangible form. In only a few minute my legs had crumbled.

Through history books I had read of tyrants putting men on the rack for torture. Maybe this was it, the rack with all its promise of anguish fulfilled. I later learned that the hips, the knees, and the ankles are all springs which when rightly used make the saddle as comfortable as an armchair. But there was no co-ordination among the springs that day. Indeed, the springs were not functioning; they were out of order.

The hips were the first to go; they froze in excruciating pain. Each lunge of the horse made it seem as if the muscles in the hips were being torn asunder. I felt like a man who was being quartered. The pain shot down the leg to the knee. The knees and the ankles ached under the hammering from the saddle. Each movement of the horse was like a knife thrust in the thigh. There was no relief. On and on we went, through patches of willow where the branches raced across the cheek, cutting hard into the skin.

On and on my horse raced, like a demon through a wilderness. Shortly we came to Cuitan Creek, a yard or so wide with a dark lava bottom. He vaulted this as if he were winged, landed on the other side, and kept on going at his terrible pace without missing a beat. He galloped recklessly through rock fields. Then he started to scrape the trees as if to be rid of his helpless, frightened rider.

The "whoas" had long ceased. I was silent and grim. For me the problem was one of survival. Leaving the horse in safety by my own volition was out of the question. My legs were paralyzed. I could not have dismounted by myself had the horse been standing still. To fall under these pounding hoofs was a frightful thought, but even more frightful was the thought of losing face before my pals. "You couldn't take it, eh?" Or darker thoughts never uttered, "Maybe the guy should have stayed home. Let's not have him the next time."

We soon came to Coyote Creek, where later I caught eight- and ten-inch cutthroat and rainbow. This creek, with its dark lava bottom, is eight or ten feet wide. My horse would not be denied. He jumped that too, hurling me against the cantle as he left the ground and then pitching me against the horn as he landed. I hung on, though I did not recover from the shock. Then the demon ran uphill the remaining 200 yards to the meadows, almost tossing me over his rear as he lurched frantically up the side of the ravine.

How I hung on I never knew, but hang on I did. It was not over twenty minutes, I suppose (though it seemed an eternity), from the time we started until we reached the meadows. Then we shot through a grove of fir and were at the edge of a beautiful expanse of green grass, a half-mile wide and a mile and a half long. "It's all over," I thought. "I finally made it."

Not so. We were at the meadows; but off to the left I saw the disappearing tail of Elon's horse. The gang was heading for another camping place. So on we went, at a dead run, for another half-mile, my anguish increased by the respite that had come so close but yet been denied.

At last I saw the camp. It was at the junction of Coyote Creek and the Little Klickitat near the lower end of the Meadows. As my horse slowed to a trot and then to a walk, I became as nonchalant as I knew how. Easing him over to a high rock, I stepped gingerly out of the saddle. I stood there regaining my poise as we bantered back and forth. I was so lame I could hardly walk; and that lameness I could not conceal. But even cowboys limp, and my limping did not cause me to fall from grace.

My legs, however, ached and trembled. They seemed paralyzed, and I wondered if the old trouble had returned. The answer was not long coming. For I wiggled my toes and knew at once that I was all right. But could I walk? Would any one laugh?

Yet those worries were overshadowed by one that was even more serious. My posterior was in a most painful condition. I could not conceal it much longer. The four-mile gallop had worn raw spots on my buttocks—raw, burning spots that clung to my trousers. I needed medical attention badly. I announced the fact. While my announcement produced great merriment, there was no ridicule. I was a casualty and some casualties were expected.

Off came my trousers for an inspection. The decision was that I was to lie on my stomach and receive medication. A large rock, as big as a grand piano, stands near the junction of the two creeks. On that rock I lay while my three youthful pals gleefully attended to my wounds and in due course patched me up in commendable style.

I remember that we had a wonderful supper that night. We also had a big campfire in the open grassy flat that lies in between the mouths of the Little Klickitat and Coyote Creek. There were delicacies from home, cookies and cake. The food came horseback too, so there was no stinting.

The sixteen-mile hike and the four-mile gallop had made me very hungry. I ate my fill and excused myself from kitchen duty that night, promising to do double duty the next day. I was sore and weary and tired beyond compare. My legs were so lame they ached.

I put my bedroll down on the grass by the Little Klickitat. As I slipped between the blankets, Elon came over to me. He was of slight build and not more than five feet six. His hair was brown, his eyes hazel. He always had a cheerful word for everyone. He took pains to see that his companions were comfortable. He seemed to find joy in doing little things for his friends. Then his eyes would dance and a note of tenderness would come into his voice. This night he leaned down close to me and quietly said, "Say, fella, you're OK. You sure can go it the hard way."

I swallowed a lump in my throat and murmured thanks. Pride swelled in my heart as I lay for a moment looking at the myriad stars that hung so close to earth it seemed they could be touched. The Little Klickitat sang softly to me. I went to sleep triumphant. Those whose opinion I valued more highly than any on earth had rendered their verdict.

Chapter VI *Indian Flat—25 Miles*

IT WAS late afternoon on a clear August day. My brother Art and I were walking with packs on our backs on the high ridge west of Cougar Lake. We were en route from Fish Lake to Dewey Lake. We were on what is now known as the Pacific Crest Trail that runs from Canada to Mexico.

We had camped the night before at Fish Lake, which is the head of the Bumping River and 13 miles from the dam at Bumping Lake. There we made our beds of white fir boughs on a patch of white clover next to a prospector's log cabin that had stood for years on the northern shore of the lake. We had slept late and had a leisurely breakfast. We aimed to make Dewey Lake the next night, which by our reckoning was only 11 or 12 miles distant. So there was no need for hurry.

Fish Lake is about a quarter of a mile long and perhaps not over 75 yards wide. Beavers have built dams at the lower end and turned a part of the meadow into marshland. The lake has always seemed so narrow when I stood on its shores that I have thought I could throw the traditional silver dollar across it. Fish Lake, like Bumping Lake, lies close to the divide of the Cascades; hence it's a damp place. There is usually a drizzle for a few hours if one stays as long as a week end. As a result the mosquito thrives there and lingers longer in the summer than in the lower lakes in the Cascades. But there are compensations for those discomfitures.

Fish Lake is an intimate body, like a pond in one's own pasture. It lies in a valley not much wider than the lake itself. It's a small place, a one-party campground. Rich grass fills the meadow. Three kinds of fir surround the lake—red, white, and balsam; and there is a scattering of cedar among the fir. There are cutthroat trout in the lake, and rainbow in Bumping River that runs out of it. The cutthroat we caught on this trip were 10- and 12-inchers, black spotted. They were as brilliant as a sunset when we slipped a forefinger through the gills and lifted them from the water. They were fighting fish, next to the rainbow in the will to live. Fish Lake was a fertile and productive mother. It was rich in algae and insect life. For a small lake it produced over the years wonderful specimens of cutthroat. Kitty Nelson one day in the years of which I speak caught 16 cutthroat there that weighed a total of 20 pounds.

There has long been a stand of tall snags around the lake. They were killed by fire years ago and rise as giant skeletons of supple trees that once bowed gracefully before the strong northwest wind. Today their beauty is gone. They have none of the moisture that marks all life. They absorb none from the earth, and hence they offer a good supply of dry wood for the camp.

At dusk, deer and elk step noiselessly through the woods, scan the meadow for their enemies, then tiptoe to the marshy land for food and water.

I have seen the meadow a mass of wild flowers in July. Cinquefoil or fivefingers, buttercups, dwarf dandelions, and monkeyflowers for yellow; lupine, violets, and asters for blue; strawberry, a species of pentstemon, and snapdragon for pink; clover and cottongrass for white. An abundance of cottongrass has indeed made the marshy land on the far side of the lake look like a miniature cotton field transplanted from some rich Texas bottom land.

This morning the charm of Fish Lake detained us until midmorning.

Art and I had been at Fish Lake before. But the country beyond it to the west was unknown. We were exploring. From the contour map we knew that the trail out of Fish Lake climbed a ridge, but we had no notion how steep it was.

It's an old sheepherder's trail that takes the shortest route to the top. There are no switchbacks with an easy grade of 10 or 15 degrees on which one can hold a steady pace. The grade of this old trail must be around 40 degrees. It rises for 1500 feet or more. That puts the ridge which the trail finally reaches around 6000 feet, for Fish Lake lies at an elevation of 4650.

On this August morning it was slow going up the steep pitch. Our horseshoe packs that we carried over our shoulders weighed 30 pounds. We had been out a week; we had come up from the Tieton by the Indian Creek Trail and passed through Blankenship Meadows and the great plateau at the foot of Tumac Mountain that is dotted with dozens of lakes—Twin Sisters, Fryingpan, Snow, and others too numerous to count. So we were hardened to the trail. But the rise out of Fish Lake slowed us.

The basic secret on such climbs is the breathing. The professional mountaineer is an expert. The lungs are the carburetor. As the air thins out, and the oxygen decreases and the carbon dioxide accumulates, inhalations and exhalations must increase unless the motor is to drop to an idling speed. Above 10,000 feet some breathe five times or more for every step they take. The increase in respiration varies with the individual. Once the required rate is discovered, coordination between breathing and walking is possible. This takes time, patience, and practice. But it turns out the mileage under pressure.

At this time I had not mastered the technique. I climbed the hard way. I suspect I practically lunged at the hillside; at least I went in spurts, taking a dozen steps or so and then stopping to pant. In this way Art and I took almost two hours to master the ridge.

It was a clear August day with no wind. The horseshoe pack hung over my shoulder like a weight of lead, twice as heavy as its 30 pounds. The sweat welled up under it and rolled down my spine. I saw it dripping from Art's nose. Our shirts were wet through. When we stopped to get our breath, we bent over and leaned forward toward the hillside, silent and bowed like beasts of burden. Thus we dropped our sweat in the trail's dust and expended ourselves on the mountainside, expecting each small shelf above us to be the top. We were exhausted at the true top. There, beside a spring under an ancient western hemlock, we dropped our packs and rested. I was proud of my legs. They had given me no particular trouble.

Among the grasses in the damp earth around the spring were scatterings of the spring beauty, with its five delicate pink petals. It looked like a lost thing in this rugged environment. It was exquisite, seeming to belong where tender hands could care for it. But here it had weathered the wind and frost and snow of ages, and the ravages of man and beasts too. The porcupines dig its roots for food. I have admired the porcupine's choice, for these roots are excellent as filling for a bread-and-butter sandwich—as good as water cress.

The bearberry or kinnikinnick was also scattered along the ridge in thick carpets that held the soil in place. This low shrub, with its reddish bark and pink urn-shaped berries, seemed more in place here. Perhaps its leathery leaves, which the Indians used for smoking, tanning, and dyeing, gave it a hardier appearance. But whatever the reason, it, like all other species of the heather family, seemed at home on these rugged ridges. At one time we often mistook the bearberry for the low-bush huckleberry before the berries had matured. But we learned to leave the berries alone. They are flat and dry to the taste. Indians, however, dried them and used them in soups. And deer, elk, grouse, and bear are fond of the berries when they mature in the fall.

Art and I lay perhaps a half-hour in our amateur botanical study while we rested from the climb. Then we moved along to the west toward Dewey Lake. It's easy going. Since there is no substantial gain or loss of elevation, a steady pace can be maintained. The trail winds in and out along the base of high cliffs that form the backbone of the ridge. It works its way through red fir, balsam fir, occasional cedars, and western hemlock of giant size. Of all the trees the hemlocks dominate the ridge. The sheer cliffs, the towering hemlock, and the balsam fir, pointed like spires to the sky, give this ridge a cathedral's majesty. That feeling is accentuated by the numerous basins that lie on each side of the trail and from whose edges the mountainside drops off 1,000 or even 2,000 feet into grim canyons.

We had gone only a few yards along the top when Mount Rainier burst into view, so close it seemed to tower over us. Then the trail swung to the eastern slope of the ridge, cutting Rainier from sight.

In the distance to the east was Bumping Lake, the home of Jack and
Kitty Nelson. It was a deep blue that afternoon, as friendly and inviting as those two delightful hosts of the Cascades. A little farther
along the eastern slope and directly below us on the right were two
other lakes. At a later time I camped at the second one on a site
called Two Lake Camp and heard the elk bugling and the coyote
yapping at the break of dawn.

A mile or so farther on is a sheepherder's short cut that takes off
to the right, crosses the narrow hogback of the ridge, and drops down
into Cougar Lake at the base of House Mountains.

Art and I took none of these inviting side trips this August day.
But we did loiter. We stopped again and again to pick the low-bush
huckleberries that were at their peak. We had been out a week and
craved sweets above all else. So from time to time we sat in the
midst of one of these huckleberry patches and gorged ourselves with
the sweet fruit.

The ridge abounds with springs and creeks, at every one of which
we saw signs of deer. And once we saw fresh bear tracks, six inches
or more across. Every time the trail swung across the ridge to the
west so that Mount Rainier came into sight, we stopped to look as
if we could not get enough.

The result was that it was soon late afternoon and we were still
about two and a half or three miles from Dewey Lake. The magic
charm of the ridge had such a hold on us that we decided to look
along its narrow backbone for a place to camp; and presently we saw
a small open shelf of a few acres a short way below us on the left of
the trail.

We descended to explore it. We found a spring with clear, cold
water. The shelf had a carpet made of alpine bunchgrass, heather,
and moss. Balsam fir, with its needlelike spires, rimmed its edge.
There was a scattering of dry wood for a campfire. The western rim
of the shelf dropped off 1000 feet or more in a steep incline to a
tangle of wilderness. Mount Rainier rose over us. We commanded
the whole scene as if we were on the roof of a cathedral. No more

perfect place to camp on a clear August night could ever be found. Here we threw off our packs.

We dug out the spring so that it would be wide and deep enough for dipping, knowing that the roily water would settle by the time camp was made and we were ready to start supper. We went above the trail and dragged down branches and logs for our fire. Only then did we unroll our packs.

We took great pride in these packs. We did not know about rucksacks or pack baskets, so we never used them. Once I tried the pack board with the forehead strap, and once the Nelson pack. But I found the horseshoe roll more to my liking. Each would take one-half of a canvas pup tent which would serve as the outside cover of the roll. Inside would be the blankets (two in each pack) and the food. And we designed a method for carrying food that suited our needs. We took the inside white cotton bag of a sugar sack, washed it, and then had Mother, by stitching it lengthwise, make three bags out of one. We'd fill these long, narrow, white bags with our food supplies. The sacks, when filled, would roll neatly up with the blankets. Each end of the roll would be tied with rope, later to be used for pitching the pup tent. Then the roll could be slipped over the head onto the shoulder.

We could not pack fresh meat, not only because of its weight but because it wouldn't keep. Canned goods, ham, and bacon were too heavy to carry. We would, however, take along some bacon-rind for grease. We'd substitute a vial of saccharin for sugar and thus save several pounds. Into one white sack we would put powdered milk; into another, beans. We'd fill one with flour already mixed with salt and baking powder and ready for hot cakes or bread. In another we would put oatmeal, cream of wheat, or corn meal. One sack would be filled with dried fruit—prunes or apples. Another would contain packages of coffee, salt, and pepper. Usually we would take along some powdered eggs.

On the outside of our packs would be tied a frying pan, coffee pot, and kettle. One of us usually would strap on a revolver; the other would carry a hatchet. Each would have a fishing rod and matches. Thus equipped, each pack would weigh between 30 and 60 pounds, depending on the length of the trip planned.

We also took along a haversack which we alternated in carrying. In it were our plates, knives, forks, spoons, lunch, and other items we wished to keep readily available. It hung by a shoulder strap on the hip opposite from the horseshoe pack. The one who carried it was indeed well loaded.

Art and I had oatmeal, scrambled eggs, bread, and coffee for supper, and ended up gnawing on dried prunes for dessert. We did not pitch the pup tent that night. There were no trees on the small shelf between which we could stretch the ridge rope; and there was no threat of inclement weather.

The sun was setting when supper was over and dishes were done. I walked to the edge of the shelf to watch the last light leave the cold shoulders of Rainier. The mountain seemed close enough to put out my hand and touch. Up, up, up it rose, eight or nine thousand feet above me. Its eternal ice fields looked down, threatening and ominous because of their intimacy. The great, dark shoulders of lava rock that crop out among its ice and snow stood stark and naked in all their detail—mightier than any fortress, bigger than any dam or monument that the hands of man could erect.

Alongside that view I felt as if I were no more than the pint of ashes to which some day every man will be reduced. That dust, I thought, when scattered on the gargantuan shoulders of Rainier would be as insignificant as a handful of sand in an endless ocean.

It is easy to see the delicate handiwork of the Creator in any meadow. But perhaps it takes these startling views to remind us of His omnipotence. Perhaps it takes such a view to make us realize that vain, cocky, aggressive, selfish man never conquers the mountains in spite of all his boasting and bustling and exertion. He conquers only himself.

The sun, which had sprayed the ice and snow of Rainier with the colors of the spectrum, had now set. Rainier stood alone in silhouette, bleak and gray in the dusk. The mood of the mountain took hold of me.

Why was this peak called Rainier? Its Indian name was Takhoma, for one of two wives of an Indian chief. The other wife, Metlako, gave birth to a son. Takhoma remained barren. Jealousy grew in Takhoma's heart. She resolved to kill the boy. Metlako, learning of the plot, left the lodge with her son, like Hagar of old, and would not return. The Spirit Chief stepped in and settled the affair by turning Takhoma into a mountain. He threw around her shoulders a white, cold mantle so that the fires of jealousy would not burst forth from her breast.

There may have been some reason to name Mount Adams after John Adams. He was, of course, our second President, and part of the tradition of America. But he did not in my view have as much claim to it as Klickitat, who, indeed, had been transformed into the mountain. Teddy Roosevelt's name would be more fitting than Adams', since Roosevelt represented some of the daring and adventure of the west. But Rainier seems greatly out of place. Captain George Vancouver chose the name in 1792. It is the name of a British admiral, Rear Admiral Peter Rainier. Vancouver did the same for Mount St. Helens. That peak bears the name of the British Ambassador to Spain in 1792. And later in the same year Lt. Broughton of Vancouver's expedition named Mount Hood for a British admiral.

None of these men, so honored, ever saw the mountains that bear their names. None of them ever set foot on the Cascades. They never perspired on these slopes or slept in the high basins on beds of fir boughs. They never fished for cutthroat or rainbow in the streams or lakes or stalked a deer on the ridges. They never saw the delicate *Sidalcea* on the slopes of Darling Mountain or the fields of squawgrass in Blankenship Meadows. These men were total strangers to the Cascades and to America as well.

The Indians had for thousands of years hunted their slopes, drunk their ice-cold waters, and lived in their shadows. Yet of all the major peaks in the northwest range of the Cascades, only one has retained its Indian name. That is Shuksan, the Place of the Storm Wind, which is near the Canadian border.

There were no white fir boughs for our bed that night. They are the best for mountain mattresses, because their needles grow out from opposite sides only and thus produce flat branches. Jack Nelson of Bumping Lake always called them "mule feathers." Once I asked him the reason.

"Well," he said, "the best mattresses are stuffed with feathers, aren't they? A mattress of white fir boughs is the best in the mountains, isn't it? Well, can you think of any animal that would grow feathers like those fir boughs except a mule?"

The night we were camped on the little shelf looking on Rainier we did not seek boughs for our bed. The meadow seemed soft enough, and for two tired lads of twelve and sixteen, the ground is not so hard as to ruin rest. By the time we turned in, the wind was blowing on us from the ice and snow fields of Takhoma. It would be a cold night and the heat of a bonfire would be dissipated. So we let the campfire die and put rocks and branches on the edges of our blankets, throwing the two pieces of the tent over us as a windbreak.

I slept fitfully. I had thought my legs had stood up well the day before. But this night they twitched behind the knees. Moreover, the wind never died; and the bed got draughty no matter how we arranged the blankets. During the dark hours I was sitting up a dozen times, it seemed, tucking them in. Each time, before I settled down again, I looked once more at Takhoma—a sentinel of the night, a mother watching over her brood.

We naturally were up at the first streak of dawn. Within the hour we had breakfast: prunes (which we had put to soak the night before), more oatmeal, scrambled eggs, and thick pancake bread, which we washed down with strong black coffee. In less than an hour, camp was broken, the coals of the fire were out, and we were ready for the rest of the trip to Dewey Lake.

Before we started, we sat down to study our contour map. We

were in new terrain and we wanted to be certain we did not get off onto false trails. As we studied the map, we noticed that we might save half a day by a certain short cut. The trail swung down the ridge about four miles to Dewey Lake. Our plan had been to sample the fishing there and then push on another four or five miles to the American River.

We could see that if we left the trail a half-mile or so ahead and plunged down the mountainside to the right, we would pick up one of the headwaters of the American River. We would have several miles of trackless forest before we hit the trail that leads from Dewey Lake to the American River by way of Morse Creek, but we would save about six miles.

We said good-by to Takhoma, shouldered our packs, and headed west along the Pacific Crest. In a half-mile or so the trail drops down to a small lake on the left which forms the headwaters of Deer Creek. It then swings to the eastern edge of the ridge and in a quarter-mile comes to a wide meadow on an open hillside.

The hillside was filled with patches of low-bush huckleberry that were heavy with ripe fruit. We dropped our packs and sat on the ground and once more ate our fill. Some of the berries were twice as big as a pea. We tossed them down by the handful, hungry for the sugar that the sunlight had stored in them. We put about a pint in our coffee pot, hoping to make sauce for supper and to simulate huckleberry cobbler by pouring the sauce over the thick bread which we baked in the frying pan.

The berries were not the only attraction of this open hill. Stubby mountain ash was scattered along its edges. Pods of the lovely avalanche lily, that blooms almost before the snow uncovers it, lined the trail. The purplish pasqueflower or western anemone was in seed, its styles turned into oval plumes that looked as soft as silk. There were lupine and asters in blue splotches as far as one could see. Cinquefoil was scattered in small clumps on all sides. Western valerian and knotweed were everywhere. The coarse and ugly hellebore, whose root is poisonous but pregnant with magic qualities according to Indian lore, laid claim to more than its share of the ground. Scotch bluebells, the flowers that Dayton rightly says have an "atmosphere of floral aristocracy," were around, nodding in the morning sun with a gracefulness and simplicity that few wild flowers have. But the showiest bloom—the one that caught the eye—was the squawgrass.

My favorite place to see it has always been the Blankenship Meadows. Perhaps that is because Blankenship Meadows is one of my favorite places in all of the Cascades. When I have stopped on its edge I have realized how the early homesteader felt who, coming to a rise of land and looking at a rich valley at his feet, knew at once he had found a place he wanted to call his home. That is the appeal those meadows on the plateau beneath Tumac Mountain have always had to me. They are the meadows that clumps of the peaked balsam fir decorate with the most striking colonnade effect of any place in the Cascades. There are fresh springs among them. In early summer a great carpet of flowers extends indefinitely. The squawgrass grows in great patches here. Its creamy blossoms make even deeper the rich green of the balsam fir.

The squawgrass is not as thick on the ridge above Fish Lake as it is on the lower reaches of the Cascades. But the few scattered patches in evidence this August day dominated the scene. This plant, which is not a grass, is more typical of the eastern slopes of the Cascades than any wild flower except the cinquefoil, lupine, paintbrush, and phlox. Its stem stands from two to four feet high, shooting up from a mass of broad, densely tufted leaves. At the top of the coarse stem are cream colored, plumlike spikes, shaped into a round cone that ends in a nipple. Elk, deer, horses, and cattle seem to like it, for as I walk or ride the trails I notice that the blossoms of the plant that lie within reach have been nipped off. But the botanists say that the plant, like every member of the bunchflower tribe of the lily family (including deathcamas, false-hellebore, and hog asphodel), is more or less toxic and that squawgrass has caused losses of stock. Bears dig up the tuberous roots in early spring and eat them. The roots when boiled make soap; hence the secondary names of beargrass and soapgrass.

The height of the stem and the size of the blossom make squaw-grass overshadow everything in any meadow. It deserves its name, the "Great White Monarch of the Northwest." It is as startlingly beautiful in a meadow of the Cascades as dogwood is on Connecti-cut's hillsides.

Squawgrass was important in the life of the northwest Indians. They carried on a considerable commerce in it up and down the Columbia. It is part of the historic produce of the Cascades. Lewis and Clark and later David Douglas wrote about it. Clark stopped at the mouth of the Yakima in October, 1805, and ate a salmon cooked for him by Indians in a basket made of squawgrass. The basket was watertight. The water it held was heated by dropping in hot stones. That winter Lewis wrote at the mouth of the Columbia that the baskets of the Indians "are formed of cedar bark and bear-grass so closely interwoven with the fingers that they are watertight, without the aid of gum or rosin." And, according to Lewis, these baskets were "of different capacities from that of the smallest cup to five or six gallons." The squawgrass baskets served double duty for the Indians—they were hats as well as cooking utensils and buckets. As a result of its great utility in that economy it was given the name *Xerophyllum tenax*, which means "the dry leaf that holds fast."

Art and I sat in this beautiful mountain garden perhaps an hour. Below us was a heavily wooded canyon bounded a few miles on the east by another ridge. The ridge we were on ran to the north a mile or so and then jutted out into a great elbow. On the far side of the elbow was the Rainier Fork of the American River. If we followed the stream in the canyon below us until it joined Rainier Fork and then followed the American River down to where Morse Creek poured in, we would pick up the American River trail. It was apparent that our reading of the contour map had been accurate. By going cross-country we would take the hypotenuse of the triangle and save time and mileage.

The first part of the descent was on a gentle slope. We went down through the open hillside where we had tarried so long, pushed through stands of mountain ash and Douglas maple, and entered a stand of balsam fir. It was perhaps 1500 feet to the bottom of the ravine; and once we were in the woods the decline became more precipitous.

A man with a pack on his back is like a horse with a rider—he has an element of unbalance that must be reckoned with in every step. Moreover, two or more men working their way off trail down a steep mountainside owe a special obligation to keep bunched together or widely scattered so that rocks loosened by one will not come pounding down to kill or maim the other.

Steep slopes of pinegrass are slippery. One has to dig in his heels at every step as he goes downhill. It is hard on the knees; it is dangerous, especially with a pack, to go fast. Momentum is easy to gain and hard to lose on a mountainside. When one is loaded with a pack, loss of balance even for a second can cause disaster. When one is afoot with limited food supplies and is several days from civilization, a sprained ankle can be a calamity.

We had slippery pinegrass under us for the first 500 feet or so. Below us was a yawning pit, heavily wooded, with occasional outcroppings of basalt. For several hundred feet we worked our way through shale rock and around cliffs. We came to a field of boulders which, loosened perhaps by frost from some high crag, had found precarious resting places on this mountainside. We soon wound through them and left them high above us as we found more gentle slopes below and made faster progress.

All the way down we saw many fresh bear tracks. These were the tracks of black and brown bears, which, though fearless on the attack and ever ready to raid a cabin or a tent, are keen-scented animals and difficult to approach in the woods. They avoid man wherever possible.

We saw fir trees whose bark near the ground was almost gone, because buck deer had rubbed the velvet from their horns and polished them on the tree trunks. Fresh prints of deer were common as we came closer to the bottom of the ravine. Once I saw a black pine whose bark was gone ten or fifteen feet above the ground —the work of a porcupine who in winter walked along a snowdrift and ate the bark as a beaver would circle a tree. And willow trees carried the marks of browsing by deer.

Presently we heard the murmur of the stream that ran down the ravine to the Rainier Fork of the American River. We made our way to it over down timber and through a thick stand of fir. There on a spit of sand we threw down our packs, lay on our stomachs, put our faces into the clear, cool water, and drank as young animals. It was a fast-water creek running over rocks into clear liquid pools. We sat on the sand bar, resting and listening to the murmur of the stream. A light wind was in the treetops making them sway and sing. All else was quiet.

I saw on the opposite bank a great mass of Canada dogwood or bunchberry. It was only six inches high and covered the bank thickly, as ivy does. Its minute flowers encircled by four creamy white, petal-like bracts were in bloom and enlivened this damp spot of monotonous green. Its edible red berries—called pudding berries in New England—would bring a dash of high color to this spot in the fall.

There was mixed with the dogwood a host of the pure white alpine beauty, a fragile lilylike flower with thin, soft leaves. The two flowers together made the stream a place of enchantment. The reward of our descent was already great. The loveliness of the Canada dogwood and alpine beauty had filled the canyon for centuries. Yet we were probably the first humans ever to enjoy it.

We doubtless were in woods never before traversed by man. This was the unexplored wilderness—no roads, no trails, no blazes, no signs. This was domain even far off the beaten path of Indians. This forest was primeval, untouched, unseen. Trees fell and in a generation or more were turned into duff. New trees sprang from fallen seed, reached with their thin tips through a colonnade of evergreens for a slit in the sky, pushed lesser trees aside, and in time were reclaimed, as man is reclaimed, by Mother Earth.

The humus at our feet was made in that fashion long before Daniel Boone or Lewis and Clark went through trackless forests of their day. Long before America was known by Europe, soil had been building in this ravine. We probably were its first witnesses. But before us was

the evidence of the process. One giant Douglas fir was stubbornly re-
sisting its return to dust. It stood here as a sapling when Columbus
was searching for our shores. The top of its broad trunk still held firm
above the earth. But the mark of crumbling was on it.

A trail, like a road, brings a sense of ease and relaxation. Men have
passed by here before, one says; so all is well. But a journey on foot
through the untouched wilderness brings different impressions. Man
is now on his own. No one has gone ahead. This is new, untouched
domain, full of hazards and dangers. On this trip Art and I looked
for some visible sign of danger—a bear coming through the brush, a
cougar slinking along the creek bottom, a bobcat lying watchfully on
an overhanging limb, even a porcupine waddling up a hill. But we
heard or saw nothing but pine squirrels and chipmunks. The un-
tapped, unexplored wilderness was, as usual, filled with no danger but
the traveler's apprehension.

I think I captured, that August morning in this unchartered canyon, some of the feeling that Daniel Boone, Lewis and Clark, Jim
Bridger, and other early travelers must have had in their explorations
beyond the frontier. Under those circumstances man walks quietly,
his nerve ends alert to pick up even slight warnings of danger. In that
environment he returns to primitive man who stealthily walked the
ridges and traversed the canyons, who hunted and was hunted, and
yet survived all others to rule the universe.

We did not tarry long at the creek but pushed on rapidly, avoiding
thick brush and working our way down to the junction of Rainier
Fork. We reached that point two hours after leaving the top; and in
another hour we found the place where Morse Creek joins the American River. We crossed it and shortly came to the trail that led down
the Naches to home.

We were now on one of the main trails of the Cascades and could
make time. But before settling to the hard grind, we took off our
packs and tightened the ropes. We also removed fine gravel that had
got into our shoes in our descent. Then we had lunch—pieces of pancake bread we had cooked at breakfast and carried in our haversacks,

what remained of the huckleberries we had carried in the coffee pot off the mountain, and clear cold water from American River.

The trail for about a mile below Morse Creek was a dirt road. A mining company had extended its road six miles down the west side of the Cascades from Chinook Pass. The construction was designed as an inducement to Yakima County to bring the road up from the junction of American and Bumping rivers. It was called the Normile Grade. The day we tramped it nature had practically reclaimed it. It was wider than a trail but only a shadow of a road.

The historic Indian route from Yakima to the coast had been up the Little Naches River which joins the American to form the Naches about four miles below the mouth of the Bumping River. It was up the Little Naches that Captain George B. McClellan looked in vain for a pass that would take the Northern Pacific over the Cascades. It was down the Little Naches that Theodore Winthrop came in 1853. He called it a "harsh defile at best for a trail to pursue," a canyon of "stiff, uncrumbling precipices," "sombre basalt walls" that were "sheer and desperate as suicide" (*Canoe and Saddle*).

It was that route that the first wagon train traveled in 1853 from Franklin County, Indiana, to Olympia, Washington. David Longmire, an old-timer in the Yakima Valley, made that trip as a boy. Case has told the story in *The Last Mountains*. This was the first wagon trip over the Cascades north of the Columbia. The route was new and untried. The party was moving on the edge of winter. On the west side they were blocked by cliffs and there was no way down or around. So they killed oxen and from the skins made leather ropes. With these they lowered their remaining oxen and wagons to safety below. They got off the mountain just in time to escape death by starvation or exposure.

Jack Nelson and other old-timers with a faithful eye to history lost their fight to have the new highway follow the Little Naches. Long after the August day of which I speak the present paved highway was constructed. It follows the Normile Grade over Chinook Pass. Years later I traveled that highway by motorcar. It is the most picturesque of all paved mountain roads, either by sunlight or by moonlight, that

I have seen. Twenty miles beyond the junction of Bumping and American rivers it crosses Chinook Pass. At that point the road is only a few miles from Dewey Lake, which lies to the south and which was our destination in the trip just described.

I think a slight resentment filled me as we roared along at 50 miles an hour on a trail where as a boy I had plodded so long and hard on foot. The inclines up which I strained with my pack in the early years meant nothing to those who occupied the car. The streams that I had waded, the mud of the marshlands that had sucked at my shoes as I sloshed through it, were covered with culverts and bridges and so would never have meaning to these hurried travelers. The motorist would indeed be going much too fast to get even a glimpse of the low patches of the creamy Canada dogwood on a meadow's edge, or to see in some shady recess of the woods the dainty rose-colored deer orchid or calypso, or to catch in lush meadows of the valley the gleam of dark blue larkspur or the flaming hues of the Indian paintbrush, or to find in grass the exquisite scarlet gilia, shooting-star, or dogtooth violet. He certainly would never hear the whir of the grouse going through a thicket ahead of him, or get the thrill of coming across fresh cougar or bear tracks in a wilderness. Those too soft to take to a trail were now whisked along with ease over terrain that, for me, should be reserved for the hardy. Those whose progress on a trail even without a pack would be slow and painful could now inhale their tobacco in a journey freed of all exertion. Thus had the wall of a wilderness been leveled and desecration by man made easy!

These were sentiments I expressed as we whirled along, doing in thirty minutes what with extreme exertion I could do as a boy only in a day.

"But aren't there other trails on which young fools can exhaust themselves?" my companion dryly asked. Of course there were. And this Chinook Pass highway was a special blessing to thousands. Yet a slight resentment at its existence lingered on.

While Art and I were eating lunch at Morse Creek on the Normile Grade, I made a secret resolution which was quite unfair to him. I had been thinking about my legs. I wondered how strong they really were. This was one of several mountain hikes I had been on; and each one had been an achievement. I knew my legs were improving. The day before they had stood up well under the pull out of Fish Lake. Apart from the twitching of the muscles below my knees that night, there were no other symptoms. I was stronger each summer. But how much stronger, I wondered.

As I studied the contour map I estimated we had come about ten miles that morning. I knew there was an excellent camp ground at Indian Flat, two miles below the junction of the American and Bumping rivers. From where we sat on the Morse Creek trail that was a good fourteen or fifteen miles.

"I wonder if we can do fifteen miles in three hours," I said to myself. "Certainly we can do it in four."

Then I made my secret resolution: we would camp at Indian Flat that night.

"We must get going if we are to make camp by dark," I said to Art.

It was about two o'clock when we headed down the American River on the Normile Grade. It was not water-level travel all the way; there were ups and downs. But the trail and the short stretch of the old road were easy by mountain standards. We had good footgear: thick socks, close-fitting shoes more than ankle high, and hobnails. So I set the pace at five miles an hour—a very fast one even without a pack.

How long I maintained that pace I do not know, probably not many minutes. The muscles along my shinbones set up a protest. There was a caustic tone in Art's words, "Where's the fire?" The pace soon slackened perhaps to three miles an hour. But once that speed was set, I tried to hold it all afternoon. We walked until dusk with no interruptions except for stops to drink at pools along the river. The pace was steady; we never relaxed even for a moment.

It was a long and weary trail, and dusty, too. Fine dust rose with every step and eventually sifted through all our clothes and filled our nostrils. There was no breeze; the sun had baked all moisture out of the hillside and it bore down on us, hot and stifling. All conversation ended. I could hear only the roar of the river, our footsteps, the rattle and clanging of the utensils tied on our packs. Mile after mile we trudged, looking neither right nor left, alert not to lose by some careless step the rhythm of our long stride. I was in the lead; Art kept close on my heels. We had gone about six miles when we came to Pleasant Valley—an excellent camp.

"Why isn't this OK?" Art asked.

"There's a better one down the line," I said.

So we swung through Pleasant Valley without breaking our walk. Then he inquired how much farther we had to go that day. I was noncommittal. In another half-mile he asked again. When I dodged a reply, he pressed me.

"Just a few miles," I answered. As we trudged on, the inquiry "How much longer?" became more frequent; the tone of his voice more dissatisfied.

I knew how he felt. A great weariness had overtaken me too. But I had made my secret resolution and for me it was do or die. My light-hearted responses to the constant question, "How much longer?" concealed my own feelings. I too was tired; and it took self-control not to be curt and sharp.

By late afternoon the questions had ceased; we had each got a second or third wind and were traveling on some hitherto undiscovered sources of energy. The pack was hanging more heavily than ever on my shoulder. A numbness began to creep through my back muscles, as if they had received a light injection of some anesthetic. As the shadows in the valley lengthened I walked as an automaton. My legs seemed more like stilts than part of me. They were almost without feeling; and the feet seemed weighted down by heavy clogs.

I remembered, as we pushed along, a chapter in one of Cooper's books. It told of the pursuit of a frontiersman by Indians; how he kept his pace all through the heat of the day and finally, by sheer endurance, eluded his pursuers in the dusk. My pursuers were the lengthening shadows. By dark I would be encompassed; and there would be no escape because of my fatigue. Was I too weak to stand the pace?

The pace continued to be a frightful one, though it may have dropped to a slow walk. The shin muscles of my legs were aching like a tooth with an exposed nerve. A small pain commenced above my eyes and soon the pounding of my heels echoed in my head. I longed to stop and rest; I wanted to sleep and never move until to-morrow. But I pushed on.

After a while the legs and head became impersonal objects, like things belonging to someone else. So I went on, my eyes on the trail, my head down. My legs were numb. I was almost unaware of my sur-roundings. On and on, mile after mile. I had to see what my legs could do.

At the junction of American and Bumping rivers we struck the dirt road. Two miles to Indian Flat.

"How about here?" said a tired voice in the rear.

"Not yet," I said. On we went, until at dusk Indian Flat loomed up as if out of a dream.

We dropped our packs and lay on them, exhausted. How long we stayed there I do not recall. We were aroused by a tantalizing smell—the smell of bacon, flavored with wood smoke. That raised us to our feet. Another party was making camp across the meadow. Our light rations always kept us on the edge of hunger on these mountain trips. The smell of bacon cooking over an open fire was therefore irresistible.

It was dark by the time fir boughs were gathered for our beds, and wood collected for the fire. We made camp by the edge of a stand of white fir and yellow pine. We were far too tired to spend much time in cooking. Normally we'd have caught a mess of trout for the frying pan. But we were much too weary. We were tempted to beg a meal from our neighbors, but pride or some standard of independence was a barrier. So we cooked our own supper. It was frugal: oatmeal, pan-cake bread, milk (powdered), and dried prunes. The smell of our neighbor's bacon almost made our own food unpalatable—and, worse, the oatmeal was burned. We ate sparingly in spite of our hunger. Then after putting beans to soak for tomorrow's meal, we crawled into our bedroll, our hunger whetted rather than satisfied.

I woke with a splitting headache. I lay for an hour, hoping it would cease. But it continued unabated. When I got up and walked about,

I felt sick at my stomach. The exertion of the day before had con-tributed to my suffering. But the headache must have been com-pounded from inner tensions as well as fatigue; for dreams vaguely horrible had occupied me in my sleep. All night I had seemed to be hunted by some evil pursuers. There were boys my age peering and taunting me, and older people watching and nodding their approval. I would almost escape the scene and then these pursuers would catch up with me—and I would be too weak in the knees to get away.

I lay down on my fir bough bed, too ill to move. Soon my brother, whose spirits I had somehow sustained the day before, awakened. Even as a youth he was tall and rangy, headed for six feet or more. His legs were long and agile. This morning his light brown, almost reddish hair, was in a tangled mass. He had slept long and hard. Now he was refreshed and hungry as a bear. I was secretly proud of his performance, and envious of his strength. He had outdone me.

He cooked himself a big breakfast, did the dishes, and put the beans to boil. I did not feel like eating. The only food I wanted was soup. "That's it, tomato soup," I thought. My longing for it was so acute, it became an obsession. We had no soup of any kind. I asked my brother if he would try to borrow soup from our neighbors.

He disappeared and was gone an interminable time. I was at first annoyed at his delay, and then anxious for him. It took him an hour to return. Then he came, breathless and excited, saying a bull had chased him.

"What did you do?" I asked.

"I went up a tree," he said. "That's where I've been all this time." His blue eyes glistened in his excitement.

"And the soup?" I asked.

He pulled out from under his shirt a can of tomato soup. He heated it, as he told me of the bull that chased him: the roar of the beast, the quivering nostrils, the horns, the red eyes, the pawing hoofs. His description was so vivid that I too could see the flames coming out of the monster's nose.

I ate the soup—every drop of it. And having eaten it, I fell asleep.

I woke at noon, hungry for beans and heavy food, and ready to push on. I was refreshed, and neither stiff nor sore.

Inwardly I felt a glow because of my achievement. I had walked 25 miles with a 30-pound pack in one day. My legs had stood up. I had conquered my doubts. So far as my legs were concerned, I knew that I was now free to roam these mountains at will, to go on foot where any man could go, to enter any forest without hesitation.

THE following summer with less premeditation I gave my legs a more severe test. One day Brad Emery and I walked more than 40 miles in the Cascades with packs on our backs. It was early June just after high school was out and before the cherries were ready for picking. We took that opportunity to have a week together in the Cascades. We went by stage through Wiley City and past the Ahtanum Mission and the Narrows to Tampico. There we caught a ride to Soda Springs. Then we put the horseshoe packs over our shoulders, took to the trail up the North Fork of the Ahtanum, and headed for the Klickitat Meadows, 16 miles distant. We planned to camp there that night.

Not far up the North Fork the old trail divided, the left fork going over the southeastern shoulder of Darling Mountain and down to the Meadows, the right fork climbing to the very top of Darling. We were chatting as we walked along and overlooked the branching of the trail. We took the wrong fork, and did not realize it until the increased pitch of the trail in a quarter-mile or so told us of our error.

We then decided to abide by our mistake. Our contour map showed that the trail we were on went over the top of Darling, turned north onto Short and Dirty Ridge, and dropped to the South Fork of the Tieton not far from the Tieton Basin. The tops of both Darling Mountain and Short and Dirty Ridge were new territory for both of us. We decided to explore them. We pushed on. Darling Mountain stands at 6972 feet, which meant we had close to 3500 feet to climb before we reached its peak. The trail at once told us of its trials, for it climbed almost without respite.

Peattie, in *Forward the Nation*, tells the unforgettable story of Sacajawea, the Indian squaw who helped to guide Lewis and Clark over the Rocky Mountains to the Pacific. He tells how she worshiped mountain flowers which in her words are "the spirits of those children whose footsteps have passed from the earth but reappear each spring to gladden the pathway of those now living." The eastern slopes of Darling Mountain would bring joy to her heart in the spring and summer. Here will be found one of the greatest flowering of plants in all the Cascades.

I have seen on those slopes larger fields of lupine than anywhere else—acres and acres of lupine, some of it mixed color of blue and white, but most of it blue—a brilliant mantle covering an entire hillside. Mixed in with the lupine but less conspicuous are a great variety of pentstemon, small and large, dwarfed and tall, blue, purple, and even rose colored. At various elevations bloom the scarlet gilia or wild honeysuckle, delicate as a hothouse orchid; bronze bells or mission bells with their adderlike tongues; the Indian hyacinth, pale violet, delicately scented; the small, dwarfed saxifrage with its soft white flowers and tiny roots which in time can cause great rocks to crumble as its name suggests; the low, dark blue larkspur, poisonous to cattle; the scarlet trumpets of the tall, graceful columbine offering special invitations to the humming birds; the weedy, bright yellow dandelion; the yellow arnica with its drugstore smell; blue Jacobs-ladder with a yellow throat; the blue gentian that Gentius, King of Illyria, found to be useful in medicine; the sego-lily or cats-ears, whose petals are like satin on the outside and hairy like a kitten's on the inside; the pollen-laden tiger lily, its rich orange spotted with brown; Bishop's-cap, whose petals remind Haskins of "five-pointed, translucent green snowflakes"; western wallflower, whose clinging quality and whose habit of flowering all summer long have made it from ancient days a symbol of femininity; St. Johns wort, whose spots are supposed to show on the day when St. John was beheaded; wild candytuft, lousewort, duck bill, fleabane, goat chickory, *Bahia*, wooly yellow daisy, Fendler's Arabis, *Eriogonum*, cinquefoil, paintbrush, cowherbs, pussy-paws, western valerian, deep blue monkshood, sage mint, knot weed, and a host of others. I believe that a Peattie or Dayton between

May and August could indeed find all the wild flowers of the Cascades on Darling's eastern slopes.

The one I found that I liked best was the Oregon mallow or *Sidalcea*. It flourishes there in the bunchgrass. It's a wild hollyhock from one to two feet tall, with miniature petals of pink. The petals have a fragile, translucent look. The flower is sparing with its loveliness, opening only a few petals at a time and saving some of its delicate beauty for those who will travel the trail later in the season. Even in the wilds there is a touch of domesticity about the *Sidalcea*. It carries me back to barnyard fences, garages, back porches, and garden walls where the hollyhock has been part of my life. There is a suggestion about it, as it leans to one side on Darling's slopes and bends before a light breeze, that it would like to be reclaimed and live with people in yards and gardens. It does indeed transplant easily and thrives under cultivation.

Brad and I left most of the wild flowers behind us when we started up the steep trail. It was a late season. We had supposed that the soft chinook had melted the snow that powdered Darling Mountain in great drifts during the winter; but we soon discovered we were wrong. There was a lot of snow in the ravines and under the trees; the trail was still damp with its moisture; and the air was chill as if it were coming out of the open door of a cold-storage plant. It was like raw March and April weather. The warmth of the lava rock and sagebrush hills in the valley had not yet reached these slopes. Patches of snow soon appeared in the trail; and it was not long before our shoes were wet through. But it was good weather for exertion. We climbed the 3500 feet with our 30-pound packs with hardly a stop.

We were greatly discouraged because of the snow; and we grumbled about it as we climbed. It meant wet ground for camping, poor fishing, and restricted hiking. But it offered advantages too. This was the first time that I had seen the glorious avalanche lily. This day I saw its tender shoots coming up right on the edge of the snow, sometimes even through a thin layer of snow. And then within a few feet or even inches of a snowdrift would be the delicate flower itself.

It's an *Erythronium*, clear white with an orange center, the flowers two or three inches across. Alpine basins will produce whole acres of this dainty flower. I have seen great meadows on the shoulders of Rainier and Hood filled with it. That sight is breath-taking. But even small patches of it under high rock cliffs, on open slopes, or at the edge of great snowbanks, have the same effect on me. And they always bring me to a reverent halt. The size of the flower, the delicacy of its texture, the gracefulness of its stance, make it one of the most wondrous of all the creations of nature. It never ceases to be startling to find something so exquisitely beautiful and delicate growing in the raw, cold atmosphere of a snowdrift.

The avalanche lily has more than my adoration; it also commands a great respect. For this flower spurns the lowlands. It does not survive transplanting. Unlike its cousin of golden hue, the glacier lily that I have found in great abundance on American Ridge above Bumping Lake, the avalanche lily has an aversion to gardens. It grows in a rugged environment; there and there alone it thrives. Like man, it needs a challenge to reach its full fruition. Its stimulus is the raw wind, cold thin earth, chill nights, and icy waters of the Cascades.

Thus the snow which dampened our enthusiasm for this mountain trip brought rich rewards. It introduced me to this fragile but stouthearted beauty of the high mountains.

There is a narrow, hogback saddle that connects the eastern end of Darling's top with the western end. The wind had cleared this saddle of all snow. But as we crossed it we saw ahead of us on the higher western end of the mountain great drifts that covered the trail. They were 15 to 20 feet deep. We worked our way around them and over, and slowly came to the western edge of Darling's top. It was late afternoon on a clear day. There was not a cloud in the sky. Brad and I stopped near the spot where a State Forest Service lookout tower now stands, threw off our packs on an outcropping of lava rock, and drank in the view.

This is without doubt the most commanding view in the Cascades. To the east and the southeast were glimpses of the valleys around

Yakima and Toppenish, gold and brown in the distance. Way to the south, deep in Oregon, the cold snowy shaft of Mount Jefferson loomed through a light haze. Then came Mount Hood—the one that Lewis and Clark called the falls mountain or Timm Mountain— touching the sky with its broad-bladed shoulder that ends in a sharp peak. Adams was next—high humped and rounded, friendly and intimate. Beyond it and to the right was St. Helens, a touch of fleecy cloud at the top of its white cone.

Running south between us and Adams was a rough gash in the earth, the deep, serpentine canyon through which the Big Klickitat finds its way to the Columbia at Lyle, Washington. North of Adams was the jagged, snow-capped line of the Goat Rocks running in a northwesterly direction for 15 or 20 miles. North of it was mighty Rainier, dominating every peak and ridge in the range. To our north stood the jagged Tatoosh Range, the high rounded American Ridge, and other ranges that seemed to go on endlessly as waves in a vast sea until they finally were absorbed in the thickening haze of the horizon.

Below us to the south, west, and north was a tumbled mass of peaks, rocks, and pinnacles. Valleys and ridges ran every which way, as if they were built without design or relation to the whole; and yet they all fitted as huge blocks into the gargantuan pattern of this tremendous range.

It was this view that led Theodore Winthrop to write in 1853 that "civilized man has never yet had a fresh chance of developing itself under grand and stirring influences so large" as that presented by the panorama of the Cascades (*Canoe and Saddle*).

The view, like the one of the delicate bitterroot and of the fragile avalanche lily, has always led me to disagree with Edgar Allan Poe's statement that he did "not believe that any thought is out of the reach of language." When I stand at this viewpoint, I am filled with a medley of emotions. I feel a challenge to explore each ridge and valley, to climb each snow-capped peak, to sleep in each high basin, to sample the berries and fish and all the other rich produce of the wilderness. It is the feeling that he who first topped the Blue Ridge Mountains or the Rockies must have had when he looked west and

saw valleys untouched by the plow and a primeval forest that had
never known an ax.

These peaks and meadows were made for man, and man for them.
They are man's habitat. He has eyes, ears, nose, and brain to understand them. He has legs and lungs to take him anywhere and everywhere through them. Man must explore them and come to know
them. They belong to him; yet they will eventually reclaim him and
rule beyond his day as they ruled long before he appeared on the
earth, long before he stood erect and faced the sun.

The mountains are harsh and cruel. But unlike man, they are not
revengeful. Their anger comes in a great flash flood or an avalanche
that roars off the mountain on wheels of death. But then it is gone
and over with. It does not linger on like man's anger, which festers
and grows in his heart and then gushes out in a great Hitlerian burst
of premeditated and planned destruction. Buck deer may lock horns
and fight to the death for domination over the herd. Yet they do not
plan wars or plot programs to dominate the forest. These beastly
quarrels are short-lived and very much to the point of self-preserva-
tion. Only man has feuds, and plots the destruction of his neighbor
or an entire race.

When one stands on Darling Mountain, he is not remote and apart
from the wilderness; he is an intimate part of it. The ridges run away
at his feet and lead to friendly meadows. Every trail leads beyond the
frontier. Every ridge, every valley, every peak offers a solitude deeper
even than that of the sea. It offers the peace that comes only from
solitude. It is in solitude that man can come to know both his heart
and his mind.

Brad and I had no choice but to camp on the top of Darling Mountain all night. The western and northern slopes were covered with
snow. The remaining hours of daylight did not leave time enough to
make a descent to any of the valleys below us. We selected an open
space between snowdrifts where there was a stand of whitebark pine,
and there pitched our pup tent and built our fire.

The top of Darling is decorated with clumps of the whitebark pine.

This is the pine whose seeds the birds seem particularly to relish. In seasons when the cones are full I have seen the camp robbers feverishly tearing the cones apart for the seeds. And as the camp robbers worked the tops of the trees, the ruffed grouse followed on the ground to catch the seeds that fell. On the exposed dome of Darling the whitebark pine are dwarfed and twisted. Great snowdrifts press upon them for a large portion of the year. The severe northwest wind whips them almost continuously, so each tree is bent and wind-blown. But it has the capacity few other trees have to withstand the fiercest storms. Hence it is practically the only tree that stands on the exposed dome of Darling.

On this mountain top a whitebark pine may be 200 years old and still be short and puny, stunted in growth. But it has the seasoning of scores of summers in its fiber. The ax bounces off it as if it were a species of hardwood. It has grown tough and rugged from a century or more of contests with the elements. It always reminds me of the wind-blown trees that the Knights of the Round Table, according to Tennyson, looked for among the crags as wood from which to fashion spears for their tournaments.

We cut a dead whitebark pine of this tough variety for our fire. There was no white fir anywhere around—the tree with the flat branches that make an excellent mattress. The leaves or needles of the whitebark pine grow all around the branch in bundles of five and make a coarse and bulky mattress. But we laid our blankets on them more for protection from the damp ground than for the comfort a mattress is supposed to bring.

We melted snow for cooking, finished supper before all the stars were out, and put beans to soak for tomorrow's breakfast. The wind came up. It was not the warm chinook that comes from the southwest. It came from the northwest with the chill of ice in its breath. We built a brisk fire to dry out our shoes and socks that had become soaked in the snow; and we tried to sit close to it to keep warm. But we finally gave up, put logs around the edges of the pup tent to impede the wind, and went to bed early.

It was a cold, cold night. I napped fitfully, chilled and uncomfortable on the mattress of whitebark pine boughs.

We rose by the break of day and put on the beans that had been soaking all night. They, along with pancake bread and coffee, were to be our breakfast. But before that breakfast was eaten we had learned that cooking at a high altitude could be a slow process. We were camped at about 7,000 feet. Boiling water is not very hot at that elevation. We had no pressure cooker. So all we could do was to keep the pot bubbling. This we did for over four hours, and still the beans were only half-done. The day was wasting; we were impatient to get off the mountain into the lowlands where we hoped to fish. So we started on the beans anyway. The outer part was done; but the inner core was as hard as plaster. Though we chewed and ate some of them, for the most part we spat them out as we would cherry pits. It was perhaps the most unsatisfactory mountain meal I ever had.

We broke camp then. Down the western slope of Darling Mountain was a snow field almost a mile long and dropping perhaps a thousand feet or more in elevation. It offered us an acceptable route, since it led to the South Fork of the Tieton where we wanted to go. The snow was what skiers call "corn" snow, hard and coarsely granulated. We had no skis, but we did have a frying pan apiece.

"Why not use them as toboggans?" asked Brad.

The idea was to sit in the frying pan, hold the feet up, lean slightly backwards, and, keeping the handle to the rear, use it as a steering rod. The problem of balance was complicated by the horseshoe packs around our necks, which became awkward and unwieldy when we were seated.

Brad started off. The frying pan which he used as a sled bit slightly into the crust of the snow. He was soon going like a flash, rocking crazily from side to side, the ends of his horseshoe pack bobbing along on the snow. He had only a short run of 100 feet or so when he turned sideways and then rolled over and over. He finally dug his foot in the snow and ended up half-buried in the mountainside. His blue eyes were laughing as he brushed snow out of his hair. I followed suit and repeated his performance. I tried again and landed head down with my pack buried with me and only my feet free. Thus we rolled and slid off Darling Mountain, yelling and laughing and shouting as we went. We were on and off the frying pans a dozen times or more. We had snow in our shoes and down our necks. Our hands were cold and raw from the rough snow; and our pants were wet. But the bottoms of our frying pans shone like new silver dollars.

We camped that night at the base of Darling, by a falls close to the confluence of Bear Creek and the South Fork of the Tieton. The latter was swollen from the snow and white with raging water, so we did not even attempt to fish it. We usually had good luck fishing the South Fork at Conrad Meadows, which was above us a few miles. We headed up there the next morning, hoping without much reason that the stream would be more moderate at that point.

Conrad Meadows is a good name and address in the Cascades. James H. Conrad, the man who homesteaded it and ran cattle in it for years, has a long-legged, clear eyed, friendly grandson, Norman Conrad, who runs cattle there today. Conrad Meadows is a mile or so long and perhaps a half-mile wide. It lies about 4000 feet above sea level. There are beautiful clumps of aspen in it and scatterings of black pine. We used to see knee-high grass there in early summer. The South Fork usually has a bit of the milk of glaciers in it, for a goodly portion of its supply comes off the Goat Rocks. But Conrad Creek, which joins the South Fork at the eastern edge of the Meadow, is always clear and cold. We would usually camp at that spot.

It was a friendly and hospitable camping place. Less than ten miles to the west, standing way above an intervening ridge, is the rugged nose of Gilbert Peak of the Goat Rocks, inlaid with a streak of glacial ice and snow. There it stands alone, dominating the horizon. Gilbert Peak, seen from the low-rimmed Conrad Basin, is an invitation for exploration. It has always drawn me like a magnet. It has always lifted my heart. A peak that only nudges the sky with its nose, leaving the rest concealed, has peculiar appeal. It suggests that what lies beneath, hidden from view, may be valleys and lakes of unusual mystery, basins and meadows of romance, glaciers agleam with breath-taking thrills. Such is the special invitation that Gilbert Peak extends from Conrad Meadows.

There was more than beauty in those meadows. The South Fork was a good rainbow stream. Deep pools; long riffles; banks shaded by pine, fir, and willow; fast, cold water; a stream 30 to 50 feet wide—this was the South Fork. Here we developed our skills as fly-fishermen. Here we found a generous food supply of fat, fighting rainbow.

But the June day we arrived there the fishing was poor. Snow water filled the river and we had little luck. We decided against taking the trail through the steep draw on the south to the Klickitat Meadows, which had been our original destination, for its stream too would be full of snow water. So we watched the sun set over Gilbert Peak, broke camp the next morning, and headed down the South Fork to the Tieton Basin, some 12 to 14 miles to the northeast.

Along we went on the easy down trail lined with lupine, vanilla leaf, huckleberry, cinquefoil, snowberry, and snowbrush not yet in bloom. We never stopped once as Brad, in the lead, set a good pace of three to four miles an hour. We crossed No Name Creek, Bear Creek, and innumerable smaller streams that in midsummer are rivulets and that now were freshets. We went through a grove of aspen and yellow pine at Minnie Meadows, crossed Middle Creek and Grey's Creek, and soon dropped into the Basin.

We camped that night at McAllister Meadows near the junction of the North Fork and South Fork of the Tieton. To the north were Westfall Rocks and Goose Egg Mountain. Between them Rimrock Dam has since been erected to form the great reservoir that buried McAllister Meadows forever under its waters. To the east were the sheer cliffs of Kloochman, where once Doug Corpron and I almost lost our lives. In the shadow of these mighty fortresses we had afternoon fishing in the North Fork. But it too was poor because of the snow water. As a result we decided to head for Fish Lake, where we were almost certain to get fish. It is a small, shallow lake whose waters are warm by early summer. Accordingly the next morning, shortly after sunrise, we started up the Indian Creek Trail.

One branch of this trail goes to the headwaters of Indian Creek just below Pear Lake, climbs to the Blankenship Meadows, passes Twin Sister Lakes and drops to Fish Lake—a good 18-mile hike. There is a fork in the trail about half-way to Pear Lake that leads west, passes near Dumbbell Lake, crosses Cowlitz Pass, skirts Fryingpan Lake, and, joining the trail out of the Twin Sisters, drops to Fish Lake. This was known as the Sand Ridge Trail. It was the one we decided to take.

We followed the North Fork of the Tieton through Russell Ranch, climbed out of the Basin on the right side of Indian Creek, passing Boot Jack Rock on our right. We were on the lower reaches of Russell Ridge until we came to the Sand Ridge Trail about seven miles from our starting point. Here the trail turns west, crosses Indian Creek, and climbs precipitously almost a thousand feet. At this point we struck snow. It was soft and slushy and it wet us through. We struggled in it for an hour or more, frequently losing the trail and expending energy far out of proportion to our progress.

We sat down on a ledge of rock for rest and consultation. Our decision was to turn back, to camp that night in McAllister Meadows, and the next day to go down the Tieton River to the Naches, then along the Naches to home.

We made an early camp in the Basin. It was not yet dark when we were eating our supper. Suddenly we said, almost in unison, "Why not go home tonight?"

Since then I have seen the same thing happen over and again. Men in the mountains, nearing the end of their trip, have an urge to cut it short by a day or two and bolt for home. For some reason the pull of home at once becomes overpowering and irresistible. And a man headed for home, like a horse headed for oats in his stable, is headstrong and unreasonable.

Once made, the decision to push on that night became irrevocable. We hurried to do the dishes and reassemble our packs before dark. They were already light, as we had been eating from them for about five days. We made them even lighter by leaving behind all the food except dried prunes and dried apples (which we put in our pockets and munched through the night) and some flour which we could use to bake bread if need be.

It was dark when we started. There was no moon; but the stars were out. We soon left Goose Egg Mountain as a great dark splotch against the western skyline, crossed Milk Creek, and keeping it on our left worked our way along the edge of a hillside until we descended to the Tieton River.

The trail crossed the river a mile or so later. The night was cold and the Tieton was filled with snow water. The water was frightfully cold as it swept above our knees in midstream, licking at the bottoms of the packs. We gained the other side with much splashing and muttering. My shoes were full of water, my teeth were chattering, I was chilled to the heart.

We stopped on the far bank to stomp and try to shake some water from our trousers. Then a chill cramp hit my leg muscles. Brad too was seized. If there had been any doubt whether we would push on, the cramps in our legs and our shivering and shaking settled it. It was plain that it would take hours for us to thaw and dry out in camp. The best way was to keep moving.

We covered thirty miles in those eight hours or more of darkness. It was the most drab and dreary hike I ever took. Many times I have come off a mountain in the dark or walked the high ridges in the blackness of night. Usually there is an exhilaration in it, for then most of the animals of the woods are on the move and all one's senses are quickened. But this night was oppressive.

All the way down we were in the narrow Tieton canyon whose walls rise a thousand feet or so on each side. The bottom of such a canyon is naturally dark. It was a Stygian pit the night we traveled it. Shortly after we started, clouds had blotted out the stars and I could not see a hand in front of me.

The trail along the Tieton was in truth a dirt road at the point where we crossed the river. It grew still wider as we moved down the canyon. Most of the time therefore we walked abreast, never speaking, stumbling occasionally over a loose rock. The Tieton was high,

as I have said. Soon we came to a portion of the road that had been
overflowed. There was no detour we could find in the darkness. So
for the second time we waded the icy water. More cramps made walking still more painful. But we had to keep moving to prevent the
cramps from getting worse.

How many inhabitants of the darkness may have seen us I never
knew. I saw none of them. A screech owl protested our invasion of
the canyon. There was an occasional slithering sound in the dry
grasses beside the road. But though rattlers infest the lower reaches
of the Tieton, I heard none that night—it was too cold perhaps for
snakes as sensitive as rattlers to be abroad. A piercing wind at our
backs whirled and howled through the funnels of the canyon. It
whipped the willows that lined the road so that occasionally they
touched our faces.

Several hours before daybreak, we began to see against the sky the
vague outline of the hills that rose on either side. This was the first
break in the darkness that had enveloped us the night long. The
dimly lighted skyline at once became a guide. My eyes were more
and more upon it. Over and again I said to myself, "Surely, the next
turn must mark the end of the canyon." My hope increased as the
skyline of the hills brightened. But on each turn the hope vanished;
ahead another few hundred yards was another twist in the ravine.
The canyon appeared to go on without end—and so it seems even to
this day when I drive this canyon or any other like it. Each bend was
like the bend behind, each was only the forerunner of a bend ahead.
We were on a treadmill, plodding on and on but standing still.

Brad was a stout hiker. There was the mark of determination on
his sharp features, an impression verified by his deep and almost gruff
voice and by his shock of unruly light-brown hair. He stood about
five feet ten and was all muscle. He was short-legged and sturdy. He
usually set the pace on our trips. He seemed to me to have endless
energy, and I was always proud to be able to keep up with him. Brad
was the pace-setter this night. It was a slow steady pace, the pace of a
plodder, the pace of one who is distributing his energies over a 40- or
50-mile stretch. It was the pace of marching men, like the one I be-

came acquainted with in 1918. It was steady, on and on, left, right, left, right, through the night.

I was proud of my legs. They were so tired they felt numb. But they never failed. They did not cry out in anguish nor did they ache. The plop, plop of my feet sounded far away, remote, impersonal. I went down the canyon in the darkness, shoulder to shoulder with Brad. I was an automaton that had been set for a course and never missed a beat.

The dawn came stealthily. As the gray of the sky increased, the wind died down. Rocks and bushes and trees for the first time became recognizable, not in detail but as identifiable blotches on a landscape. Then they emerged in daylight, stark naked in their poverty. For we had left the pines and fir and green hillsides far behind us. We had left the Tieton and were in the lower reaches of the Naches canyon.

Mount Cleman, sterile and dry, was on our left. Its deep ravines, washed out by thousands of rains, looked in the dim light like folds of flesh on the face of an old, old person. So far as the eye could tell, the hills on both sides of the canyon were bare except for cheatgrass, bunchgrass, and sage. But as the sun rose, a soft green tinge touched them—the light green of tender shoots and of the myriad wild flowers that were scattered in the sage and grass. There were cottonwoods and oak in the draw and sumac and elderberry bushes by the river which gave a sparse greenness to the bottom of the canyon. A magpie appeared; but no other bird or animal greeted the dawn with us. The raven usually comes at this hour as the scavenger who picks up the carcasses of rabbits killed by the traffic of the night, but none was on hand this June morning.

Now we could get our bearings. We were on familiar ground, and realized at once that we were only three or four miles from Naches. We paused briefly for a rest, taking off our packs and stretching out on the side of the road. We did not plan to go to sleep; but we did. We could not have slept long, for the sun was not yet up when we were awakened by the clattering of a truck. It was a truck en route to pick up cream from farms in the Naches canyon. We rose, startled and unsteady, when we saw it bearing down on us as we lay sprawled with our feet in the road itself.

Once aroused we pushed on; and knowing that our goal was near, we picked up our pace. It was not long before there was a song in my heart. The sun was above the rim of hills to the east when I saw the village of Naches. Acres and acres of green alfalfa fields and scattered apple orchards lay before us, a friendly oasis in the desert. Only one who, in his great suffering throughout the night, despaired that morning would come, could have welcomed this sunrise more than I. I was so relieved to have the dark ordeal behind me that I did not appreciate how great was my fatigue. Since it was Sunday, no lunch counter would open until 8 o'clock. It was now about 6:30. And the train—known as Sagebrush Annie—that would take us to Yakima, would not go down until 11 o'clock. After 8, when at last I had my fill of ham, eggs, potatoes, and toast, an overwhelming drowsiness claimed me. I fell asleep on the station platform and was awakened by the clatter of the train.

The next I knew the conductor was shaking me. I was home, saying good-by to Brad. In spite of my fatigue I put the horseshoe pack over my shoulder and walked the half-dozen blocks to my home with a spring in my legs. I was happy at heart if not in the flesh. I had walked with a pack over 40 miles in one day. I had walked the whole night through. I was proud of my legs. I wanted to shout "Look at my legs! Hear what I have done!" Remember, I was a boy. I wanted to laugh at the guys that said I had puny legs. I wanted to take them to the hills for a contest—an endurance contest, if you please. Brad and I could outwalk anyone in the valley.

And then I went to bed and slept from that noon until the sun was high the next day.

When I awoke, the doubt was gone forever. The achievement of walking 40 miles with a pack in one day had banished it, just as the sun rising over Naches had absorbed the long fingers of mist that hung over the hayfields yesterday morning.

Chapter VIII   *Deep Water*

THERE are many lakes to the north and west of Mount Adams. Often, like Surprise Lake below Gilbert Peak, they are dark and deep and lined with thick forests of pine and fir that run to the water. Others are hardly more than potholes. There is one such in a meadow near the southeastern end of the ridge mounted by the famous Goat Rocks. It is not more than 100 yards long and 50 wide. It lies in a high meadow of heather and alpine bunchgrass. It is fringed by dwarfed whitebark pine and Alaska cedar, both stunted by the altitude and wind. It lies not more than a stone's throw from a perpetual snowbank. Yet, under a July sun, the upper layer of its water was at times almost tepid. So Doug Corpron and I dubbed it Warm Lake. It was for us boys a friendly water hole. But I always felt an ominous spell hanging over the dark, tree-mirroring lakes when I traveled the Cascades as a boy.

Part of my feeling was owing to the Indian legends. It was said that spirits or genii lived there. The gods controlled the formation of rain. If the lake waters were in any way disturbed, the gods who resided there would send rain to plague the offenders. As a result the Indians would not throw rocks into such lakes, or drink from them, or water their horses there. And, most assuredly, they never would bathe or swim in them. At least that is the legend as it came to me.

That legend alone, not to mention the eeriness, was enough to keep me from those shores. Some of the lakes even seemed spooky when I looked into them from a ridge. In my youthful imagination, a swirl in the middle of the lake might well have supernatural significance. According to the Indians, that was supposed to be one way in which the spirit who lived there made his displeasure manifest.

In some lakes of the region there were supposed to be beaver women, or water nymphs. It was said they would come half-way out, sometimes holding a baby. As a boy, I took them also on faith; but I never even imagined I saw one.

The case of the sea serpent on Bumping Lake was different. This lake is about four miles long. Its natural size was much smaller. But about 1910 the United States Reclamation Service built a dam below the lake to impound water for irrigation. As a result a great timbered area was inundated. When the reservoir is full, there is a winding expanse of beautiful blue water. When it is down, stumps of the old forest, waterlogged driftwood, and mud flats stand exposed in ugliness.

One day a few of us boys were walking the trail that leads along the northern shore of Bumping Lake to Fish Lake. Bumping Lake was brimful. It was raining; and a strong east wind was producing whitecaps at the western end of the lake.

Suddenly one of the boys cried out, "Look, the serpent!" And there a hundred yards or so offshore was some object in the lake which in the haze of the storm did look like a huge snake playing on the surface of the water. What it was I never knew—probably a half-submerged log or a long, sinewy branch. But I was an easy convert to the serpent theory. The Indian legend was that an evil spirit inhabited that lake. He was a monster that reached up from the dark waters, grabbed unsuspecting fishermen, and took them with him to the darkness of the bottom. He would turn himself into floating logs, submerged branches, or trunks of trees, the better to deceive a passer-by. Hence even if what I saw on that rainy day was a log or a branch, it still was consistent with the serpent legend.

The Indians kept away from Bumping Lake. In the 40 years that Jack Nelson lived there he only saw four Indians at the lake. They came for a ride in a brand new car, not to fish.

So the tales concerning these deep lakes of the Cascades increased my wariness of all mountain lakes.

The case of Warm Lake, below the Goat Rocks ridge, was different. It was in the open, like a swimming pool in a lawn. Its water was so clear that I could see the rocky, sandy bottom far out from shore.

No dark depths were there to warn me. And at no place did it appear more than twenty feet deep. There was nothing ominous about it, and, as I have said, its surface water was warm, although it lay close to a snow field. As boys we planned a night there whenever possible, for there is nothing more attractive than a bath after a week's exertion on the trails. And there is the same novelty about swimming in comfort next to a snowbank as there is skating outdoors on artificial ice at Sun Valley on a warm day in July.

We would bathe and swim in this lake for a whole afternoon in July or August. Our pattern was to take a dip, then lie naked in the heather sunning ourselves, and then return to the water for more splashing and shouting. Yet I never got far from the bank. I remember being there with Doug Corpron and watching him. He would dive in with a running jump from the bank, coast part of the way across the pond under water, then come up to the surface, swim to the far bank and, without stopping, swim back. He'd shout to me, "Come on! It's fun!"

He had a round face that always seemed cheerful and content. And he had brown eyes that exuded confidence. He stood about five feet ten and even as a boy was on the plump side. He'd stand on the bank of the little lake, toss his head to shake the water off, and smooth down his shock of dark-brown hair. Then after a moment's rest he'd dive in and be off again. He seemed to me to be as much at home in the water as a porpoise or a seal.

I hugged the bank, wading and splashing water. When I had my picture taken in this pond, I made sure I had only my head sticking out. But I did it by kneeling in shallow water. Once or twice when I tried to swim, a feeling of panic swept over me. I would freeze and become rigid, unable to move my legs. I would gasp for breath and strike out with my arms. My legs would hang straight down in the water and I would be unable to move them. Even when I walked in water over my waist, the panic would seize me and I would have to go to shore.

No one ever knew this. I naturally was ashamed of it. It all fitted into fears that had become established in my imagination. I thought it had something to do with my puny legs, since they became useless once I got into deep water. That fact puzzled me. I often said to myself, "It's funny that I can walk and run and climb with my legs, but not swim with them." But once the panic seized me in the water, I had no command over them. I suffered intensely as I fished the streams and lakes of the Cascades, or as I bathed in Warm Lake.

The worry grew and grew, as only a specter can. It made every expanse of water a source of anxiety and yet a challenge. It was at once an invitation to overcome the fear and a fear that I would never succeed in doing so. My aversion to the water was, indeed, mixed with a great attraction for it. Often I would be mesmerized by it and stand on the edge of a pond or a pool, looking into the water as if to draw from its depths the secret of its conquest of me. It was the master; I was the servant. That created a resentment which developed in my heart; and the more helpless I was in conquering my fear the more intense the resentment became. The waters of the rivers and lakes were great attractions; but as one can have an appetite for food to which he is allergic, so the waters to which I was drawn filled me with apprehension.

I knew the origin of my fears. They went back to the day I almost drowned. But I thought it took only will power and courage to overcome the fear that drowning had instilled in me. I learned years later that the early fears of childhood work through the sympathetic nervous system, which does not depend on will power for its functioning. When the man says "Yes," the sympathetic nervous system will often say "No" and send him helter-skelter in the direction opposite from where he decided to go. If this goes on long enough, a man can conclude he is irrational or end up frustrated and desperately ill with an illness that no medicine can cure.

It had happened when I was ten or eleven years old. I had decided to learn to swim. There was a pool at the Y.M.C.A. in Yakima that offered exactly the opportunity. The Yakima River was treacherous. Mother continually warned against it, and kept fresh in my mind the details of each drowning in the river. But the Y.M.C.A. pool was safe. It was only two or three feet deep at the shallow end; and while it was nine feet deep at the other, the drop was gradual. I got a pair of water wings and went to the pool. I hated to walk naked into it and show my skinny legs. But I subdued my pride and did it.

From the beginning, however, I had an aversion to the water when I was in it. This started when I was three or four years old and Father took me to the beach in California. He and I stood together in the surf. I hung on to him, yet the waves knocked me down and swept over me. I was buried in water. My breath was gone. I was frightened. Father laughed, but there was terror in my heart at the overpowering force of the waves.

My introduction to the Y.M.C.A. swimming pool revived unpleasant memories and stirred childish fears. But in a little while I gathered confidence. I paddled with my new water wings, watching the other boys and trying to learn by aping them. I did this two or three times on different days and was just beginning to feel at ease in the water when the misadventure happened.

I went to the pool when no one else was there. The place was quiet. The water was still, and the tiled bottom was as white and clean as a bathtub. I was timid about going in alone, so I sat on the side of the pool to wait for others.

I had not been there long when in came a big bruiser of a boy, probably eighteen years old. He had thick hair on his chest. He was a beautiful physical specimen, with legs and arms that showed rippling muscles. He yelled, "Hi, Skinny! How'd you like to be ducked?"

With that he picked me up and tossed me into the deep end. I landed in a sitting position, swallowed water, and went at once to the bottom. I was frightened, but not yet frightened out of my wits. On the way down I planned: When my feet hit the bottom, I would make a big jump, come to the surface, lie flat on it, and paddle to the edge of the pool.

It seemed a long way down. Those nine feet were more like ninety, and before I touched bottom my lungs were ready to burst. But when my feet hit bottom I summoned all my strength and made what I thought was a great spring upwards. I imagined I would bob to the surface like a cork. Instead I came up slowly. I opened my eyes and saw nothing but water—water that had a dirty yellow tinge to it. I grew panicky. I reached up as if to grab a rope and my hands clutched only at water. I was suffocating. I tried to yell but no sound came out. Then my eyes and nose came out of the water—but not my mouth.

I flailed at the surface of the water, swallowed and choked. I tried to bring my legs up, but they hung as dead weights, paralyzed and rigid. A great force was pulling me under. I screamed, but only the water heard me. I had started on the long journey back to the bottom of the pool.

I struck at the water as I went down, expending my strength as one in a nightmare fights an irresistible force. I had lost all my breath. My lungs ached, my head throbbed. I was getting dizzy. But I remembered the strategy: I would spring from the bottom of the pool and come like a cork to the surface. I would lie flat on the water, strike out with my arms, and thrash with my legs. Then I would get to the edge of the pool and be safe.

I went down, down, endlessly. I opened my eyes. Nothing but water with a yellow glow—dark water that one could not see through.

And then sheer, stark terror seized me, terror that knows no understanding, terror that knows no control, terror that no one can understand who has not experienced it. I was shrieking under water. I was paralyzed under water—stiff, rigid with fear. Even the screams in my throat were frozen. Only my heart, and the pounding in my head, said that I was still alive.

And then in the midst of the terror came a touch of reason. I must remember to jump when I hit the bottom. At last I felt the tiles under me. My toes reached out as if to grab them. I jumped with everything I had.

But the jump made no difference. The water was still around me. I looked for ropes, ladders, water wings. Nothing but water. A mass of yellow water held me. Stark terror took an even deeper hold on me, like a great charge of electricity. I shook and trembled with fright. My arms wouldn't move. My legs wouldn't move. I tried to call for help, to call for Mother. Nothing happened.

And then, strangely, there was light. I was coming out of the awful yellow water. At least my eyes were. My nose was almost out too.

Then I started down a third time. I sucked for air and got water. The yellowish light was going out.

Then all effort ceased. I relaxed. Even my legs felt limp; and a blackness swept over my brain. It wiped out fear; it wiped out terror. There was no more panic. It was quiet and peaceful. Nothing to be afraid of. This is nice . . . to be drowsy . . . to go to sleep . . . no need to jump . . . too tired to jump . . . it's nice to be carried gently . . . to float along in space . . . tender arms around me . . . tender arms like Mother's . . . now I must go to sleep. . . .

I crossed to oblivion, and the curtain of life fell.

The next I remember I was lying on my stomach beside the pool, vomiting. The chap that threw me in was saying, "But I was only fooling." Someone said, "The kid nearly died. Be all right now. Let's carry him to the locker room."

Several hours later I walked home. I was weak and trembling. I shook and cried when I lay on my bed. I couldn't eat that night. For days a haunting fear was in my heart. The slightest exertion upset me, making me wobbly in the knees and sick to my stomach.

I never went back to the pool. I feared water. I avoided it whenever I could.

A few years later when I came to know the waters of the Cascades, I wanted to get into them. And whenever I did—whether I was wading the Tieton or Bumping River or bathing in Warm Lake of the Goat Rocks—the terror that had seized me in the pool would come back. It would take possession of me completely. My legs would become paralyzed. Icy horror would grab my heart.

This handicap stayed with me as the years rolled by. In canoes on Maine lakes fishing for landlocked salmon, bass fishing in New Hampshire, trout fishing on the Deschutes and Metolius in Oregon, fishing for salmon on the Columbia, at Bumping Lake in the Cascades—wherever I went, the haunting fear of the water followed me. It ruined my fishing trips; deprived me of the joy of canoeing, boating, and swimming.

I used every way I knew to overcome this fear, but it held me firmly in its grip. Finally, one October, I decided to get an instructor and learn to swim. I went to a pool and practiced five days a week, an hour each day. The instructor put a belt around me. A rope attached to the belt went through a pulley that ran on an overhead cable. He held on to the end of the rope, and we went back and forth, back and forth across the pool, hour after hour, day after day, week after week. On each trip across the pool a bit of the panic seized me. Each time the instructor relaxed his hold on the rope and I went under, some of the old terror returned and my legs froze. It was three months before the tension began to slack. Then he taught me to put my face under water and exhale, and to raise my nose and inhale. I repeated the exercise hundreds of times. Bit by bit I shed part of the panic that seized me when my head went under water.

Next he held me at the side of the pool and had me kick with my legs. For weeks I did just that. At first my legs refused to work. But they gradually relaxed; and finally I could command them.

Thus, piece by piece, he built a swimmer. And when he had perfected each piece, he put them together into an integrated whole. In April he said, "Now you can swim. Dive off and swim the length of the pool, crawl stroke."

I did. The instructor was finished.

But I was not finished. I still wondered if I would be terror-stricken when I was alone in the pool. I tried it. I swam the length up and down. Tiny vestiges of the old terror would return. But now I could frown and say to that terror, "Trying to scare me, eh? Well, here's to you! Look!" And off I'd go for another length of the pool.

This went on until July. But I was still not satisfied. I was not sure that all the terror had left. So I went to Lake Wentworth in New Hampshire, dived off a dock at Triggs Island, and swam two miles across the lake to Stamp Act Island. I swam the crawl, breast stroke, side stroke, and back stroke. Only once did the terror return. When

I was in the middle of the lake, I put my face under and saw nothing but bottomless water. The old sensation returned in miniature. I laughed and said, "Well, Mr. Terror, what do you think you can do to me?" It fled and I swam on.

Yet I had residual doubts. At my first opportunity I hurried west, went up the Tieton to Conrad Meadows, up the Conrad Creek Trail to Meade Glacier, and camped in the high meadow by the side of Warm Lake. The next morning I stripped, dived into the lake, and swam across to the other shore and back—just as Doug Corpron used to do. I shouted with joy, and Gilbert Peak returned the echo. I had conquered my fear of water.

The experience had a deep meaning for me, as only those who have known stark terror and conquered it can appreciate. In death there is peace. There is terror only in the fear of death, as Roosevelt knew when he said, "All we have to fear is fear itself." Because I had experienced both the sensation of dying and the terror that fear of it can produce, the will to live somehow grew in intensity.

At last I felt released—free to walk the trails and climb the peaks and to brush aside fear.

Chapter IX   *Fear Walks the Woods*

As FAR as the forces of nature are concerned, there are only two serious dangers in the mountains. The animals can be put aside, for they try to avoid man. The grizzly may be an exception; but it has been my experience that one can get into trouble with the black or brown bear only if he succeeds in maneuvering himself between a mother and her cubs. I have met timber wolves on trails when I was unarmed and have always been able to stare them down. The cougar is the hardest of all animals to see and seldom attacks a man. The bull elk when he is with the cows is probably the most dangerous of all animals in the woods. But the chance of conflict with a wild animal in the hills is not so great as the chance you take in traffic when you walk the city streets.

The forest fire and the avalanche are different. They are two risks that, at certain times of the year, always look over the shoulder of one who knows the mountains and travels their trails.

The forests of the Pacific Northwest can become kindling. In long periods of drought the trails lie thick in dust, ankle deep and as fine as flour. Pine and fir needles become as combustible as paper. A campfire, unless circled with a trench, can spread along and under the surface. The chain that drags a log in lumber operations may scrape a rock and make a spark, igniting almost at once a whole forest. A cigarette or match carelessly tossed by the side of the trail can do the same. Lightning may make a flaming torch of any of the resinous evergreens. Even one spark can cause irreparable damage—a smouldering fire whipped to a blaze by a slight wind, racing up trees and through forests faster than a man can run, killing all life with its hot tongue, leaving behind desolation and a sterile earth that will not produce crops of timber for a generation or more.

Rangers, guards, and lookouts of the Forest Service are on edge in these dry spells. Douglas C. Ingram was a grazing examiner of the Forest Service. He was an outstanding field botanist. One day he sent in to Washington, D.C. from southwest Oregon a new species of *Silene*, a wild flower of the pink family. The species he sent is the handsomest of the western *Silenes*—gray-green leaves topped by deep cherry-red flowers. On August 17, 1929, Dayton had it named for Ingram: *Silene ingrami*. Ingram never knew this, for a few days earlier he had died fighting a forest fire.

The fire was on Camas Creek in the Chelan National Forest of eastern Washington. Lightning had struck a pine tree. A trench was put around the fire after it had burned 160 acres. It seemed the danger was over. But the next day the wind picked up live embers and carried them across the trench. They fell within a few feet of the fire fighters. The freakish wind whipped the fire so crazily that the men could not stop it. Before morning the fire had covered 5,000 acres and was still raging.

A large crew was brought in, including Glenn Mitchell and Ingram. When the fire trapped a dozen of the men, Ingram led them into a small clearing and sat whittling sticks and telling stories. His cool leadership banished their panic and restored reason. But all this time the fire was leaping toward them. This was not a ground fire; it was a crown fire that traveled the tops of the trees—the kind of a forest fire that often goes faster than a horse can run. If the men had run, the flames would have curled around their shoulders and burned them to cinders. Ingram was ready for the emergency. As the fire sped toward them, Ingram had the crew lie flat. The fire leaped over them and went its mad way. Then Ingram led them safely to camp.

A couple of days later the men were about to be trapped again. Ingram pulled them out and took them to a high ridge to eat lunch. Since conditions had not improved, he then sent them back to camp. Ingram and Ernani St. Luise remained behind to look for Glenn Mitchell who, they thought, had gone down the ridge. They had not traveled far before the wind blew up the fire. The fire was below them. An inexperienced person would probably have retraced his steps. But as Glenn Mitchell told me, "Anyone who has fought fires knows that they run uphill whenever there is a chance." Mitchell knew what a forest fire would do, for this same day a crown fire had made a fast run up the ridge where he was working. A hot wave of flame and smoke barely missed him.

Ingram also knew forest fires. His decision was to get around the end of the fire and below it. But as Glenn Mitchell said when he described this fire to me, "This was one of those phenomenal instances when the unexpected happened." The fire did not travel uphill or down. It burned a strip about a mile wide and three miles long on a level contour. It was going faster than Ingram and St. Luise could walk. Hurry as they did, they could not get ahead of it. Progress was slow because of the rough terrain and down timber. The freak wind increased to a gale, and whipped the fire up the ridge towards them. It came with a roar, curling over the trees and along the tops. Its long, hot tongue licked the earth and turned it black.

Ingram and St. Luise saw it coming. They picked out a fairly open, yellow pine slope where there was not much to burn. They lay down together, faces to the ground. A wall of fire and smoke, fifty or more feet high, raced up the slope, faster than a horse could run. It lay over the men for a second or two like a fiery blanket, burning their clothing and blackening their skin. Then it was gone in a flash, roaring like a winged inferno to the top of the ridge.

Ingram and St. Luise probably were suffocated from lack of oxygen. They may have been suffocated even before the fire reached them. A near-vacuum, with the heat of a furnace, is often formed in the path of a raging forest fire.

The avalanche of snow has left its scars on most of the ridges of the Pacific Northwest. It often carries whole forests with it, tumbling tall pine and fir as if they were matches and rolling huge rocks before it. There are many scars of avalanches in the Cascades. There are even more in the Wallowas.

The Wallowas lie in the northeast corner of Oregon. They have peaks in the 10,000-feet zone such as Eagle Cap, Matterhorn, and Sacajawea. The ridges of the Cascades are for the most part soft, rounded, and heavily wooded, and run around 6,000 feet. In the

Wallowas they are mostly jagged backbones, made of a granitic rock and averaging around 9,000 feet in elevation. Some are so narrow on the top that a horse cannot be ridden along them. Many of the canyon walls of the Wallowas are sheer rock that has been polished by glaciers—slopes that have a 30-, 40-, or even 60-degree grade. For all practical purposes they are straight up and down. Thus the Wallowas have become known as the Switzerland of America.

It is indeed unusual to see a canyon in the Wallowas whose walls have not been scarred by slides. Some slides have left swaths three or four thousand feet long and a quarter of a mile or so wide. Sometimes they have had such tremendous momentum as to carry across the canyon a half-mile and then up several hundred yards on the other wall, leveling everything and grinding great rocks to powder. One such slide took place a dozen years or more ago about a half-mile above Turkey Flat on the Lostine River not far from our cabin.

A slide of such proportions can crush a house as if it were a cardboard carton. Selecting a location for a cabin therefore requires care. Some of the most beautiful sites lie at the mouths of draws that can, and do, spew thousands of tons of snow, rocks, dirt, and trees into the valleys.

John Muir once reported snowslides that wiped out lakes in the Sierra. I know one such in the Wallowas. High on the ridge west of our cabin on the Lostine River in the Wallowas is Mud Lake. It lies under a granite wall that rises at a steep angle 1000 feet or more above it. The lake was known for its five- and six-pound eastern brook trout. Today it still has trout; but most of the big ones disappeared in a snowslide in the spring of 1948. The slide came off the granite wall, carried through the lake, and crushed trees 50 yards across the meadow on the far side. As it swept through the lake it took water and fish with it, as one would empty a wash pan with the palm of his hand in a quick sideward movement.

Anyone who has stood on a hillside watching a boulder rolling down toward him has seen a rockslide in miniature.

One day in June in the early forties, I was on my way by horseback to Frances Lake in the Wallowas. The lake is usually at its best three weeks after the ice is out. There still was much snow up high. But the lake, which lies over the ridge to the east of our cabin, is one of the earliest lakes to go out in the spring. It has three-pound rainbow in it, a lure that offsets the steep and treacherous trail that reaches there. The trail rises about 4,000 feet in a mile and a half. The last 1500 feet are in fairly open terrain and rise at a grade of around 40 degrees.

I had worked my way on horseback to about 500 feet from the top of the ridge. The climb is strenuous and I had stopped many times to let my horse blow. Once while he rested I alighted and turned him sideways, to tighten the cinch. I had finished with that and was standing at his head, holding the bridle in my hands, when I heard a noise. I looked up and saw a boulder, weighing at least 50 pounds, jumping and hurtling through the air, headed my way.

It had been loosened by some animal, probably a bear that went up the wooded stretch over the saddle ahead of me. The boulder wobbled on its course, careening first to the left and then to the right like some wanton dervish bent on destruction. To run was dangerous: the footing was unsure, time was short, and there was no way of escaping the wide arc the rock was commanding as it bounded unpredictably from one side to the other on its downward course. My decision was instantaneous—to stand still.

In the split second or two which it took the rock to reach me, there came back to me the vivid memory of a funeral service twenty-five years earlier in Yakima. A prominent citizen had died in a mysterious manner. The church was packed and I, a boy of fifteen, slipped in and stood at the back, more out of curiosity, I think, than respect. Standing there, I heard an eloquent minister describe the strange passing of the deceased. It was, he said, as accidental as that caused by a huge rock which, started by the casual step of some animal, comes hurtling off a mountainside to strike an innocent and unsuspecting traveler strolling in the valley below.

Was the drama of that sermon to be staged on the mountainside before my own eyes? But the rock was on me. I could feel its breeze and almost its fury as it roared under the belly of the frantic horse at a speed greater than he could ever run.

My heart was still pounding as I watched it roll on and on a thousand feet or more down into the abyss below.

An avalanche of snow has ten thousand times the alarm that anything else in the mountains can produce. I saw one in action on the same ridge some ten years ago.

Before the trail starts up the steep stretch of mountainside where the bounding rock came down on me, it crosses a ravine. This ravine runs to the top of the ridge, 1500 feet or so. It is a V-shaped ravine about 50 feet across. It has been washed by thousands of rains and polished by innumerable slides. And it collects great rocks as the peaks that tower over it crumble and crack under the action of the frost.

In June 1940 I was on this trail headed for Frances Lake. When I reached the ravine, it was filled with snow—eight or ten feet of it. The snow was getting so soft that my horse would sink deep in it. So I dismounted and led him across the 50-foot span of snow. The trail then climbs sharply about 30 or 40 feet. I went that far on foot and stopped to mount.

Then without warning came the slide. I heard the first roar as it started near the top of the ravine. It picked up rocks and snow as it poured down the funnel, gaining momentum as it neared. Rocks as big as pianos were traveling ahead of it. Other rocks, small and huge, were caught up in the snow and debris. By the time it reached me the slide was 50 feet wide, 20 feet deep, and 100 yards long.

The vibration shook the mountain itself. The roar was that of a hundred express trains in a tunnel, of dozens of thunderstorms on an echoing hillside.

It rushed past, almost at my feet. It looked like a mad monster, roaring to destruction. Tons of wet, dirty snow hurled great rocks in the air as if they were pebbles. The whole churning mass seemed to have been tossed by some frenzied beast. The rocks on which I stood trembled as it passed. The slide moved on and on down the mountain until, with a shattering of trees in the forest below, it stopped. All was as silent as if death itself had passed through the ravine.

The fears of forest fires and avalanches, the only mountain fears that have any substantial basis of fact, are not the ones men usually take with them into the wilderness. The things they fear in the woods are in large part the same kind of things they fear in the city. The things they fear hold no intrinsic threat. They are as harmless as a frown, a knife, a skyscraper, a great cliff, or lightning. They are symbols of things that are terrifying.

Some fears may represent a person or place or event that was painful or frightening in childhood. The water of the lakes and rivers of the Cascades was such a symbol to me, as I have said, until I finally conquered the fear of drowning. Some, like a knife or office building or cliff, may be an invitation to death, by suggesting injury either to one's self or to another. Others, like lightning, may quicken feelings of guilt by suggesting long fingers of a revengeful god that reach down from the heavens to punish the culprit.

I have known people to go to bed and cover themselves with blankets when an electrical storm came. I have seen them filled with terror when the lightning struck and the thunder rolled. These people suffer real agony when they are on a mountainside and the storm breaks. Then there is no place to hide, no shelter. Man then stands in the open like the pine and the fir, without cover or protection. Like them, he is a good lightning rod.

Some of these mountain scenes of electrical storms can be either beautiful or terrifying, depending on one's conditioning. A few years ago I brought a pack train out of the Minam in the Wallowas up the Glacier Trail to Long Lake. A storm was rising from the south as we started the steep climb out of the Minam. We were perhaps 1500 feet above the river when the storm broke on the opposite ridge, some five air miles away. For a while sheet lightning played among the clouds. Then forked tongues struck at the ridge. In rapid succession—almost as fast as one could count—lightning hit three trees. And as each tree was hit it burst into flames like a match. It was one of those rare and exquisitely beautiful scenes that one could ride the trails 50 years or more and never see. For some people, however, there would be in it no beauty but only terror.

Being lost in the woods is for many people the most frightening experience of all. The very thought of being lost strikes fear, and casts a shadow over many mountain trips. It is so powerful a force that in spite of its subtlety it can produce a quick sweat or cause other discomfiture to the uninitiated. I do not pretend to know the various elements from which that fear is compounded. They probably vary among individuals. But ignorance is probably the mainstay of the fear. Lack of familiarity with the mountains, and with their ways, can create panic. Knowledge of their sources of food and shelter, and the manner of finding one's directions without a compass, points the way to survival. This creates confidence. But confidence is the product of experience.

Being lost in the Cascades or the Wallowas is not, of course, as dangerous as being lost in the Maine woods. I remember a few years back, leaving Gordon Frazer's lodge on the shores of Square Lake in the northeast corner of Maine, and striking through the woods a few miles to a trout stream. I had spent many a day in the woods; but I saw at once that these were woods that presented a different and more acute problem. The terrain was low rolling; there were no peaks or high ridges to give a bearing. And once I was in the woods, there were many stretches so thick with spruce and balsam fir that I could not even see the sky.

To the untrained eye they had a sameness that could be woefully misleading. By studying moss and bark and the lengths of branches, one could determine, without the aid of a compass, which direction was north. But it was plain that he would have to be on intimate terms with those woods, and know them throughout their farthest reach, to walk them with assurance and confidence. Gordon Frazer was such a person. We went to our trout stream by day, and returned in the dark as surely as the taxi driver finds the station for the new-corner in a strange city. But I never spent enough time in them to feel that I would be master if I were there alone.

The case of the Cascades and Wallowas is different. If one is lost in them, there are ridges to climb to find the directions; and once on top there usually is some major peak to serve as a landmark. Even if the higher points are hidden in clouds, there is often some lake or ridge to mark a bearing on a map. Yet that is not always true.

In 1948, I was camping with friends at Fryingpan Lake, which lies on the wide plateau above Bumping and Fish lakes. Conelike Tumac Mountain rises in the middle of this plateau and dominates it. There is no surer guidepost in the Cascades. But the morning when we broke camp at Fryingpan, a thick mist hung over the plateau, blotting everything from sight that was not within 50 or 100 yards. The low-lying fog was as thick as pea soup. No landmarks were left. Only the dark shapes of trees loomed in the mist, and they all looked alike.

Katherine Kershaw and Johnny Glenn took the pack train down the trail to Cowlitz Pass and Dumbbell Lake. Elon and I planned to go cross-country about two miles to Twin Sister Lakes and then cut back cross-country to Cowlitz Pass, traveling two sides of the triangle while the pack train took the hypotenuse. We studied our maps and headed the horses we were riding in the direction where the Twin Sisters lay. We traveled half an hour or more in the mist and discovered we were almost back at Fryingpan. We started again. Once more it happened. We started a third time. Again the horses returned us to Fryingpan.

They were circling with us, looking for the other horses. The circles they were making were wide, gentle arcs. There were no landmarks to guide us. Hence it was not easy for us to keep them on the compass. We finally gave up, conspired at Fryingpan, and picked up the roundabout trail that leads to the Twin Sisters.

In the mountains horses often circle on their riders. It's a natural thing to do. A hungry man who passes a restaurant that exudes odors of ham and eggs is likely to circle back if the next block takes him to the edge of town and the blackness of night. A lonesome man will do the same. Horses are in that sense only human.

Horses are more reliable than men, however, when all landmarks are blotted out. Some men have a keen sense of direction when walking blindly in the woods, but the majority do not. Even Bob Bowman lost his directions in the woods. Bob was as good a woodsman as the mountains have produced. He spent most of his life in the Wallowas and knew them in detail. The trail that leaves the Lostine canyon a short distance below our cabin, goes over the high ridge to the west through Brownie Basin and Wilson Basin, and then drops to the North Minam Meadows, was originally laid out by Bob and appropriately carries the name of Bowman.

Bob was a storyteller of note. He was present in 1942 at the cabinwarming and told tall tales that even his friends doubted. He told, for example, of the lady who was fishing for redsides in the Wallowa River. She had boots on and was standing in the river with a pitchfork. When a school of redsides came by, she would scoop them up with the fork and toss them on the bank.

"In a little while," said Bob, "so many redsides swam up the river that they knocked her down."

And after a respectful pause, he added: "Those fish would have drowned her but for me. I went in and dragged that good lady from the river."

But the story of what actually happened to Bob, himself, topped even his tallest tale. It happened in the North Minam Meadows. He and Roy Schaeffer had been hunting deer. They had shot a buck deer high on a ridge overlooking the meadows. It lay 1500 feet or more up the ridge at the base of sheer cliffs. Roy went for the buck, taking one horse with him and leaving the pack train with Bob. He told Bob to wait for him in the meadows.

Bob tied the horses to trees, built a fire, and sat down to wait. He had only the horses and a flask of whiskey for company. Darkness soon came, the hours passed, the flask at last was empty, and Roy did not return. Bob began to think he had misunderstood Roy. So he tied the pack train together again and started down the valley on foot, leading the horses and looking for Roy. In a half-hour or so he saw a bonfire ahead of him in a grove of trees.

He stopped and shouted, "Hullo!" There was no answer.

Again he shouted at the top of his lungs, "Hullo!" No one answered.

Once more he yelled, "I say, hullo over there!" Still no answer.

By then Bob was put out. Cupping his hands, he bellowed, "Well, don't answer if you don't want to, you long-nosed, old goats."

A few hours later Roy found Bob far up the canyon.

Roy laughed when he told me the story. "You know," he said, "the next morning I proved to Bob by his tracks that he had been yelling at his own bonfire the night before."

The trips my brother Art and I took into the Cascades as boys worried Mother sick. To her the idea of being lost in the mountains was terrifying. But it was a matter of no great concern to us—even when we were lost, as once we were. I was seventeen and Art thirteen. We were on foot in the Cascades with our horseshoe packs. We had left Fish Lake and climbed the ridge to the trail that leads to Dewey Lake. We were on the ridge somewhere southwest of Cougar Lake when we got lost.

It had rained at Fish Lake the night before and the air was heavy with fog. Visibility was not more than a hundred yards or so. Rainier was blotted out; and so were the towering cliffs that decorate this majestic ridge. There were no landmarks left; and we were not very familiar with the territory. We had left the trail, looking for low-bush huckleberries. Instead of returning to the trail the way we had left it, we went forward at an angle, expecting to pick it up on our right. We came to what we thought was the trail and followed it. It turned out to be no more than a deer run. If we had taken the pains to find even one blaze, our trouble would have been saved. We should in any event have been wise to our error, for in a mile or so the path we were following started down a canyon on the left. A careful look at the contour map would have shown that Dewey Lake did not lie in that kind of domain. But we went on our way, ignorant of our error.

We dropped at least 1000 feet. The pitch of the canyon wall was precipitous. I began to have doubts about the trail, because it looked more and more like a deer run. But it was hard to concede an error of this kind, especially when it meant climbing a thousand feet or so with a pack up the steep canyon wall that we had just come down.

We were almost to the bottom of the canyon when the deer run petered out. It was plain that we had come the wrong way. By then it was dusk and there was no use turning back. We had seen no water on the ridge for several hours. We did not know whether the trail lay to the north or the south of us. We were turned around and needed time and daylight to reconnoiter. It was better, we thought, to camp in this canyon. At least there would be water. We could not see it because of the thick brush that filled the draw, but we could hear it running. We thought there would be a place to camp in the ravine. In the morning we could get our bearings.

When we reached the bottom it was almost dark. We were in brush so thick it was practically impassable. We thrashed through it for fifteen minutes or so and made no progress. It was now deep dusk and we were lost. I did not have the least idea which way north was. I looked up at the sky but it was filled with clouds. I looked for peaks, but every landmark was shut off from view. There was only the dark hulk of the canyon walls on both sides. I knew only that we were somewhere in the Cascades; but I could not have pointed to the direction of Mount Adams if my life had depended on it.

We sat and talked. We were in a fix, but we were not panicky. As the dusk turned to darkness we said that perhaps our wisest course would be to sit on our packs and wait for dawn. The thought was oppressive, for we were tired and hungry, and a chill had swept through the canyon. Without a fire, the night would be long and cold and depressing. We decided to have one more try at it. We must have fought the brush for a half-hour more and probably made 50 feet. By then the night was black. I was about ready to call it quits and to sit in the brush all night. We were getting nowhere, and exhausting ourselves in the process.

I was in the lead; and as I strained to look ahead I saw a white streak a dozen paces away. I made for it, came up to it, and saw that it was a spit of white sand, free of brush. It was not more than ten feet square; but it was close to the creek that came down the ravine. And it was big enough for two boys.

There we pitched our tent, built a fire, and cooked supper. The campfire lighted up this wild and desolate place and gave it friendliness. I had been apprehensive at being lost and depressed at the thought of lying in the brush all night. Now that feeling disappeared and I was at ease.

But that was temporary. As we sat eating our meal around the small campfire, I began to study our situation. We were literally hemmed in. There was no escape in the darkness. The brush had proved to be almost impassable. There was no trail. We were lost. I suddenly felt trapped. We were tight in the embrace of the darkness and the brush. As I looked over my shoulder the surroundings began to take on a menacing aspect. The brush that hemmed us in on our small spit of sand seemed to me like long, dark fingers stretching out to crush us. The hulk of the mountain, which towered above us, seemed ready to swallow us.

We sat there, as teen-age boys will, acting unconcerned and jovial even when fear clutched the heart. Suddenly out of the brush came the most frightening cry in the mountains—the screech of a cougar. The cry was close by, so close that I thought the cougar would be on us any second. Shivers passed through my body. I think my hair stood up. Art's face looked white as a sheet.

When I recovered my wits and reflected, our situation seemed hopeless. We were trapped. The brush was impassable. We could not escape over the 2000-foot barricade of the mountain. We could not even hide, for the brush was on three sides of us and it concealed the cougar.

The ten-foot spit of sand was our cage for the night. The situation of the zoo had been reversed. The cougar could roam at will and survey the victims cornered in the cage by the creek. He could stalk us—and then pick us off, one by one, whenever he chose. He would probably wait until we were asleep and then spring on us.

These were the fearful thoughts in my mind. Many times since I have awakened to find the tracks of a cougar not far from my bedroll or tent. But I did not know in those early days that a cougar is the most difficult of all animals to approach in the mountains and rarely attacks man.

Now the cougar screeched again. It was a bloodcurdling screech—a cry that pierces the heart and creates a state of near-panic to the uninitiated. The screech seemed to come from behind our pup tent. My fright was increased by the realization that we had no weapons, except jackknives.

Then Art and I thought of the fire. All animals were supposed to be afraid of fire. If we kept one going and hugged it close, we'd be safe. So we decided to build our fire as big as we could and feed it with wood all night.

You get more than warmth from a campfire in the woods. It can transform a desolate ridge or canyon into a home. It drives away forebodings and worry. One who is nervous when sitting in a dark patch of woods relaxes when a campfire is burning. He draws near it, not for warmth but for friendship. It's an ally, a companion. It reinforces courage. It pulls men together, becoming a bond between them. And it helps cast off the apprehension of dangers lurking in the outer rim of darkness.

Wood was our problem this night when we were lost. We went to the creek's edge and cautiously looked up and down. it. We saw down timber along the shore not more than 25 feet away. Keeping close together, we anxiously waded the creek and dragged a quantity of limbs and logs close to our pup tent. We moved the fire as close to us as we dared and then retired. Art and I took turns replenishing the fire throughout the night.

The screech of the cougar came again and again. Every time he screeched he seemed to be right next to the tent. I imagined I heard his catlike steps. I even imagined I felt his breath against the canvas walls.

The night was endless. I kept an open jackknife in my hand all night long. We got no real sleep until the first streak of dawn was in the sky. Then we slept hard for several hours and woke relieved that the menace of the night had passed.

We cooked breakfast in warm sunshine on the spit of sand and then started the long pull out of the canyon. It took us most of the morning to get back on the ridge. The country to the north was new and strange. We had come from the south, so we worked in that direction. But it was not until midafternoon that we found a trail that bore our footprints of the day before. Then we were on the ridge, not much west of Fish Lake. So Art and I thought, but never knew for sure, that we had slept in the deep canyon of Panther Creek the night we were lost.

Whenever I walked the trails as a boy, it never occurred to me that the wilderness itself might be a menace—that it could swallow and hide a person for all time. Even when we were lost at the bottom of Panther Creek, the sense of being lost produced no panic. The only real menace seemed to be the bloodcurdling cry of the cougar that echoed and re-echoed in the narrow walls of the dark canyon. Yet, having been lost and having come out on my own, I do not think that the fear of losing my way in the unknown wilderness ever did enter my heart.

My unconcern has been best expressed in a poem of Robert Frost which I recently saw for the first time in *The Mind on the Wing* by Herbert West:

> Have I not walked without an upward look
> Of caution under stars that very well
> Might not have missed me when they shot and fell?
> It was a risk I had to take—and took.

That philosophy can make exhilarating many experiences that hold a great potential of danger. With that philosophy man can find interest and adventure in unexplored canyons, even when he has lost his way and has no peak or compass to guide him.

Chapter X   *The Campfire*

THERE was deviltry, practical woodcraft, and serious talk on these early pack trips. The tomfoolery was uninhibited. The woods are a good place for man or boy to shout and yell. Everyone accumulates steam that is hard to blow off. There is nothing quite so good for that ailment as a lusty bellow at the top of a mountain ridge or at the base of a towering cliff. There is no neighbor to be disturbed. There is no sensitive or fidgety person who might translate such sound into either a breach of the peace or a sign of approaching insanity.

Our boyish shouts and shrieks echoed off the cliffs of the Cascades. We pushed each other from logs into pools of water. We poured cold water down unsuspecting necks. At dusk we stretched a rope or a vine ankle high across the path to the creek, so that our pal would fall flat on his face as he went to get water for cooking. When that happened, bedlam broke loose in the woods.

This horseplay took even more robust forms. Once three or four of us were camped on the edge of Goose Prairie a few miles below Bumping Lake. It had been a miserable trip. We had had rain for over a day and the camp was soaked through. We dubbed the place Camp Rain-in-the-Face, for we had no tent and our blankets had absorbed all the drippings from the trees. Our bedrolls were soaked through. In the morning when we crawled out of our doused blankets, we looked as if we had been dragged in a lake behind a boat.

The consequence was a gloom over the camp which I decided to dispel. While I cooked breakfast, I planned my strategy. I served my companions, and while they were seated on the ground eating, I brought them coffee in big tin cups. When cleaning the rainbow trout cooked for this meal, I had reserved the heads, and when I poured the coffee I had put one head in each cup.

I watched the faces as the boys ate their trout and pancake bread and sipped their coffee. One boy finished his plate, put it on the ground, took his tin cup of coffee in both hands and slowly drank it. Soon he took a deep draught. I saw his face turn white. The expression was one of shock, nausea, and disgust. Peering out of the coffee at the bottom of the cup were the cold, glassy eyes of a trout. He let loose with terrible imprecations. At once the calm of Goose Prairie was broken by a riot. The gloom that had settled over the camp was gone.

Once when we were camped at Fish Lake, we took possession of the prospector's cabin that stood on its shore for some twenty years or more. It was raining and the cabin, though beginning to disintegrate, offered a measure of shelter. It was a one-room cabin, built at the time there was prospecting for copper on the range behind the lake. It had once been chinked with mud, but that had cracked and largely fallen out. It originally was furnished with chairs, bed, table, and cupboard that were plain but beautifully tooled. In the woods men are wantonly destructive of property such as cabins. It is hard to understand why. Those who are respectful of their neighbors' property at home take liberties with a cabin or shelter in the mountains. In fact they may tear it apart and use the wood for fuel. The lovely furniture of this prospector's cabin had been carried away or used for firewood. Hand-hewn cedar shingles had been torn off the roof for kindling. The floor had been removed. Finally the walls themselves were torn down and the logs used for campfires. Today not a trace of the structure remains. Man consumed it in its entirety, as a termite would do.

When we took possession of this cabin on the rainy day in question, its floor was gone and there were open places in the roof where some shingles had been removed. But the cabin was comparatively dry and the dirt floor, with a little cleaning up, was most presentable. More important, the cabin had a cookstove with a stovepipe running through the roof.

We soon had the cabin cleaned and a fire going in the stove. There was good companionship. We'd sleep warm. There was already the aroma of fresh coffee and trout from the stove. There was rain on the roof; there was contentment in our hearts.

The stove at first drew extra well. Supper was not done, however, when it began to smoke. Nothing would effect a remedy; no matter how we fixed the drafts, the smoke rolled out. It poured through all the holes in the cabin. We opened the door, but we got no relief. We would step out into the darkness to dry our eyes and get our breath. But the rain which had started again would soon send us back in. Finally, we were overcome.

Half-blinded by the smoke, coughing and sputtering, we were driven outdoors. When our eyes had dried and our lungs cleared, we surveyed the situation. There was smoke coming out the door, the holes in the roof, and a thousand cracks in the walls. But no smoke was coming out the chimney. I was hoisted up to see why. I found that someone had surreptitiously placed a saucepan over the top of the stovepipe.

We looked around. There were only three of us—the guilty one had disappeared. With shouts we set out to find him. He was not far from the cabin, behind a tree. We mauled him and rolled him and roughed him up. But the punishment was tempered with mercy as well as prudence. We did not throw him in the lake until the sun was high the next day.

On these early trips we learned something of woodcraft. There is skill even in making a good bed of white fir boughs. The boughs should not be cut too long, since the branches should be no thicker than a pencil. The coarse, bare end of the bough should be pressed down toward the ground and be overlapped by another bough. If time and care are taken and a plentiful supply of boughs is used, a bed that is most fragrant and fairly soft can be built. Three layers should be used as a minimum; six layers are more than twice as good as three.

We learned to chop a stick of wood by leaning it on the far side

of the log, not on the near side. If it is put on the near side, the ax
or hatchet may well follow through into the foot. If it is put on the
far side, the force of the blow is into the ground.

We found that a lump of pine rosin, neither too soft nor too
brittle, made a bitter but fairly adequate chewing gum for dusty
trails.

We discovered how to start a fire by rubbing sticks together. But
it was too slow a process; and we were clumsy at it. We would do it
only as a stunt. The Indians twirled sticks somewhat in the manner
of a brace and bit. That was quite efficient. I never mastered their
technique.

Starting fires outdoors without paper can be a drawn-out job,
especially in wet weather. The first problem was to find a dry stick
or chip. Theodore Winthrop, who crossed the Cascades in 1853,
camped one August night in a storm not far south of the Klickitat
Meadows. He found bits of punk and dry fuel in a natural fireplace
hollowed in an ancient ponderosa pine. He built his fire inside the
tree—a dangerous thing to do, as he found out, for soon the whole
tree was ablaze.

A hollow tree, however, is a good place to find a dry chip with
which to start a fire. More often than not we would have to chop
such a chip from the inside of a small log. We would take the chip
and with a sharp knife reduce it to shavings, leaving each shaving on
the stick. Thus we would have a piece of wood fashioned like a
comb. The comb of shavings would hold a flame for a few minutes
and so serve the function of paper or dry leaves. With that as a base,
we could use dry pine cones or bark, or any other light material, to
get a sizable blaze going. Jack Nelson always called these chips "prayer
sticks." Once I asked him why. "Well," he replied, "you light them
and then pray." For quick fires (and for all fires in damp weather)
we would take the time to search out pieces of pitch wood. Then
we would have a fire in a jiffy.

Today there is the sheepherder stove which weighs about 40
pounds and ties easily on the side of a pack horse. It has an oven
and a draft at the rear. The lengths of stovepipe chimney telescope

one into the other and go inside the stove for packing. The stove is about 29 by 14 by 8 inches. It can be put on stakes at any height desired above the ground. And a person can cook as well on it as on any wood stove at home. At least the pies, puddings, fish, and potatoes I have seen come out of its oven have tasted along the trail as fine as any I ever had in the city.

In the early days when we carried all our equipment on our backs, we did our cooking over open fires. When it came to such food as beans, requiring long cooking, we would hang the kettle on a stick which was supported at either end by a forked stake. The stakes could be raised or lowered depending on the intensity and height of the fire and the rate of cooking desired. Flat rocks arranged in and around the fire would hold the coffee pot and small kettles for oatmeal, prunes, and the like. The frying pan for bread and trout would be managed by hand or propped at an angle against a rock.

There are few trees that shed rain throughout a hard storm of a day or two. Close examination will show that most evergreens turn up slightly at the end of their boughs. Those trees therefore drip "inside" in a hard rain. But there are occasional trees—red fir, for example—that shed water even though rain falls for three or four days. It may take a long search to find one, but there are such. The boughs of this tree will have tips that either are flat or turn down. And they shed water better if the tree leans slightly. A bedroll under such a tree will stay dry during any mountain rain.

An Indian once told me, "White man make big fire and stay cold. Indian make small fire and stay warm." What he meant was that if he built a fire so small that he could squat on its edge and hold his hands over it, he could stay warm. There is wisdom, backed by centuries of experience from the mountains and the plains, behind that observation. But we youngsters were more romantic than wise. When our campfire was going and supper was cooking, we would start a bonfire near by. We'd build a trench around it so that fire creeping through pine needles would not consume our camp while we slept. We'd pile on logs and branches and watch the blaze mount higher and higher. The surrounding pine and fir trees would be illuminated and stand as dark curtains, reflecting the light of the fire. Above them sparks would go dancing toward the stars. Behind them would be the opaque darkness of the forest.

That darkness became familiar to us. We walked the trails at night without fear. We knew the sounds of the woods: the creaking of a pine as its top moved in a night breeze; the screech of an owl; the crack of a stick as some porcupine or other inquisitive prowler carelessly scouted our camp; the howling of the coyote on a distant point of rock. When these interrupted the chorus of crickets or frogs from a near-by pond or marsh, we were not startled. They were as familiar to us as the sound of a horn above the drone of city traffic. The screech of the cougar was different; but we seldom heard him, and we came to learn that he, too, would not molest us.

These fires at night brought cheer and fellowship. We would talk of the happenings of the day and of the plans for tomorrow; of the perplexing problems of school and of home; of the men of the valley whose examples we did not care to emulate. As the sparks rose to the tops of the trees and disappeared into the firmament, we would dream dreams that only boys can dream.

Maybe some day I could take Gifford Pinchot's place. He helped create the Forest Service. I often saw its men in the mountains, riding the trails—strong, long-legged rangers, clear-eyed, robust men. If I went to forestry school and learned all the knowledge of the woods, I too could be a ranger and from there work up to Pinchot's place. I could carry on his fight for conservation. He loved the mountains; so did I.

Maybe I could be a reclamation engineer. There was the vast Moxee country east of Yakima, where the Rosa irrigation project now thrives. A lawyer got Mother to invest in a Moxee irrigation project all that was left from Father's estate after funeral expenses had been paid and our house was erected in Yakima. Everything was lost. Perhaps I could figure out a way of bringing clear, cold mountain water down to that desert land of the Moxee.

Doug Corpron was sure he was going to be a doctor. Perhaps I would be a lawyer. I'd often slip into the courtrooms of Yakima. Judge E. B. Preble presided in the State Superior Court, Judge Frank H. Rudkin in the Federal District Court. From a rear seat I would observe the trials. Judge Preble was a quiet, unobtrusive man. Judge Rudkin was a commanding figure, with a massive forehead and deep voice. The stillness seemed to be extra deep when he entered the courtroom. There seemed to be goodness in these judges. I sensed they knew where the truth lay and that no force on earth could deflect them from it. O. E. Bailey, an insurance man, had been to Washington, D.C. and seen the United States Supreme Court in session. He said the same was true of it. He said there was no appeal from its rulings except to God.

I was not greatly impressed with some of the town lawyers, though I did not know them. Some whom I saw in action in the courtroom seemed either pompous or shifty. Some seemed to have snide tricks up their sleeves. The Indians would have called them fork-tongued. They did not seem to have truth in their hearts. I was a harsh critic and probably often unfair. Later I came to know men like George McAuley and Judge Thomas E. Grady. These were men with warm and spacious hearts and with deep insight into people. They saw more in law than a game of wits. But when I sat in the Yakima courtrooms, listening to civil and criminal trials, I often vainly thought I could do better than the lawyers I saw in action.

Maybe I should go into public life. There was Hiram Johnson in California and William Borah in Idaho. I could hear their booming voices way out in eastern Washington. They seemed to know the truth. They were not cowed by anyone. They were free, independent. They were clean, strong men like Gifford Pinchot.

In those days Hiram Johnson seemed to me a Sir Lancelot on a crusade. He was crying out against railway opinions rendered by railroad judges and against the hold that corporate interests had on California. He campaigned for conservation, workmen's compensation, women's suffrage, and an eight-hour day for women. He drove grafters from legislative halls. He made one think that government was something a State should be as proud of as it is of its homes and schools, or of its rivers, trees, and mountains.

Borah was crying out against the trusts and monopolies in sugar, steel, lumber, copper. He inveighed against the money trust. He opposed the concentration of financial power that made it possible for a few bankers to produce a panic or win an election or sway a legislature. He was for the income tax. He too was a symbol of good government and a foe of corruption. He stood on the side of the underdog.

The story was that Borah had saved a Negro from being lynched. The man was in jail in a town not far from Boise. Borah got an engineer to take a locomotive out of the roundhouse at Boise late one night and run him over to this town. Borah barely got there in time. He ran to the jail where the mob was tearing down the door. Standing on a box, he talked. At first the rioters were sullen and threatening. Then, meek and shamefaced, they melted away into the night.

There was a man, this Borah! A great lawyer, too! If I could only talk like him!

These were the things we discussed around dozens of campfires on the high ridges above Yakima. It seemed, in fact, that I had to escape the town to see my personal problems more clearly.

There was time for reflection in the solitude of the mountains. The roaring bonfire of the camp would draw out our innermost secrets and longings. Sometimes we would talk until only a glow of coals remained of a roaring fire. A crescent moon would appear above a distant peak. The long dark fingers of the pine and fir reached higher and higher in the sky as the fire died down, and the stars drew closer to the high shoulders of the Cascades. A brisk breeze would come down off some glacier of Adams or Rainier. A chill would sweep over the camp. Then we would know that we had put off sleep too long.

Chapter XI   Indian Philosopher

WE NEVER saw many Indians on these early pack trips. Once in a while there would be some squaws, or "squars" as Clark of the Lewis and Clark expedition would have said, fishing for trout in the Big Klickitat. More often we would see squaws high in the mountains and off the Indian reservation, picking huckleberries. They would have a pack train of eight, ten, or twelve horses. Each horse would carry two five-gallon kerosene cans. They might be camped on one spot a week or more while they scoured the surrounding slopes for berries. Brad and I used to say that while these five-gallon John D. Rockefeller cans brought light to the people of far-away Asia, they also brought huckleberries to the Yakimas.

The Indians of the Pacific Northwest held huckleberry festivals. These were ancient celebrations, in the nature of Thanksgiving. They had a religious character and were inaugurated with devotional chanting and drumbeating. Then the first berries picked were passed around and sampled. Coyote had decreed that no one should eat the berries before the service was over. If he did, there might be no crop another year. Feasting and merriment followed. Each Indian then was free to pick and eat. Usually the squaws did the work. Some berries were dried and used for winter food, though they were chiefly eaten fresh. They have always been important to the Indians, but they have been used even more extensively in modern than in ancient times.

The squaws would shout and gesticulate whenever we stopped for huckleberries on a slope where they were picking. We never were sure what they meant. Brad often said they were telling us to clear out, that we were on their private domain. I told him I thought he was too severe in his judgment. Maybe they were warmhearted, hospitable women who were inviting us to dinner. Although it happened often, we never did find out what they had in mind. We did not understand their language, and we never entered their camp to ascertain whether an invitation had been extended.

It was seldom that we met an Indian brave in the mountains. But there was one I met twice in the Tieton Basin. Though I spent many hours with him, I never knew his name. He was a full-blooded Yakima and proud of his race. The first time was one July morning when I was fifteen or sixteen. I believe it was Brad who was camped with me in the Basin for several days. He went downstream to fish; I went up the Tieton River. Here in a clearing I saw an Indian camp. A tepee was pitched. On scaffolds, constructed out of willow branches stretched between pine trees, salmon were drying. Several dogs sounded the alarm at my approach. A squaw and three children appeared. Then striding across the clearing toward me came the husband.

He resembled the picture I have since seen of Kamiakum, the most famous of all chiefs of the Yakimas. He was a large man, with a dark, massively square face, and a reflective look. He was tall for a Yakima, nearly six feet. He was probably in his late twenties. His walk was graceful—more of a glide than a step. He had a spear in his hand.

He greeted me with a smile and said, "Fishing?"

"Yes."

"Trout?"

"Yes, trout."

"You should catch salmon," he said. "They are much better. Come, I will show you some I have caught."

He went back across the clearing to the scaffolds, with me at his heels. There he or his squaw had laid some 20 salmon out for drying. They were 20- to 40-pound fish, split open and lying in the sun. The flies were bad, and the squaw had built a smudge of green willow. The fish would be partially smoked as well as dried. Later they would be packed on horses and taken down the valley to this Indian's home on the edge of the reservation.

When it came to fishing, the Yakimas from time immemorial concentrated on salmon: Wik-a-nus. They and the other tribes in the Columbia River Basin leaned heavily on it for their food supply. What I saw that July day, Lewis and Clark had seen. When Clark visited the confluence of the Yakima and the Columbia on October 17, 1805, he found the Yakima filled with salmon. The Indians had split their captured salmon open and were drying them on scaffolds in "great numbers."

The salmon is hatched in fresh water, starts to the ocean soon after hatching, and returns to the same river four to six years later to spawn. It goes back to the stream where it was hatched and there completes the cycle of its life. I have seen them 400 miles from the ocean, high on the eastern slopes of the Cascades in a tributary of the Yakima so narrow I could jump it. These were 30- to 50-pound salmon, bruised and battered from their long journey up the Columbia to the Yakima, and then up the Yakima into its tributaries and headwaters.

The Yakimas and other Northwest Indians have spots where they have fished for salmon from time immemorial. There were three main places: Sunnyside Falls and Prosser Falls on the Yakima, and Celilo Falls on the Columbia. The natural falls at Sunnyside amounted to no more than a good riffle, but they have since been improved by the government. Both there and at Prosser the salmon are caught by spearing as they jump. At Celilo they are dipped with nets on long poles.

There are of course legends about the salmon and these falls. The Bridge of the Gods, which long ago spanned the Columbia shortly above Bonneville, fell into the river, creating a dam which the salmon could not negotiate. Coyote saw the peril to the people who depended so much on salmon for food. He went to work, clearing out a channel through the barricade so the salmon could once more seek the headwaters. Then to complete the job he went down the river and herded the salmon upstream through the channel.

At times Coyote formed a dam to block the salmon. Thus, if he fell in love with a maiden and she refused to marry him, he might in revenge form falls that the salmon could not get over. He did this several times on some of the tributaries of the Columbia, but never on the Yakima.

But Coyote was for the most part beneficent. He realized, for example, that the people would be greatly aided if the rivers had falls which the salmon must jump. For when the salmon are in the air, they are easier to spear or net. That is why Coyote constructed the falls at Sunnyside, Prosser, and Celilo.

On this July morning I stood by the Indian's side admiring the salmon hanging on the scaffold. I turned and asked, "How did you catch them?"

"With a spear," he said. "Come, I will show you."

We walked up the Tieton to a grassy knoll by a deep pool.

"You stand and watch," he said. "Salmon will come."

Lewis and Clark, as they traveled the Columbia River Basin in 1805, saw Indians fishing for salmon with spears. In the *Journals*, Clark describes the way the Shoshones of Idaho did it: They employed a gig or bone on a long pole; "about a foot from one End is a Strong String attached to the pole, this String is a little more than a foot long and is tied to the middle of a bone from 4 to 6 inches long, one end Sharp the other with a whole to fasten on the end of the pole with a beard [barb] to the large end, the [y] fasten this bone to one end & with the other, feel for the fish & turn and Strike them So hard that the bone passes through and Catches on the opposite Side, Slips off the End of the pole and holds the Center of the bone."

This Yakima's spear was built in almost exactly that manner. It was made of fir, about five feet long and tapered at each end. A bone perhaps four inches long, with a sharp point and barb, fit snugly over one end of the spear. But the bone was detachable. A leather thong, tied one end to the bone and the other to the shaft, held the bone when it was detached. But the Indian did not fish in the Shoshone manner. He stood as motionless as a statue on the edge of the pool, his eyes never leaving the water at his feet, the spear poised in his right hand. The pool was four or five feet deep. The water was clear and smooth.

I saw a flash in the pool. The spear struck. The next I knew the Indian had both hands on the shaft of the spear, lifting a salmon out of the water. The bone, which was in the salmon beyond the barb, had detached itself from the spear. The weight of the fish was on the leather thong that hung from the shaft. A 30-pound salmon was thrashing at my feet. The Indian hit it with a club; a tremor or two passed through its body; then it was still.

This fish had been as shiny as a new silver dollar when it came into the mouth of the Columbia from the Pacific Ocean 400 miles away. Now it was as dark as the Tieton's bottom. It was bruised and battered. Large gashes lacerated its skin. Hatched in this stream four to six years earlier, it had come back to its birthplace to spawn and die. It was short of its journey's end by not more than a few miles, or perhaps only a few rods, when it was killed. It had escaped the gill nets of the commercial fishermen at Astoria and Hood River on the Columbia, eluded the dip nets of the Indians at Celilo Falls, dodged their spears at Prosser and Sunnyside on the Yakima, and outwitted all natural enemies in the rivers. Yet man—its most potent enemy from time immemorial—was waiting in ambush at the destination toward which some instinct had directed it.

But there is no place for romance when man is foraging for food. Other salmon would elude my Indian companion on the Tieton, skillful as he was. Nature was profligate with the supply of spawning stock. Enough would get through to assure perpetuation, even on the Tieton.

The Indian dressed the salmon and hung it in a willow tree. He returned to the edge of the pool where he had speared it. In half an hour he had two more. I watched him closely, but each time my eye was so slow that I saw only a flash. Yet in that split second he had seen the salmon, calculated the refraction of the water, and driven home his spear unerringly.

Years later Roy Schaeffer told me of the even greater skill of a Nez Perce who fished the Wallowa River in eastern Oregon for salmon. This Nez Perce sat astride a horse, with a spear such as I have described, to one end of which a coil of rope was attached. He watched a pool thirty or more feet on the opposite side of the Wallowa River. When he saw a salmon dart into the pool, he let fly his spear. Before the spear had reached its target, he turned his horse and started away from the river. The spear would strike home, and the horse, continuing on its way, would drag the salmon from the river.

I spent the whole day on the Tieton with my Indian friend. After he had speared three salmon, a thunderstorm came up and a light shower spattered the Basin. I think it was more an urge to loaf and talk than a desire to avoid the storm that led him to suggest that we seek shelter. So we stretched out in a thick stand of jack pine and waited the storm out.

I asked him about rattlesnakes. He said that once the rattlesnake was a monster with three heads and three tails, each tail having many rattles. This giant rattler killed many people. Coyote, to save the people, cut off two heads and two tails. Now he can't hurt the people so much. I asked if there were rattlers in the Tieton Basin. He said he thought not, that they did not get up so high in the mountains. Then he told a strange tale which I later found in various forms in the lore of the Indians of the Pacific Northwest.

A flood was coming to engulf the earth and wipe out its inhabitants. The Spirit Chief, Tyhee, hastened to save his people. He came down from the heavens and appeared before a medicine man. He told this good man to shoot an arrow into a cloud near Mount Rainier, then to shoot a second arrow into the butt of the first arrow, and then another into the butt of the second, and so on until a chain of arrows reached the ground. The people and their animals were to climb up the arrows and escape the rising floodwaters.

The medicine man did this; and the Yakimas climbed the chain of arrows to safety. Following them came the animals. As the medicine man looked down from above, watching the animals climb the chain of arrows, he saw the rattlesnake bringing up the rear. After all the good animals had passed to safety, the medicine man broke the chain of arrows. The rattlesnake tumbled back into the floodwaters, which by then had reached the shoulders of Mount Rainier. That is why the rattlesnake is never found at high altitudes in this region.

I told my Indian friend that we boys had been told that the reason the rattlers were not found at these altitudes was that they were sensitive to cold and could not stand even the cool summer nights in the Cascades.

He smiled and said, "That may be true. But that's not what my grandmother told me."

I asked him if it were true about the animals climbing the chain of arrows.

He smiled and asked, "Do you believe the story of Noah?" .

"Noah?" I asked. "Do you know about him?"

"Oh, yes," he said. "The Fathers taught me that."

My Indian friend knew of the mission on the Ahtanum. He had been to Catholic schools in the Lower Valley. He had finished high school. He owned some rich bottom land along the river, and for several years had tried to cultivate it. But he said he was not a very good farmer. The soil was ideal for truck farming and excellent crops could be raised. He was not expert at plowing and hoeing and irrigating. He tried to work hard. His mind wandered, however, and he longed to be riding the ridges, stalking a deer, or lying in wait on the Tieton for a salmon to dart into a pool.

He had talked his problem over with the Father. The Father agreed that he should lease his land and follow in the footsteps of his ancestors. Now he had cattle on the range. When the chinook blew across the ridges, he would start his cattle across the foothills to the mountains. As the snows melted he would take them higher and higher. When the first snow fell, he would start the return to the foothills. Meanwhile he would spear salmon and kill deer on the reservation and put away food for the winter months.

There was a silence, and then he said, "I do not know the onion, the tomato, the asparagus. I do know the salmon, the deer, the horse, and the steer. The Father says to do what I can do best. That is why I hunt and fish and ride the range."

After another pause he said, "It takes many different trees and shrubs and grass to make a forest. It takes many kinds of animals to fill the woods. The bear, goat, cougar, coyote, deer, and elk are all different. Wouldn't it be bad if all the animals were alike? It takes many races to make the world. Wouldn't it be bad if all people were the same? My skin is brown; yours is white. You can do things I can't do. I can do things you can't do. Some of my people think we're better than the whites. They say that the white man gets strong when he has Indian blood in him. Some of your people think they are better than us Indians. Maybe so. But no white man can spear salmon better."

I sat whittling and listening. The storm had not abated. Sheet lightning played across the skies and thunder echoed off Goose Egg Mountain and Kloochman Rock. There was a long silence.

"Tell me some more of your fairy tales," I said.

He replied as quickly as his spear had hit the darting salmon. "If you knew my grandmother, you would know that she would never tell fairy tales." But there was a twinkle in his eye. We both laughed.

He was still for a few minutes; then he told me the story of the giant tick (Upsha) who had a contest with Coyote. It was a long, rambling tale. It ended with Coyote putting a curse on the tick, so that thereafter he would not be able to kill animals but could only crawl in their hair and suck their blood.

I asked him about the Painted Rocks. There are several lava cliffs in eastern Washington bearing relics of ancient paintings. Some are on the west side of the Columbia about a mile or so above Vantage Ferry. The ones I knew the best were those at the gap that the Naches River wore through the hills just west of Yakima. There on smooth walls of black lava are picture writings in pigments of red, white, and yellow. They have lost some of their clarity and brilliance with time, but remnants remain. No one knows for sure what they mean, for the Yakimas had no written language.

My Indian friend told me about the god of medicine that painted the rocks. And he told me the story painted on the rocks at the Naches gap: a tragic love story of Strong Heart and Morning Star who leaped to their deaths from the top of those palisades.

"Tell me more," I said.

"Only one more, and then I must go. If I talk with you, how can I get salmon for my family?"

There was a roll of thunder far away to the south, sounding as if it came off the distant crags of Mount Adams. He looked up and said, "Do you know about that?"

"About thunder?" I asked.

He nodded.

"No. Is there a story about thunder?"

He told me a wondrous tale of the fight between Coyote and Thunder (Now We Na Kla). Thunder at one time was vengeful in this area, striking people down with fire and shaking the ground so hard that it trembled. People were so frightened they hardly dared enter the woods for deer or stand on the rocks for salmon. The story of how Coyote mastered Thunder was intricate. It ended with Coyote holding him to the ground and beating him with rocks and clubs. Then Coyote put a curse on him: he could thunder only on hot days; he could flash his lightning in the sky but could not kill the people.

My friend smiled and said, "Lightning seldom does damage in our country, as you know. You see, Coyote really is our friend."

By then the sun was gone. We returned to the river and parted. He gave me a big-brother slap on the back. I watched him almost reverently as he worked his way noiselessly through the brush. I slept that night on a bed of white fir boughs at the foot of Kloochman Rock, dreaming of a friendly Indian that had stepped right out of a page of one of James Fenimore Cooper's tales.

I did not see my friend again that trip, since we broke camp early in the morning and headed for the Indian Creek Trail that leads to the high lake country. I was back in the Tieton Basin, however, early in July the following year. We had come down the trail of the South Fork and were camping in the Basin for our last night out.

It was early afternoon and I had gone up the Tieton to catch a mess of trout for supper. I came across a camp—Cub Scouts, I believe. The boys were allowed to go in swimming in one particular section of the river. Here the water was not over two or three feet deep; and ropes had been stretched above and below the section not only to mark it but also to add to its safety.

There were a number of boys in the water. Nearest me was a lad of ten or eleven who was standing up to his waist. He was fat and chunky, and timid about the river. Suddenly he let out a blood-curdling yell and dashed for the bank of the river as fast as the rough bottom and his tender feet would allow.

I stopped him and asked what was wrong. There was panic in his face. Something had been after him. I asked him what. He said something slimy had tried to catch him by the leg.

I heard a chuckle and looked around. Here was my Indian friend of the previous summer. Making a wavy motion with his hand he said, "A salmon swam between his legs and slapped him as he went through." By then the lad, still terrified, was running back to camp. He was the only one who saw no humor in the episode.

My Indian friend and I sat down to visit. He said the salmon were running strong in the Tieton; that he had several dozen drying already. I screwed up my courage and inquired:

"Could you teach me how to spear a salmon?"

My heart overran with joy when he said he would. He took a green fir bough five or six feet long. He peeled and scraped it until it was smooth; he tapered it at each end. He had an extra tip made of deer bone and an extra leather thong to fasten the tip to the shaft. He apparently carried these as emergency supplies. He soon had the shaft fitted into the socket of the bone and the thong tied fast to the bone and the shaft.

We went along the Tieton until we came to a likely pool. He put my spear in the water, showing how it appeared to be broken and saying I must therefore aim several inches above or beyond where the salmon seemed to be. We stood still as statues. He had my spear poised. My heart pounded with the excitement of the moment. Soon there was a flash and my spear in his skilled hands lifted a salmon.

I could hardly wait to try my own hand. He gave me the spear and told me to wait at this pool. He went upstream. I felt more comfortable with him around the bend of the river. His expert eye on my amateurish performance would be most embarrassing.

I waited, my spear poised to strike, my eyes were on the water. Minutes passed. Then there was a flash. My spear drove home; but I hit only the bottom of the Tieton. I readjusted the bone tip and waited again. In a half-hour or so there was another flash and my spear hit the water. Once more I speared the bottom of the Tieton. Again it happened and again.

I decided I needed more instruction. So I went upstream a quarter-mile or so and found my friend. He had speared three salmon since I saw him. I stayed with him for about an hour, watching him spear two more. By then I thought I knew the technique. So I went upstream and found water that seemed ideal.

Here was a pool with a sandy bottom where a salmon could be easily spotted. There was brush on each side which made handling the spear difficult; but there was a log across the river at the head of the pool, and above the log a great deal of driftwood had collected. The pile of brush resembled a beaver dam except that the pool was on the downstream side. I worked my way out on the log until I was over the middle of the stream. I crouched on the log, my spear lifted in my right hand. I watched the water like a hawk. The pool was about five feet deep. It was a dozen feet across and extended above the log about twenty feet. From my vantage point it was easy to see any fish that entered the pool.

I had not been on the log many minutes before a salmon darted in. I drove the spear down towards him with all my strength—so much that I lunged right into the water.

In those days I was still frightened in deep water, let alone under it. I couldn't swim; and once immersed my legs became rigid. I had dropped the spear as I fell, and I grabbed for overhanging brush. I caught hold of some willows and pulled myself to shore, shivering and shaking.

I looked across the river. My Indian friend was doubled up with laughter. He had retrieved my spear, and he shouted to ask if I wanted it back. I finally saw the humor of the situation, but I made a gesture indicating I never wanted to see the spear again. I shouted thanks for all he had done and started for camp to dry out. I had gone about 50 yards or so when I heard a yell. I turned around and there was my friend holding up the biggest salmon yet. It came from the pool in which I had been doused.

That night as I lay under the blankets listening to the wind in the tops of the pine, I thought about these Indians. Some called them an inferior race. Perhaps my friend would not do so well in my Latin class, but in the woods he was a champion who walked in the footsteps of great ancestors. He was from a race that lived in a world full of spirits. Their gods were exacting and revengeful. Every manifestation of nature had a hidden meaning. His was a race trained to conceal emotion and to develop an impenetrable exterior. My friend had these qualities. But under the influence of the new environment —church, school, and the community at large—they had acquired a different significance. They were still present, though not dominant. Like his color, they were qualities that gave flavor to his personality. They were vestiges of culture from an ancient day. They gave him a suggestion of mysticism, as the trace of sage in the Tieton gave it a touch of enchantment.

This Indian was justly proud of his race; he had discovered an important secret of success. He knew that as a Douglas fir cannot possibly become a cedar or a sugar pine, similarly he could not be recast into another image. He could be only himself. Once a man accepts that fact, his yearnings become geared to his capacities. He knows his strength as well as his limitations. He may be unknown and unsung; but being wise, he has found the road to contentment. Like the mountain laurel, or snowberry, or sage, he pretends to be no more than he is. By being just what he is, and no more, he contributes a unique and distinct flavor to his community. He is not likely to have a neurosis that produces physical ailment or social maladjustment. Thus did I have a lesson in philosophy.

Chapter XII *Sheepherders*

BILLY McGUFFIE is a Scot with the love of heather and bluebells in his heart. He's a thin, lean man of dark complexion, with sharp features, sparse hair, and a twinkle in his eye. He was born and raised in Scotland. When a young man the lure of America caught him. He got his passage. And at long last the boat steamed into Ellis Island.

There was excitement and the warm glow of hospitality on arrival. There in New York harbor stood the Statue of Liberty, on its pedestal the wonderful message of welcome:

> Give me your tired, your poor,
> Your huddled masses yearning to be free
> The wretched refuse of your teeming shore.
> Send these, the homeless, tempest-tossed to me;
> I lift my lamp beside the golden door.

Billy knew that he was welcome; he was the poor. One of seven children, he was born at Lagginmoore in Wigtownshire. He wanted to see the world. When he left Ellis Island he had ten dollars in his pocket. His departure from Scotland had made him sad; he had been seasick all the way across. Now he was so homesick that he could not bear to leave the boat, his last contact with home.

I once asked him, "Why did you leave the boat, Billy, if you felt that way?"

Billy replied, "They wyled me oot o' steerage wi' a bowlfu' o' parritch."

Billy ended up in Yakima. "Holstein" Davis, who owned a dairy ranch in the Moxee, saw Billy the day he arrived and offered him a job milking cows. But, Billy's folks had dairy cows in Scotland, and he replied, "I cam five thoosan' miles tae get awa' frae lookin' a coo i' the face."

The following day Billy hired out as a sheepherder to Andy

Wilson. By the following August he was in the high basins under Mount Rainier. This land became a new home to him. Here was the finest welcome possible: heather and bluebells and sunsets over rocky crags.

Billy herded sheep for three years. Then he entered partnership with Wilson, and later with Sandy McGee. At one time they owned 20,000 sheep. Over the years, all of the valleys, meadows, and ridges west and north of the Klickitat became familiar to him. They were to Billy the Scotland of America; they became his second love. His heart was always light as he tramped the high basins under Mount Adams. He found humor in the vicissitudes of sheepherding. He brought back to the valley tall tales of his exploits.

Billy is a storyteller. His yarns have the unique flavor of a brogue, which with him has a wide range. One evening at Double K Ranch, Goose Prairie, Washington, we were before the fire listening to Billy roll the r's. Jack Nelson leaned over to me and whispered, "Billy's got a marble in his throat." And so he has.

Billy was aggressive in coming to the defense of the Scotch when an issue was made as to their parsimony. I asked him the reason for it and he told me his story of Jock McRae:

"One summer nicht John Duncan McRae, a freen o' mine, and I went into Spokane, dirty and thirsty, from a weary job a'loading sheep. We went into a pub and had a drink. As we came oot we met up with a Salvation Army street corner meetin'. As we paused there a moment, a Salvation Army lassie with a tamboreene walked up to Jock for a donation. 'What dae ye want, lassie?' Jock asked. 'Some money for the Lord,' she replied. With a twinkle in his eyes, Jock countered, 'How old are ye, lassie?' 'Eighteen,' was her answer. Jock said, 'Well, I am eighty-seven and will be seein' the Lord lang afore ye and I'll just gie him the penney mysel'.'"

There was a pause and then Jack said, "It all goes to show that the Scotchman isn't stingy; he's just cautious."

Bears have long been an obsession with Billy. He came across many such marauders during his sheepherding days. They gorged on his sheep and caused him much damage. Once a bear tastes sheep he becomes a killer. He raids the bands repeatedly. His appetite is never satisfied. Such a bear becomes the foremost enemy of the sheepherder.

Billy has many bear stories. He tells how he caught one running up a tree, grabbed him by the hind legs, and held him until Sandy McGee got a gun. But the story I like best is Billy's tale of the bear and the Irishman:

"I was tendin' sheep in the Mount Adams country a wheen years syne when Irish Dick, one o' the maist strappin' an' strangest herds I ever kent, caught a wee black cub bear. The neist time Irish Dick gaed tae the toon o' Toppenish what lies by the water on the Indian Reservation, he brocht the cub wi' him an' cowpit' it off tae a saloon keeper for a quart o' whuskey. Dick himsel' was nae taetotaller.

"The new owner tied the bear tae a post for a wheen years but ae dae the bear brak awa' an startit' oot tae see the toon. As he daunered doon the middle o' the main street wi' his chain danglin' frae his thrapple, a' the toonsfolk ran awa' oot o' his sicht and hid themsel's, a' but Irish Dick who happened tae be in the toon that dae and was roarin' fon frae ower mony drams o' whuskey. Irish Dick was nae a' bit feart o' his auld frien', sae he grabbit the cub by the back o' his thrapple an' ca'ed oot 'Whoa.' But the bear either didna ken his auld frien' or was scunnered o' him for havin' troked him intae slavery for a bottle of whuskey.

"Nae matter the cause, the mon an' the beast were sune rowin' aboot i' the stoor an' glaur o' that Indian Reservation toon, first tare an' then thither on tap. Sure the place o' the tulzie was cloudit' wi' stoor an' only the angry pechin' o' the bear an' the Irishman's dirlin' voice could be heard.

"At laist, when the noise stoppit' an' the stoor had a' faun doon, the folk wha had hid themsel's frae the bear keekit oot an' saw the bear tied like a grumphic wi' Irish Dick sittin' on tap, his body streamin' wi' bluid, an' nakit for a' but his heavy buits. The bear was pit back tae his post no muckle the waur for his fecht, but Irish Dick, his body bleedin' an' torn, wad hae nae doctor's aid."

"What ever happened to Irish Dick?" I asked. "Did he die of his wounds?"

"Fifteen years aifter the braw auld Irishmon froze tae his death i' a box caur," Billy replied.

Billy had conquered all the adversities of the Cascades in fair weather and in foul. But his greatest triumph was when he made his Buick run on mutton tallow. It's a true story; and this is the way Billy told it to me:

"It was a dae i' the autumn o' 1915 when the win' blew cauld wi' angry sooch. Motor caurs were gey few an' clatterin', an' horses were as frichtit o' them as the Indians lange syne were feart o' the West'ard march o' the white man. Roads were fit alone for four-fitted beasties that dinna' min muckle holes and sand.

"It was in su' a like dae that my auld frien' Sandy McGee, ma wife, an' masel' startit oot i' ma new Buick caur up intil the Klickitat country which lies couthie again' the sprawlin' sides of Mount Adams. We were hurlin' up tae the sheilin's on the moors whar ma sheep feed at the back end o' the year.

"As we traipsit alang about seventy-five miles frae home and the nearest repair shop in Yakima, what did we dae but strike a muckle big stane whit brak the oil pump off ma brent-new Buick, an' a' the oil i' the ceelinders cam' skalin' oot. Bein' o' pioneer stock I had tae ca' upon the gear to han', so I gaed aff on fit tae ma reist sheep sheilin' aboot twa miles awa' whaur I found some car'board an' oot o' it I cut a piece that fittit in whaur the missin' oil pump was supposed tae be. Lookin' aroon' I found an auld rubber boot that had been thrown awa', frae which I made a gasket to seal the bottom. Then, wi' twine pu'd oot o' flour sacks, I made the job strang. Then I prayed tae the Almighty it was ticht an' firm eneuch tae haud.

"After a' this I killed a sheep, fried the tallow oot i' a huggie ower a campfire, and timmed it oot into a wheen auld cans, aye found in thae times wherever the herds had been bidin' a while. As tomato, pea, sauerkraut, and coffee cans were filled wi' hot tallow, I kept the fat meltit' by puttin' them neist the fire. But the tallow frae the can I first filled, which I believe was labeled 'Alaska Red Salmon,' was timmed ower the tap o' ma reinforced car'board floor and allowed tae cool and harden, an' forbye tae fill the cracks and crannies ma hasty work had left.

"When a' the cans were filled wi' hot tallow, I timmed it quickly intae the crankcase and we startit back doon the twistin' mountain roads and got hame with nae mair fash at a'.

"Of course, the Buick Company made a muckle ado aboot the event. The story was tell't in newspapers and magazines a' ower the land. I was even offert tae travel wi' a' expenses paid tae for awa' toons, but nane o' that for me. I had tae bide here and herd ma sheep."

Billy, like many a Scot from the old land, is a ubiquitous character. While he adjusted himself to the ways of his adopted country, he retained not only his Scottish way of speech but also the hard granite of Scottish independence and integrity. That is the real flavor he brought to his community. Billy is the king of all sheepherders. No more jovial, lighthearted, friendly man ever walked the Cascades. I did not know him when I traveled the trails as a boy. I met him in later years when I revisited the Cascades. He has no counterpart among sheepmen that I ever knew.

One night at Billy's home in Yakima I asked him why he had turned to sheepherding when he arrived in Yakima. There was a twinkle in his eye as he replied, "I was born glowerin' at a lamb, an Ayshire coo, and a bill. I likit the lammie best."

Even in the early days there were cattlemen in the mountains, especially in and around Conrad Meadows and the Tieton. But we seldom saw them and rarely had any contact with them. It was the sheepherders whom we came to know. They were a motley crowd.

The sheepherders wintered in Yakima. There were wild yarns about them. Johnny Glenn, of Naches tells one that is typical: Two sheepherders holed up in a rooming house in Yakima for the winter. They consumed such quantities of liquor they became "snaky." One morning one of them was walking down Yakima Avenue. A friend stopped him and said, "Say, Joe, do you know that your buddy is up there at the rooming house, suffering from delirium tremens?"

"Sure, I know it," replied Joe. "When I left a little while ago, I saw the snakes crawling all over him."

We never ran into alcoholic sheepherders. But we did encounter a few odd ones. They started with their bands of sheep on the lower foothills in March or early April. By August they were well up the high ridges of the Cascades, where they stayed until the first snow. It was in these remote places we came across them.

Each sheep outfit had a herder and a packer. The herder stayed with the sheep all the time. The packer traveled back and forth between a base camp and the sheep camp, bearing food and other supplies to the herder. When in camp with the herder he usually did the cooking, tended the pack string, and did the other chores. The common story was that the packer was sent along to keep the herder from going crazy. The tales were tall about herders who finally cracked under the incessant ba-a-a, ba-a-a, ba-a-a. Some herders after weeks alone with the sheep ended up daffy—some muttering to themselves; others becoming mute with a glazed look in their eyes; some wandering aimlessly in the woods with loss of memory; others queer and affected, shunning the company of people as they retired to some lodginghouse in the valley for the winter.

I never verified these stories. A packer would tell us that his herder was "nuts." But those statements had to be taken with salt, since packer and herder were often on unfriendly terms. Yet the stories persisted.

Gwen T. Coffin, editor of the *Chieftain*, weekly newspaper of Enterprise, Oregon, recently gave the legend quite a twist. He wrote:

We hired out one time for a summer's job herding sheep out in the good old Uncompahgre country, Colorado. The boss took us out about 40 miles from nowhere, gave us a few rudimentary instructions on how to get along with sheep, and left us alone with about 1500 of the bawling animals. After about 48 hours with nobody to talk to and no sound except the baaing of sheep, we thought we were going loco. So we ditched the whole business, hooked a ride to town and forthwith cancelled any ideas for further association with sheep.

And so, said Gwen, a person with that experience can understand and appreciate the plight of the sheepherder depicted in the following item from the *Tribune* of Lewiston, Idaho:

Whoever heard of a cougar herding sheep? Wendell Stickney swears he saw one.

Stickney, a herder employed by Jack Titus, Snake River grower, said he was hiking up a trail to Lightning Creek. He saw about 35 sheep approaching him on the trail.

Behind them, he insists, was a cougar, an animal notorious as a sheep killer. The big cat, the herder said, with all the skill of a trained dog, ambled behind the herd. He cuffed those who got out of line, and moved back and forth behind the group to keep stragglers moving.

Stickney said he hid behind a tree until the animals had passed.

Then he shot the cougar with a pistol.

Gwen summed it up as follows: "Yup, we quit the sheepherding business before we saw cougars herding any of the animals."

The mental stability of the sheepherders was of no concern to us when we walked the trails with our horseshoe packs. We eagerly sought dinner invitations from them regardless of their sanity; for the food they served was a relief from our monotonous diet.

We made bread by cooking batter in a frying pan. The bread was in effect a hot cake an inch or more thick. It was filling, if not nourishing. But after the first day or two in the woods it was not appetizing.

Beans, baked in a pot with pork and dark molasses, can be the queen of all dishes, in the woods or anywhere else. But beans boiled, with only salt added, can quickly acquire a unique monotony.

There can be no finer breakfast dish than oatmeal served with sugar and thick cream. Oatmeal served with saccharin and powdered milk is still fair. But when oatmeal carries the burden of breakfast and also pinch-hits for potatoes at suppertime, it begins to lose its prestige.

At a housewife's touch, dried prunes or dried apples can be transformed into delicacies. But when they are boiled and eaten hot day after day, or munched in dried condition, they cease to be food in about a week. From then on they have only one value, and that is medicinal.

Powdered eggs at the hands of a skilled chef can be made the base for tasty dishes. But powdered eggs under our inexpert management were always pasty and flat. We held them in contempt and took them along only because the food we could carry in a horseshoe pack was limited.

Trout always helped. But trout is not filling like beef, mutton, venison, or grouse. It takes red meat to give quick energy for grueling outdoor work. The early chronicles of the West often relate how weak and famished men drank the warm blood of freshly killed deer, mountain goats, or sheep to restore their sagging energies. We were never as hard pressed as that. A kettle of beans would put us over any mountain. But a week on the trails would make us starved for meat and for sweets. There is where the sheepherders came in; and they never failed us.

The sheepherders invariably served mutton in the dinners they cooked for us. Sometimes it was mutton freshly slaughtered for the occasion. The stomach of a growing boy is a bottomless pit; and if, being accustomed to a meat diet, he is put on starches for a week, he'll wolf any meat that is put in front of him. At least that was our experience.

These sheep camp dinners always included potatoes, sometimes cooked sheepherder style (steamed with bacon and onions), but usually boiled. We would douse them with thick slices of butter and powder them with salt and pepper. We ravenously devoured all vegetables, for the lowly bean was the only one in our packs.

Sometimes the sheepherder would serve slices of soft white bread brought in by a pack train from a base camp miles below in the valley. More often than not he would have jelly and jam and syrup; and we used them without restraint. Dessert would sometimes be cheese and crackers and coffee. More often than not it would be fruit from a tin can with gingersnaps or chocolate cookies. At these meals we were gluttons, stuffing ourselves and making up in one meal for all we'd missed in our meals along the trail. Then we'd throw logs on the fire and sit and talk far into the night.

During these early days I met one sheepherder whom I thought was crazy. He was a chap called Frenchy. The packer invited my brother and me to dinner one July afternoon when we were traveling the Conrad Creek Trail above Conrad Meadows. We gladly accepted. We pitched our pup tent not far from the sheep camp and after a respectful interlude put in our appearance. We were scrubbed and clean and ready to eat packer and herder out of their larder.

We were fully two hours ahead of suppertime. The packer prepared a late one, timing it for the hour of darkness when the sheep at last bedded down. Only then would the herder leave them. That would be about 8 o'clock this July night. And eight o'clock is a late dinner hour in the mountains.

By eight the herder had not come. He had not appeared at eight-thirty. It was getting on to nine and the packer said we might just as well eat. After we had started the herder appeared.

He was a short stocky man with a gray Vandyke beard. He spoke with an accent. As he walked into the circle of light of the campfire he said with a note of impatience in his voice, "Who dees boys?"

The packer explained that he had invited us to dinner, that we were camped in the meadows, that we brought fresh news of the outside world, and so on.

There was a pause, and Frenchy said, "Bah."

The packer handed him a plate stacked high with food. Frenchy knocked it from his hands onto the ground. "Where's de hot milk?" asked Frenchy.

"On the back of the stove," said the packer. Frenchy took the kettle of hot milk, tore off a third of a loaf of bread, dunked the bread in the milk, and wolfed it in silence. Then he drained the last of the milk from the kettle, threw the kettle to the ground, blew first one nostril and then another with his fingers, and stalked off into the darkness.

I looked at my brother; he looked at me. We had never up to then failed to receive a royal welcome in any camp in the mountains. We had never in town or on the trail had such a rude host. There was silence for a while and then I asked, "Where'd he go?"

"To bed," said the packer.

"Did we insult him?" I inquired.

"Naw, he's nuts," said the packer. "Fact of the matter is, he may be getting better. Those are the first words he's spoke to me in many a day. You guys stick around and Frenchy may *talk* his head off. The dirty little rat, I may knock his snooty little head off soon."

We soon retired, hoping to get up early and see Frenchy. Though we were up before the sun, Frenchy was gone. He apparently had got up in the dark, before dawn. He had cooked himself breakfast and rejoined the sheep as they were beginning to stir.

The packer told us about Frenchy at breakfast. Frenchy was a Basque from Oregon. He and the packer had had many quarrels, the most recent one over an Indian squaw. The night before our arrival Frenchy had drawn a knife on the packer. The packer, a rangy Texan, had knocked Frenchy out. The bad blood remained between them. The packer was leaving for good. As we were doing the dishes he said, "Frenchy ain't going to kill this packer. But I would like to poke the fat little pig again, just for fun and good luck."

When our packs were rolled and tied and we were ready for the trail, the packer had his string of horses partly saddled. We watched him until he finished. Then he swung into the saddle and started south on the trail that led back to the Ahtanum. We waved good-by. Sombrero in hand he shouted, "Look out for those damn sheepherders. They're mostly nuts."

We turned west on the trail that led to the Goat Rocks. We had not gone a half-mile when we saw sheep slowly working their way up the slopes to the north. Below them on a rock by the trail sat Frenchy. His 30-30, the famous sheepherders' gun, lay across his knees. He apparently did not see or hear us until we were close to him. He sprang to his feet, his rifle in one hand, his eyes ablaze. He quickly turned on his heel and, shouting some imprecation, started up the slope toward the sheep. We quickened our pace and looked over

our shoulders at him as we swung along the trail with our packs. I
do not think we felt at ease until we were high on the shoulders of
Goat Rocks under the shadow of Tieton Peak and Devils Horns.

Brad and I once came across an unsanitary sheepherder who was
camped above Conrad Meadows. It was late afternoon when we spied
the smoke from his camp on the eastern edge of a small clearing.
This sheepherder had left his dogs to guard the sheep, while he returned to camp to cook an early dinner—his first meal since daybreak.

He was on his knees kneading sourdough bread in a pan when we
walked into camp. He greeted us effusively and told us we must stay
to dinner. We accepted at once, tossed our horseshoe packs to the
ground, and sat on them to rest and watch the sourdough operation.

Brad and I soon doubted the wisdom of our quick acceptance, for
we saw at once that the man's hands were filthy. He used his fingers
to blow his nose, first one nostril, then the other, followed by a wip-
ing of his hands on his overalls. Then he would return to the
kneading.

Brad and I looked at each other with horror. But retreat never got
beyond a faint suggestion in our minds. The lure of a bounteous
dinner in a sheep camp after a week of beans, oatmeal, powdered
eggs, frying-pan bread, trout, and dried prunes, was too great. We decided that the cooking would probably kill all the germs. And so we
laid our fir bough beds in an adjoining grove and pitched our pup
tent. We washed and scrubbed extra hard, I think, as a sort of compensation for the unsanitary habits of our host.

The dinner was one of the best I ever ate.

Visitors were welcome in the sheep camps because the herders were
lonely men. From June to October they would see few outsiders.
They longed for news of the outside world; they usually longed for
companionship. We would sit and talk to them far into the night.
Our talk ran not so much to the mountains and their mysteries as
to the affairs of men in Yakima, Chicago, Washington, D.C., Lon-
don, and Berlin. As a result we learned little of the mountains from
these sheepherders.

Occasionally one would tell us how he dealt with a marauding bear or coyote or how he lost some sheep from eating a poisonous plant. He frequently would relate his fishing exploits.

It seemed that the sheepherders we met were poorly equipped for trout fishing. I do not remember seeing a fly, bait, or casting rod in any sheep camp high in the mountains. The sheepherder always had hooks and some line; and he cut a willow for his rod. With grasshoppers, periwinkles, or frogs for bait, his needs sometimes would be satisfied. But those crude methods did not always deceive the wily trout. Then the sheepherder would seek our advice. We would give him flies and leaders and explain their use as best we could. We would tell him about likely pools and lakes on his itinerary. I think we told the sheepherders more about the mountains than we learned from them. And we also conducted seminars in current events around their camp fires.

It was late summer in 1914. I was fifteen and entering my junior year in high school that fall. The apples in the Yakima Valley orchards had been thinned. The cherry, apricot, peach, and pear crops had been picked. Apples were yet to come and school would soon open. I saw a chance to get away for a week and took it.

As I was rolling up my horseshoe pack, I had an idea. I would be gone a week or more. I planned to enter the Cascades through the Naches and the Tieton and go back into the lake country beyond Cowlitz Pass. I would most likely run into a sheepherder in that region, for sheep by this time would be getting close to the highest ridges. The papers carried big news—news of war in Europe. So I decided to take recent issues of the Yakima *Daily Republic* with me. I put several in with my blankets and also a recent issue of the weekly magazine, *The Outlook*.

A few days later I was skirting a meadow on the east side of Cowlitz Pass when I saw fresh sheep droppings. I stopped several times to listen for the barking of a dog; I kept looking for the curling smoke of a campfire. There was not a sign of life. There was no sound except the chatter of a red squirrel at the top of a balsam fir near the trail's edge. So I decided to scout the southern edge of the meadow.

It was about two hours before sundown and I did not want to miss a sheep camp.

I left the trail and went south across the meadow. I had almost reached what seemed to be its southern edge when out of a small grove of fir came a half-dozen sheep dogs. They sounded like a hundred demons. My instinct was to retreat. But reason replied in the negative. So with quivering flesh but to outward appearances with firm steps and steady voice, I met them and spoke to them, walking all the while toward the clump of balsam fir out of which they had raced. They kept circling, yapping at my heels. But some of the viciousness had disappeared from their barkings. Their protest at my approach was now more formal than aggressive. Then came the voice of their master. He had emerged from the clump of fir and gave a command intelligible only to him and to them. They became silent, and one beautiful Australian sheep dog jumped and licked at my hand.

The sheepherder who greeted me was a middle-aged man with a full brown beard. His eyes were blue and kindly. His face was bronzed, and when he took off his hat I could see that his tan ran up his massive forehead and into the bald spot on the top of his head. He looked a little as I imagined Walt Whitman must have looked. This man was tall, long-legged, long-armed, a wiry, rangy man who appeared to be equal to any challenge of the mountains. His voice was resonant, with powerful carrying qualities even in ordinary conversation. It was a voice that came back to me four years later as I drilled and marched in the uniform of the United States Army.

He greeted me with "Hi ya"; and extended a hand as gnarled and tough as the alpine fir that dotted the ridges to the west. He invited me to his camp. It was on the far side of the grove of fir and faced the edge of a smaller meadow I had not seen from the trail. Firewood had been split and piled near his tent. There was a crude table made of small pine and fir logs.

As I walked into camp, two or three camp robbers that apparently had been stealing bread from inside the tent flew up. My host turned his dogs on them; and the shepherds went through the futile exercise of pursuit, with much barking and wagging their tails. Then at a soft, almost inaudible command, something like "All right, boys," they stopped and curled up in the shade.

It turned out the packer had left on the previous day for supplies. He would be back on the day after tomorrow, when camp would be moved beyond Cowlitz Pass to the west. The sheepherder, whose name I never knew, had come back to camp to start a fire and cook supper. I was invited to dine with him. We would eat before dark. Then he would go to the sheep, which were in a small basin beyond a low ridge to the west. When they were bedded, he would return and we would talk.

"I haven't seen a paper for four months," he said. "So you will have to bring me up to date."

He lighted a fire and started supper. I brought him cold water from a fast-flowing spring that fed a rivulet that wound its way through this small meadow for 100 yards or so and then poured out into a soggy, swampy expanse of grass and reeds. I made my camp close by his big tent and collected white fir boughs for my bed.

By that time he had his pots on the fire. I handed him the Yakima newspapers and the copy of *The Outlook*. He thanked me, and after a pause said, "Will you do me a favor? Read me the paper while it is still light."

So while he cooked supper, I read the most recent paper, headlines and all, starting with the left-hand column on the front page. Most of it was news of war—the Kaiser, the Huns, the English Channel, Flanders, the Tricolor, the Marseillaise, the Rhine. It was deep dusk when I finished the first page. Supper was about ready.

"Thanks, son," he said. "Now bring your plate and get some mutton chops, potatoes, and peas. There's bread and butter and jelly in the tent. Do you like your coffee real stout?"

When I started to eat, he left with his dogs to tend the sheep. He was back in an hour or less. As he was filling his own plate, he said, "Son, do you think you can see to read me some more?"

So I lay on my belly by the campfire and read on and on as he ate. When he had finished, we did the dishes.

"Now we'll build up this fire a bit and hear the rest of the news," he declared.

It was a still, clear night. There was a touch of fall in the air. I sat close to the fire. He cross-examined me. He not only wanted to know about the war; he wanted to know about baseball, the price of hogs, sheep, cherries, and hay, the news of the valley, of Woodrow Wilson whom he admired, Congress, Teddy Roosevelt, and Pershing. I could not answer all the questions he asked, though I tried to give him a synopsis of events during the summer of 1914.

After he had pumped me dry, there was silence. There was not even a murmur in the tops of the fir that guarded the camp. There was the crackling of the fire and the faint sound of the snoring of one of the dogs. All else was quiet. The stars hung so low that they almost touched the firs.

My heart was filled. There was hard work in the valley. There was freedom in the mountains. There seemed to be endless opportunities ahead. I saw my future shaping up in vague outline. I had some family responsibilities, but I had no worries or doubts or fears. I felt a place awaited me in America. I felt I belonged here and that I was part of something exciting and important.

The war in Europe? It was as remote as the typhoon that swept bare an island in the South Pacific whose name I could not even pronounce. War in Europe? That should not concern any one here. Hasn't Europe always had wars? Even a Hundred Years' War? The war was remote, as foreign as a flood in China or a revolution in Persia.

That is why, I think, the evening in the meadow below Cowlitz Pass remains so vivid in my mind. For as I sat in silence thinking of the war as something wholly removed and apart from our world, the sheepherder spoke, "Well, you boys may have to finish this."

I was startled. I plied him with questions. Why should a war in Europe affect us? How could fifteen-year-old boys finish a war? Why would America want to fight in Europe?

We talked into the night by the campfire on the edge of the lonely meadow in the high Cascades. My host did not have much formal education, but he was informed and highly intelligent. He could make a complicated thing seem simple; he had the capacity of putting seemingly irrelevant things into a pattern. Or perhaps it was an ability on his part to make one see things his way. He was indeed exciting. He gave me my first seminar on war. He told me why it was that this war would soon be "our war."

This was the most unsettling talk I had ever heard. I was back on the trail early in the morning, striking down toward Indian Creek, Kloochman Rock, the Naches, and home. As I swung along in silence, the words came back to me, "You boys may have to finish this."

Brad, Elon, Doug, and I? Perhaps my kid brother Art too? Would we have to kill people with knives and guns? We fifteen-year-old boys, who loved everything that moved in the mountains, who swore we never could kill a doe or a fawn, would be killing people soon? The guy must be nuts! Another daffy sheepherder!

Then I remembered the last scene with him. He had cooked me a great breakfast—ham and eggs, potatoes, hot cakes with butter and syrup, and coffee. I had washed the dishes and assembled my pack. I stood on the edge of the meadow facing the east as I said good-by. There was gentleness in his voice. He placed a hand on my shoulder and stood in silence a moment.

"You will make a good soldier. A kid that can lug a pack over these ridges can go anywhere Uncle Sam wants to send his army."

Then I'd pick up the cadence—one, two, three, four—left, left, left-right-left—as I marched down the trail to home and my junior year in high school. That is how I marched out of the Cascades on the last wholly carefree trip I ever had in the high mountains.

I entered Whitman College at Walla Walla in the fall of 1916. When war involved America in 1917, it swept that campus as well as every other spot in the country where youth was congregated. Men in uniform appeared. Some of them were upperclassmen back at the fraternity house for a week end before leaving for some unknown destination. Friends with sealed orders in their pockets were saying good-by with moist eyes. There was much swearing and boasting and bravado. America was going to "clean up a few alley rats." It wouldn't take long. The whole thing would be over in no time. The Kaiser is probably "shaking in his boots already." America is plenty tough. These Huns will be "mighty sorry they started this fight." It won't take long to finish it. "We'll teach them."

That summer I went into the Cascades on a short pack trip. But the mountains seemed strangely lonesome. I was turned down for aviation. Brad was in the air corps. A letter from him had arrived from Texas. As I walked the trails the sheepherder's words of three summers ago echoed through me: "You boys may have to finish this." We would finish it, too. Until that was done, there would be no satisfying pleasure in the high mountains. There was work to be done, a war to fight.

With thoughts like that, the pack trip was an unrounded experience. It was like a hurried excursion through a house that is about to be closed to make sure water is not running, lights are off, electric irons are unplugged. And as one goes from room to room, pulling a shade or tightening a window, he hears the car outside waiting to take him to the station. He is reluctant to go but he is glad to be out of the lonesome place. The front door is about to close when he decides to take one more look in the kitchen. It is hard to leave, yet there is no enjoyment in staying.

By the next summer I was at the Presidio, being drilled by an old army sergeant. "Left, right, left, right, left, right"—on and on for hours. Then at the day's end the fog would roll in from the ocean and I would go to my cot in the barracks and rest. And as I lay there, I'd often think of my sheepherder friend below Cowlitz and hear him say, "You boys may have to finish this."

Once that summer I was down by the docks of San Francisco watching a troopship load. The men marched aboard in silence. No one was there to see them off—no band, no music, no friends. There were many youngsters, eighteen and nineteen years old now but fourteen or fifteen when the sheepherder talked to me. Each face was serious. There was a tenseness in the air. This was a serious business, not an excursion. I knew what they were thinking, for I was part of them. They were thinking about cutthroat trout or rainbow trout in a stream like the Klickitat, the golden reflection of a sunset behind some mountain such as Adams, the Saturday night crowds of the streets of a small town, the tolling of a church bell, the quiet and solitude of the deep woods.

They also were thinking that they'd be back soon. But in the back of their heads was the thought that they might not.

As I marched in the training camps, I remembered Logan Wheeler. Logan was the first of my friends to die in France, killed in action at the Meuse Argonne. Logan had worked in his father's creamery. He had wavy chestnut hair and brown eyes that had joy and laughter in them. He was full of life. He walked as if there were springs in his heels. He was always on the run, always cheerful and friendly. His girl friend was a lovely creature whose name I forget.

A few days after news of Logan's death reached Yakima I met this girl on South Third Avenue. She was coming from a store, with a package under her arm. Grief had cast a pallor over her beautiful face. She walked as if wounded. I choked up. I only nodded. I stopped for a second, touched her arm and hurried away. As I passed, she broke down and wept. It was then I realized, for the first time I think, what it meant when a war became "our war."

Chapter XIII   *Trout*

TROUT fishing for food is different from trout fishing for sport. When a man needs trout for supper, he is not going to observe the niceties that sport fishermen respect. He is after his trout in the most direct way open to him under the law. He may, indeed, catch a trout with his bare hands. That's not too difficult when the fish is under a bank or in moss in a small stream. One must tread softly so as not to disturb him. The hand must enter the water quietly and slowly and at a distance from the trout. It must be brought up under him gently. A trout loves to have his belly rubbed. After a few tender strokes he can be hoisted from the creek.

As boys we used every lawful way we could to catch trout. They were the only regular relief that we had from our diet, except huckleberries and grouse. We quite frequently found huckleberries. Less frequently we had grouse, for there were not many times when it was lawful to shoot them. Even then they could not be had with regularity, since the only weapon we had was a revolver.

Once Brad and I had been out a week or more. We were climbing on the abrupt trail out of Conrad Meadows towards the Klickitat Meadows. Brad was ahead, carrying a .22 revolver. We were in a stand of tamarack. A grouse flew to a branch almost over our heads. Brad whipped out the revolver and fired, one, two, three, four. With each shot the grouse said "oik," stretched its neck as if to discover where the noise came from, and held its seat on the branch.

There were two bullets left. Brad handed it to me. I took two shots and missed; each time the grouse said "oik." It sat still while Brad reloaded the revolver. It acted like the man in the sideshow who has his head through a hole in the canvas and is quite confident no one in the crowd is skilled enough to hit him with a baseball. Brad now took careful aim; in just one shot he snipped off its head. The fat grouse fell at our feet.

We drew it at once and lashed it to a pack. That night in the Klickitat Meadows we stewed it. We ate all of it, every morsel but the bones. We fried two pans of bread and dipped the bread in the juice. Grouse anywhere, anytime, is close to the top of the menu; but no grouse was ever more delicious than this particular one. The succulent meat had an Elysian quality, better than mortal man deserved.

Since we depended so heavily on trout for food, we fished seriously. We did not have the leisure in which to play with the various methods of fishing. We often reached a camping place at dusk. There would be a half-hour or so for fishing. If we were to have trout for supper, the catch must be fast.

We unwittingly took a leaf out of Izaak Walton's *The Compleat Angler*. I learned years later that he advised to fish for trout downstream with a short line. He advised also, when fishing with a fly, "if it be possible, let no part of your line touch the water, but your fly only." That is, I believe, known in England as dapping. Izaak Walton called it to "dape or dap."

Dapping with a fly was almost a surefire method for us. But it will not work in every place. In many pools a person who lets only his fly touch the water will most certainly frighten any trout there. The ideal place is in the white water at the head of a riffle. It makes no difference whether the stream is 12 feet or 12 inches wide. If either a wet or a dry fly is allowed to dangle in the white foam, it will probably be taken by any trout that happens to lie there in wait. At any rate that was the quickest, surest way we knew.

I think I had my best luck dapping with a coachman bucktail or a McGinty. But almost any standard fly would do the trick: queen of the waters, Jack Scott, brown hackle, gray hackle, black gnat. We caught rainbow and cutthroat up to 14 inches this way. Those are not the largest trout in Western waters. But in any water a 14-inch rainbow or cutthroat is a champion.

If the stream had no such riffle, more time and exertion would be required. Then I would use a wet fly and fish with a long line downstream, working the fly up and across the pools. Or I would let it drift down an eddy and slowly retrieve it. When fishing with a wet fly, I learned to lead the rainbow or cutthroat a bit when it came for the fly, i.e., to pull the fly away. That seemed to increase the appetite.

Our fishing was mostly on streams. But when I fished a lake I also used a wet fly. Dry-fly fishing was too involved for me. I did not have a double-tapered line. I sometimes used fly oil to make the flies float. But my leaders were only three feet long, and a wet submerged line would soon pull the fly under. I learned to fish the rise—that is, to drop the fly, when possible, on the swirl caused by a feeding trout. I found that if the fly was placed at once in the middle of the circle, a strike was practically assured.

When the trout were not feeding on the surface, I went down for them. A split shot or two near the end of the leader would carry the fly 10 feet or more under water. Sometimes I used an ordinary wet fly, waiting perhaps two or three minutes for it to sink before starting to pull in. Then I retrieved it in short, easy jerks in an effort to simulate an insect swimming to the surface.

More often I would use a woolly worm. They simulate the nymph or naiad that is swimming to the surface in order to spread its wings and fly. A nymph has no unfolded wings; it is the larva intermediate of the egg and the fly. So the woolly worm has no wings. It is merely a hook whose shank has been wound with various kinds and colors of wool, hair, yarn, or leather. As Crowe, in The Book of Trout Lore, says, "Take an Alder or Zulu; clip off most of the hackle, wings, and tail, and you have a nymph as realistic as many sold at your favorite tackle counter." When the woolly worm is drawn slowly up from the bottom four or five inches at a time, it resembles a nymph seeking the new freedom of the air.

Our fishing as boys was not exclusively with flies. We used them whenever possible because they were more convenient. Bait had to be caught; we could not bring it in with us in our packs. Moreover, one grasshopper would usually catch not more than one trout, whereas one fly would catch a dozen or more.

But when flies didn't work, I resorted to bait. In the Cascades,

an occasional frog could be found in the meadows, as by the Klickitat. I would hook him through the lips and ease him gently into
the water at the head of a deep pool. He would not usually go many
feet before a rainbow or cutthroat would rise to take him.

An Indian told me that the best way to catch trout was with a
spoon. He said that the spoon should be baited with a piece of under-
belly of a small trout. He was meticulous about the precise piece.
I asked him about it. There was an authoritative finality to his reply,
"Closest I can get to bait with sex appeal for trout."

The bait I usually used was either a grasshopper or periwinkle.
I learned, as most boys do who go fishing, that the best time to catch
grasshoppers is in the morning when the dew is on the grass and
their wings are wet. I caught the periwinkle in shallow water along
the edge of a creek or a lake. In August nothing but their black, inch-
long, pebble-covered silken cases are likely to be found in the waters
of Western mountains 4,000 feet or more in elevation.

The periwinkle or pennywinkle is the colloquial name for the
caddis worm. It is the nymph or naiad of the caddis which, in the
region of which I speak, usually hatches in late July. It makes a
wonderful bait for trout in the streams and lakes of the Cascades—
better, I think, than the grasshopper.

Izaak Walton recommended dapping for trout not only with flies
but also with bait. He suggested a line two yards long with a grasshopper on the hook. He said to stand behind a bush or a tree and
"make your bait stir up and down on the top of the water." He
added, "You may, if you stand close, be sure of a bite but not sure
to catch him."

As boys we unconsciously emulated Izaak Walton in our bait fishing too. I also dapped with grasshoppers and had great success.
Somehow I had better luck with them in pools without white water,
and my luck in whirling pools was better than in pools that were
calm.

When it came to periwinkles or caddis worms I fished differently.
Then I would put on light lead and cast at the base of a riffle or
pool. After a pause of a minute or two, I'd pull the line in a few

inches at a time. It was indeed the same method I used when fishing with the woolly worm. The periwinkle was the real nymph, the woolly worm the artificial one.

I learned these skills almost entirely in the high Cascades. There was fishing in the valley. The rainbow trout in the Yakima River then, as now, were extra large. But it is a treacherous stream, deep and fast. The Naches was quite accessible in its lower reaches, and I occasionally fished it. But my main desire was to get to the higher altitudes. Up in that wild and remote country two or three of us would have whole lakes and streams to ourselves. There we could fish with knowledge that no one had preceded us through the pools to disturb the trout.

The Klickitat Meadows are the most ideal spot for boys God ever created in the wilderness. They are about a mile and a half long and a half-mile wide. Now they can be reached by road; but when I first camped there, they were about 16 miles into the Cascades by trail. They are in a basin 4600 feet high. The view from the edge of the timber where the trail emerges is reminiscent of New England. The basin might be tucked away in western Connecticut or Massachusetts or even in Vermont or New Hampshire. The hills that rim it are soft and low lying. The sole peak in view is Bear Mountain to the west, and from that angle it suggests an Eastern rather than a Western mountain.

This natural mountain meadow looks as if it had been cleared and planted with grass. There are only a few trees in it. The Little Klickitat, lined with patches of willow, meanders through, growing in size as first the Diamond Fork and then Coyote Creek flow into it. It can be jumped at many points, and at no place is more than a dozen feet or so wide. There are pools in it, but none that is deep and treacherous. A boy can explore this meadow and discover all its secrets, and those of the river too, without risk. There are mosquitoes during most of the summer, but no insects, reptiles, or animals that need be feared. There is no more hospitable place in the mountains.

It's the most ideal place to learn trout fishing that I know. When I went there as a boy, there were rainbow and cutthroat in the river—

Montana black-spotted cutthroat. Neither they nor the rainbow ran much over six or eight inches, trout of manageable size for boys. Boys can learn the secrets of a stream with that kind of fishing. They can experiment; and none of their attempts will be costly. They run no danger of losing tackle and little of breaking rods. Through trout of that size they can come to intimate terms with a mountain meadow and a mountain creek and lay the foundation for greater conquests.

I caught my first trout in the Klickitat Meadows, on a fly—a coachman, I believe. I was thirteen then. It was a rainbow, about eight inches. As I held the twisting, struggling fellow in my left hand, my body tingled. I felt the struggle even in my toes. Here was a champion, a fighting heart if there ever was one. He was clean and sleek and committed to life. I could not kill him. He desired life as much as I and was not badly hooked. I returned him to the water.

Since then I have released many trout. But this one was the only one I released for sentimental reasons only. As I have said, the urge for sweet, tender trout to round out our starchy diet was great. I learned early to kill trout. I learned to clean them by slitting the belly lengthwise and snipping the tendons that hold the gills to the head. When that is done, one downward movement removes gills and intestines together. I learned that the offal pollutes the water if thrown into it and therefore should be buried on the shore.

Having learned the secrets of the trout, I acquired new confidence in my ability to survive in the mountains. My food supply was surely obtainable from the creeks and lakes; hence the fear of being lost and starving was not a factor in these trips.

Chapter XIV   *Fly vs. Bait*

FLY-FISHING for trout has no equal. And of all the fly-fishing, the dry
fly is supreme. The dry fly floats lightly on the water, going with the
current under overhanging willows or riding like a dainty sail on the
ruffled surface of a lake. It bounces saucily, armed for battle but looking as innocent as any winged insect that rises from underneath the
surface or drops casually from a willow or sumac into a stream or
pond.

There is the split second when the trout rises to the fly—an in-
stant that is flush with tenseness. The trout may rush from the bottom so hard that he leaves the water, as a salmon does when, fresh
from the ocean, he jumps over and again to free his body of lice. Or
the trout may come up to it gently and take it in his lips softly, as a
lady would a cherry. Or he may more discreetly whirl under it, sucking it down to him as he turns in the excitement of the hunt.

However it happens, the heart stands still. There is the tenth of a
second when the trout has the fly in his lips and before he rejects it
as false. The anxious thought races through the mind: Have I too
much slack line on the water to set the hook? If the reflexes of the
fisherman are fast, and no slack line is on the water, then he sets the
hook in a flash. A trout so hooked is not hurt, for it is usually his
lips alone that are involved. Thus he has the full use of his energies
and an excellent chance to get away. The game's the thing, with
victory going to the one most skilled. One three-pound rainbow
caught on a No. 12 or No. 14 dry fly with a 2x or 3x 9-foot leader is
worth three or four caught with worms or salmon eggs or on the
hardware of spoons or plugs.

It was experience with bug hatches that committed me to fly-
fishing. I saw my first one at Fish Lake, headwaters for the Bumping

River in the Cascades, on a warm July day when I was a boy. My brother Art and I had walked in from Bumping Lake and tossed off our hot horseshoe packs. We were lying on the shore, dozing. There was not a cloud in the sky and the lake was smooth. In a little while a breeze came up, causing a lapping of water at our feet. It was seductive. But before we had a chance to drop off to sleep, I heard a splash. I bolted upright and saw before me a calm and quiet lake come suddenly to life. A bug hatch was on. The nymphs or naiads of a species of the mayfly had left the bottom of the lake, worked their way to the surface, and spread their wings. Thousands of them were now playing the surface of the lake, rising, then falling and dipping the surface, flitting in pairs, dropping fresh eggs in the water. They seemed to be rushing to sow the seed that would perpetuate their line, lest the brief and hurried minutes of their own lives be expended on less important matters.

An old dugout canoe at Fish Lake went with the prospector's cabin that stood there for years. It was fashioned from a cedar log in the manner in which the Indians of the Pacific Northwest made their boats. It was constructed, I believe, by a prospector, though it looked pretty much like the Indian canoes that Lewis and Clark described in their *Journals*. We carried it to the lake and settled down to fishing. We fished a wet mayfly. We started fishing in the nick of time, for the hatch was over in thirty minutes, ending as abruptly as it had started. But in that time we got a dozen cutthroat, eight to twelve inches.

The bug hatch is as old as insect life. The eggs laid on or above the water sink to the bottom and lie dormant for a period. In the case of mayflies it will be a few days, a few weeks, or a few months, depending largely on the species. The nymph or naiad that emerges from the egg hides in the bottom of the stream or lake, or hangs to rocks in swift currents, or swims in quiet water, or burrows into the mud. During his incubation he lives on other aquatic insects if he has the appetite of a stone fly or a caddis, or on plant tissue, algae, and diatoms if he is a vegetarian like the mayfly. During his incubation he molts repeatedly, each molt bringing him closer to maturity. The period of incubation varies. The mayfly will often remain a nymph or naiad for three years.

Nature is prolific in her supply of this form of fish food. The species of the various flies are great in number; the order of the stone flies and salmon flies has over 1200 species, the mayflies about the same, the caddis flies around 3600, and buffalo gnats about 300. They all are amazingly fertile. Female stone flies may lay 5000 or 6000 eggs apiece. Even so, the margin nature has provided for survival is not great; the eggs, nymphs, and flies are prey for every fish and for other aquatic animals as well.

When the conditions are just right, there is a strange stirring of life down in the bottom of the lake or stream. The period of incubation is over. The nymph slowly swims to the surface, where it crawls onto a rock or branch or spreads its wings and flies. Then the mating starts, and new eggs are dropped in the water. The life of the fly may be as brief as a few hours. That is true of the mayfly. For if the mayfly hatches at sunset, it will probably die by dawn.

Izaak Walton observed that "Those very flies that used to appear about and on, the water in one month of the year, may the following year come almost a month sooner or later, as the same year proves colder or hotter." Fish biologists estimate that in the three summer months there will be, on the average, a bug hatch every two or three hours on the inland waters of the Pacific Northwest. There is no dry fly box in any pocket that can match all those flies. That is why a fly-fisherman is always adding to his collection against the day when he will see the hatch of a new fly. And he may carry those flies for years and never see their counterpart on the water.

In July 1940 Jim Donald and I were fishing the Deschutes River above Bend, Oregon, near the point where Fall River pours in. In that stretch the Deschutes is a deep, quietly moving millrace. There was no sign of life on the river, not a rise as far as the eye could see. Suddenly the redsides began to roll on the surface. A bug hatch was on. The flies were so dark and small that we could not see them at first. They were a species of the black gnat. I had no artificial fly as small as those on the water. But Jim had in his kit a collection of Nos. 22 and 24, which are so tiny that it is hard to thread them at any time let alone in the dusk. There was a reward for Jim's foresight. He soon had a pound and a half redside on the tiny No. 24 hook. He played him for a half-hour; and it was dark when Jim finally brought him to the net.

No bug hatches are more exciting than those I have witnessed when wading a stream or the shallow water along the shores of a lake. Silver Creek meanders at 6000 feet through pasture land about 20 miles below Hailey, Idaho, a town memorialized by Nancy Wilson Ross in *Westward the Women*. It has no white water, but purls along like a millrace. It is as broad as a city street and from 3 to 12 feet deep. Some of its bottom is covered by small gravel, but most of it has a deep stand of grass, weeds, and moss. This is an ideal rainbow stream. It is, I think, the best dry-fly stream for rainbow in the United States.

Jim and I were fishing Silver Creek in waders on a late evening one July. We had gone to the stream on the heels of a heavy thunderstorm. There was at most an hour of fishing before dark. We took to the stream shortly above the Point of Rocks.

There are two ways to fish Silver Creek with dry flies. One is to use as short a line as possible, dropping the fly on the near side of the stream and letting only the leader touch the water. This is a modified version of dapping, but it can be used successfully only on those portions of Silver Creek where the fisherman is concealed by tall grass or willows. It takes a strong heart to work the stream that way. One often cannot see his fly, which intensifies the shock to the nervous system when a two- or three-pound rainbow strikes. Then the fisherman is apt to set his hook too late.

Blaine Hallock taught me the better way. It is to quarter the creek downstream. Upstream casting is poor, for there is neither white water nor riffles in Silver Creek; hence the shadow of the line will most assuredly be seen. Silver Creek fishing is delicate fishing. One must come down on his trout with great finesse. When one quarters the creek downstream, a flip of the tip of the rod will feed out more line without disturbing the fly. In that way one can get a long, long float, 50 yards in some places, 30 yards in most places, before the fly is pulled under by the weight of the line. It is at the end of those long floats that the trout is apt to take the fly.

One who is slow in setting the hook will not get Silver Creek trout. And any trout hooked at that distance is usually lightly hooked. I have met no dry-fly fisherman with more finesse and skill than Blaine Hallock—to me the old maestro. But I have seen him lose 12 of 15 Silver Creek trout that he hooked at the end of a long float. Even so he brought three rainbows weighing between two and four pounds to the net that day, which was three times what Jim and I together had.

This evening in question Jim and I were quartering Silver Creek. We each had one trout weighing a pound and a half or less. But the strikes had slacked off and it looked like the trout had left the surface for that day. Suddenly a bug hatch started. We never identified the fly and had none to match it. It was a small species of salmon fly. We were in water well above our waists. We could see the nymphs coming to the surface and emerging full blown from the water. A stream that we had thought to be close to dormant burst into frenzied activity. Rainbow, five pounds or better, were rolling within reach of our fingers. Smaller rainbow were jumping. Millions of flies were bubbling from the water. The river was alive, as far as the eye could see, to the left and right. Hundreds of trout were making the river boil. They began to jump and roll within inches of us.

Both of us acted as if we were in a state of semishock. Jim finally found a second or third cousin of the fly that was hatching. He caught a one-pounder in the midst of the turmoil. And the hatch stopped as suddenly as it had started. The flies melted away in the grass and reeds. The creek became quiet. There was no splash or swirl to break the silence. The creek had 30 minutes of frenzied activity and then, as if exhausted, became dormant.

Izaak Walton listed as his artificial flies the dun, stone, ruddy, yellow or greenish, black, sad-yellow, moorish, tawny, wasp, shell, and drake. "Thus have you a jury of flies likely to betray and condemn all the Trouts in the river." If Izaak were alive today he would, I am sure, add the Hallock killer.

Blaine Hallock for years watched what fell off the willows at the water's edge, and put together a fly unique in the Pacific Northwest. The prospectus on the fly, written by the inventor himself, is worthy of the SEC files. Blaine wrote me as follows:

I am sending you under separate cover a few trout flies which are locally known as "Hallock's Killers." They were made especially for you but I am sending these few only because, in the hands of one not thoroughly familiar with their deadly qualities, and proper method of use, they are really dangerous. Should you be fishing from a boat and are out over the water where trout are known to abide, extreme caution should be employed in affixing the fly to the leader. You should hump over the fly, concealing it in the pit of your stomach and between the folds of your coat, preferably getting down on your hands and knees to the end that the fish cannot possibly see the fly during the operation. Perhaps the better method is to carry a tarpaulin or blanket under which you can crawl while handling the fly. If you are angling from the shore, you should be careful to get well back from the bank, say 75 or 100 feet, and if possible conceal yourself behind thick brush or a big tree. Trout have been known to attack these flies with such vigor and accuracy and to leap such phenomenal distances when seeing the lure that they usually gulp the fingers, sometimes even the hands of the angler, inflicting deep cuts and lacerations with their teeth.

Izaak Walton wrote that his "jury of flies" was not indispensable, that "three or four flies neat and rightly made, and not too big, serve a Trout in most rivers, all summer." Each fly-fisherman would be likely to have a different list of indispensables. Haig-Brown in *A River Never Sleeps* says that your favorite fly is "the one you'd fall back on if you were to have no other, something like the one book you'd take along to a desert island." Two of his are the Gammarus fly and the brown and white bi-visible, flies that he has not used for years, since he already knows they will catch fish under most conditions. For trout, my dry flies include the Hallock killer (giving full discount to Blaine's prospectus), the coachman bucktail, the blue upright, and the gray hackle with red body. And my wet flies are the coachman, black gnat, woolly worm, and caddis.

While it is a great day for the fly-fisherman when the trout are on the rise, it is often necessary to go down for them. Jim Donald and I put in our first appearance on the South Fork of the Madison several years ago in late July. We had fished Elk Lake, Montana, which lies not far from the Idaho line. We had seen 19-pound rainbow taken on a troll. But the best for us on flies was a seven-pounder plus a miscellaneous collection of smaller rainbow in the neighboring Hidden Lake. It was hard, slow work on the lakes, painfully slow in the hot sun that beat down the whole of the windless days we spent there. We decided to repair to a stream where fishing conditions were less likely to be affected by the weather.

We chose the Madison from the reputation it enjoyed; and the next noon checked in at an auto camp in West Yellowstone, Montana. That afternoon we sought out the South Fork. To our dismay it was almost as much a lake as the waters we had left, for Hebgen Dam had transformed a mountain stream into a long slough. We fished hard, using most of our tricks. We fished dry and wet. We got a few small trout but none worthy of the reputation of the Madison.

The next day we sought local advice. Our guide turned out to be a men's-suit salesman for a mail-order house. Each of us ended up being measured for a suit on the banks of the South Fork. (They were good suits, too.) But before that had happened we had experienced the finest nymph fishing we had ever known.

Our guide put us in deep pools. The water was well up to our armpits, almost at the top of our waders. Our feet were on small gravel. We used the woolly worm in various colors at the end of a nine-foot leader, with only the weight of a swivel attached at the head of the leader to carry it down. We would cast out, wait a minute or two for the woolly worm to sink, and then start a slow retrieve. We would take the line in with the left hand, an inch or two at a time, coiling it in the palm as the slack accumulated. By midafter-

noon the two of us took thirty trout. We killed five, returning the
rest to the river. The smallest one caught weighed two pounds, the
largest two and a quarter pounds.

It was delicate fishing. If we had had our afternoon skill in the
morning, we would have had more than the thirty. Jim yelled like
an Indian at his first fish. Well he might. It broke water, stood on
its tail, and shook its head trying to dislodge the woolly worm. I
am stirred from the lethargy of an armchair even at the memory of it.
"A rainbow!" I shouted. But I was wrong. It was a German brown
acquiring rainbow tactics in the cold waters of the Madison.

There is hardly a fisherman who does not discover something about
trout, bass, steelhead, or salmon that those before him did not know.
Lads a hundred years hence will find the answers to questions that
have stumped all who preceded. For the calculus of water temperature, humidity, the moon and sun, the wind, bug hatches, and the
like are too involved for any one man to compute. Izaak Walton
about three hundred years ago put the problem in the following way:
"Angling may be said to be so like the Mathematicks, that it can
never be fully learnt; at least not so fully, but that there will still be
more experiments left for the trial of other men that succeed us."

I have often seen trout or bass at the bottom of a pool and dangled
bait before their noses without results. Yet sometimes, if I were
patient, and held the bait right in front of the fish for five minutes or
more, I would be successful. I remember such a case when I was
bass fishing in Lake Wentworth, New Hampshire. I was anchored in
thirty feet of water off Turtle Island in a pool where I seldom failed
to take bass. For bait I was using crayfish that are native to the lake
and which I caught with my hands. This day the lake was mirrorlike.
There was no breath of air; and the sunlight fell with the full intensity
of July.

For several hours I had been unable to interest any small-mouthed
bass in the crayfish. I peered over the edge of the boat and saw a
bass poised directly below. I lowered a fresh crayfish until it hung
suspended in front of the bass's nose. The crayfish, hooked through

the tail, was waving his claws menacingly at the bass. The bass did not move. That went on for five minutes or more. Then the bass lunged at the crayfish. He seized it from the side and slowly turned it in his mouth so as to swallow it tail first. When the tip of the tail was in his mouth, I set the hook. The bass was transformed into a mass of energy. He came straight up from the bottom of the lake as if he had been shot out of a cannon. He came so fast I could not begin to take the line in on the reel. He hit the surface about a foot from the boat and jumped. The force of his jump carried him some three feet in the air; he gave a side twist, shook his head, and landed in the boat—a pound and a half of fighting-mad bass flesh.

One July day I had whipped the shore water of Green Lake in the Wallowas for several hours with a variety of dry flies. I should have had my limit, but only three or four trout were in the creel. I was standing at the meadow's edge on the south side of the lake wondering what to try next. As I stood there perplexed, a 15-inch eastern brook slowly swam in to shore. When he was two feet offshore in perhaps eight inches of water, he turned and stopped, perfectly poised and facing the depths. He was not more than three feet from my boots.

I decided to have some fun with him. I reeled in my line, leaving only the nine-foot leader free of the ferrules. I looked in my fly box and spied a McGinty. Playing a hunch, I greased it with mucelin and tied it to my leader. All this time I had not moved my feet; but my arms and hands had been active. Yet my trout was not in the least disturbed.

I risked disturbance, however, when I swung the rod out over the water so as to dangle the McGinty in front of his nose. Even then he was not frightened. When the McGinty touched the water, he had it in a flash. I set the hook and my trout was in deep water fighting for his life. That trout violated all the rules man had made for him.

The bait-fishermen are not only vociferous; they are probably in the majority. The debate between them and the fly-fishermen has been going on for centuries, and will never cease as long as there is a trout pointed upstream in a riffle, waiting to see what the river brings him.

One summer day I came out of the Wallowas with a creel filled with 12 to 14-inch rainbow caught with a dry fly on the Big Minam. I ran into a newspaperman whose curiosity was excited by a glimpse of the catch. I told him of the Big Minam, which rises from the south end of Minam Lake in the heart of the Wallowas. It flows for 40 miles through one of the prettiest mountain valleys the Creator ever fashioned. It is fed on its course by several good streams—the Little Minam, Rock Creek, the North Minam, and Elk Creek. Dozens of other smaller creeks flow into it and it is fed by hundreds of springs. The valley is narrow—a quarter- to a half-mile wide. The mountains rise on either side 2000 to 3000 feet.

There are great stands of ponderosa pine in the valley. There are huge fir trees, red and white, and towering tamarack on the slopes. Jack pine is scattered here and there in groves so thick no tree can get beyond the spindling stage. There is now and then a touch of spruce and once in a while a yew tree. On the tops of the ridges are scatterings of mountain-mahogany, excellent browse for deer. And in the ravines are alder, willow, and hawthorn. There are whole acres of snowbrush along the mountainsides, filling the valley with its sweet perfume in June and July.

This is excellent elk country—Rocky Mountain elk introduced from Wyoming in 1912. And wise and crafty buck deer watch over the valley from the base of granite cliffs that mark the skyline of the mountains.

In years past the Big Minam has been one of the best trout streams in America. There were streams that had larger rainbow in them, but none harbored lustier ones. Moreover, few streams are more exacting on the fly-fisherman. The water is as clear as water can be. It runs for the most part over sandbars and bright gravel. Detection is easy; delicate fishing is required. One should let a pool on the Minam rest at least five minutes after catching a trout from it.

This is the discourse I was giving my newspaper friend—bragging

a bit as I held the trout up one by one. When I had finished he said,
"You caught them on bait, I presume."

"Bait?" I snorted. "There ought to be a law against fishing for
trout with bait."

My statement was on the wires that afternoon, and Ben Hur
Lampman, editorial writer for the Portland *Oregonian*, saw it the
next morning. Ben is more than editorial writer. He is a fisherman
extraordinary. He is something of a botanist and biologist. He is also
a philosopher.

Ben has a plaque entitled "The Angler's Prayer" with a verse
inscribed on it that reads:

> Lord give me grace to catch a fish
> So big that even I,
> In talking of it afterward
> May never need to lie.

The story of how that prayer on Ben's plaque was answered is told
by Ben himself in the greatest fish story ever written. It is entitled
"Them Two Guys Is Nuts." It tells how Ben caught a 120-pound
sturgeon, 6 feet 10½ inches long, in Blue Lake, Oregon, after a battle
of 2 hours and 15 minutes. I mention the story only to indicate that
the primordial man is strong in him—so strong that he tossed out
the poet when I endorsed the dry fly. Ben sat down and wrote the
following editorial.

Tarrying briefly at La Grande on his way to the fine fishing of the
Wallowa Mountains, where are lakes with almost incredible trout, Associate Justice William O. Douglas, of the Supreme Court, held that in
fishing for trout there can be no sport unless the artificial fly is used, and
preferably the dry fly. . . .

But the associate justice neglects, we think, to consult a most distinguished precedent which in piscatorial matters has all the weight of
the English common law. The authority is one that cannot properly be
ignored in the handing down of such a ruling, for surely it is generally
conceded to govern these instances, and the name that it bears is warmly
luminous in English letters. It may seem tedious to cite Izaak Walton,
but none the less there is a duty in the instance, for Walton is Walton,
as one might say Blackstone is Blackstone, and not to be altered by in-

dividual prejudice or personal inclination. This ethical pillar of what one might term the common law of angling, the veritable father of the code, sets the associate justice, one fears, at naught.

We have no intent to reverse an associate justice of the highest tribunal, nor should we know how to come about it with privilege and decorum, but it ought to suffice to refer to the code of the angler as written by Master Walton, wherein a considerable part of the chapter on trout fishing is devoted to the employment of baits, which portion takes precedent over the equally authoritative discussion of using the artificial fly. Izaak Walton was lyric in his praise of the gentle, which is the common maggot, and of the dewworm, the lobworm, the brandling, the marsh worm, the tagtail, the flagworm, the oak worm, the gilttail, the twatchel and many another. He gives explicit and well-nigh affectionate instructions for their culture and care before he turns, with scarcely less of delight, to treating of the grasshopper, the minnow and the caterpillar. All these, and their manipulation, are in the classic *corpus juris* of the ethics and practice of trout fishing. (People v. Trout, 1 Walton 78)

It seems, clearly enough, that in his ruling on fly-fishing the associate justice is reversed by a still higher court. . . . The error is not in individual election of a certain method, which is as may be, but rather in the implication that trout may be honestly acquired in no more than the one manner. And Master Walton is so obviously to the contrary.

Ben was right in marshaling eminent authority to his side. Izaak Walton endorsed bait for trout. Izaak listed, in addition to those cited by Ben, the beetle, black snail (slit open), and any kind of fly including the lowly housefly. Izaak preferred the grasshopper dangled on the surface of the water. But my son Bill and I bettered the great Izaak one summer day in the Wallowas.

We were camped at Long Lake and had gone over to Steamboat Lake for a day of fishing. Steamboat lies close to 7000 feet. It has an island that faintly resembles a steamboat; hence its name. It lies surrounded by granite ridges. They rise from 1000 to 1500 feet on the east, west, and south; and a few hundred feet on the north. They are steep rock walls, studded with whitebark pine, Engelman's spruce, and alpine (balsam) fir that have managed somehow to extend their roots into tiny crevices, splitting the granite as the roots grow in strength. These are smooth rocks, polished by glaciers.

A lush meadow lies at the south end of the lake where one can find in July and August a purple monkeyflower, the fireweed, daisy, buttercup, larkspur, Scouler St. Johns wort, and pleated gentian. Through this meadow a stream wanders in serpentine fashion and pours clear, cold water into the lake. The waters of the lake wash the other three granite walls. The granite is here and there streaked with marble. The light stone seems to draw out the deep sapphire of the lake.

Bill and I had been fishing with dry flies. We had three or four eastern brook of from 10 to 13 inches and a rainbow or two around 10 inches. But the going was slow. So I started my son on mastery of the roll cast. He was standing on the southern shore at the edge of a rock that is as wide as a paved street and slopes gently into the water. Suddenly a swarm of grasshoppers came over our shoulders from the southwest. They covered the rock. A high wind blew them out on the water. Then began an extensive, an amazing rise. The only thing comparable to it that I have seen took place in a different medium. At the Malheur Bird Refuge near Burns, Oregon, one July evening I saw hundreds of redwings diving and swooping over swarms of dragonflies that filled the air above the marshes of Malheur Lake. What the redwings did to the dragonflies, the trout did to the grasshoppers at Steamboat Lake. And each scene was equally animated.

The water immediately in front of us became alive with fish. Big trout—two- or three-pounders—rolled under the grasshoppers, sucking them under with a swirl. Smaller trout left the water, jumping again and again for the fresh bait, gorging themselves. There were literally hundreds of swirls and splashes extending farther and farther into the lake as the wind carried the hoppers away from the shore. It would have been impossible to draw a circle three feet in diameter that did not include a rising trout.

The temptation at such a moment is to give the trout what is being offered—to bait hooks with grasshoppers or even to add a grasshopper to a fly hook. But a grasshopper on a hook does not sit as nicely on the water as a grasshopper with his freedom. So we decided on a different course. We decided to try the Hallock killer and to fish it dry. The underbody of the Hallock killer has a yellow-green tinge that is very close to the color of the grasshopper. It was this underbody that the trout would see.

We greased our Hallock killers with mucelin and cast out. Our dry flies rode high and saucily on the surface, bobbing with the riffle that the wind had kicked up. They were surrounded by live grasshoppers, a half-dozen grasshoppers within inches of our flies. In a flash each of us had a strike. The trout chose the Hallock killer over the real thing. We caught trout as fast as we could cast. We caught trout as long as the grasshoppers pulled trout to the surface. The largest was an 18-inch eastern brook. My son, fourteen at the time, caught him. In view of the angle of decline of the rock into the water, I decided against the use of a net. So Bill beached it. It was wholly out of water on the rock when the hook became disengaged and it regained its freedom. It was fully 18 inches long and any fair-minded jury would concede it two pounds.

Blaine Hallock is a purist and the de facto head of the Dry Fly League of the Pacific Northwest. He wouldn't use bait on trout if his life depended on it and would expel anyone from the League who was caught doing so. At least that's what I thought. Jim Donald also proclaimed to be a purist. But he proclaimed it so vociferously that he raised doubts in my mind, like the lady who protested too much. One day my doubts received reinforcement. I was searching Jim's tackle box, with his permission, for a leader. In a box at the bottom of the kit I found several interesting specimens.

One was a grasshopper. I held it up accusingly.

He said, "Must have jumped in and died."

Beside the grasshopper was a shrimp. I held it under his nose and asked, "How do you explain this?"

Jim said, "Brought it along for my lunch."

I looked under the grasshopper and the shrimp and found an artificial mouse. I then had him dead to rights.

On our return from the fishing trip I put the matter to simon-pure purist, the old maestro, for a ruling. I cast into poetry the brief that I filed. It read as follows:

In days long ago the true dry-fly addict
Never once cast a covetous look
At a worm or a frog or a mouse or a hog
Or at varmints which lived in the brook.

The fly which was dry was a symbol to him
Of a skill which was noble and fine
He was careful to note it was always afloat
All the feathers, hook, leader and line.

He cast in the pool where the granddaddy lay
He waited and followed the float
For the surge and the splash, the thrill of the flash
Of the trout which seemed big as a boat.

But now it appears a decay has set in
In lieu of a speck of a fly
A piece of raw meat that a trout likes to eat
Meets the test if it's greasy and dry.

And all that is spun from the tenuous thread
That a thing which is dry and will float
In fact has a wing though it's only a thing
With four legs and a tail—like a goat.

Alas and alack—and believe it or not
Things have come to a terrible state
Black gnat and gray hackle, and all dry-fly tackle
Are usurped and dethroned by King Bait.

Oh ye who have erred I beseech ye, repent!
Raise your eyes from the earth to the sky!
Leave the mouse to the cat—forsake ye the rat!
Keep your fly like your powder, son, dry!

The old maestro's ruling came in due course. He replied in kind:

If cows can dance the rhumba on an ice pond,
    (And once a cow did jump over the moon)
If listening to the brook a felon's yet fond,
    (Per Gilbert's rhythmic operatic tune).

If men who have a thirst may speak of dryness,
　　(And feeling dry is worse than getting wet.)
It may be said with no pretense of slyness
　　That lubricated mice may win the bet.

To fly may not imply the use of pinions.
　　A flag may fly from any breezy height.
So men may disagree in their opinions,
　　And every one of them may still be right.

There are so very many ways of flying.
　　There are so very many kinds of flights.
There are so very many sorts of dryness,
　　Let's give the oiled mouse his Bill of Rights.

Now you and I may scorn the lowly varmint,
　　But scorning cannot rid us of the pest.
So cast aside your black judicial garment,
　　Commune with God—and He will do the rest.

Thus did even a purist fall from grace.

My son Bill and I were fishing Silver Creek, Idaho, one September day. On the upper reaches is a large slough, some thirty yards wide and a quarter-mile or more long. There we took our positions, side by side, he up to his armpits, I well over my waist.

It was a squally day, fifteen minutes of gusty wind followed by a half-hour of quiet. When there was no wind the surface of the slough was glassy. Then conditions were too delicate for fly-fishing; for the shadow of the line sounded an alarm to the rainbow. In those periods of quiet we would get out of the water, work our way up the bank that bounds the slough on the south and study it. What we saw at one such time startled us. A school of two dozen or more rainbow swam by us. They were on a lazy cruise. They were not more than 25 or 30 feet away. We got a close look. There were eight better than 30 inches long, a half-dozen more were over 24 inches and the rest from 16 to 18 inches. It was an armada, thrilling to behold.

When the next breeze came, we waded quietly into the water and cast toward the spot where we imagined the cruising rainbow to be. We were fishing dry and had changed from a gray hackle to a bucktail coachman. Within an hour I had three of those big fellows on. There would be a swirl under the fly and the hook would be set. But I was either a trifle slow or a trifle fast. Not once did I set the hook securely. There would be a run, a dorsal fin cutting the water, a jump, a surge—and then a slack line.

At last I was discouraged, and decided to forsake the slough for the stream. Bill promised to follow me shortly. Several hours passed and he had not showed up. Slightly concerned, I started upstream where I had seen him last. Pretty soon someone came running and shouted, "Your son needs help. He's got a big one on."

"How big?" I asked.

"About 10 pounds I think," was the reply.

Waders are ungainly even for walking. They never were designed for running. But run in them I did. I stopped only once in the half-mile or more, and that was to borrow a net from another fisherman. Neither Bill nor I had one, and a net would come in handy even though the trout should turn out to be but half of 10 pounds.

But I arrived too late for the battle. There was Bill, wet to the neck, with a grin on his face, and a rainbow that was slightly over 16 inches in length hanging on his right thumb.

When I left him he had forsaken the fly. He waded the neck of the slough in water up to his chin, changed to a reel with nylon line, and fished as Sandy Balcom, manufacturer of pipe organs in Seattle, had taught us.

Sandy uses a 4- to 6-pound clear nylon line, 300 feet long, with a backing of 8- to 10-pound nylon line also 300 feet long. His leader is 3 feet long, 1¾ to 2¼ pounds strength. His hook is a No. 8 or 10 single-egg type. He puts on two salmon eggs, the lower one having only the faintest part of the hook point showing. There is buckshot on the leader to carry it down. The bait is allowed to settle on the bottom and is then stripped in very slowly. Sandy has delicate fingers. He can make a few passes over the bottom and know at once its character. He can make bait the king under practically any fishing conditions I have known.

Bill played the rainbow he caught with the salmon eggs at least

40 minutes; and when the last ounce of energy was gone from the rainbow's stout heart, he turned on his side. Bill then slipped a finger through the gill and the battle was over.

As we walked through the willows to the road where our car was parked, I saw in my son's eyes an excitement I had not seen before. I knew there had been awakened in him an instinct that has been carried in the blood stream of the race since man first lowered a net in the ocean or first stood by a pool with a spear waiting for the flash that heralded the arrival of a salmon or trout.

Chapter XV   A Full Heart

I STOOD at daybreak one August morning on the ridge above Diamond Lake in the Wallowas. We were camped at Tombstone Lake and I had risen early to find and explore Diamond, which lay below me 800 feet or more in a deep pocket of the mountains. The dark sapphire of its water, its remoteness from the trail, the steep slopes surrounding it, the fir that almost hid it from view—these combined to give it an air of mystery in the faint light that preceded the sunrise. The view stirred in me a feeling of eagerness and suspense that I have experienced again and again on coming to a ridge overlooking an unexplored lake in the wilderness.

I hurried down as though I were late for an appointment, intent on rainbow cruising the surface for food. Where were the deep pools and the best feeding grounds? I thought of one-pounders and four-pounders. Would the big ones be at the end of those logs lying in the water?

I thought I was alone, so it was startling when I saw a buck deer, two does, and a fawn going around the lake ahead of me. I wondered what bugs might be on the water and what flies to use. A rise showed fifty yards from shore—a swirl under something white. The circles expanded themselves as they reached toward shore, and all was quiet again.

As I began to whip the surface with my fly, great expectations filled my mind. This was a remote place that perhaps only a half-dozen people a year ever reached. It was largely unexplored water. "There may be four-pounders here," I thought. So I matched my wits against the imaginary champion, and changed from fly to fly until a bucktail caddis brought a pound-and-a-half rainbow to the net.

The sun had not been on the lake an hour when I had to leave. I

had climbed halfway up the steep mountainside when I sat for
a few minutes on a granite ledge and looked down into Diamond. I
felt then as one does when he meets for the first time an interesting
person. One gets only an inkling of the full personality, and this
slight acquaintance whets his appetite. This was the beginning
of a friendship; Diamond had much to offer and I had a longing
for its offering.

Lakes, like people, have personalities. It takes time and patience,
but if one goes about it the right way he can get on intimate
terms with a lake. Lake Wentworth in New Hampshire was such a
lake to me. I discovered on my own every good bass pool that it
harbors. Some are near points of islands, some are in unsuspected
spots offshore where a ledge is concealed 30 or 40 feet below the
surface. Others are in sandy stretches where the bass like to cruise.
One is in the least likely place of all—three feet of water a few
yards beyond a marshy shore. Here at sunset I would anchor both
bow and stern, cast out a live minnow hooked lightly through the
lips, and watch for the dorsal fin of a bass as he came viciously for
the bait in the shallow water.

I knew the ledges and rocks of Wentworth as one knows his own
property. I could safely feel my way across it in darkness as one
would navigate his living room or work his way across his pasture
without a light. I swam off its shores; and I swam great distances
between its islands, two miles or more. I felt the warm surface water
and the chill of a current coming from some spring in the middle. I
knew the winds and what to expect of them. I knew the wet east
wind and the three-day blows out of the west. And I knew where the
bass were feeding at those times.

Wentworth was a friend, like Long and Steamboat and Frances of
the Wallowas later became: and like Fish and Bumping and Fryingpan of the Washington Cascades had been earlier.

Friendship with a lake is likely to be more placid than friendship
with a river. It is also more easily cultivated, for rivers are unruly,

headstrong, and violent. Yet the river holds the greater charm for the fisherman. The reason is complex. A river can completely change its character in a few hours. Some of the most striking examples are the streams that run off the western slopes of the Olympic Mountains in Washington into the Pacific: the Quinault, Hoh, and Quilla-yute. This is an area of great rainfall, as much as 140 inches a year. A heavy rain for a day or so can raise those rivers a foot or more. When that happens, the character of the pools and riffles changes radically.

Each pool in a Western river is a study in hydraulics. Unlike a swimming pool, it is not understandable merely in terms of a top, bottom, and sides. It is a whirling mass of water. The current may run at varying speeds at the different levels. The volume of water affects the course of the current. Cutthroat, steelhead, and salmon have different feeding habits. To know where they are is one thing; to know how to reach them in a particular pool is another. The newcomer cannot know these things. It takes familiarity and observation.

A river is on the move in more ways than one. The rocks are always rolling. They roll for miles and become rounded like those of the Naches in the Cascades. The sand they grind shifts from place to place. Each pool changes from season to season. Spring floods wipe out log jams and sandbars, altering not only the character but the location of pools and riffles. When ice goes out it may take with it whole beds of algae and moss, as it has done in Silver Creek, Idaho, thus transforming long stretches. The process works in reverse when a spring flood carries tons of silt from a hillside or meadow and dumps it over beds of algae and moss, as I have seen done in the Wallowas in East Eagle Creek and in the Minam. Favorite feeding grounds for trout are rendered sterile and the design of the river refashioned.

So it is that the character of a river, unlike a lake, is most inconstant. It can be one thing in September and quite a stranger the next June. The technique of fishing the pools must be learned anew each year. Every spring is a new adventure, no matter how often a man returns to a stream. Moreover, a stream is not so moody as a lake. When the riffles leave the surface of a lake and a dead calm settles over it, the fish are usually less active. But in calm days or in windy ones the river is vibrant with activity; it is not dependent on outside forces to stir it to life.

Of all the rivers, those that connect immediately with the ocean, such as the Campbell on Vancouver Island and the Quillayute on the Olympic Peninsula, have the strongest appeal. They have the cutthroat, steelhead, and salmon that run in from the ocean. These migrants constantly renew the life of the stream and fill each pool with expectancy. These streams are not fished out. They run either through primitive country without towns or mills to pollute them or race to tidewater through undespoiled land in national parks or forests.

The pool has a strange attraction for man, whether it is against the shore of a lake under overhanging willows or formed in a river from logs or rocks. Any quick movement of life in its dark depths gives it magic. The shadows that run through it, the blurred outlines of a log, the streaks of white sand, suggest forms and movements of life. The imagination can indeed make a sterile pool an enchanted spot.

When man wades a river he becomes as much a part of it as the logs, the rocks, the fish, the water ouzel. There is the pressure against the midriff. He balances as he leans into the current and pushes his legs through it. It can be especially treacherous, as in the lower Deschutes of Oregon in early summer, when one misstep would send a man whirling to oblivion in an avalanche of white water. It can be comfortable and relaxing in streams such as East Eagle of the Wallowas and the Klickitat of the Washington Cascades. When man wades a river, he returns to the water as all good hunters of fish have done from time immemorial, and comes up to his prey from behind.

There is a thrill in traveling on fast water in a boat or canoe. The white waters of the Rogue or McKenzie in Oregon or of the Quinault or Quillayute in Washington have challenge throughout for one who fishes them in that way. The craft barely misses huge rocks close to the surface as it shoots down narrow channels through which the river pours. Submerged logs reach out clawlike to rip the bottom from the canoe. One gets relaxation in the wide expanses of calm below the roaring falls or cascades. And then comes a rapid, giddy run through flat water in which the boat bounces like a cork along a current. These experiences fill every moment on our Western streams with tenseness. Then man is not only pitted against fish; he matches wits with a river. There are few greater exhilarations in the woods.

It is better that a lad face adventure on a stream or lake than risk the more subtle dangers of the poolroom. The streams and lakes do not breed juvenile delinquents.

Every stream, every lake I have ever fished is packed with memories not only of the fish I caught but also of my human companions. I remember them and their yarns and our experiences together far better than I do our fish:

—A. T. Hobson, Montana rancher and for many years Secretary of the Reconstruction Finance Corporation, before a campfire at Cheval Lake in the Wallowas, teaching a group of songsters verses of "The Tattooed Lady."

—Palmer Hoyt, publisher of the Denver Post, dismounting at Frances Lake, in the Wallowas, after an exhausting ride over one of the worst trails ever traveled by man or beast and muttering, "If they are shooting suckers, I'm it."

—Jimmy Conzelman, famed football coach and advertising man, coming down horseback on the selfsame trail in the dusk and saying, "They should keep horses attached to beer wagons like we do in St. Louis. They are one thing a man should never straddle. And those escalators in Penn Station in New York City aren't so bad either, if you get what I mean."

—Dick Neuberger, of journalistic fame, lying on the shore of Tombstone Lake in the Wallowas after a hard 26-mile ride and saying, "Be sure, boys, to put the slab at my head."

—Jim Donald, Oregon lawyer, bellowing like a bull elk as he bathed in the icy Minam at dawn.

—Gene and Frank Marsh, Oregon lawyers, and the late Merle Chessman, newspaper publisher of Astoria, singing "The Loving Cup" in the moonlight on the banks of the Deschutes.

And there was also the willow thrush. It was dusk, and I was walking the trail along the Minam River returning to camp at Granite Crossing. There were trout in my creel. I was wet and weary, ready for a cup of hot mulligan and bed. The roar of the river was in my ears. Suddenly there came the wistful notes of the willow thrush. I never saw the bird. I could not quite locate the thicket of willows from which it was serenading. I stopped at least five minutes to listen. When I turned to go, there was new strength in my step. The haunting melody of the little brown thrush followed me to camp and lingered until dark.

One of the most memorable experiences happened on a fishing trip to Bear Lake in the Wallowas early one September. Lauten McDaniel, oil distributor and garageman of Wallowa, and his son Keith arranged to meet me and my son Bill at the lake for three days of fishing. Lauten and Keith went in with horses by way of Bear Creek. Bill and I took a pack train out of the Lostine, up the Bowman Trail to Brownie Basin, then to Chimney Lake, and on up to Hobo Lake, one of the highest lakes in the Wallowas—8300 feet. At Hobo Lake the trail ends.

Some 800 feet or more above us was a granite ridge we had to cross. We slowly picked our way up it, and at last looked down into the Bear Creek Saddle. There are spots along that ridge where one can find gentle slopes down the other side, but we chose the least favorable. The slope was steep—45 degrees or better—and covered with loose rock. There were ledges to skirt and rolling rocks to avoid. The going got too rough for riding, so we dismounted, each leading a saddle horse and a pack horse. The pack on one horse loosened, and before I could climb up the steep slope to fix it, it had swung under his belly. The horse bolted and bucked, scattering food, kettles, and sleeping bags 500 feet down the mountain. We wasted precious time collecting them and repacking the horse. It was black when we reached Bear Lake, and we were disappointed because we had counted on the evening for fishing. That night the weather changed. Fall had set in.

We fished the next day and the following one with little success. Bear Lake, in the fashion of high mountain lakes, had turned virtually dormant. We took a few eastern brook, a couple around 12 inches, but none of any size. From a fishing viewpoint the trip failed. But it was a congenial group; there were happy campfires at night and choice food; and the meadow was carpeted with alpine speedwell and pleated gentian. One night before we retired the moon rose over the granite peaks that stand guard on the east. The light gave the rockslides opposite us a glistening sheen and turned them into tumbled seracs from an ancient glacier. We watched a golden gleam dancing in the water as we sat late talking of personal things.

The next day we broke camp. We returned by way of the Bowman Trail, our creels empty. A rainstorm broke as I led the pack train out of Wilson Basin to the top. When we arrived at the saddle, with Brownie Basin 500 feet below us, it was still raining but with the sun over our shoulders from the west. Suddenly a rainbow formed immediately in front of us. It was so close one could almost have thrown a rock through its arc. One end of it was anchored on the northern edge of Brownie Basin, the other a half-mile distant at the southern edge. Both ends in the same mountain meadow! Two pots of gold at our very feet! As I stood there drinking in the scene, I remembered what Ben Hur Lampman once wrote:

Quoth Justice Douglas of the United States Supreme Court, on arriving in Oregon for his vacation, "I am going where I can find the largest fish." Ah, but when the largest fish has been found will it be caught? We commend the jurist for his judicious employment of language, for he does not declare that he will catch the aforesaid fish, to have and to hold, but merely that, he, William O. Douglas, will repair to its favorite vicinage. Yet it is not unlikely that Justice Douglas, who plies a deft rod, will catch him a very fine fish. We believe him, however, on reliable report, to be a better fisherman than this. We believe that fishing itself is all in all to him, and not merely the fish.

How is that? Duffers and dubs, sir, frequently come home with the largest fish of all, while Waltonian merit seemingly goes unrewarded. To hook, play and land the largest fish is not necessarily proof that one is a master fisherman. We remember a jaunty novice, equipped with the cheapest of rods, reels and lines, who was single-egg fishing a green eddy in the glorious Rogue. On the gravel beside him lay a huge steelhead—a noble fish to dream about. "Did you catch this fish?" he was asked wonderingly. He bridled at the question. "Who else do you suppose?" he countered truculently. "Well—er—did he fight much?" The novice stared scornfully at his interlocutor. "Not with me he didn't, mister: I hauled him right in!" You, see, that's what we mean.

Unless we have been woefully misinformed about his attitude toward fishing it is our opinion that Justice Douglas would fish for any manner of fish, in any sort of water if need be, while his heart rejoiced. He prefers trout, of course, and who doesn't? So, we suspect, did Master Walton, yet he found merit in "the chavender or chub." Doubtless he, too, preferred trout, we say, but he could be happy with either, "were t'other dear charmer away." What every fisherman learns, soon or late, is that a full heart is better than a full creel.

It was a cold July day in 1948. The snow had been particularly heavy the preceding winter. There were seven feet of it on the level around our cabin in the Wallowas on April 15, and two feet of it were still there on May 15. When I arrived from Washington, D.C., in mid-June, the snow was gone from the Lostine canyon but big drifts hung on the ridges and blocked all trails. Aerial reports showed the high lakes wholly or partially frozen. It would be a brief season for fishermen, and almost as brief for the trout. There would be only a few weeks for the bug hatches on which trout fatten. July would be almost gone before the water was rid of its icy chill, and September frosts would be on the heels of the dog days of August.

Green Lake is one of the first of the high lakes to open in the spring. It lies 7100 feet up, nestled under granite crags of the ridge that bounds the North Minam Meadows on the south. The mountains rim it in horseshoe fashion, the north side being open. That side of the lake laps the edge of a great saucer. Almost 2000 feet below the rim is the North Minam. The mountain drops off from that edge in a great tangle of lava rock and conifers, as wild and broken terrain as one can find in the mountains. This pocket in the Wallowas is a high shelf. One sits high in the heavens on the edge of this lake. At the south side of the lake is a rich meadow with a small stream that in late August is only inches wide but ice cold. This is an ideal place to camp. There is feed for the horses; and if they tire of that, there is the sweet mountain fescue or bunchgrass (*Festuca viridula*) on the ridges above.

There are conies (carrying Stanley Jewett's name) in the rock slides to scold and chatter. There are does and bucks on the rim; and there are cougar and coyote to hunt them—hunters that know no law against taking does and fawns, hunters that have no legal limit on the kill. If one watches carefully he may see the gray-crowned rosy finch, the red crossbill. He might even see the Rocky Mountain pine grosbeak, a ruffed grouse, or possibly a fool hen (Franklin's grouse).

The water of the lake is deep green from the rich algae that cover its bottom and give it its name. The fish are especially sweet. They are eastern brook, fat and lively. Isaak Walton said, "If I catch a trout in one Meadow, he shall be white and faint, and very like to be lousy; and as certainly if I catch a Trout in the next Meadow, he shall be strong, and read, and lusty and much better meat." I think I could take a taste test and find the one Green Lake trout in the frying pan. They have the sweetest taste of any eastern brook I have eaten. One of them is worth a half-dozen of any others I have known.

These fish were a part of the magnet that drew me over the mountains. I left our cabin around 5 A.M.—an early start because the snow promised slow travel. Normally it takes three hours to go the seven miles to the North Minam Meadows on horseback. My daughter Millie set the record for that trip when she was sixteen—the time when Dick McDaniel was thrown from a horse and had a concussion. Then Millie rode Lightning out to Lapover for a doctor in an hour and a half, without putting the horse beyond a walk. I would be lucky to make the trip in four hours this July day. Brownie Basin lies about

2000 feet above the Lostine. This morning it was filled with drifts of snow. Towering over it are jagged granite cliffs. There was a stark grandeur about them. Huge avalanches of snow perched on their shoulders, with ten-foot drifts all the way to the top. The saddle, half as wide as a city street, was filled with broken blocks of snow more than a dozen feet thick. Below the saddle to the west are Wilson Basin and John Henry Lake. The sun was high and John Henry was sparkling as if a million mirrors were casting light on it.

The hillside snow was too soft for horses, so I walked, leading Dan. We both floundered in it for a half-mile or more and did not leave it until we reached the basin, a rich meadow dotted with pine and fir and lying about 7000 feet high.

Here I saw young whitebark pines, bent even as the bunch grass from the pressure of heavy snow that had burdened them that winter. Hundreds of them had been crushed under the terrific weight, some never to straighten again. I remembered one in particular, a whitebark pine 15 or 20 feet high. It bowed at a crazy angle; and so it would be shaped throughout its life. But already it had turned its tip straight as an arrow to the sky. It reminded me of England, crushed under the burden of war but raising her proud head to the sky where freedom lives.

I went down the pitch of trail that leads to the North Minam Meadows—the old Bowman, which dropped off the mountain like a spiral staircase. It often lay thick in powdered dust in August. Today it was wet with snow water and had been heavily washed and gouged by spring floods.

In the Meadows I found elk grazing, and I heard coyotes yapping at them from the mountainside. From Wilson Basin the trail had been lined with flowers and shrubs in bloom. The Meadows were ablaze with colors, wild flowers rioting in the late spring that had suddenly arrived in the Wallowas. The North Minam River was so far over its banks as to transform the Meadows into a lake. Dan had to swim the middle stretch. I held my feet on his shoulders, and the water lapped at my saddle seat.

We went into the woods on the other side and found the Culbertson Trail to Green Lake—most of it a treacherous series of cut-backs that climb for a mile at 45 degrees or more. I leaned forward against Dan's neck and rested him frequently, since it was his first strenuous exercise of the season.

There was much down timber that had to be cut away, for we were the first travelers of the year. There was a lot of snow at the lake. But the water itself was clear of ice and snow; and so was the half of the meadow nearest the lake. There was not a sign of life on the surface. I took a yellow and black woolly worm from my box, tied it onto a nine-foot gut leader, and at the head of the leader put a small split shot. Usually I trim off the fuzz, leaving only a shank wound tight with wool yarn, but this time I left it on. On the retrieve from the first cast I had a strike. On the fourth I had an 11-inch eastern brook. In short order I caught six trout, ranging from 11 to 13 inches.

I kneeled by the icy brook to clean them. Then I appreciated for the first time the full glory of the meadow. The grass was beginning to appear, only a quarter- or half-inch above the ground, not yet high enough for a horse to take in his lips. Ahead of the grass were the buttercups. The meadow was golden with them in the late sun. There were spots of star moss on some of the rotten tree trunks. Hellebore, its leaves all furled in conical shape, was beginning to poke its head out of the ground, but no other plants were in evidence.

At the lower altitudes there were many flowering plants and shrubs which I stopped to pick on my return. I had no plant presser along, so I put them in my fish basket on top of the trout my woolly worm had seduced from Green Lake. It was a rich collection I had made.

Serviceberry, chokecherry, red willow or dogwood, elderberry, currant, and snowbrush were the shrubs in bloom. Yellow columbine, stickweed, pussytoes, western valerian, skunk cabbage, tall groundsel, sweetroot, western wallflower, wild rose, windflower, miner's lettuce, alumroot, twinberry, heartleaf arnica, wild carrot, buttercup, yellow violet, sheep bluebells (liked more by sheep and cattle than by horses), Solomon's-seal, several pentstemon, strawberry, Richardson's geranium, Oregon grape, yarrow, forget-me-nots, larkspur, honeysuckle (gilia), and lupine—these were the wild flowers I picked in the dusk.

The most fragrant of all was the snowbrush (*Ceanothus velutinus*), sometimes known as tobacco brush, mountain balm, and sticky laurel. It is popularly called chaparral, a term applied loosely to describe various types of shrubby vegetation. Chamise is its prototype on the desert. As Walt Dutton of the Forest Service once told me, "It's chaparral if you can't ride a horse through it; chamise, if you can."

Snowbrush comes into a region on the heels of a forest fire and often takes over. Many of the snowbrush areas of the Northwest are almost impenetrable. They are a nightmare to fire fighters. The shrub can't be pulled because it is too deeply rooted. It can't be chopped readily because it is too loose and springy at the base. But it can be snapped off easily—if one knows how—because it is extremely brittle at the ground level. Digging a fire trench through it is a fine art, as the men of the Forest Service know.

Deer like to bed down in snowbrush and they browse somewhat on it. Cattle and horses leave it alone; and it is far down on the menu of an elk. The resinous varnish of its leaves adds to the inflammability of the shrub. The leaves contain volatile aromatic oils which on a warm sunny day give off a pleasant odor. When crushed they have the fragrance of cinnamon.

This July day the snowbrush had been in bloom for most of the way along the trail from Lapover to the North Minam Meadows. Acres of it had surrounded me. Its odor in bloom is more fragrant than the locust or the lilac or any other blossom I recall—sweet and penetrating, subtle and suggestive. Its fragrance seemed to fill the whole canyon of the North Minam. I last saw it when I was on the lip of the Lostine canyon on my way home. It was dusk; 1000 feet or more below me was a vast yawning pit lined with fir and pine and filled with a haze that made it seem miles deep. I stopped Dan for a moment. An evening breeze swept off the mountain from the west. It carried the perfume of the snowbrush with it. That fragrance made this darkening canyon a place of enchantment, a land where only imagination can carry a man.

Coming through Brownie Basin I had heard the wheezy notes of the white-crowned sparrow. Now from some undisclosed thicket came the sweet song of Audubon's hermit thrush—the delicate singer who, as Gabrielson and Jewett once put it, produces "the music of the stars."

These were my memories as I unsaddled Dan at the barn and entered our cabin. Friends had arrived during my absence. They were seated before a roaring fireplace. They gathered around me at the sink as I separated flowers from fish under the glare of a gasoline lantern. In that light they could not see the glory of my botanical collection. I was too tired to describe the beauty of the scenes I had witnessed on my trip. But the memories of this journey were so poignant that I laughed out loud when a friend who prefers a soft chair by the fire said, "So you rode twenty miles of rough trail for six trout?"

Chapter XVI   *Goat Rocks*

"This wind blows right through you!"

Elon and I were standing on Old Snowy of the Goat Rocks—8200 feet high in the Washington Cascades—shouting to each other in a strong northwester. Canyon walls, lined with glacial ice, snow, and rocks, dropped away 3000 feet on two sides of us. We had approached Old Snowy from the north, following a hogback of dark lava rock ranging in width from a few yards to a foot. This hogback rose and fell like any healthy backbone, causing us to gain and then lose altitude. It was a clear August day, and our spirits were high. As we stood on Old Snowy's peak the wind was indeed blowing through us.

Kay Kershaw of the Double K Ranch and Johnny Glenn of Naches had packed us in. We had come from Bumping Lake. We stopped briefly at Fish Lake and camped the first night at Fryingpan Lake, where the evergreens and deep grass were so heavy with rainwater they looked slightly frosted. The next day we dropped over Cowlitz Pass, the divide between the Bumping and the Tieton watershed, and rode all day through clouds of thick mist. We skirted Benchmark and Otto Busch lakes and went past dozens of small ponds that appeared and disappeared through whirling fog.

All during the morning I hoped the mist would rise. Below us on the left, buried in fog a thousand feet or more thick, were Clear Lake and all the valleys and ridges of the Tieton. They were old friends I had not seen from the vantage point of this high trail for thirty years. I was anxious to look at them again and to renew my acquaintance. By early afternoon my wish came true; and the sight I saw made me sorry it had.

Leech Lake was bathed in sunshine. It is a wilderness lake with pure, deep blue water, lying in a thick stand of conifers just above White Pass. But man had desecrated the spot. The Forest Service shelter, a shingled lean-to, had not been cared for. Part of it had been used for fuel; and strewn around it were piles of tin cans, paper, cardboard boxes, and bottles. I wished I could recall the mist that had plagued us all morning, draw its curtain, and hide this scene from view.

We camped that night at Slipper Lake, which is in a small basin just below the top of Hogback Mountain. The heavens were clear; and the sun rose the next day in a sky untouched by clouds. Though I knew the view from the top of Hogback would be unobstructed, I was not prepared for what I saw when the pack train finally wound its way there.

Directly below us was Shoe Lake, a half-mile or more long, in form and size the left shoe of Paul Bunyan. It lies in a sparsely wooded basin rimmed by hills on three sides; and it almost spills over the rim on the south. Directly opposite us to the south, 10 or 15 miles away, were the Goat Rocks. I often had seen these Rocks as a boy from both Darling Mountain and Conrad Meadows. I had climbed Gilbert Peak many times. But those approaches were from the southeast, where the view is more restricted and the angle less advantageous. So my long acquaintance with Goat Rocks had not prepared me for the startling panorama they now presented.

Before us was the full stretch of them, forming 15 or 20 miles of jagged and snowy skyline athwart our path. To the left was Devils Horns—without doubt the head of the devil in prone position. Two great horns at the top of the brow were plain to see; a long, sharp nose dominated the face; there was a twist of evil in the mouth; and the chin seemed to be covered with coarse hair. To the right and slightly closer was Tieton Peak, looking as if it had been designed as a pyramid and then abandoned when half-finished. Then came Gilbert Peak, with its long, black fingers of rock rising like jagged beams in the sky. To its right were the sedate Ives Peak, shaping up by more conventional lines into a soft, rock point, and Old Snowy with a sharp crest rising above powdered shoulders. To the extreme right was the dark wall of Johnson Rock. This jagged knife of skyline dominated the scene. A bit of the crest of Mount Adams could be seen over Old Snowy. But there was no other snow-capped peak to share with Goat Rocks even part of the grandeur.

The view filled me with unrest. I wanted to head at once for those peaks, to camp in the valleys below them and to explore their basins and ridges. The invitation had an urgency at least partly owing to the uncertain weather.

"This is the day to be on Old Snowy," I thought, as I scanned the skies for signs of more fog and rain.

The country between Hogback Mountain and the Goat Rocks is a gargantuan washboard, dropping and rising, dropping and rising over the ridges. It finally ends in McCall Basin, which wise range management of the Forest Service has preserved as one of the loveliest of all mountain meadows. We did not camp there this trip, but climbed the ridge to the northwest and dropped down the other side to West Camp. Here we were at the headwaters of the Clear Fork of the westward-flowing Cowlitz. It is the best basin the northern slopes of Old Snowy offer as lodging to visitors. There is clear cold water and dry wood for man; there is good grass for the horses. Sharp outcroppings of the Goat Rocks tower over the camp.

Elon and I climbed Old Snowy the next day. We had been experimenting with the pressing of wild flowers. We had no regular presser, so we brought along the telephone directories of Los Angeles and Seattle, which proved fairly satisfactory. Each was held by hand-screws between covers of plywood and tied on our saddles. We had collected specimens of flowers and shrubs all the way from Bumping Lake, specimens too numerous to list. We admired most those flowers that were somewhat new to us and rather rare in this region: the yellow monkeyflower from Fish Lake; a species of rose pink pentstemon we found below Cowlitz Pass along a trail lined with blooming western laurel; the delicate white flowers of the tall, leafy Sierra rein orchis from the southernmost meadows of the plateau north of

Leech Lake; the tiny alpine speedwell and the orange-anthered saxifrage which filled the Shoe Lake basin; and a few tiger lilies we saw before we dropped into McCall Basin.

The things we had seen in 60 miles of mountain trails were as nothing compared to what we saw on Goat Rocks. It was the eighth of August, 1948, when we climbed Old Snowy; but the season was a late one. The flowering was at its peak.

The flowers of Goat Rocks probably are unequalled anywhere in the Pacific Northwest for massed effect. Whole basins are carpeted with them—acres upon acres. The Cascades abound with these natural gardens. Blankenship Meadows below Tumac Mountain is one. They will be found on the sides of Rainier, Adams, and Hood, as well as on the Goat Rocks. The sight of 10 or 20 acres of avalanche lilies in bloom is breath-taking. There may be a whole hillside of deer's-tongue, paintbrush, or cinquefoil. An entire basin may be covered with the shooting star or the speedwell. The stream that feeds it may be lined with the yellow monkeyflower as far as the eye can see. These flowers are all fragile, and their colors are delicate. No matter how often I see them I am amazed at their capacity to thrive in this rigorous environment, for the altitude ranges from 4500 to 7000 feet.

Though the wild flowers of the Wallowas equal in variety and beauty those of the Cascades, the massed effects are not so common there. One day Gabrielson and I were discussing the reason for it. He pointed out that lava rock soil was predominant in the Cascades and granitic rock soil in the Wallowas. Lava rock soil has phosphorus and potash in addition to calcium. Moreover, volcanic soils are characteristically dark in color. This gives them heat-absorbing qualities that favor the distribution of flowers to higher altitudes than would otherwise occur.

The theory commends itself because in the Wallowas the meadows that rest on lava rock (which was uplifted when the mountains rose) are the ones that show massed effects of wild flowers comparable to those in the Cascades. Probably, also, the greater rainfall in the Cascades is a factor. The Wallowas are much less humid; their weather is more continental than coastal.

But again, no place for me is richer in memories of massed wild flowers than the Goat Rocks. I remember a trip Doug Corpron and I once took to Gilbert Peak when we were boys. We camped by Warm Lake, where I finally conquered the fear of drowning. The snow had not been off the meadow for more than a few weeks. It was ablaze with flowers.

Most numerous of all were the white and red heather, which seem to like acid or sour soils the best. John Muir called the white heather "hardy" and "adventurous." He wrote of the red heather of the Sierra, "No Highlander in heather enjoys a more luxurious seat than the Sierra mountaineer in a bed of blooming bryanthus." The same may be said of the red heather of the Cascades, whose shrubby and wiry stems extend an invitation to stop and sit. These are not the "bonnie heather" of Scotland, yet they have great charm. Their bell-like blossoms give a blush to an alpine meadow. According to Dayton, the ptarmigan love to eat them.

This day Doug and I saw dozens of other flowers mixed in with the heather. They spread at our feet as rich, thick, and bright as those in the most decorative of Chinese rugs. Doug was studying botany at the time and knew most of them by name. We marked out a spot about three feet square. We got down on our hands and knees and made a count. There were 30 kinds of flowers in that narrow space. I remember only the white and red heather, violets, buttercups, saxifrage, pleated gentian, Indian hyacinth, and dwarf phlox. Hues of pink, yellow, and blue made this high shelf below the gaunt and grim rock seem warm and vibrant. No formal garden was ever prettier.

When Elon and I climbed Old Snowy we collected over 50 specimens of wild flowers, even if the numerous species of a particular genus such as pentstemon, lupine, or monkeyflower be counted only as one each. There were acres of Indian paintbrush on the shelves of Old Snowy, paintbrush of three or four different shades of delicate red that only a master artist could mix. Indian hyacinth and cinquefoil were blended into tapestries. In every basin were streaks of white and red heather as far as the eye could see; there were on every hand splashes of white, pink, yellow, blue, and violet.

But the plants that held us most were the dwarf lupine and dwarf phlox. These were high on Old Snowy above the green basins where the paintbrush flourishes. They grow mostly in the coarse dark sand that covers the high shoulders of Goat Rocks. It was partly, I think, the contrast of the light blue of the lupine and the white and lavender of the phlox against the gray, drab soil that was so impressive. But it was also the fact that these dwarf flowers were matted in patches all along Old Snowy, and almost to its top, like coarsely woven but brilliant scatter rugs laid at random.

The dwarf lupine is one of a large genus that may have 100 or so species. Lupine takes its name from the Latin word for wolf, because it was thought to devour the fertility of the soil. Such is not the fact. These members of the pea or legume family enrich the soil, as farmers knew in the days of ancient Rome. Lupine has been prominent in literature from the time of Virgil. David Douglas was enamored with the genus. Perhaps more than any other flower it caught the eye of those who traveled the Oregon Trail in the early days. Lupines are known as poisonous plants. The roots of some species eaten raw are toxic, but the Indians and some of the early explorers baked or roasted them for food. The seeds of many species are poisonous to stock, especially sheep.

The dwarf lupine (Brewer's lupine) we saw on Old Snowy was true to the lore of the genus. It was flourishing in skimpy soil. But it was not the cause of the poverty of this alpine land. It had the magic power through the nodules on its roots to draw nitrogen from the air and to transmit it to the soil. It was committed to the task of making the ground fertile at 7500 feet. Its light blue gave zest to the project. Its leaflets, spread into palmate circles, made the plants prim and neat in contrast to the rough habitat where they thrived.

The dwarf phlox is perhaps the most intriguing flower I have seen at the very high altitudes of the Cascades. It apparently needs little soil. It thrives in a crack of lava rock. With such a tenuous hold on life, it sends out its thick mat of lavender and white over a rock sur-

face several feet square. It is probably at least first cousin to an xero-
phyte, for it grows in dry, windblown spots. Certainly the high
shoulder of Old Snowy is as near a desert as high mountains can produce, having all the bleakness the hardy dwarf phlox seems to
demand. Gabrielson has said the phlox "hate wet feet." On Old
Snowy they are buried under deep drifts in the winter and catch the
large amount of rain water the clouds spill over Rainier and Adams.
But the coarse sandy soil drains rapidly, producing the poverty of
conditions under which they flourish.

In McCall Basin on the previous day we had seen many signs of
bear and elk. This morning we saw elk tracks almost to the top of
Old Snowy. We saw fresh bear tracks at the lower reaches of a snow
field that runs off toward McCall Basin—tracks almost six inches
wide. There were many signs of mountain goats: tracks, droppings,
and hair.

These rocks are the ancient home of the goat. Not far south, perhaps 40 miles as the crow flies, the Klickitat and the White Salmon
rivers tumble into the Columbia. Lewis and Clark, in October, 1805,
saw in that vicinity Indians wearing robes of the goat, which Clark
described as follows: "the wool of which is long, thick, & corse with
long corse hare on the top of the neck and back something resembling
bristles of a goat, the skin was of white hare, those animals these
people inform me by signs live in the mountains among the rocks,
their horns are Small and Streight."

The Rocks, rich with lichen and moss, apparently are ideal for
these animals. Tender shoots of wild flowers grow far up the peaks.
And there is alpine bunchgrass down around 6000 feet where the
tree line runs.

Many times as a boy I saw these mountain goats silhouetted against
the sky on the ledges above Meade Glacier on Gilbert Peak. The
slightest movement toward them and they would be gone in nervous
jumps over the rim or behind rocks. I have seen billies working their
way across the sides of seemingly impassable cliffs on Tieton Peak,
where a slip would mean a fall of 1000 feet. In late summer I have

looked down from Darling and seen goats grazing with elk on the back of Short and Dirty Ridge some 30 miles from their habitat on Goat Rocks.

On the top of Gilbert Peak is a rock cairn; and in the cairn is a copper capsule placed there by the Cascadians when the peak was dedicated in 1949. The capsule contains a parchment scroll and other historic data relative to the peak. Previously there had been a tin can in the cairn, containing a pencil and notebook where all who climbed were expected to write their names. The book we wrote in as boys is now gone; but a new one, dating from the thirties, has taken its place. A 1948 entry relating to goats indicates that one party saw 30-odd in a herd, and one climber put his camera within a few feet of a billy.

A similar treat almost came to Elon and me the day we climbed Old Snowy. We started from West Camp and had worked our way up perhaps 500 feet, with over 2000 to go. The slope was a stern 60 degrees. I was ahead on hands and knees, scrambling through dense alpine fir at the foot of a cliff we were skirting. I had cleared the fir and had only a few more feet to climb before I could round the end of the cliff. A fleck of sandy dust from behind the cliff whisked by my face. In the moments it took me to look behind the rock, the goat had gone. I knew it was a goat, for in front of me were his tracks, fresh as a pie just out of an oven.

We saw many surprising creatures higher on the slopes. To begin with there was the slate-colored junco. At first we saw this bird standing alone in the snow fields, intent. Then we saw him in a good-sized flock, whirling and wheeling above the snows. We soon discovered what he was looking for: dead flies half as big as the housefly, and dead mosquitoes. The juncos, like the gray-crowned rosy finches, benefit from the refrigeration of the high snow fields and search out frozen insects that have perished on their migrations. Five hundred feet below the crest we saw a chipmunk that flicked his tail and disappeared in a thick mat of prostrate juniper. In the coarse sand by a patch of phlox were big black spiders, very much alive. A host of white butterflies hovered over a light blue mat of dwarf lupine. Then from the great void came a host of grasshoppers, almost 8100 feet in the air on the narrow spinal column of Old Snowy. These grasshoppers, we thought, should be on the shores of Packwood Lake, which we could see far below us to the west, or on the edge of some other water where they could flirt with fish.

The greatest surprise of all was the hummingbird, which we first saw a hundred feet or so below the top. We were virtually on that narrow, peaked spot when it darted at us as a fighter plane attacks a bomber, or a junco a hawk. It came within a few feet of my face, then swooped and disappeared, only to return again and again. She who had gone so far to build a safe home resented even a friendly visit.

We sat half an hour or more on top, watching the slopes on either side for signs of goat, but with no reward. Our ridge tapered towards the north, its farthest nob looking like a hillock, though it was a steep mountain. I often had climbed it to find the obsidian rock the Indians used for arrowheads. The obsidian lay exposed there in the sunlight, its small flaky pieces looking like bright, shiny bits of new asphalt.

Below it to the west was Egg Butte, a lone pillar in a deep canyon. Towering over Egg Butte was Johnson Rock, cold and ominous. At this angle it showed only a cliff of a thousand feet or more, dark and forbidding, filled with deep harsh crevices running virtually straight up and down. This year the snow had filled most of them; and its brilliance made the blackness of the basalt cliff even more imposing. The crags of Ives Peak and Gilbert Peak were now near neighbors to the south.

"What cliffs for expert rock climbers," Elon said. And we fell to talking of our earlier adventures on these peaks.

Elon and I took a difficult route up Gilbert Peak on a later trip in 1948. The easy course follows the righthand edge of Meade Glacier to its head, then climbs a rock escarpment, bears left up a large snow field, turns right at the southeastern base of the peak, and follows the back of a bladed edge of lava rock to the top. The difficult route, which Elon and I chose, kept on the left side of Meade Glacier. This course led laterally across steep snow fields where we should have had

ice axes and alpenstocks, as the snow was more than half turned to
ice. We had to dig toe holds with our shoes for every step we took.
Our ankles and toes ached from the digging. Our pace was that of a
tortoise—no more than a hundred yards an hour. There was no great
danger from falling except the risk of being skinned and bruised from
a 500-foot slide onto the rough ice of Meade Glacier. But we chopped
safe steps across the 400-yard expanse. At last we came to cliffs that
had to be climbed. For these we used a rope. It was here that Elon
went ahead, risking his neck to scale the cliffs. Then he dropped a
rope to me so that I might pull myself up the wall with hands and feet.

But that route borrowed trouble. The climb up Gilbert Peak, like
the one up Old Snowy, need be no more than a stiff jaunt for legs
and heart that are stout. For the mountaineer it is no more than
training ground for peaks like Adams and Rainier.

We found ample room in the early days for horseplay on these
slopes. We would hurry to the top so we could race crazily down.
We would sit at the top of the snow fields, hold our feet up, and slide.
Sometimes we lost control, rolling over and over on the inclines and
ending in some snowbank, wet through. Years later—thirty years later,
in fact—I did the same with my son and Elon and Horace Gilbert.
We came sliding down the edge of Meade Glacier in a shower of
flying snow, shouting and laughing and shrieking. It was still fun.

In our teens we rolled huge rocks off Gilbert Peak. It was thrilling
to watch them go crazily down over the snow. They would disappear
under the brow of some ledge and reappear hundreds of yards farther
along, bouncing and hurtling through space. Once four of us were in
a party that climbed the peak. One lad rolled a boulder over his hand
and cut it badly. He bled profusely and soon fainted. The three of us
stood him on his head, holding his feet in the air until we knew by
the commotion he made that he was once more conscious.

I mentioned this to Elon the day we were on top of Old Snowy.
And he shouted at once, "Rolling rocks *is* fun!" And so the two of us
rolled great rocks onto the fields below and watched them boom
down the pitch—down, down, down until they disintegrated into

small pieces or disappeared as small specks. We made bets as to whose rock would roll the farther. As they raced madly down the mountainside we'd yell and shout: "Come on Downer," "Come on Buster," each cheering his own rock on. That, too, was still fun.

These peaks of the Goat Rocks are not high as Western peaks go; they are around 8200 feet. But no mountain I have been on, not even Adams, creates the same feeling of height. The highest point on Gilbert Peak is like a crow's-nest at the top of a long mast. There is not room for more than a dozen people. Up there one has the feeling that the nest rides at the top of the heavens and rules over the whole domain of the Cascades. The sides drop directly off into steep canyons plastered with glaciers on the east and with rocks on all sides. When one peers over the eastern edge he looks almost straight down a thousand feet or more. It's an eerie feeling in a gale, and the sensation is only slightly less heady when one stands in a gale on the pyramided peak of Old Snowy.

The day Elon and I stood on Old Snowy, the wind came up from the northwest, strong and cool, as if Rainier itself had generated it in some deep ice cavern. It ruffled our hair, billowed our shirts, and fluttered our pantlegs as though we were standing before a giant fan. It flicked specks of sand from the ridge as it licked its cool tongue first one way and then another into the recesses on the leeward side of this backbone of rock. It whined through the broken escarpment of the ridge, whirling madly around each pinnacle or finger of rock.

Patches of prostrate juniper dot the ridge, closely matted, running vinelike over the sandy ground. Dwarf whitebark pine is scattered among the juniper—knee-high trees, 15, 20, or even 30 years old, hanging tenaciously to life and growing almost imperceptibly on the rocky ridge. The wind trilled through this juniper and dwarf pine, first softly, then more loudly; finally in a great crescendo it roared down the snow fields and glaciers of Old Snowy to play a symphony in the distant evergreen slopes of Darling Mountain.

Elon shouted, pointing below, but half his words were blown away as quickly and completely as a handful of sand disappears when

thrown into the ocean. Thinking he might have seen a goat, I un-
holstered my Luger revolver and fired eight times at a boulder some
70 feet below me. I hoped to kick out any animal that might be there,
so Elon could take a picture of it. The sound of the shot was absorbed
in the wind as if the pistol were muffled. There was no echo, just a
faraway explosion that might have come from a distant peak. The
noise and smoke of the gun were gone as quickly as the powdered
dust of the rock I had peppered with lead.

Elon, who had started down the ridge, came back and stood beside me. Throwing his arms toward the sky, he yelled: "How wonderful to feel the wind blowing through you on a high ridge!"

This was the wind that had whipped up the fires the hot lava flows
ignited tens of thousands of years ago. Too, it had cooled the molten
lava as it reached out with its hot tongues and inundated the land
as far as 100, 200, and even 400 miles into Oregon and Idaho. It was
the wind that had carried the chill of glaciers   gion when
ice crept down from the north to fill the valle   ent of the
redman came floating down on its wings to t   eaver, the
mammoth, and the camel thousands of years be   was born.

I leaned against the wind and talked with Elo   d was not
only tireless, it was timeless. Old Snowy, which   ked so enduring and eternal, was young compared with th   geological
time Old Snowy was indeed only the creation   brief moments. By that standard Elon and I were like wi   l the wind
whisked into oblivion. We were indeed as temp   fleeting as
shouts floating down deep corridors of the sky a   once in a
vast void.

As I stood in the cold gale peering into the steep canyons, the
froth of life seemed to blow away.

I thought of vain men, pacing up and down on the platform,
waving their arms, filling the air waves with their noisy complaints.

I thought of clever men gaining advantages by trick and cunning.
I thought of men who by manipulation got verdicts and judgments
and wealth they did not deserve.

I said those things to Elon and went on to say that nature was a great leveler. Men fighting a blizzard on the plains or an angry storm at sea at once became equal. The same was true when they walk the trails or climb mountains. The fact that a person lived on one side of the railroad tracks rather than on the other made no difference. Poverty, wealth, accidents of birth, social standing, race were immaterial. When man is on his own, mother's accent, father's prestige, grandma's wealth don't count. Neither does the turn of a phrase or a perfect voice. Tricks and boasting are of no account in surviving the adversities of nature.

Old Snowy has no deceit or cunning. It welcomes and receives man on his merits. It aims neither to destroy him nor to flatter his ego. It is as genuine and as impartial as the northwester. It is a symbol of real freedom, of real equality. "Freedom and equality are the ideals that America represents," I said. "That is the symbolism of Old Snowy in a world where infinite evil works hard to get permanent footing."

Such was the lecture I delivered on the high ridge of Goat Rocks. Then like all orators I turned to my audience for approval. Elon was the most friendly, attentive one a speaker ever had. He shouted at once, "Right you are."

Then I thought of all the beehives of intrigue every nation has. These are the factories where endless energy is expended in whittling down one man or woman, in building up another. Ambitions are encouraged and generated. The strength of one man becomes the source of insecurity of another. A campaign to destroy the dominant one starts. Destruction of a man becomes a profession. Subtle propaganda spreads through receptions, cocktail parties, and dinners. It seeps into columns and editorials. It gets into broadcasts on the radio and into news stories. The business of destroying a character becomes a full-time job. The business of building up a man also becomes a profession; heroes are manufactured by those who make that their business.

I remembered the man who was paid $100,000 to fill the papers with smears on me when I was in the midst of my Wall Street reform program. I remembered sly, clever little men who planted editorials here and there to discredit their competitors, who tried to manipulate public officials, who even sought to influence courts. I remembered those who whispered that F.D.R. was insane—that being crippled he was only half a man.

I remembered men who pleaded in court with great feeling and compassion for human liberties and freedom—men whose voice was the voice of humanity, but whose hand was the hand of a group of exploiters.

All that, I thought, is the froth of life that would disappear on the wings of the northwester on Old Snowy. It would be gone as quickly and as silently as a shout in this gale. The wind would whip away intrigue and scheming. It would clear the air of the vain boasts of men. The petty politician would stand naked; and in his nakedness his character would be revealed. The peddler of gossip would be deprived of his pen and his smirk; he would stand whimpering and friendless. Schemes would fall helplessly from men's lips on this rocky ridge.

Man stands here as I imagine he stands on Judgment Day— naked and alone, judged by the harmony of his soul, by his spiritual strength, by the purity of his heart.

I was brought back to earth by Elon. "Daydreaming?"

"Yes," I boomed. "Dreaming of all the phonies I have known whom I would like to see up here on these peaks all alone."

"Do they live in Washington, D.C.?"

"A lot of them."

"Well, I have a few pet ones right here in the Yakima Valley. Let's start on them and—" The rest was whisked away in the gale. We laughed and turned our faces to the narrow hogback below us that was the trail to camp.

When I reached the lowest ridge from which I could see Old Snowy I turned, clicked my heels together, threw my shoulders back, and did what a hard-boiled sergeant at the Presidio in 1918 had taught me to do before a superior: I saluted.

Chapter XVII   Jack Nelson

JACK NELSON is as much a part of Bumping Lake as the Federal
reservoir. The reservoir, impounding 38,000 acre-feet of water, was
the first of six built by the Bureau of Reclamation to service 400,000
acres in the Yakima Valley. It was finished in 1910. Jack was its
first gatetender, a job he held until he retired in 1946.

Jack was born in New York City of parents born in Scotland.
He is stocky, white haired with warm blue-green eyes. By training he
was a pharmacist. At the time the reservoir at Bumping Lake was
being constructed he worked in a drugstore in Yakima. He went up
to the lake and applied for the job of gatetender but was turned
down. Only a married man would be considered.

"Give me a week," said Jack. The Bureau agreed. That Saturday
Jack rode the weekly stage from Bumping Lake to Yakima—65
miles. He was looking for a wife. He found her. She was a cook in
a restaurant in Yakima. She was the lovable Kitty who came overland from Nebraska as a youngster and lived not far below Grand
Coulee Dam where her parents homesteaded. Jack and Kitty were
married and back at Bumping Lake the next Friday. Jack got the job
of gatetender. Thirty-seven years later he told me, "We came up here
on our honeymoon, Kitty and I, and we've been on it ever since."

Since retirement in 1946, Jack and Kitty have remained at Bumping Lake during the summer and most of the winter. They have
cabins they rent. The cabins and a dining room were built in the
early years, somewhat in self-defense. Jack and Kitty long have been
known for their hospitality. Their cabin was near the road's end.
There the trails took off into the high Cascades. It was only natural
for one to stop at the Nelson's cabin, the last contact with civilization along the frontier.

Kitty had a cup of coffee and doughnuts or coffee cake for every-one. That was the way she first greeted me, in 1912 or 1913. I came up the road in a hard rain, headed for Fish Lake. I left my horseshoe pack on the Nelson's back porch and stood in the kitchen, dripping water on the clean floor, while I sipped Kitty's hot coffee out of a big, thick cup of white china. Jack sat by the stove, made light of my discomfiture, told of the glories of the mountains, and spoke of the exciting adventure of walking the trails and discovering the secrets of the woods.

Somewhat the same thing happened to every traveler who went that way. If it was mealtime, an extra plate would go on the table for him. Jack is most generous. "He'd give a friend anything he had," said one admirer. "He'd give away everything but the lake. He couldn't give that away because it belongs to Uncle."

Kitty's cooking and Jack's conversation were irresistible. The lists of acquaintances broadened into lists of friends and these friends were unwittingly on the way to eating Jack and Kitty out of their sustenance. So the cabins went up and the Nelsons remained solvent.

Jack's job in the summer was to operate and maintain the reservoir gates and keep the outlets free of driftwood. Summer and winter his responsibility was to maintain 23 miles of telephone line. He also kept the weather records, including snow measurements.

Bumping Lake is a wet spot. The average annual precipitation is about 44 inches. The average snowfall is 204 inches. The heaviest snowfall was 40 feet in 1915–16. One February, during a 36-hour period 62 inches of snow fell. The blizzards that sweep the canyon are dangerous to anyone caught in them. Sub-zero weather is common, the average minimum being 5 degrees above. As Jack often said, this was "no place for a sissy." The closest neighbors were 23 miles distant. From November to April, Jack and Kitty were on their own. At such a time the telephone was most important, for it was their only contact with the world. Their mail was left with the neighbors 23 miles away. The letters were read to Jack and

Kitty over the phone. If they wanted to send a letter, they telephoned the message to these neighbors, who wrote it for them.

As a boy I heard Jack's stories of the winters at Bumping Lake. There were tales of hardship and adventure. One I will never forget: One January Jack had gone down the road 16 or 17 miles to repair a telephone-line break. He finished the job and at night returned to his halfway cabin at American River, 11 miles below Bumping Lake. It was still snowing the next morning, so Jack telephoned Kitty and told her he couldn't reach the lake that day. Three feet of fresh snow had fallen on top of three or four feet of old snow. Jack decided to break trail with his skis as far as he could and return to the halfway cabin that night. But he was able to travel only a few miles and back that day, for the snow and wind never ceased. It looked as if he'd be snowed in for a week.

Jack then had a brain storm. He telephoned Kitty to close the gates of the reservoir that night. Bumping River would be dry by the next morning and Jack figured he could go up the river bed on foot. That night Kitty closed the gates. Next morning Jack skied the few miles over the trail he had broken the previous day, stacked his skis, and started up the river bed. This was about 7 o'clock. He discovered that 9 or 10 miles below the dam the water was not entirely out of the river. His feet were soon in it, for the exposed rocks and gravel were coated with glare ice and the going was treacherous. Jack traveled steadily but carefully, often getting into water up to his knees. "That was when my hair would nearly raise my hat off," Jack once told me.

He was soon chilled through by the icy water. The wind whipped snow into his face. He was numb. He had to stoop to the gale to walk. He dared not stop, for he knew he would freeze to death before he could ever start a fire. He took 8 hours to go 8 miles. He was then at Goose Prairie, 3 miles below Bumping Lake, and it was darkening. Kitty would be worried, so Jack in spite of his great weariness increased his pace and fought off the drowsiness and cold that threatened to enfold him. Soon he saw footprints in the river bed that Kitty had made earlier in the day when she had been down the river looking for him. He found skis and poles stacked for him under a tree. And just as he reached them Kitty appeared with a lantern she planned to hang there as a beacon.

When Jack tells the story today, he is filled with a great emotion. Once I commented on it. He said, "When Kitty and I met that evening in the blizzard we fell into each other's arms and cried, unashamed. Our meeting put to shame the romance of any embrace that ever followed the minister's words: 'I now pronounce you man and wife.' Our love was never more devout than in that moment of rescue."

"But Jack, you had enough experience to know that the river route would be treacherous and dangerous," I said.

"I know," said Jack. Then after a silence he added, "Shows what a man will do to get home to a lady named Kitty."

There is the New England imprint on Kitty even to a slight twang in her voice. Her features are sharp. There is friendliness in her hazel eyes. Her clear skin shows the touch of many suns. Her high forehead and silver hair give her a patrician look. She is a person of few words, but those are always to the point. She is an expert fisherman. She knows the trout and seldom fails to get her quota. She likes best to go to the high lakes of the Cascades and sleep on their shores. Jack calls her "one of the oldest living campfire girls." She has long been hardened to the life of the woods. One day at Cougar Lake she and her companions saw seven bears. Kitty chased three of them out of camp in the early morning.

Usually Kitty had to do her fishing at Bumping Lake. She would fish from a boat an hour every day, if she could.

"Did she always catch fish?" I asked Jack.

"Almost always. And when she didn't, she'd always have an interesting report of what she had seen."

"For example?" I pressed.

"An osprey or fish hawk putting on his diving act—hundreds of violet-green swallows performing with graceful swoops."

Kitty is a woodsman in every respect. Snowshoes and skis are her familiars. Many times she has gone down the river on skis alone.

And now, at the age of 71, she still covers the trails of the Cascades on horseback. To this day she and Jack ski the 12 miles from Bumping Lake to American River in the dead of winter. Early in 1949 they made the trip in five hours, double the time it took them in their thirties but still a record for people in their seventies.

Bumping Lake was a lonely spot during the winter. But Jack is not one to eat beans and hibernate. His mind always has been active. He has broad intellectual horizons. A catalogue of his library would suggest that the owner was a professor of history or political science or perhaps of English literature. There are Adam Smith and Stuart Mill; all of Shakespeare, Wordsworth, Dickens, Thackeray; the Harvard Classics; Baker's life of Woodrow Wilson; Toynbee; American history books, particularly history of the Pacific Northwest and chronicles of Lewis and Clark; books on trees and shrubs and flowers; books on Indians. Jack is an omnivorous reader. He would hold up his end of a conversation in almost any drawing room I am acquainted with from Yakima to Park Avenue.

When Jack had a book in his hand and Kitty at his side, he was happy. The winters were long but not boresome. It had only one monotony and that was food. The meat was pork in a barrel. The only green vegetable was cabbage. Once I asked Jack about that diet. He replied, "You know, by the first of March I'd be willing to cut a man's throat for a green onion."

Jack is a student and a philosopher. He has seen enough of the footsteps-of-spring and the larkspur, the avalanche lily and Indian paintbrush, snowslides and sunsets, blizzards and hummingbirds, and all the raw material out of which the great universe is fashioned to know that man does not have many of the answers to the secrets of life. And so he can trip an upstart with a gentle question or inspire a sensitive and inquisitive lad with an offhand suggestion of mysteries unseen or unsolved. Jack's first article of faith is that there is a Force or Being wiser and more potent than man. Jack often has been called the Hermit of Bumping Lake; but the Sage of Bumping Lake is more fitting.

I knew him first as a storyteller. He is not a garrulous man. At times, however, he will hold forth for hours, spinning tales in a way that would compete with storytellers of any age. He is a Scot and at times a dour one. But he was expansive more often than not, and from these talks I built up a supply of yarns of the Cascades.

Jack talks with childlike simplicity. There is not a trace of warning in his face or voice as he spins on. I liked to think all of his tales were true. But Kitty would say, "You don't believe everything he says."

Fascinating characters played roles in his tales: Uncle Tom Fife, Wildcat Matheson, Beaver Bill, Bacon Rind Dick, Pete Cresci. There was Six-Fingered Pete who, indeed, had twelve fingers and twelve toes. These were flesh-and-blood people who frequented the mountains. One or two Jack "would not trust with last year's calendar." But most of them were warm and lovable characters. And I felt I knew them all from the stories spun around them.

I remember best Jack's story of Charlie the Swede. Charlie was watchman on certain mining properties at Gold Hill on the American River. He went to Yakima and spent all his money on a big drunk. As he was recovering from his spree he started home for Gold Hill. It was winter, and after he reached American River his travel was on snowshoes.

Charlie had a trapper friend, Jack Campbell, who ran his trap line up American River. So he decided to inspect the traps as he went along and save his friend a trip. The first trap held a lynx. Charlie killed the lynx, reset the trap, threw the lynx over his shoulder, and continued on his way. He shortly came to a second trap with a lynx in it. He killed it also, threw it over his shoulder, and pushed on. When he reached the third trap, it also held a lynx.

"Wonder if I'm seeing things," Charlie mused. "Maybe that whiskey got the best of me."

But so far as he could tell the lynx was real and alive. So he killed it and put the three of them over his back and mushed along. In a while he came to the fourth trap. He could hardly believe his eyes, for it too had a lynx.

"Now I know I've been drinking too much," said Charlie. So, squeamishly, he hung up the three lynx he had killed and went on to Gold Hill, leaving in the trap the fourth one he thought he had seen.

A few days later he met Jack Campbell. He told him the story and ended by saying, "You know, Jack, I'd have swore I killed three lynx. But when I saw the fourth one in your trap spitting fire at me, I knew I had the D.T.'s. I gotta lay off that whiskey. It really had me."

When Jack Campbell got to the traps, he found three lynx hanging in a tree and a fourth in a near-by trap.

As he finished the tale Jack Nelson said to me, "Shows what a man's imagination can do to him in the woods."

I believe it was Jack who first told me of Wawa, the giant mosquito. Kuykendall suggests that the finding of the bones of the pterodactyl in this region may have been the origin of the legend. (The History of the Pacific Northwest). In any event, Wawa was bigger than a man and had a strong, swordlike bill three or four feet long. Anyone who came near him was doomed. He would run his bill through his victim and suck out the blood. He had killed so many people that Coyote, benefactor of the Indians, became alarmed and decided to destroy him. One cold day Coyote went to Wawa's lodge and asked whether he might build a fire for Wawa's comfort. Wawa, suspecting no trick, invited Coyote in. Coyote built a huge fire, then quickly smothered it, filling the lodge with smoke. Wawa lay down on the floor in order to breathe. Coyote at once split open his head with a stone knife. Out of Wawa's head came a swarm of mosquitoes of the size we know today. Since then the mosquito has not been able to stand smoke. Thus Coyote not only rid the land of a vicious enemy of the people; he also taught them the best protection against mosquitoes is a smudge.

But according to Jack the smudge is good only against the current crop of mosquitoes. It is of little avail against those that winter at Bumping Lake. Give a mosquito a couple of winters in that hardy climate and he comes out highly aggressive, immune to insecticides, trained in the art of using a smudge as a smoke screen for attack, equipped with a bill that has a point as sharp as diamonds, and with armor that will survive all but a direct hit behind the ears. Jack had many a rough night with these veterans. He likes to tell about the time he was asleep in the tent where he had his bed for 35 years. A flock of these hardbitten insects invaded. Jack knew that orthodox methods of getting rid of them were of no avail. So he arose, lighted a candle, and stalked them. When he maneuvered one into a corner of the tent he would quickly put the flame to it. There was no other sure-fire way. In this manner Jack stalked and killed 12 in 30 minutes. There was one mosquito remaining. He was the granddaddy of them all. He was so wise and agile it took Jack a full 10 minutes to corner him. Jack finally maneuvered him into the top corner where the walls of the tent met the ridge. Jack was about to use the torch, when quick as a flash the mosquito turned and blew out the candle.

The whole region from Bumping Lake to Fish Lake is ideal for the mosquito. It is damp and moist during most of the summer. But better still is the plateau above Bumping and to the south— the plateau of many lakes, the marshy meadow land that Tumac Mountain overlooks. Among these is the beautiful Blankenship Meadows, rich in wild flowers and decorated with the loveliest balsam fir of the whole Cascades. On the early maps Blankenship Meadows is called Mosquito Valley. And the name was most appropriate, for here the hardiest of all the Cascade mosquitoes grew and thrived.

According to Jack they are the best breeding stock in the region. Some person with a devilish mind carried some of them down into the valley, crossed them with woodpeckers, and produced what Jack calls a swamp angel. It has the woodpecker's size and skill and a mosquito's temperament and appetite. The swamp angel comes out when it rains and attacks with a vengeance.

From Jack I had my first stories of Paul Bunyan and the Blue Ox. Puget Sound was dug by Paul Bunyan to be the grave of Babe, the ox. The Babe was sick and no medicine would cure him. Paul was sad as he dug the big hole. The dirt he threw up became the Cascade Range. He was almost finished when the Babe got into a supply of wood alcohol and epsom salts and suddenly revived. The Babe rose to his feet, still attached to Paul's bunkhouse and hot-cake griddle, and went off lunging and snorting. The hot-cake griddle hit the Cascades at the place where the Columbia River now runs and dug out the Columbia gorge.

Goose Prairie, three miles below Bumping Lake, is a natural meadow of a few hundred acres set in a thick forest of pine and fir. In June it is ablaze with color. Acres of lupine paint huge streaks of blue across it. There are lesser streaks of yellow and white and red. At such a time Goose Prairie is richer and more varied in color than any of man's creations.

The Goose Prairie flower I saw as a boy that I remember best is the vanilla leaf—or sweet-after-death. The leaves when drying do indeed have a sweet odor, for they contain some coumarin. Its slender cluster of white flowers stands high on a single stem that rises above one leaf divided into three broad leaflets like the strawberry. They have no petals or sepals, only naked stamens and pistils. The plant is sometimes called the butterfly, for when the center leaf is removed the two side ones resemble a huge butterfly with wings spread. The plant carpets the region around Goose Prairie. It is found in the shade along the road as well as in the meadow. It is the finest of all mountain grass or leaves in which to wrap trout.

Goose Prairie was the homestead of Tom Fife and his father John who laid their claim in 1886. They came to this country from Fifeshire, Scotland in 1866, and first worked in the coal mines of Pennsylvania, later moving to Wyoming where they prospected for a while. Then followed two years' work on the Mormon Temple at Salt Lake City. They pushed west, came up the Yakima Valley, passed through the town itself, and headed up the Naches Canyon, where the quiet and cool of the fir and the pine beckoned. They soon came to Goose Prairie and at once laid claim to it as a homestead. Not many years later Tom christened it for a lone goose that visited the meadow one evening and stayed the night.

Today Goose Prairie has a store and a post office, and is most famous for the Double K Ranch where Kay Kershaw and Pat Kane give dudes of all degrees a warm welcome, and show them on skis, on horseback, or afoot the glories of the Cascades. The Boy Scouts fine camp at its northwest edge was a gift from Tom Fife.

Tom loved Goose Prairie with all the love man is able to bestow on land. From the beginning it was a symbol of freedom for him and his father. Here the grass is knee-high in June. The air is pure and clear. Old Scab, Buffalo, and Baldy watch over the meadow from the south. At dusk there are deer on its edge. Scotch bluebells reign. There are rainbow in the Bumping River, whose clear waters carry even in midsummer the chill of snow and ice. Here a man can be free. He can trap and hunt and fish and run stock if he wishes. There is no bell or whistle to summon him to the mines.

Tom built a small 7-by-9 cabin with a fireplace at one end where the cooking was done. He had but one book, and that was a collection of Bobby Burns' poems. Tom lived there most of each year until his death in 1922. When Tom's father died in 1890, Tom made a coffin of tamarack and dug the grave. But the coffin was too heavy to be lowered alone, so Tom walked 23 miles to get a man to help him place the casket in the grave. Today Tom lies buried beside his father.

I saw Tom Fife many times when I was a boy. He seemed a gruff man, but those who knew him say he was warm and friendly and understanding. According to Jack Nelson, his heart was "as big as a frying pan." One day Tom returned from Yakima with a badly needed pair of shoes. Some miners stopped at his cabin on their way out prospecting. Tom was a prospector. He had mining claims at Gold Hill on the American River, and on the Rattlesnake. None of them ever panned out, but he was sentimental about them, naming the first one Blue Bell in memory of his native land. Tom knew the ways of prospectors, their problems and their adversities, and the long trail down which these prospectors were headed. When he saw that the shoes of one of the party were virtually gone, Tom presented this unknown character with the new shoes.

By commercial standards Tom was not a success, for he probably made but a few hundred dollars a year. Even his cougar traps baited with chickens did not work. But there was always a pot of beans on the stove; and any wayfarer was welcome to share them.

Jack likes to tell about the Christmas dinner he and Kitty had at Tom's cabin. They had been down to the American River to fix up a ramshackle log cabin as a halfway house for winter use. When they had cleaned it, plugged up ratholes, and put in a supply of firewood, they loaded their packs and started the return on skis to Bumping Lake. They were weary by the time they had traveled the nine miles to Goose Prairie. Uncle Tom stuck his head out of his cabin and called to them to come and "break bread" with him. A big black pot hung over the fire, steaming an odor that was most appetizing. Tom with pride removed the cover and told his guests to take a look.

"It was an eyeful," says Jack. "There, full life size, floated several pine squirrels with heads, eyes, and toe nails intact."

"Red squirrel mulligan," is what Tom called it. They ate it with fresh scones and coffee.

"No Christmas dinner ever tasted better," says Jack.

Kitty adds, "Let's say none was ever more unique."

Shortly before his death Tom decided he must do something for his adopted country. The utmost expression of his affection could be made only by a gift of that which he prized more than anything else— Goose Prairie. But how could Goose Prairie be useful to America? One day an idea came to him. It was a wonderful idea. He must tell someone. So he raced the three miles to Bumping Lake to break the news to his closest friend, Jack Nelson. He burst in on Jack, breathless.

"I've got it! I've got it! I know what I can do for my country. I will give a part of Goose Prairie to the Boy Scouts. They can learn to be men up here." The old man choked up, with tears in his eyes. He could say no more. Thus did a mountain meadow reach deep into the heart of a Scot.

Fifes Peaks lie north of Goose Prairie. They are sheer cliffs with jagged points rising above a ridge. They stand erect and confident and proud like Tom Fife himself.

One day I was walking the shores of Bumping Lake with Jack Nelson. He was showing me the trees, which are to him "the greatest of all inanimate things." Bumping Lake lies too high for ponderosa pine, but somehow a couple of them do grow there. Red and white fir flourish in that area; so does the balsam fir. The western hemlock, mountain or black hemlock, tamarack, Engelman's spruce, yellow cedar, lodgepole and whitebark pine, and yew trees are there. Jack touched each one fondly.

We stopped by a balsam fir that pointed spirelike to the sky. He commented on its beauty and we admired it. He turned to me and spoke movingly of his friend Tom Fife, a man he loved and admired above all others. And he ended by saying, "Well and often do I remember when Tom called my attention to some bit of beauty—a dash of color on the hillside, a shapely tree, a flower. He spoke with such reverence that anyone could readily sense the depth of inner feeling that went into his expression of adoration for nature."

There was a quaver in Jack's voice as he spoke. His eyes were moist. He was silent for a while. In a few minutes he said, "You know, Bill, some people have urged me to paint the beauties of nature that are here. After a fresh snow the hills are clear cut and the trees are bent with a burden of white. Then Mother Nature invariably wears blue and has most of her diamonds on. In the fall the tamarack and willow and Douglas maple set the woods on fire with color. There is the beauty of an electric storm with Nelson Peaks standing illuminated for a split second against a pitch-black sky. There is an evening when a soft mist floats over the lake, gradually blotting everything from view."

"Why don't you try to paint some of those scenes?"

"I can't paint nature, Bill. I can only paint men and women."

I walked straight into his trap. "I didn't know you painted men and women, Jack."

"Sure I do. 'Men' over one door and 'Women' over another."

That is Jack's way of escape when some great wave of sentiment threatens to overpower him.

Jack directed the work at a CCC camp in the Cascades during the thirties. He had charge of a group of young men shipped out of the eastern industrial centers, lads who had known only the morsels of life. If they did not snatch and grab, they would go without. With cunning and deceit, like Coyote, they survived only by outwitting others. Life for them was an appalling insecurity, with the result that they developed aggression, pessimism, distrust of every living soul. They had never known, since they left their mothers' arms, human kindness and warmth. People had always barked and snarled. Friendliness was a stranger. Jack tells of one chap by the name of Farrel, who had been a window washer in Brooklyn. One day the strap that was holding him broke and he fell four stories into the courtyard of an apartment house.

"That didn't knock me out," said Farrel. "Just dazed me. But it left me some ugly scars."

"What happened?" asked Jack.

"Well," replied Farrel, "I naturally did some groaning. What burned me more than anything was a woman on the second floor. She poked her head out the window and yelled, 'My husband works at night and tries to sleep in the daytime and I want you to quit making so darn much noise down there.' "

Jack saw a transformation take place in these men. Gentler qualities appeared. Aggression diminished. When pitted against nature they became mellow. There is no place for cunning or deceit when man is against the forces of gravity or has a Douglas fir to contend with.

"Many phases of CCC were too expensive," says Jack. "Some were waste. But the fact that the boys were kept as Americans was worth the cost. Otherwise they would have been leaning on the corner lampposts or sitting in criminal courts. The Seabees benefited later from the CCC training of these men, and the Forest Service program was advanced at least 25 years. The durable benefits to the nation and the individual boys were immeasurable."

This assignment Jack prized. For he could mold men and their characters in the deft way his hands could guide the sapling tamarack so it would grow 200 feet straight toward the sky.

Jack at some time may have been on a horse, but for years he has gone afoot. He explained it by saying a man on foot sees more and learns more than a man on horseback. The morning's newspaper of the woods is indeed more legible to the man afoot. The mark of the bear, cougar, deer, elk, coyote, or porcupine that preceded him are plain to see. Miner's lettuce or spring beauty or the tender scarlet gilia might be missed by the man on horseback. Even the flycatcher's nest could go unnoticed, or the caddis hatch on the stream, or the flight of the eagle through the woods, or the coral mushroom.

While writing this chapter I received word that Jack had broken three records: he had hunted deer, ridden a horse, and slept in a sleeping bag. Primordial man has strange quirks in Jack. A deer is too much a thing of beauty to hunt. As for sleeping bags—well, they are too civilized. "In the woods I always leaned against a tree for sleeping," said Jack.

I once asked him what he would do differently if he had his term of years at Bumping to serve over again.

"Up here we have always been 65 miles from a dentist; and for many years a good share of that mileage could be covered only by foot. If I had it all to do over again, I would have all my teeth pulled at the start. Then, if any of them started to ache, I'd ship them down by parcel post for repair."

Two years after Jack retired I drove up from the Double K Ranch to call. He was in a happy mood. He talked for hours, telling old stories and entertaining me with varied yarns from his rich folklore. Then for several minutes there was quiet. I asked him what final paragraph or sentence he would write about his long life in the mountains with Kitty. He reflected for several minutes and then he said: "Bill, people can't live as long as Kitty and I have under these peaks without knowing there is some Supernatural Force that rules over us all."

After a long pause he continued, "The birds of Bumping Lake show His amazing handiwork."

Then he told me of his study of birds. He had classified 63 different kinds that he had seen at the lake in the summer. These covered a notable range: ouzel, junco, heron, pipit, thrush, swan, loon, jay, grouse, tanager, finch, wren, robin, sandpiper, killdeer, kingfisher, crow, swallow, siskin, chickadee, raven, bluebird, dove, vireo, eagle, vulture, grosbeak, woodpecker, flicker, owl, sapsucker, hawk, warbler, blackbird, crossbill, nuthatch, hummingbird, sparrow, duck—all as neatly classified as Ira Gabrielson or Stanley Jewett would have managed it.

I asked him about birds that are winter residents at Bumping Lake. He had seen more than 30, including the ouzel, belted kingfisher, blue heron, merganser, winter wren, black capped chickadee, chestnut-backed chickadee, Steller's jay, Canada jay, magpie, raven, rosy finch (the ones that love a building made of logs with the bark on), pileated woodpecker, red-shafted flicker, red-breasted sapsucker, white tailed ptarmigan, great gray owl, Cooper's hawk, sharp-skinned hawk, Clark's nutcracker, native pheasant or ruffed grouse, Franklin's grouse or fool hen, blue grouse, crow, western goshawk.

Jack spoke of the birds with tenderness. Top billing went to the water ouzel or American dipper. It needs open water but there is usually some throughout the winter at Bumping Lake.

"There's no need to feed it in the wintertime," said Jack. "It walks deliberately into water and disappears without effort, using its wings to fly under water." This bird over and again had dived for my dry fly when I cast for trout in the Bumping River years ago. I asked him why he had such great affection for it. "Bill, it can sit and teeter on an icy boulder on the coldest of days and sing its heart out to you. One loses all thought of discomfort when this prima donna gives her music."

The number-two spot, according to Jack, goes to the winter wren, a tiny bundle of energy and rarely still. "The volume of its music always makes me stare when I see the midget that is producing it."

During the winter Jack gets on intimate terms with the chickadees and Canada jays or camp robbers. They sit on his hand or hat and eat their daily ration. The nest of the Canada jay has long piqued his curiosity, but he has never found one. He has seen these birds in March gathering moss, bits of cloth, cotton, and so on, and leaving for higher elevations. Jack has tried to follow them to their nests without success. They disappear from Bumping Lake for two months or more. Those that return seem to be adults.

I asked about the summer birds. "The Beau Brummells of the summer are the western tanager and the western evening grosbeak. It's a wonderful sight to see up to 250 grosbeaks in one flock in the fall of the year."

It's the pileated woodpecker that gives Jack and Kitty the most company throughout the year. "He's got a wingspread of two feet," said Jack. "And he's handsome." He went on to say that this bird is one of a family making a living with their heads. The woodpecker is the first one up in the morning, followed closely by the robin.

"His sledge hammer blows on a dead tree on a frosty morning can be heard a mile. I've seen him become so interested in digging for worms and grubs in rotten stumps that I've walked to within five feet of him."

After a pause Jack added, "Noisy neighbor, this woodpecker. But I wouldn't be without him."

It was the 10th of January, 1947, and 12 degrees above zero. Jack's successor at the reservoir, C. R. Ford, saw a strange bird sitting on the dam at the lake. He walked to it, took it in his hand, and carried it in to Jack, who recognized it as an oyster catcher. It lived only a short while.

"That bird," said Jack, "was 135 miles from salt water. The weather had been foggy for a week on the coast and this black oyster catcher had become bewildered, crossed the main divide of the Cascades, and landed exhausted on the dam."

Jack finished talking of his birds with this: "Years ago someone wrote that birds are little feathered bits of God. Nothing more appropriate could be said."

Outside the cabin we stood looking to the south. The sun was low, painting the edges of clouds in brilliant colors. Jack touched my arm and pointed to Nelson Peaks. They were touched with fiery red that flamed only for a moment. Then the curtain was drawn and Nelson Peaks disappeared.

The sun went down and we returned to his cabin to sit by his fireplace watching the sparks of pine logs go up the chimney. At last he said:

"When man can look at mountain peaks with a deep sense of his own littleness and still have faith—

"When man can learn how to make friends with others and how to keep friends with himself—

"When man can hunt birds and deer without a gun—

"When the moonlight on a mountain lake or a snowcapped peak breaking through storm clouds brings calm and peace like the thought of one much loved and long dead—

"When man knows how to pray, how to hope, how to love—

"When man can find the time to stop and look at the grass and trees and mountainsides and come to know them and call them friends—

"When man can see the handiwork of the Creator in the bluebells, spring beauty, and avalanche lilies and in the water ouzel, winter wren, and woodpecker—

"When man can feel the sense of eternity even in the wind that blows from the northwest off Rainier—

"Then man has found contentment and harmony and peace."

That is indeed what I learned when I sat as a boy at the feet of Jack Nelson in the wilderness at Bumping Lake over thirty years ago.

Chapter XVIII   *Roy Schaeffer*

The last words Franklin D. Roosevelt spoke to me were "How are Thunder and Lightning?" This happened at a Sunday luncheon at the White House three weeks before his death. Luncheon was over and he had transferred to his wheel chair. The attendant was wheeling him away when he turned and asked the question.

Thunder and Lightning are horses. Thunder belongs to my son Bill and Lightning to my daughter Millie. We acquired them in a curious way.

Back in northeastern Oregon, my wife and I were building our tamarack log cabin on the Lostine in the Wallowas. Roy Schaeffer, who runs a dude ranch near by, was in charge of the project. Fonzy Wilson, whose work with ax and saw is superb, was head carpenter. The walls and roof were finished, but no windows or doors were in and the floor had not been laid. At the end of a July day we were sitting on nail kegs, listening to Roy tell of the Nez Perce Indians who had the Wallowas for their ancestral home. Roy revered Chief Joseph, whose land had been wrested from him in one of the nation's least honorable undertakings. While Roy talked, a stranger came down the path through the woods. His Levis and his walk showed him to be a cowboy. Roy seemed to know him, for the two spoke. The stranger joined us but sat in silence for the better part of an hour.

Then my son, who was about ten, came up from the river where he had been fishing. At the first break in our conversation the stranger turned to him and said, "Got a horse, sonny?"

Bill shook his head.

"Like to have a horse?"

Bill's eyes lighted. "Sure would."

"I've got a horse for you, sonny."

Perhaps from some Scotch impulse I spoke up, hating at once what I asked: "How much, stranger?"

"How much? I just gave the boy a horse."

We went down to get the horse in a few days. He was a three-year-old chestnut, racing and snorting with tail high, on the range north of Wallowa. The stranger was Dan Oliver, and the horse we named Thunder.

Several weeks after Dan gave Thunder to Bill, Millie came up to the cabin for a few days where Roy, Fonzy, and I were still working. At the end of one day I built a campfire outside and cooked supper for the children. During dinner Roy turned to Millie and asked, "Did Bill tell you about his horse?"

Millie is the horseman of the family. She can ride like an expert and hold up in any competition. She has an understanding of horses given to few. Knowing them, she is unafraid and is their master. The idea that her younger brother had a horse when she had none was preposterous. If there was a horse in the family, it had to be her horse. She turned to me:

"Bill hasn't got a horse, has he, Dad?" And there was a note in her voice that asked me to tell her that Bill certainly did not have a horse.

But I nodded, "Yes, he has a horse."

The effect was worse than if I had slapped her. She burst into tears and sobbed, "Why does he have to have a horse when I want one?"

So I told her of Dan Oliver and Thunder. But the sobs did not stop. A wind came down the canyon and stirred the tips of the jack pines at our backs, a chill wind for early August. I threw a log on the fire and we sat around it. Millie's plate was untouched as she sat with her face in her hands staring into the flame.

Perhaps ten minutes passed when Roy put down his cup, stood up, turned to Millie, and said, "If Dan Oliver can give Bill a horse, I can give you one."

Millie was on her feet, dancing up and down and shouting, "Where is it, where is it?"

"In the North Minam Meadows."

"Let's go get it! Let's go right now, Daddy."

A few days later we rode the seven miles over the mountain range to the west and down into the North Minam. Roy had a dozen two-year-olds at pasture there, and he rode up the meadows to find them. In a while the horses broke through the woods at the edge of the clearing, stood for a second, and then stampeded across it.

"Take your pick," shouted Roy. And Millie picked a slim-legged, light-footed sorrel—the one with the most fire in his eyes. She named him Lightning.

I told President Roosevelt the story that winter, and he said, "You're doing all right for a Scotchman."

"Not as well as I would like."

"You mean you are looking for a third horse for nothing?" he asked.

"Exactly, Mr. President. And when I thought of people who might give me a horse, I kept thinking of you." He threw back his head and laughed in his hearty way.

Roy Schaeffer is the same kind of warmhearted, generous person Franklin Roosevelt was. With a man in need he'd share his last slab of bacon, his last pound of coffee, and in the mountains he'd care for him and expect no reward. The suggestion of a reward would, I think, hurt. He is indeed one of the few I have known who like to give more than to receive. He will die as he was born, poor in worldly possessions.

Roy Schaeffer is the man I would want with me if I were catapulted into dense woods anywhere from Maine to Oregon. He knows Oregon best, but in any forest he would be king. For he is as much a part of the woods as the snowberry, the mountain ash, or the buck deer. The woods are part of him. Above all men I have known, he would be able to survive in them on his wits alone.

Roy is quiet and unassuming in any crowd. He is tall—six feet two. He is big—240 pounds. His eyes are blue. And his hair, now thinned, was once a wild and unruly shock. Roy's parents were the first white people married in Wallowa Valley. He was born there January 5,

1888. It was 60 degrees below zero that day. The rugged scene into which Roy was born is symbolic of the environment through which he has moved during his life—a life on the plains and in the high mountains of eastern Oregon. He has worked long hours deep in the Snake River canyon in the heat of summer when the lava rock of the canyon walls turned it into an oven night and day; he often has slept in a hollow in the snow at the top of the Wallowas with a blizzard howling overhead.

He married Lucy Downard in 1908 and for the honeymoon took her to Bear Creek Saddle in the high Wallowas. This saddle is a great rolling meadow about 8000 feet up, at the head of Bear Creek, surrounded by low-lying rims of hills gripped by jagged fingers of granite. They hold Bear Creek Saddle close to the clouds. At the time of his marriage Roy owned a band of sheep. He left them at Bear Creek Saddle while he hurried down to Wallowa to claim his bride. They returned at once on horseback to the sheep camp. From that time Lucy has shared the hardships of Roy's life and also has brought him five children—Charles, Annamay, Ivy, Dorothy, and Arnold—all of whom love the mountains as do Roy and Lucy.

Roy owned this band of about 900 sheep for six years. During that time he came to know both the summer and winter ranges of the Wallowas. He sat in snow, rain, and sunshine on their hillsides and saw the life of the mountains at work. The mountains became as familiar to him as a factory is to a man who works there.

After Roy sold his sheep he was a jack-of-all-trades. But most of the jobs took him to the back country. He was the champion of sheepshearers. He sheared by hand 200 sheep a day and better. He is a strong man; but sheepshearing taxes the strength. Bending over, holding the animal, working the shears through the tough wool—this is killing. Of all jobs, it came close to exhausting Roy's great energy.

Between sheepshearings came a variety of jobs on farms and in lumber camps, with a few winter months in Union Pacific roundhouses repairing locomotives. "That work," Roy once said to me, "was the part of my life that was wasted." He loves the outdoors and it is punishment to assign him to inside work. Most of his days have been spent in the mountains taking fishing parties to high lakes and hunting parties to high ridges or deep canyons. In the winters he has done much trapping for marten. In 1934 he bought Lapover, famous dude ranch of the Wallowas.

Roy's strength is prodigious. His hands are like hams. Each of them is so strong it could crush a man. Taking hold of it is similar to grasping a wild steer by the horn. There are many stories of his feats and most of them have a Paul Bunyan touch. One fall he and three others were hunting deer in the Grande Ronde canyon. Roy became separated from the others. He rejoined them late in the afternoon to find that one had shot a buck. The three men had worked out a scheme for division of labor in getting the deer out of the canyon. One would carry the rifles while two would carry the buck. Roy met them as they were resting for a short climb. He tied the four legs of the buck together, slipped his rifle barrel underneath the knot, raised the rifle to his shoulder and started up the canyon wall. It was a good 2000 feet to the top. The buck weighed 185 pounds dressed. Roy stopped a few times on his way up but he finished ahead of the other members of the party.

Many years ago he figured he was spending $120 a year for chewing tobacco, which was too much for his budget. He decided to short-circuit the retailer and manufacturer and go directly to the producer. He wrote to Hawesville, Kentucky, and found a man who for $10 would send him a good sized box of unprocessed tobacco. It is the leaf and stem of the tobacco plant, dried but otherwise just as it comes from the field. It comes in three strengths: mild, strong, and extra strong. Roy orders the extra strong. For $10 he gets a supply that lasts a year. He takes the plant and crushes it into a coarse powder and carries this in a cotton bag that Lucy made for him.

This tobacco is powerful. Though many have tried no one but Roy has been able to chew it. He has bet that no one else can chew it for a half-hour and so far no one has won the bet. One man who chewed Roy's tobacco only ten minutes spent all night behind the chicken coop. Roy's reputation has spread. No one bums a chew off him. He also smokes this tobacco in a pipe, and has yet to find a smoker who can inhale it.

The habit of chewing tobacco has affected his speech, so that he does not move his lips when he talks. He probably could have been another Edgar Bergen if he had tried, for he speaks from the stomach. It is a deep guttural sound, hard for the newcomer to pick up. But it has great carrying power. I have been 100 yards from him in the woods and heard what he said even though he did not raise his voice. He talks as I imagined, when a boy, that an Indian would talk.

Roy is an expert shot with a pistol and rifle. He can take his six-shooter and hit a horsefly with one shot at a distance of 30 feet. One evening I saw Roy with his 30.06 hit empty shells that we threw high in the air. He never missed. He can do better than that. I've seen him take a .22 Remington, throw out a shell, load the gun and hit the shell with the second shot before it hit the ground. Roy has seldom missed his buck even at 500 yards.

Roy has a great respect for the animals that inhabit the forests. Coyote is the exception. Coyote plans his campaign of killing with some of man's thoroughness. Roy has seen coyotes station one or more of their band at the bottom of a draw while one went to the top of the ridge in search of a deer. The deer, once jumped, raced down the ridge with the coyote in full pursuit. When the deer reached the bottom, tired and weary, there would be fresh coyotes lying in wait to take the next leg of the relay.

In hard snow, the coyote takes a heavy toll of deer. He runs on top, while the deer keep breaking through. So the coyote gradually gains on the deer and quickly snaps the tendons in its rear legs. The deer is down, and the coyote is at its throat in a flash. Roy has known one coyote to kill 20 or 30 deer in a winter day in that way, taking a few mouthfuls from each carcass. For the killing is not primarily for food; the coyote kills for the joy of killing. He hamstrings elk as he does deer when he finds them wallowing in deep snow.

Roy is for the extermination of the coyote. "If man wants deer to hunt," says Roy, "he must eliminate the coyote. The deer cannot long stand to be hunted by both."

And so January finds him at Salem, Oregon, talking with legislators in an endeavor to get a bounty placed on coyotes—one sufficiently attractive to make every farmer's boy in the county look for a coyote den when spring rolls around.

Roy and I were hunting in the Snake River country, camped on Lightning Creek several miles above its mouth. Lightning Creek runs into the Imnaha, and the Imnaha runs into the Snake about five miles below the confluence of the Imnaha and Lightning Creek. These waterways flow out of the most deeply scarred and rugged canyons of the continent. Hell's Canyon of the Snake, a dozen miles or so above the mouth of the Imnaha, is indeed the deepest canyon of the continent—2000 feet deeper than the Grand Canyon. It is 7900 feet from the lip of the ridge to the surface of the water. Here the Astor overland party foundered. Here Captain Benjamin Bonneville was turned back. Here the Snake is one of the most treacherous of all rivers to run.

The Lightning Creek canyon in which we were camped is no ordinary canyon. The valley at points is a quarter-mile wide, with the canyon walls rising 2000 to 3000 feet. Centuries of erosion have exposed on either side layer after layer of dark lava rock, each from a few feet to 20 or 30 feet thick. The north slopes of these canyon walls are carpeted with the famous Idaho fescue (Festuca idahoensis), and the south slopes with bluebunch wheatgrass (Agropyron spicatum), the bunchgrass that is found on the hills out of Yakima, the most important indigenous grass of the Pacific Northwest. These grasses stand a foot to two feet high in the Snake River country. At a distance of a few miles they look like the nap of a yellow-green velvet that flows softly over the canyon walls.

Here and there thick stands of pine and fir make dark patches on a light green landscape, sometimes sprawling the whole length of a deep draw or lying in a thick mantle over the shoulders of the range.

The slopes and hill crests have only straggling evergreens to adorn them. It is as if a forest were sown with an uneven hand.

Sheltered ravines holding springs or a creek cut ugly gashes in the canyon walls. They always have shelter, for even where the pine and fir are absent they are filled with willow, cottonwood, alder, elderberry, sumac, and chaparral. This vegetation forms a spine of high brush that runs the whole length, crawling 2000 to 3000 feet up the hillside like a sinewy green serpent. There are rattlesnakes in the draws and on the rimrock.

There are several ways to hunt this country. One is to send a member of the party circuitously to the saddle at the head of one of the draws. He goes a roundabout way so as not to disturb the deer that may be in the draw. After he is at the top, another hunter goes directly up the draw. The deer go out ahead of him at the saddle, where the ambush is laid. That is the way my son and I like to hunt that country. Another method is to work up the mountain along the side of a ravine, rolling rocks into it in order to flush any deer that may be bedded down. That is the way Roy and I hunted on this particular October day.

We usually would be 500 feet or more above the bottom of the draw, working along its sides under outcroppings of rimrock. The rocks we rolled into the draw bounced in abandon down the slopes, weaving weird patterns in their paths. They would disappear into the brush; and in a few seconds a deep, muffled, crashing sound traveled back to us. Then the silence of the canyon would return, as if its sleep had been only fitfully interrupted. We would stand alert, looking below for the slightest movement in the ravine.

These were tense moments. I knew for the first time the feeling not only of the hunter but of the hunted. The quickened pulse as the rock plunged off the hillside; the tingling suspense as it veered first one way, then another; the pounding heart and the feel of its breath as it went rolling by. I understood the psychology of the deer: to freeze and to hold ground, to stay quiet and still as a statue, until and unless the rock came perilously close. Then and then only would a break for safety be made.

Roy must have made a close hit with one rock. A four-point buck broke into the open, coming out of the draw and onto the slope across from him. The buck first stepped softly and then in two bounds got behind a lone ponderosa pine.

"There is plenty of time," thought Roy. "I'll sit down and take careful aim."

There did, indeed, seem to be plenty of time. For the buck had 1000 feet to travel to the top, with no brush or tree or ledge to offer protection on the way up. Roy sat still for a minute or two. Then he said to himself: "That buck is staying behind the tree. I must run downhill and get my shot before he gets out of range."

Run down he did. He went off at an angle, running 50 yards or more before he stopped. When he prepared to draw a bead on the buck, the tree was still between them. Whichever way he turned the buck kept behind the tree, as a squirrel does in any park in the land when one comes close to him. In a few minutes the buck was gone with the saucy flash of his tail over the saddle. Roy had not even had a single shot at him. Later Roy said, "You know, Bill, that buck was a lot smarter than me."

Roy has a great affection for horses. When this powerful man is near a horse, he is unfailingly gentle. His hand on a horse that is ill or injured has the tenderness of a father's hand at his child's sickbed. His voice is soft. And his gentleness with horses is reciprocated. I have seen a trembling three-year-old, wild and unbroken, become calm as he touched it and talked to it in a low voice.

Roy has never owned a pair of hobbles. His horses never leave him in the hills. This means, of course, that he picks his camp-grounds with an eye to the comfort and pleasure of the horse as well as to his own. He looks first for horse feed—not for grass that horses can eat in a pinch, but for sweet and tender grass that is rich in protein, like the alpine bunchgrass that grows as high as 8000 or 9000 feet in the Wallowas. As a result, Roy's horses are never far away in the morning. A handful of oats and his soft whistle will bring them to him. From November to May they run wild in the winter range on the lower reaches of the Big Minam; but when Roy goes to get them in the spring they come right to him. Then he puts his arm around their necks and pats them, greeting them as one would a friend long absent.

Once when Roy and I were camped at Cheval Lake in the Wallowas, we took a side trip to New Deal Lake. It is a small lake of ten acres or so, in a treeless basin. It has eastern brook trout up to five pounds. Cliffs shaped somewhat like a horseshoe hem it in. Our approach was from above, which brought us to the lake from the south side. When we first saw it, it was 500 feet below us. The slope was perhaps 45 degrees or more, but it was not dangerous except for one stretch. That was a flat piece of tilted granite, smooth as a table top, half as wide as a city street, and covered with loose gravel. There was no way around it; it had to be crossed. Roy was in the lead. I watched to see what he would do. His horse stopped and sniffed the rock. Roy spoke to him and touched him lightly with spurs. The horse stepped gingerly on the granite. Then putting his four feet slightly forward, the horse half walked and half slid down the granite with sparks flying from his shoes.

"Might have slipped in these boots if I had tried to walk," said Roy in a matter-of-fact way. And he probably would have, for under his lighter weight the loose gravel would have rolled.

It was then that I thought of Jimmie Conzelman's definition of horsemanship. "Horsemanship," says Jimmie, "is the ability to remain unconcerned, comfortable, and on a horse—all at once."

One November day Roy had his hunting camp set up near the mouth of the North Fork of the Minam. It was a big party, with seven or eight tents. It was so sprawled out that from a distance it looked like an Indian camp. Smoke came from every tent. There was a big center tent where the cooking was done. A few horses stood tied to trees in an outer circle, waiting to be saddled. Three or four elk hung high above the ground from poles laid between two trees.

Roy was preparing breakfast, and as he cooked, Mac, a wise, old mule, age 35, came up and nuzzled him. When I have been at Roy's barn saddling horses, Mac has often come up behind me and given me a push with his head, urging me to the door of the barn where the oats were kept. He seldom stopped until I gave in.

Mac was a favorite of Roy's: He always trusted Mac with the delicate tasks of a pack train. Mac always carried the eggs and the liquids, or any pastry that Lucy might fix for the first night out. Mac was never tied onto a pack string. He followed behind, taking his time and picking his way. I have seen him stop and look closely at the space between two trees, trying to figure whether he could get through without bumping or scraping either side of the pack. Often he would go around rather than take a chance. He never rolled a pack. He often was late in arriving in camp behind a pack string; but he always brought his burden in safe and sound. At breakfast time he was always in camp begging for hot cakes.

This morning Roy turned to Mac and said, "Want a hot cake? Well, go away and come back pretty soon and I'll give you one."

This happened over and again. Finally he fed Mac a few.

"Now don't bother us any more," said Roy. "Go on." And with that he gave Mac a push. Mac stood for a minute and then went over to the trail that ran close by camp and started downstream.

When Roy saw Mac go downstream, he was puzzled. The horses were upstream. Lapover was upstream, up the North Minam and across a high range ruled by the jagged finger of Flagstaff Point. Downstream was the winter range and the town of Minam on the paved highway coming up from La Grande. Roy sometimes went out that way, but only in an emergency; for when he got out, he would be 30 miles by road from Lapover. That was the long way around.

"Let's see where Mac goes," said Roy.

So we followed him down the trail a mile or so. Roy finally stopped and said, "We're breaking camp and following Mac. We're moving down the Big Minam and will go out by the town of Minam. Looks to me like a big snow is coming. Mac usually knows it before I do."

We broke camp and moved downstream. Before morning a heavy

snow fell, almost 18 inches, which meant there were at least 4 feet
on the ridges. And 4 feet are far too much for any pack train.

The next night beside the campfire Roy chuckled as he said,
"Mac knew more than all the rest of us put together, didn't he?"

The high lakes of the Wallowas number 100 or more and lie at
6000 to 8400 feet. Each has a personality. Cheval is hardly more than
a pond nestling under granite peaks in a high secluded pocket. It's
small and intimate—a one-party camp. Long and Steamboat show
wide expanses of water like those in the Maine woods. They show
broad acres of deep blue water on calm days, and produce whitecaps
in rough weather. Douglas lies in the high lake basin under Eagle
Cap. Here there are granite walls mounted with spires like unfinished cathedrals. It is austere or intimate, depending on how one
comes upon it. Patsie, Bumble, and Tombstone lie like friendly,
open ponds in a pasture. Diamond, Frances, and Lee have the dark
cast of wells without bottoms, and water that chills to the marrow
a few feet under the surface. Blue, Chimney, and Hobo appear as
sterile as slate, showing clayish bottoms with no moss or grass. Green,
Minam, and Crescent are lush with algae and moss, rich feeding
grounds for trout.

Fish have been planted in 50 or more of these lakes. Roy has
packed many thousands of fingerlings in to them, carried in milk
cans and kept alive by the sloshing of the water caused by the movement of the horse or mule that transported them. Sometimes Roy
while en route to one lake has paused long enough at a smaller one
to pour in a dipper of fingerlings. Or having a part of a can left
over, he has climbed a ridge or dropped into another canyon and
planted a few hundred fingerlings in a remote pond. In that manner
dozens of lakes have received their fish. Many are nameless lakes, un-
marked on maps, with no trail to designate their locations, tucked
away high on ridges or in small basins below granite peaks. They are
deep blue sapphires in mountings of gray and green.

One summer Stanley Jewett and I were on a pack trip with Roy.
We were studying the problems of the fish, convinced that in many

instances the solution was to supply the lakes not with fish but with food, such as fresh-water shrimp or periwinkles. We were camped at Long Lake. One morning Stan suggested we take a look for mountain sheep.

The bighorns were native to the Wallowas, where they once existed in large numbers. Captain Bonneville, who wintered on the Idaho side of the Snake in 1832, reported that the bighorns were the principal diet of his expedition. But none have been seen in the Wallowas for a decade or so, and it seemed incredible. Stan thought the ridge east of Long—the rocky backbone that stands as a 1000-foot granite barrier between it and Steamboat—was where they might be.

We started up the ridge early one morning. We soon had to dismount and leave the horses, for there was a granite wall ahead of us. We were almost to the top when we spotted fresh tracks of sheep—the unmistakable imprint of the bighorn in fine sand on a ledge. We hurried to the top, thinking he might be going ahead of us. When we peered over the rim, we saw no sign of a bighorn. But there in a meadow of heather was a shallow lake of 10 or 20 acres. A breeze swept from the south and touched its surface, ripples dancing like lights in a dazzling chandelier. In the midst of the ripples there was a swirl. An eastern brook, perhaps 15 inches long, was rising to a fly. This was an eastern brook that Roy four years before had brought here in a milk can tied to a pack saddle of a mule. Now there was life in the once sterile pond. Now there was a new reward at the end of an adventurous climb for those who dared those treacherous cliffs.

The North Minam Meadows lie over the range to the west of Lapover. It is a rich bottom land, a mile or so long and a half-mile wide, coveted by every man who loves the mountains and has seen it. Fortunately it is in a national forest. It has knee-high grass for horses from spring until winter. The North Minam meanders through, spilling over marshy banks lined with tall grass and rushes. Like the Klickitat Meadows of the Cascades, it is ideal for a boy's fishing. Here he can hide himself in the tall grass a few feet from the river's edge and float his fly on the water. It will not go more than a few feet before he has a rainbow or eastern brook. They are little fellows, from six to eight inches, but they are every inch champions and right for the pan.

There are ice-cold springs in the meadow, and groves of trees for camping. In late June the valley is filled with the fragrance of the snowbrush. And from May until August most of the wild flowers of the Wallowas will be found there.

This is where Joseph C. Culbertson came to die. He acquired a lung infection from his chemical researches, and his doctors gave him six months to live. As Joe lay on his bed, trying to think of the place where he would like to spend the last months of his life, he remembered the North Minam Meadows.

"That is the place," said Joe.

His wife put their affairs in order and got in touch with Roy. It was early May, 1938, and the snow would be out of the North Minam. Roy made several trips over and set up camp for the Culbertsons—tents and store beds, medicines and provisions, all the accessories of the sickroom. When camp was established, Roy and Mrs. Culbertson went back and got Joe.

Joe was almost too weak for the seven-mile trip from Lapover by the Bowman Trail, but somehow or other he made it. For weeks he lay in a screened tent in a small grove of jack pine and Engelman's spruce at the edge of the North Fork. The Meadows are 5200 feet high and in sunshine most of the time from May to November. From his tent Joe could see deer and elk at the salt lick, and hear the willow thrush singing. Every morning he watched the sun touch the eastern rim of the canyon, with its great columns of granite rock. One morning as Joe watched he saw the sun touch one rock and transform it into a giant eagle. The breast of this eagle is slightly lighter than its crest. It stands atop the ridge and commands the Meadows.

From his place in the Meadows Joe saw storms make up around Steamboat and Long lakes and swoop down on them, often leaving snow and sleet on the ridges even in August. But they brought only a light rain to the Meadows. There would be the gentle, almost inaudible dripping of the trees during a night of rain. In the morning great fingers of mist would start moving up the canyon. By noon a west wind would have cleared the valley, and the sun would be shining on the rock eagle. Every night there was the soft music of the North Minam as it left the marshlands of the Meadows and picked up momentum for its wild and rugged journey down to the Big Minam, three miles distant.

By the time the Douglas maple, willow, and tamarack had turned, Joe had started fishing in the North Fork. In November when Roy packed him and his wife out, Joe was a new man. The Culbertsons camped in the meadows in 1938, 1939, and 1940, going in when the Bowman Trail was first open and leaving only with the first snow of winter. There I met Joe Culbertson, some six years after he went to the Meadows to die. He and his wife opened their camp to our pack train and gave us lunch. The next summer I came across Joe after I had climbed halfway up the steep trail to Green Lake. Joe had a pick and shovel and was starting to construct a new trail to the lake—one with a more comfortable grade. There was joy in his heart and tenderness in his voice as he spoke of the Meadows.

Others have experienced the same thing. Once Reuben Horwitz, construction engineer, had a long vacation coming to him. He and Janet had Roy pack them into the Meadows for a stay of several months. They camped where the Culbertsons camped. They had not been there long when Reuben was thrown from a horse and seriously injured. He ended with a long convalescence in the Meadows, and like Joe came out well.

Roy took me there in 1939 on our first pack trip together. When we left Lapover, Roy looked to the sky in the south and said, "It's a bit too blue. We're apt to have a storm." The last day or two it had been too hot for August. There had been little breeze and the heat of the valley was in it. The woods were tinder dry and the dust, pounded and churned by many pack trains, lay deep on the Bowman Trail. We rested our horses frequently as we climbed out of the Lostine canyon. The powdery dust rose around us. And when the horses stopped, sweat ran off their bellies and noses and disappeared in the dust.

We were at Brownie Basin, not far from the top of the range, when we heard thunder. The storm came quickly. Clouds moved in from the south. The heat had hung on the mountain as it does in a city long after the sun has set on a humid day. But now it was gone in a flash as a strong cold wind swept in, licking the ridges with a smattering of rain. The rain turned to snow and sleet. Before we had crossed Wilson Basin, which lies over the top on the western side of the range, the ground was white with snow.

I stopped my horse Dan halfway down to the North Minam Meadows on the zigzag trail that drops out of Wilson Basin. He turned sideways on one of the crooked elbows of the path, as I looked down on the meadows a thousand feet or more below me. They were dimly visible as through a fog, for the snow at this altitude had turned to rain and was falling soft and misty. Suddenly Dan reared and snorted and tried to run. I looked up the trail, and there coming around a bend was what appeared to be a long, dark serpent. It weaved and wiggled as it came down, and once in a while raised its head as if better to mark its course. My first impulse was the same as Dan's. But in a second I understood.

Pulverized dust can be as efficient in shedding water as the feathers on a duck's back. When it is as fine as flour, it contains an air cushion with pores too small to admit water. Thus it can become a roller that carries water off a mountainside. That is what happens when a flash flood rolls off a dry desert hillside of the west, tossing houses and barns as if they were chips. That was what was happening this August day. A great stream of water was running on top of the slick dust of the Bowman Trail. It descended the mountain in a rush. Dan did not stop snorting and rearing until he felt the familiar touch of the water on his hoofs.

By the time we reached the Meadows the rain had settled to a steady drizzle. It had a stubbornness and persistency that indicated it might be with us for days. The trees were dripping; the dampness penetrated everywhere.

Roy found pieces of pitchwood and had a fire going in a jiffy. He piled slabs of dry bark of a red fir on the fire. This is the fuel that produces the hottest fire in the mountains of the West. At once the atmosphere of a home took the place of the wet woods.

The best of all fuels in the Wallowas is mountain-mahogany. Its coals from the night's fire are hot in the morning. But there is no mountain-mahogany in the Meadows, for it grows only on the ridges. So Roy said, "Let's get some cottonwood, willow, or alder. It's a little better if it's on the rotten side. I learned that from the Indian squaws when I was a boy."

We had no tent on that trip, so before dusk Roy said, "Let's see if we can find a dry tree for our sleeping bags." He thought he could find one that would shed water for three or four days, and it was not long before he did. It was a red fir, leaning slightly to one side. It was dry underneath. There we put our bags for two days of rain, and they stayed as dry as they would have in a tent.

The third morning when we wakened the sun was rising in a clear sky. We lolled about camp, hanging out blankets and clothes to rid them of dampness. When we had finished, Roy said, "You know, a man could live in these Meadows just about forever. It's a powerful healthy place."

Then he told me about Joe Culbertson and Reuben Horwitz, and how in the old days he used to come here just to sleep off the fatigue of sheepshearing. "When God made this spot He made the air a little lighter and cleaner. He made the water a little purer and colder. He made the sunshine a little brighter. He made the grass a little more tender for the horses."

As Roy talked, three does and a fawn crossed a clearing above camp. The yapping of a coyote floated down from the ledges high above them. In a little while a bull elk, with at least a six-foot spread of horns, sauntered by, as unconcerned as a window shopper on Fifth Avenue.

"That elk would act different if the hunting season was on," said Roy. "Funny, but they know when it starts. Frighten a herd of elk during hunting season and they may leave the country. I've known them to travel 40 or 50 miles without stopping. But deer are different.

Each buck has his little domain. Maybe it's a draw or a stretch of woods a mile or so long. Wherever it is, it's home, and he won't leave it. If you're hunting him, he'll circle back to it. He'll stay in the country he knows."

Roy added: "Another nice thing about these Meadows is that they are protected by Uncle Sam. That's the way it should be. It's against the law to graze sheep here. That's right, too. Pretty soon they got to take the sheep out of these mountains. If people are to come here and fish and hunt or take pictures and climb these peaks, they'll need lots of horse feed. Pretty soon people will discover that all the feed in the high Wallowas is needed for horses and deer and elk."

It was snowing when our pack train pulled out of Bear Creek Saddle, headed toward Sturgill Basin and Stanley Ridge. It was a light snow and there was no wind, so the near-zero temperature did not bite. The snow did not melt as it fell; it powdered our hats and shoulders so that we soon were a ghostly looking procession winding among the trees of the silent forest.

An inch of snow had fallen when the pack train reached Sturgill Basin. At this point we were high above the North Minam. On the ridge opposite us was Green Lake, frozen into a great crystal turned milky by the light touch of new snow. And on the far horizon to the south the town of North Powder was only faintly visible as the storm dropped a curtain of dusk over the mountains. When the pack train pulled through the Basin and climbed to the Washboard Trail that leads to Stanley, a cruel wind with a severe bite in its teeth had come up from the southwest. It drove the finely powdered snow into the skin as if it were sand from a blasting machine.

The ridge along the Washboard Trail is cold in any wind. This trail, decorated with prostrate juniper and whitebark pine, winds along the hogback west of Bear Creek. At points the hogback is only a few feet wide, with the ground dropping 1000 feet or more on each side at a dizzy pitch of 60 degrees. In these places the wind howled on this winter day as it picked up speed from the downdraft that sucked it into the Bear Creek canyon, 3000 to 4000 feet below the trail on the right. This trail often passes along the base of jagged cliffs that rise as great hackles along the hogback. Here it is often skimpy, carved from the base of the basalt cliffs. At these places this winter wind hurled its weight against the cliffs and whirled clouds of snow into the air. Then it swerved off the cliffs and raced to the north with a whine in its throat.

Below us on the left the land tumbled in disarray into a series of sharp ravines that collect small streams of pure cold water in the spring and summer and carry them to the Big Minam. The slopes leading into them are dangerous. A single horse might pick his way up or across these steep inclines, but neither a pack train nor a horse with a man on him should venture it. One of these draws ends in Chaparral Basin some 3000 feet below the trail. At that point a sheepherder's train once rolled into the canyon. Five horses were tailed together. The rear one slipped and fell, pulling the other four with him. They rolled for half a mile. When they came to rest, down on the sharp rocks that line the brush on the lower reaches, the five horses were dead and their cargo was scattered over the mountainside. The sheepherder stood briefly with bowed head, as if in reverence at the burial of friends; then sadly he turned his horse around and headed back to get a new outfit.

Roy shouted something when we passed this place, pointing down to Chaparral Basin. Perhaps he was reminding us of the episode I have just told. But the wind was so strong his words were carried away, mere petals of snow in the blizzard.

I have often stopped here on a summer afternoon, enthralled by the view. Off to the west in the valley of the Minam is the great meadow of the Horse Ranch, where Red Higgins welcomes visitors at an airport in the wilderness. The light green of that meadow is the only break in the darkness of the conifers and basalt that line the valley—the only break, that is, except for an occasional glimpse of the blue water of the Minam itself.

This is favorite country of elk and ruffed grouse. Here I have found a vast display of exquisite pink pentstemon. Here the wild currant and black-headed cones flourish.

The ridge the trail follows runs north and turns in a great arc to the west. From a distance it seems impassable. The sharp cliffs, the precipitous mountainside, and the ravines that slash its surface in deep and ragged cuts seem indeed to be forbidding obstacles. There are in fact not many places where a trail could traverse this treacherous ridge. But some sheepman years ago picked his way around great rocks, across ledges, and under the cliffs, and found footholds adequate for one-way travel in the six miles it takes to travel the arc of the bowl. I always feel at grips with adventure when I look at this route. Every step must be taken gingerly. It is as though one were walking along a cornice of a building high above the canyons of Wall Street.

Much of the beauty of the scene had been wiped out by the blizzard of this November day. The Horse Ranch and the whole valley of the Minam were lost to view. Even the far points of the ridge we were on had disappeared. Whirling snow made impenetrable clouds in the deep pockets of the canyon below us. The trail traverses a virtual knife-edge above Blow Out Basin. Here it seemed as if the whole pack train would be blown into the void.

The wind soon pierced our heavy mackinaws, slipped under our chaps, and chilled our legs. The six miles along the rim of the basin seemed twelve. Cold reached through to the very marrow. It would have been a relief to walk, but the trail was slippery and no place for half-frozen people who could only stumble. Roy wisely kept to his horse; and the others agreed. We moved in silence, bent forward so as to soften the force of the wind that blew us against the cliffs on our right.

By the time we had cleared the rim and come out on the broad ridge above Stanley, it was midafternoon and deep dusk. Low, dark clouds had swept in from the southwest and cut the vision to a few hundred yards. On the open ridge the wind was a gale. Great swirls of snow blotted even the pack train from view. To stay in this place all night with the expectation of being alive in the morning would seem reckless to most people. Yet Roy pulled up by a clump of fir, dismounted, and said, "Guess we better camp here."

He cut two poles about 8 feet long, each having a fork at one end.

He cut another pole about 12 feet long and, using it as a ridge, lashed it into the fork of each of the other two poles. He then raised these poles and used ropes to anchor each of them to stakes. Then he took longer poles, about 15 feet long, and laid them as rafters on the windward side of the lean-to, about 18 inches apart, so that one end rested on the ridge and the other on the ground. These roof poles he lashed to the ridge with twine and rope. Next he took quantities of fir boughs and wove them through these roof poles until he had a snug thatch that was several boughs thick. He closed each end of the lean-to in the same way, weaving fir boughs through cross poles that he had lashed into places in those openings. In front of the lean-to he built a three-walled open fireplace, prying up rocks from the frozen ground and building a horseshoe-shaped wall 18 inches high with its open side toward the lean-to. A fire was started, and in not much over an hour everyone in the party was snug and warm. The horses were fed oats and baled hay we had packed in. They stood throughout the night with their saddles and blankets on for protection. Before supper was cooked the blacks and bays and sorrels were so heavily powdered with snow they were indistinguishable one from the other. We humans bedded down in Roy's lean-to. The wind howled out the night and in the morning the snow was over a foot thick. But Roy's work had been well done; there were no draughts to disturb our sleep.

Roy knows the Wallowas in winter. He has buried himself in them for a week or more, riding out a blizzard. Sometimes his shelter was a cabin; at other times it was a hole in the snow.

Roy usually ran a trap line for marten from Minam Lake to the head of the Copper Creek Basin, an eight- or ten-mile arc in the high mountains. It had to be at an elevation of 6000 to 8000 feet, because that is where the marten are found in winter. He placed each trap on a tree trunk, three to four feet above the ground. He learned about marten bait the hard way. One winter he baited his traps with the trimmings from elk meat, and as a result he lost a winter's catch. Marten do not like fat meat.

Rabbit, pine squirrel, and blue jays are the best marten bait available in the Wallowas. Marten will not touch camp robbers or flying squirrels. They love grouse, which in severe winter weather sometimes bury themselves in snow for warmth.

"We can't see the grouse," said Roy. "But the marten smells him and digs him out."

Roy would leave Lapover on snowshoes every week or so for a five-day inspection of his marten traps.

"About a quarter of the traps caught camp robbers, blue jays, and squirrels," Roy told me.

Roy's pack weighed 40 pounds or more. He always took an ax for wood and a shovel to dig a hole in the snow for lodging. He carried a frying pan, kettle, coffee pot, and a cup, plate, and spoon. He took 20 pounds of rabbit meat for bait, and a half-dozen extra traps. For food he had coffee, sugar, bacon, whole wheat cereal, potatoes, and bread. Roy never took blankets or a bedroll on these winter trips, because the weight of the pack did not permit it. At night he slept like a bear in a hole in the snow. He cut off the top of a snag and with that wood built a fire next to the snag.

Those who have built fires in deep snow know, as Gifford Pinchot observed (*Breaking New Ground*), that it promptly melts itself down out of sight, leaving only a hole with a little steam coming out. That's why Roy always carried a shovel on these snowshoe trips. He dug a pit in the snow as he followed the fire down. Since the fire was next to the snag, Roy was able to take his wood supply down with him to the bottom of the pit. In the morning he might be 15 feet or more beneath the surface. His bed was fir boughs. If it rained or snowed, he would dig an alcove in the side of the pit and crawl into it. There he could ride out a blizzard for several days.

One day, when Roy was reminiscing about these trap-line trips, he said to me, "People think snow is cold, but it isn't. It's a blanket that has a lot of warmth in it. At times birds bury themselves in it to keep warm. I've seen deer do the same thing. They keep their heads out, but they will lie in a snowdrift entirely covered for maybe 18 or 24 hours."

The mountains in the winter are cruel to man and beast. The game leaves the high country and goes down to winter range. There are no berries, roots, or other produce of the woods for food. Travel itself is hazardous. A blizzard in the Wallowas may blow 12 days and drop a swirling cloud through which man cannot see even 50 feet. Or the snow may turn to slush and cling to snowshoes like leaden weights. Then a man may not be able to walk more than 2 miles in a whole day. In cross-country travel he can readily exhaust himself, and in his fatigue at the end of a day sit down to rest and freeze to death. Roy's first principles of winter travel are: 1) Always take along a shovel and an ax; 2) get under the snow when weather is bad; and 3) go slowly at the beginning of the day, saving energy for the last few hours of the evening, for a blizzard or rainstorm may come up and change the character of the travel. Then a man's life may depend on his reserve of energy.

Throwing a diamond hitch, putting an improvised shoe on a horse, building a lean-to in a storm, carrying a sick or wounded person out of a wilderness, cooking, finding the lair of a buck deer or the den of a bear—these and any of the hundred and one experiences of a pack trip are chores that Roy handles with understanding and high efficiency. It is the competence one respects when one sees the deft fingers of a sculptor at work, or watches the sure eye of an axman, or observes a skilled mechanic at a lathe, or hears the master advocate in court. It is the extraordinary skill that one finds at the top of any profession or trade. There is a finesse and quality about it that distinguishes the skill of any champion.

When I read of the early mountain men I think of Roy. He would have been a credit to Jim Bridger or any of the early scouts. He is the caliber of man I think Captain William Clark of the Lewis and Clark expedition must have been. Clark did not know the outdoors as a botanist or biologist or geologist knew it. He knew it as a country lawyer without benefit of formal legal education may know the law. He knew his way through the wilderness, he could appraise its risks and dangers, and he knew where to find shelter and sustenance. Clark could not spell very well, and his writing shows some vestiges of illiteracy. He was not erudite, but he had wisdom and judgment.

Clark was a simple, uncomplicated man who had the knack of giving every problem in the woods a practical twist. He was the kind of man who could survive though he entered the wilderness empty-handed. He had the competence to deal with the day-to-day tasks, which, though trivial, added up to life or death. Such a man is Roy Schaeffer. He, too, could have done with credit what Clark did.

Roy was a warm admirer of President Roosevelt. Shortly before the 1945 Inauguration he got the idea he wanted to attend. He sat up in a day coach all across the country and arrived in Washington, D.C., late one afternoon. He was dressed in cowboy boots, Pendleton pants, a loud plaid shirt, a mackinaw, and ten-gallon hat. He strode through Union Station with a battered suitcase, stepped into a taxicab, and told the driver, "I want to see Bill Douglas."

Eventually he ended up at our home in Silver Spring, Maryland; and during his two-week visit he captured the town. He went to dinners and luncheons and teas; he stayed in character and wore his cowboy clothes to all of them. He stood on the White House grounds with head bared and saw Roosevelt take the oath. A lady in the crowd said to him, "It's always good to see someone from Texas."

Roy, embarrassed, said, "I'm from Oregon, ma'am."

We walked down Pennsylvania Avenue together, and reserved Easterners looked up at Roy and said with friendliness, "Hello, cowboy."

Roy would touch his hat and, as if speaking to a traveler on a high mountain trail, reply, "Hi."

He pounded the pavements of Washington with his high-heeled boots and said to my wife at night, "Walking the Bowman Trail is easier."

He slept in a bed with white, clean sheets and commented, "Never slept inside but what I caught a cold. Wish I had brought my sleeping bag. Then I'd sleep on the back porch. It's much healthier outdoors."

As a rock fish, famous product of Chesapeake Bay, was being prepared in our kitchen, he said, "If I had a big flat rock, I could build a

fire in the yard and cook the fish on the rock. Bet it'd be the best fish
you ever tasted."

At a dinner in Georgetown he turned to the hostess who in all her
life had probably never been in a kitchen and said, "These are good
biscuits you made, ma'am. Some day I wish I could dig a hole in your
yard and cook you some sourdough bread. It can be real light and
fluffy, too, you know."

One afternoon at a tea I saw Roy surrounded by a group of news-
papermen and -women. He towered above them all, as Flagstaff
Point towers over his cabin at Lapover. I saw from the expression on
his face that he was not wholly at ease. I stepped to the outer circle
of the group to discover the reason. He was being plied with questions
of politics in Oregon, prices in Oregon, industrial and social conditions in Oregon, and the run of questions a distinguished visitor from
the Far West might expect from the press of a friendly metropolitan
paper. Roy is not a man of books. His formal education is slight. He
seldom reads even in the long winter days when he is snowed in at
Lapover. But he listens to the radio; and down in the valley he hears
the talk in the poolhalls and on the street corners. He also listens
attentively to every traveler who comes up the canyon. His intelligence
is of a high order. He has insight and understanding of people and
their motives. And so he has a simple understanding of great issues—
as sound as the common sense of the common people. But he was too
timid to advance his views to the circle of sophisticated corre-
spondents who faced him at the tea. Finally I heard him say, "You
folks know all about those things. I know nothing except the mountains. Here in Washington you can write your columns and stories
and tell me what is true and what isn't. When you come to Oregon,
then it'll be my turn."

"What will you do then?" asked a lady reporter.

"I'll tell you what I'll do," said Roy with great seriousness. "I'll
blow up the air mattress of your sleeping bag for you."

In the deep woods Roy would not know how to do anyone a
greater favor.

Chapter XIX   *Food*

THERE are many things to eat in the mountains, and most of them are good. Gifford Pinchot, during the days when he rode the trails, sampled them freely, eating everything from elk to grasshopper. He enjoyed bear roasts, fried cougar, rattlesnake steaks, and stewed grouse. Once he told me the best meat of all was the chicken hawk— sweeter than quail, more tender than pheasant, and more delicate than grouse. Clark of the Lewis and Clark expedition gives some support for this recommendation. He reported that his hunters killed three hawks at the mouth of the Columbia in the winter of 1805 which they "found fat and delicious." I asked Pinchot what was the least palatable of his outdoor dishes, and he answered without hesitation: "Grasshoppers." He had cooked them in deep fat like scallops; and they were, he said, as crunchy and tasteless as fried straw.

Roy Schaeffer rates cougar higher than Pinchot did. The cougar meat is like a cat's. And according to Roy it is not far below chicken.

"Matter of fact," said Roy when we were cooking a scanty meal on a cold night at Bear Lake in the Wallowas, "cat meat's not too bad. I knew a Chinaman in eastern Oregon years ago. He ran a restaurant and served cat for chicken in all his dishes. No one knew the difference."

"How did he get his cats? Raise them?"

"No. Caught them with a saucer of milk in the alley." And after a pause he added, "You know, cougar is healthier and better than alley cats. Hard to get, though. It's a rugged, cross-country hunt with dogs."

Roy puts young porcupine ahead of lamb. He roasts it on a spit over coals of mountain-mahogany, cottonwood, quaking aspen, or willow. In his judgment it is perhaps the real delicacy of the mountains.

The best meat I ever had in the hills was blue jay. Roy and I were camped six miles above the mouth of Lightning Creek in the Snake River country. It was early October and unseasonably warm. The series of lava cliffs that formed gargantuan steps up the canyon walls absorbed the heat of the sun and warmed the canyon as a brick can warm a bed. In spite of rattlesnakes, we put our sleeping bags down in the grass by the side of McLaren's old cabin. We slept with our sleeping bags open and unzipped.

The birds and insects, like the rattlesnakes, behaved as if it were late summer. Robins, blue jays, and Hungarian partridges were there in abundance. One day I hunted Butcher Knife Creek. It tumbles 2000 feet or so down a sharp narrow ravine into Lightning Creek. It is heavily wooded in spots and is filled with thick brush to the top. I scouted its length, perspiring freely in the heat of the canyon as I fought brush and dust and rattlers for an entire morning. There were plenty of signs of deer, but not even the flash of a tail. When I got almost to the top I heard shots above me. When I reached the summit, I discovered another party camped there and learned that I, by working up Butcher Knife, had unwittingly become a beater for them. Deer had gone out ahead of me and over the saddle within range of the party camped there. One buck was being dressed.

When I came back empty-handed late in the afternoon, I discovered that Roy had spent a more productive day. He had gone up Lightning Creek with a shotgun, and flushed Hungarian partridges from a stand of sumac. As they rose, blue jays also rose. The jays, being in the line of fire, fell. We had them for supper, fried in butter. They were sweeter and more tender than any quail or other bird I ever tasted—although I have yet to determine whether Pinchot's chicken hawk is better.

Bread was important to us on our early pack trips. As I related in a previous chapter, we carried ready-mixed flour in long, thin cotton sacks and rolled them in our horseshoe packs. The recipe was Brad's:

    2 cups flour
    4 teaspoons baking powder
    ¼ teaspoon salt.

Sometimes we stirred powdered milk into it, and added fat if we had some.

The dough was mixed fairly thick, as it would be for biscuits. The cooking was done in the frying pan. When the pan was hot and greased, the dough was poured in to fill it. That meant it was about an inch thick. We first held it over the fire for a few minutes in order to cook the bottom. Then we propped it up in front of the fire to finish by radiation.

It was a main part of our diet. We dunked it in coffee. We carried it in our haversack for a noon meal. We picked the low-bush huckleberry, made a sauce, and poured it over the bread. "Delicious," was Brad's usual comment, though how much was owing to an outdoor appetite I never knew.

Sometimes, when we were lucky to have sugar rather than saccharin in our packs, we poured in a half-cup or so. I remember that Doug and I did that one night when we were camped at McAllister Meadows in the Tieton Basin. In Doug's words, "When it has sugar it's cake; when it's plain, it's bread."

As boys we made either a mush or a form of bread in the same way with corn meal. In frying it, we invariably did what no good cook would do—we let a scorched crust form, which was to us perhaps the outstanding delicacy on the early pack trips.

There is a universal quality about bread, whatever may be its color or ingredients. Like air and water and sunshine it is a part of the life of all peoples. Like the family, it is part of our traditions. Gandhi once said, "God himself dare not appear to a hungry man except in the form of bread." Ben Hur Lampman once printed a verse written by an anonymous author:

> Be gentle when you touch bread
> Let it not lie uncared for, unwanted—
> Too often bread is taken for granted.
> There is such beauty in bread;
> Beauty of sun and soil;
> Beauty of patient toil;
> Wind and rain have caressed it,
> Christ often blessed it—
> Be gentle when you touch bread.

That verse will always have a special value to those who, like myself, have marched on bread or got from it the strength to do the day's work.

There is no bread in the mountains like sourdough. Roy Schaeffer has cooked it for me many times. The night at Douglas Lake when he cooked it in a frying pan propped up in a pit is the most memorable. It had a flaky quality that would be hard to duplicate. I asked Roy for his recipe, but he said: "It's hard to describe. It's all in the way you do it."

Barney McPhillips, banker from McMinnville, is also a master with sourdough. During a hunting trip on Lightning Creek he told me, "Sourdough is an art, not a science. It requires a certain state of mind in order to be successful."

Neither Roy nor Barney can supply the state of mind. But Barney's recipe is a good starting point:

Sourdough is started by mixing potato water, milk, salt, sugar, and one-half of a yeast cake. Mix it up to a consistency that is easily stirred. The proportions up to this point are immaterial. When it has risen to at least one-half again its own volume and bubbling good, it is ready to use.

For hot cakes, mix enough flour and water with the starter the evening before you want to use it, so that it will be the right consistency the next morning to make hot cakes without adding either flour or water. Pour off enough dough for four people, add a couple of good husky teaspoonsful of baking powder, and as you mix it up pour in a tablespoonful or two of bacon grease. Then add a couple of tablespoonsful of sugar, and stir vigorously.

For biscuits, add flour and water to your starter so that the batter is as stiff as can be stirred. This should preferably be done about noon, although it is all right to do it immediately following breakfast. To make the biscuits, pour off the required amount of batter (leaving a starter, of course), add baking powder and sugar, douse them in the pan on both sides with warm lard, and put in a warm place to rise for an hour before putting them in the oven.

Both of the above recipes are predicated on using the batter every day. If it has gotten too sour, a touch of soda is necessary before mixing, both for the biscuits and the hot cakes. Care must be taken in mixing it into the biscuits or you will have rusty streaks, commonly referred to by old-timers as "too much yaller."

The *Lookout Cookbook*, Region One, of the Forest Service says of sourdough: "Sourdough bread is much more healthful as a steady diet than baking powder bread or biscuits." And it recommends sourdough for hot cakes: "Excellent hot cakes may also be made with this sourdough batter. Use more sugar than for bread or biscuits. Add a little salt, a pinch or two of soda, stir well, and drop into hot, greased pan. The consistency of the batter should be the same as when making baking powder hot cakes."

The night on Lightning Creek when Barney was discoursing on sourdough, he said, "It works better in high altitudes than at sea level. Maybe that's because camp is always at the higher altitude; and all food tastes better in the woods."

I asked him about one's state of mind—what a cook should do to develop the proper attitude. He laughed. "I knew a cook who said his skill at sourdough was due to the bourbon he drank." Then more seriously: "With my recipe and a few years' practice, a fellow should be able to build himself quite a reputation with sourdough." And then he told me some of the folklore of sourdough, including the story of the old trapper in the Oregon Cascades who in the winter took the starter to bed with him so that it would keep warm.

When I was writing this chapter I sent Barney's recipe for sourdough to Roy Schaeffer for comment. Roy told his daughter Annamay that I should be "put right on the sourdough." So Annamay wrote me saying: "Dad never uses milk in his sourdough. He makes a starter with 1 quart flour, 1 yeast cake, and enough warm water or potato water for a batter a little thicker than hot cake dough. He lets this stand in a warm place for 24 hours." That's all Annamay wrote except this. "I think one has to be in a state of mind to even tell how to make sourdough and I'm afraid I'm not in that state of mind today."

And that's about all that can be said about the art.

Apart from our bread, we had little imagination in our cooking during the early pack trips. The dried eggs we took along in powdered form were as flat and as tasteless as putty. We never mastered the art of making them into savory dishes. Memories of those eggs came back when I heard rumblings about desiccated eggs from the American servicemen overseas during the recent war. About the same time a woman seated next to me at dinner in Washington, D.C. was commenting on the waste in our Lend-Lease shipments. Eggs were her prime example. "You know what some of the Europeans did? They knew nothing about desiccated eggs. So when they got shipments of them, they fed them to their chickens." The memories of dozens of breakfasts and suppers on top of the Cascades went flashing through my mind. I remembered how flat and unpalatable our dishes of such eggs had been. I could almost taste them again. Turning to my dinner partner I said, "Madam, that's exactly what I would have done."

Damon Trout, electrical engineer of Portland, Oregon, has a recipe he calls Pennsylvania Dutch Fried Eggs:

Cube three or four slices of bread (this will vary with the number of eggs you are planning to serve). Brown in butter in frying pan. After the cubes have browned, add additional butter and break eggs over the cubes. Mix thoroughly, add salt and pepper, and cook either moist or well done, whichever is preferred.

Besides being exceptionally good, if there happens to be a shortage of eggs in camp or the bread has become stale, this will prove to be the remedy.

This recipe makes a fine dish for the woods even if powdered eggs, mixed with water or milk, are substituted.

A deluxe way of cooking fresh eggs is that which Frank and Gene Marsh, lawyers of McMinnville, Oregon, have developed:

Take large skillet, number 8 or 10, and fry slowly thick slices of ham, with fat left, so to make ham gravy. After ham is cooked, add cream to ham fat grease, drop eggs in and cook slowly to taste. Serve eggs on slice of toast with ham and gravy.

When there is only a skillet in camp, Saul Haas' squaw dish comes in handy.

Cut bacon into small pieces and fry. Add canned corn (the creamed variety preferred) to the bacon and grease. Stir the mixture so as to distribute the bacon and grease. Add eggs quickly (powdered eggs will do).

Saul knows men who, lost in the woods, lived on this dish for days.

As boys our cooking of trout was unimaginative. We fried them in grease over the open fire. That method of cooking places the trout at a disadvantage. The fishy taste is cooked into the trout, and that together with the grease (especially bacon grease) kills much of the sweetness of the meat.

Gene and Frank Marsh have a method of avoiding that result when it comes to large trout—from two to five pounds—or to Rogue River steelheads·

Clean and *skin*, cutting crosswise in four or five pieces, filet if desired. Powder slightly with flour, salt, and pepper. Fry in clean skillet with butter *only*. They are best if cooked within one or two hours after they are caught.

But in general trout should not be fried. Or if they are fried they should first be skinned—unless they can be fried in bear's oil. Bear's oil is the king of all cooking fat. It is best obtained in the late fall when the bear is in his prime. Then he manufactures thick rolls of fat that often render great quantities of oil. Roy Schaeffer once obtained 30 gallons of oil from one bear. This oil is especially desirable for bread, pies, and pastry. It also is superior for frying fish and meat. When Lewis and Clark were near The Dalles, Oregon, an Indian Chief gave Clark a quantity of bear's oil. Clark fried a salmon trout in it and wrote in the *Journals* that it was "one of the most delicious fish I have ever tasted."

Trout or salmon are sweetest if no oil is used in cooking. Boiling is an ancient method, though seldom used today on the lakes and streams of the Far West. If it is done correctly, the flavor of the meat is preserved, and is not clouded with the fishy taste from the skin.

My preferred recipe for trout starts, but does not end, with boiling. After dressing the trout, place it in boiling water for 2 or 3 minutes, depending on the size of the fish. Remove the skin, head, and bones. Add salt and pepper to taste and a bit of butter. If a broiler is available, place the trout under the flame until it starts to turn brown. In the woods the same result can be obtained by a reflector oven or, in its absence, by radiated heat of the campfire. This method frees the trout of any taint of fish oil, leaving all the natural sweetness and tenderness.

A trout or salmon (and probably a bass too, though I have never tried it) can be cooked exquisitely if it is split and lashed to a board that is propped against a fire of any hardwood. Nancy Wilson Ross (*Farthest Reach*) describes how modern Salmon Sluitum is cooked in that fashion:

> You make a good fire of any hardwood. (The Indian considered alder a necessity since alder smoke gives the salmon an added flavor.) The fish are scaled and have their heads, tails, and fins removed. The backbone is also carefully removed—without cutting the salmon—by making an incision down each side of it on the flesh side, not the skin side of the fish. The fish is then flattened out and in this position two wooden skewers are thrust entirely through it, one near the place where the head would be, and the other near the tail. These skewers must have about a ten-inch projection because they stand upright on the ground supporting themselves against a four-foot-high crossbar of wood, with sawhorse ends, which is placed above the coals. Thus, leaning on the crossbar, the salmon cook two and a half to three hours, so that the oils are driven by the heat back into the fish. Their only seasoning is salt, plus the alder smoke and their own inimitable flavor.

The Forest Service has a recommendation that can be used for any fish and is particularly good for flat fish: —— -

> Cut off the head and tail, split open the back, but do not cut clear through, leaving the fish so that it may be opened wide like a book and tacked on a plank or piece of bark. Tack some thin slices of bacon or pork to the end of the fish that will be uppermost when before the fire, and if you like, a few slices of raw onion sprinkled with pepper and salt. Sharpen one end of the plank and drive it into the ground before a bed of hot coals, catch the drippings in a tin cup or large spoon and baste the fish continually until done.

Oak or hickory are recommended. But in the Pacific Northwest mountain-mahogany, willow, cottonwood, quaking aspen, Douglas maple, or alder are usually all that are available; but they will produce satisfactory results. In the woods this method is sometimes used by preference and sometimes because dishes have been lost or left behind. That is how Roy happened to perfect the art of cooking trout on a rock.

He was at Green Lake with a party that had packed in for an overnight trip from the North Minam Meadows. When they unpacked, it was found that all the dishes had been left behind. Roy scratched his head and set about designing a method for cooking trout. He got a flat rock some three feet in diameter, propped it at an angle of 45 degrees, and built a fire against it, keeping the fire going for three hours. Then he moved the fire back about two feet, dusted off the rock, and prepared the trout. He sprinkled them with salt and pepper and rolled them in flour. The whole fish was put on the rock, without grease. The heat of the rock cooked the underside of the trout and the heat of the fire cooked the outside.

When trout is handled in this way it is dry and mealy. There is enough oil in the skin to protect the flesh. When the trout is done, the skin is curled and burned. I have found that many who dislike pan-fried trout eat great quantities of trout prepared in this manner.

There was a night at Cheval Lake in the Wallowas when Roy and I so operated. We cooked 36 trout that were from 8 to 12 inches long. There were four us, and not enough trout to satisfy everyone.

A comparable result is obtained by adding salt and pepper, wrapping the trout in the thoroughly wetted broad leaves of the vanilla leaf plant, covering the package with mud, and burying it in hot ashes and coals. Roy has an alternative. He makes a thick dough with flour as though for bread and wraps the trout in the dough. The package is buried in hot ashes and coals. The dough serves to keep the trout moist and to protect it from the fire; before eating, it is peeled off and discarded.

The champion of all recipes of this nature was discovered by Ben Hur Lampman. I report it in his words, taken from the *Oregonian*:

A man came into the office, and seated himself the other side of the desk, and said that he had recently read Nancy Morris's instruction on how to cook fish that will prove irresistible. It sounded good, he agreed, but he himself had a way of preparing fish that was far superior, although he greatly doubted if Miss Morris would give the recipe space in her column. Nor would you find it in cookbooks. Yet of all fish he remembered, it was trout cooked this way that had lingered unforgettably in memory. Why, sir, when he thought of that fish, he could hear the shouting of the south fork where it leaps down the canyon. And first, of course, if you would have such fare, you must catch your fish—nor should those be fingerlings, but deep-flanked specimens as long as your forearm, and just as they are when the net lifts them.

And then, he said, you will make a shallow depression in the sandbar and build your fire there. You ask—he repeated—if we are now at the river? Where else? To be beside the river is essential to the recipe. One piles the driftwood high, and keeps on fishing while the sand is heated and the bed of coals is formed. Now rake the glowing coals aside, and the superheated sand, and, having swathed your trout in damp paper, consign the fish to this pit. At once restore both sand and embers, and leave a small fire burning. Then keep on fishing, say for half an hour. And when you judge your trout is done, remove the embers and the sand, and lift him in his paper casing to the waiting log. Carefully, carefully now! With a flick or so of the knife point the viscera, compacted, are removed. What? Well, in those days he had always carried a shaker of salt in his creel.

And so, beside the south fork, in a slow rain long ago—he said—they had eaten such fish as that of which Walton said it was "too good for any but anglers, or very honest men." A most remarkable trout, with surprisingly little sand in it—considering—and served with the sauce of hunger, which doth surpass all else.

Salmon pemmican was from time immemorial a staple of the Columbia River Indians. Cooked salmon was pounded, salmon oil added, and the flesh thoroughly kneaded. It was crammed into salmon-skin bags which were sealed with glue. From all reports it would keep this way for several years.

Sometimes the salmon was mixed with the palatable bulbous roots of the wapato or camass. Other varieties were made with pounded serviceberries, pounded dried venison, and deer tallow. Equal quantities of bitterroot and serviceberries sometimes were mixed with fat and boiled and added to the salmon. Or meal made from sunflower seeds was added, together with fat. On occasion, unseeded berries of the chokecherry were mashed in a mortar and mixed in.

Today smoked salmon is preferred—smoked over a slow fire of willow, apple, Douglas maple, hickory, or alder. One of the best smokers of salmon or steelhead I know is August Slathar of Forks, Washington, whose smokehouse is near Maequatta—our lodge by the Quillayute River on the Olympic Peninsula.

Auggie's process is elaborate. The salmon are cut lengthwise along the backbone and then into 4-inch pieces, and washed and scrubbed. A layer of these pieces is placed in a stone crock or wooden tub, skin side down. This is covered with a light coating of salt "about twice as heavy as if you are going to fry them." Then another layer of fish and salt, and so on.

They make their own brine, and should be left in it 10 or 12 hours, depending on the thickness of the fish. Then they are taken out and scrubbed (but not soaked) in fresh water and placed on a slanting board or screen to drain for three or four hours. Wet fish should not be put into the smokehouse.

While the fish are draining, a good bed of coals is prepared in the smokehouse. Auggie suggests peeling the bark if alder is used, for that bark makes the fish strong. The fish are placed on latticed trays over the fire. It takes four to five days of continuous smoke to complete the process. The fire should smolder. Green wood is therefore better. The smokehouse should never be over 80 degrees. The process will produce good smoked salmon for anyone, though Auggie's special skill and know-how give his smoked fish an exceptionally sweet flavor.

Trout are best preserved by smoking. When they are so treated and hung in a sack near a cookstove, they will keep several weeks even in summer. That retards molding.

Smoked trout is a delicacy of the hills, and fairly easy to prepare. Roy Schaeffer and I smoked some on a July weekend in a remote part of the Wallowas; and a week later President Roosevelt was enjoying them at the White House. We were camped at Cheval Lake, a hard 12 miles from Lapover. We were catching an abundance of eastern brook trout and were eager to preserve them. The weather was hot even for the high mountain shelf, so we decided to make a smoker for the trout.

We dug two pits about 3 feet apart and 2 feet deep—one 3 feet square and the other about 2 feet square. We connected the two pits by a trench a foot wide, and covered the trench with bark. The smaller of the two pits was our firebox. Strips from tin cans were laid across green sticks that we had placed over this pit, leaving an open end in the pit where we could insert wood for the fire. We covered the firebox and the trench with dirt, driving four 4-foot stakes on each side of the larger pit and stretching twine between them. Next small hooks out of baling wire were tied along the twine at intervals of an inch or so. The trout were rubbed with a generous supply of salt and pepper on the inside flesh. (Instead of rubbing the trout with salt and pepper before smoking, some soak them overnight in a solution of water, salt, and sugar—for 5 pounds of trout, 2 quarts of water, 3 tablespoons of salt, 1 tablespoon of sugar.) We hung them by the gills on the hooks and covered the scaffold with tarpaulin. A fire of rotted pine and fir, built in the smaller pit, was kept going from Friday afternoon to Sunday morning—36 hours or better. The secret is to keep the trout away from flame and in a steady, cool smoke. A small flame should be kept burning so as to rid the smoke of gases that make the fish taste strong. The best wood is green willow, or alder with the bark peeled off, but cottonwood or quaking aspen will do. Yet even with the rotted pulp of pine and fir, our smoked trout were finer canapes than one can buy.

There is a lot of Labrador-tea in the Wallowas and Cascades. I have found it from 4000 to 7000 feet. It is usually found in damp or boggy places such as are common in the North Minam Meadows, though I have seen it in spots less conspicuously wet. It is a leafy evergreen shrub from one to four feet tall. Its oblong, leathery, resinous dotted leaves are alternate, with small white flowers in clusters at the ends of branches. There are five spreading petals. At the elevation of a mile in the Wallowas it usually blooms in early July.

This tea has long been known along the eastern seaboard. The Indians used it. Settlers took it up, and it received fame in the Revolution when the British product was banned because of the tax. It makes a mild, pleasant tea that suffices in a pinch on a pack trip. It is also a good seasoner for soups or mulligans. A handful of the leaves, put in a pot for the last five or ten minutes of the cooking, contributes a delicate aromatic flavor.

Pit roasting, an ancient form of fireless cooking, was extensively employed by the Indians of the Pacific Northwest, especially for fresh vegetables. A pit was dug two feet deep and a couple of feet wide. A fire was built in the pit until a layer of hot ashes and coals was formed; or heated rocks were placed in it. The coals or rocks were covered with a layer of wet bracken. The food was placed on top of the bracken, and covered by another layer of wet bracken, and the pit was filled with dirt. The food would be left in the pit several days. In case greater speed was desired, a fire would be built on top.

This is a method of cooking well worth mastering. It is especially handy when one has a headquarters camp in the mountains and is taking side trips. When one leaves on a Monday, he can bury Wednesday or Thursday night's supper in the ground and have it waiting for him piping hot on his return. It also will be helpful if cooking utensils are lost or left behind.

Pit roasting is a superior method of cooking. Any vegetable can be used, though some are better than others. Carrots, onions, and potatoes are, for example, good ones to include. Small sizes are preferable. If only large ones are available, they should be cut into pieces no bigger than a walnut. When meat and vegetables are cooked together, it is best to cut the meat into slices an inch or two thick. After salt and pepper are added, the entire dish is wrapped in flour sacking, wrapped again in several layers of heavy brown paper, and further wrapped in wet burlap.

The pit should be about two feet deep, with four or five inches of hot coals at the bottom. These should be coals of hardwood. I have either built the fire in the pit or raked the coals into it from a fire built on the ground. The wet burlap package is placed directly on the coals. Rocks can also be heated and placed on top of the burlap. The pit is then filled with dirt. If a thick bed of coals is used on the bottom and hot rocks on top, a meal of meat and vegetables for almost any sized group can be cooked in four to six hours. A whole quarter of beef can be cooked this way in 16 hours. That is the way we barbecue beef each July on Hart Mountain in southern Oregon for the Order of the Antelope.

A roast can be cooked that way overnight. Damon Trout, who cooks roasts of venison or beef this way, places a thin metal sheet above the roast before filling the pit with dirt.

I remember when Roy Schaeffer and I got back to our cabin late in the evening after a hard pack trip. We were tired and famished. We had come through a snowstorm on top of the Wallowas and were wet and cold. The prospect of preparing supper was not a cheerful one. Roy excused himself, saying he would be back in a minute. I saw him take a shovel and flashlight and enter the woods above the cabin. He was back in 15 minutes with a dirty looking burlap package in his hands.

"What's that?"

"Supper," he replied.

"Supper? You're fooling."

But he wasn't. Three days earlier, before we left on the trip, he had prepared this supper and buried it in a pit of coals.

"Figured we might get back late," he added.

When the scorched and dirty outer layer of burlap was removed and the brown paper discarded, there was a piping hot dish of vegetables and lamb. For a supper dug out of the ground and placed before a weary traveler of the mountain trails it was most satisfying.

Roasting meat over an open fire is an ancient method of cooking. Gene and Frank Marsh have barbecue recipes for this method that are the best I have discovered. Their recipe for beef barbecue is equally good for venison or elk:

Roll 35 pounds of boned steer beef, similar to a rolled roast. Run 6 or 8 skewers or pins ⅛ inch in diameter, 30 inches long, crosswise through center of roll, and wire skewers to barbecue irons in position to place on frames over open oak wood fire. Cook over medium fire for approximately 5 hours. Turn frequently and baste with following sauce:

   1 gallon meat stock
   2 quarts tomato juice
   1 tablespoon dry mustard

2 tablespoons sugar
4 tablespoons vinegar
1 bottle Worcestershire sauce
1 cup grated onion
1 clove garlic, minced
1 bottle catsup
1 pound butter
2 tablespoons salt
1 teaspoon black pepper
1 teaspoon paprika
few drops tabasco sauce

Make meat stock from bones and scraps of beef, boil for one hour, add other ingredients and simmer for 30 minutes. Baste hot.

Many have discovered that the best meal in the mountains for wet or dead-tired people is something that is hot, in semi-liquid form, and crammed with calories. Such a food is especially welcome to a fisherman or hunter who has exhausted himself on streams or on the crags. As the warmth spreads through his body, he will be ready to crawl into his bag or sack for immediate sleeping.

The first of these dishes I ever tasted under those circumstances was at the North Minam Meadows. One time when Henry Hess, United States Attorney for Oregon, Roy Schaeffer, and I were camped there, Henry and I took a day trip to Green Lake, high on the ridge to the south. We fished until dusk. By the time we had cleaned our fish, put up our rods, saddled our horses, and entered the thick woods that lead out of the lake, it was dark. The horses circled back on us, eager to return to the good feed they saw at the lake. They did that over and again until we were lost. We had no flashlight, and only a few matches which we decided to save in case we were stranded for the night. We finally found the trail by getting off and walking. Once on it, we stayed there by feeling the sides of it with our feet. It is only two miles to the Meadows from Green Lake, but it took us four hours.

I was tired beyond words. I had been ravenous several hours earlier, but fatigue had taken the edge off the hunger. The cup of stew Roy handed me was the most invigorating single bit of food I can recall. It is put together as follows:

Boiling beef should be barely covered with water and allowed to simmer all day long.

Potatoes should be cooked separately and added about a half-hour before serving. At the same time add one can of corn, one can of string beans, one can of peas, and two sliced onions. Add salt and pepper to taste and bring to a boil. About fifteen minutes later add a can of tomatoes, a can of tomato juice, and a dash of tabasco sauce. Boil for another fifteen minutes and serve.

This stew is served in a cup.

There is much folklore about frying or grilling steaks in the woods. I append a few observations. There is an excellent way of frying steak without grease. Wade Hall, of the Forest Service, suggested it to me. It comes in handy when there is no grease in camp or when there is someone in camp with ulcers:

Heat frying pan until hot enough to fry steak but use no lard or other grease. When pan is hot sprinkle enough table salt in the bottom of the pan to give it a gray appearance and then fry your steak as usual. The salt will prevent sticking.

Ferd Oberwinder, advertising specialist of St. Louis, showed me the best of all possible ways to cook steak. A thick bed of coals is required, preferably of charcoal but the coals of mountain-mahogany, oak, or hickory will do.

Rub salt freely into the steak, dip in olive oil or some vegetable oil, and place it *right in the coals*. Sear each side quickly. Baste with a sauce that is made as follows: 1 bottle Worcestershire sauce, ¼ pound butter, 3 nubbins of garlic, juice of 1 lemon, 1 pint of tomato puree. Turn the steak frequently, basting on each turn.

This steak has the aroma of the woods in it. It will be black and charred on the edges and will carry a delicate trace of wood smoke.

Art Abbott, of the Forest Service, who, according to A. G. Lindh, "lived and died the victim of a hearty appetite in a land of mediocre camp cooks," was largely responsible for the *Lookout Cookbook*, Region One, which has many fine recipes, and a few suggestions for pack trips such as the following:

Grease top of kettle when cooking fruit . . . and it will not boil over.

A few drops of vinegar added to the boiling water in which an egg is to be poached will prevent the egg from breaking.

If soup is too salty, add slices of raw potato. Boil and remove.

Before heating milk in a saucepan, rinse pan in hot water and it will not scorch so easily.

To prevent cheese from molding, wrap in a cloth wrung out in vinegar. Then roll in paper.

In cooking vegetables, cover those that grow under the ground; leave uncovered those that grow above the ground.

A pinch of soda stirred into milk that is to be boiled will keep it from curdling.

When you suspect that your cooking has been scorched because you have neglected it for just one moment too long, lift the vessel holding the food quickly from the fire and stand it in a pan of cold water for a few minutes. In almost every case the scorched taste will entirely disappear.

Many attractive dishes have been concocted in an unorthodox manner in the woods. On a fishing trip in North Carolina I learned that potatoes can be boiled so as to have a roasted or baked effect. To every quart of water add a half-cup of salt. When the potatoes are cooked and allowed to drain for a few minutes, they will have the mealy taste of baked potatoes.

Simple dishes appeal in the mountains. That's partly owing to the hunger that comes from the strenuous exercise. It's partly the fragrance of wood smoke drifting along the banks of a stream or wafting up from a lake shore. It's partly the enchantment of the campfire that draws people together, making each meal an important and intimate affair. Fried potatoes then move way up the list of delicacies.

In the woods, sheepherder's potatoes become de luxe. They are made in a frying pan with sliced onions and diced bacon. Water is added to keep them constantly moist while cooking. I'm not sure what appeal they might have in the city. I have been reluctant to try them for fear the enchantment might be broken. In the woods the odor of potatoes, onions, and bacon is tantalizing. And for me it is associated with sunrises in meadows where the heather is in bloom. Then the wood smoke drifts through the basin, mixing its odor with the fragrance of the breakfast and the balsam fir.

The aroma of onions cooking over an open fire is one reason, but not the only one, why Damon Trout's recipe for Pennsylvania Dutch fried onions is especially attractive:

Slice six medium sized onions and brown in frying pan. To this add 2 tablespoons sugar, 2 tablespoons vinegar and 2 tablespoons flour. This will become quite thick, so water should be added to thin to right consistency. Add salt and pepper to taste.

These are especially good served with venison liver in a hunting camp. That is what I said to Leland Hess, Oregon lawyer, when we were on a hunting trip high on Catherine Creek in the Wallowas. Leland replied: "You're right, but what wouldn't be good with venison liver?"

One July day Wade Hall and I crossed Hawkins Pass in the Wallowas to the Imnaha River. The view from the pass is the most startling in the Wallowas. This is wondrously broken country—great peaks and ridges of granitic rock, distorted as if they were born as a result of some great convulsion. The actual pass is a narrow saddle on a bleak ridge.

A distance along the ridge was a snag of ancient whitebark pine, finally destroyed after a century or more in the cruel exposure of the spot. Scattered along the ridge were bunches of dwarf pentstemon (blue beardtongue) and the showy alpine hulsea with its big yellow flower heads. All else was coarse sand and granite boulders. The few signs of botanical life were a dramatic reminder of the time it takes to reduce granite to duff or humus.

Below us to the east was granite 1000 feet high and shaped like a gargantuan bowl open at one end. High on the opposite side a trickle of water came from the rock. This was the headwaters of the Imnaha, on whose lower reaches Chief Joseph and his Nez Perce wintered. The evergreens in the bottom of the canyon were a thick mat of coarse hair.

We dropped off the ridge, followed the river, and camped in whitebark pine. The sun was turning the cliffs that command this canyon gray and green and then deep purple. We built a fire of willow, and

Wade cooked brigand steak. To do this, he cut cubes of steak, slices of onion, and squares of bacon, impaled them alternately on a sharpened stick, and broiled them over a bed of coals. The juice from the beef and bacon was dripped on bread we held under the food. The odor of the bacon and onions filled our little grove of whitebark pine on the banks of the murmuring Imnaha. The stars were out when these morsels were done. We built up the fire and ate them just as a crescent moon appeared over the range to the south.

The scene brought back memories of a time when I stopped on the ridge of foothills west of the Selah Gap out of Yakima and cooked myself a small meal—the first meal I ever had in the hills, and the most exciting. I was in my teens. That was when I went to the foothills to toughen my legs. It was dusk when I reached the northern outskirts of town and headed for the railroad bridge that crosses the Yakima River there. It was dark when I reached the top of the ridge and faced west. Some stars were out. Broken clouds were drifting in from the southwest and obscuring most of the sky. These clouds were blown by the gentle chinook that had melted snow on the ridges of the Cascades and brought the first touch of spring to the valley. This night there were scatterings of rain on the foothills, as fleeting as the clouds that raced overhead.

I came to an outcropping of lava and made a fire of sagebrush on its lee side. I had no knife or ax and therefore had to tear the sagebrush with my hands. It had a ruggedness acquired from the adversities of the desert, but after much pulling I got myself a wood supply. The shadows and flames danced against the rock as the fire whipped in the wind.

I had in my pocket a few slices of bread and a little bacon. I held a slice of bread on a stick of sage and toasted it on both sides. Then I held a slice of bacon on the stick and cooked it over the flame, catching the drippings on the bread. This was a wonderful dish. The sage was in it, and more. The fire died as I ate the sandwiches. Finally I started home. Down the ridge, the dampened sage filled the air. Now it had new meaning for me. The sage had become a part of the food, and so at last it had become a part of me.

Chapter XX   *Snow Hole*

THE day before Thanksgiving, Roy Schaeffer, Henry and Myrtie Hess, and I were going into Lapover. The town of Lostine was wet and cold; and the warmth of the big stove at the rear of Crow's general store was hard to leave. The Wallowas that reach almost to the edge of the town were covered by a lowering sky. A flurry of snow struck as we started up the canyon in Roy's truck. There was an inch of snow at Pagan Bridge. And at Pole Bridge, which is eight miles from Lostine and eight from Lapover, there were a half-dozen inches.

From that point the road climbs abruptly, skirting the canyon walls and winding through lodgepole pine and tamarack. The snow thickened the farther we penetrated the mountains. The Forest Service guard station at Lake Creek, four miles short of Lapover, was under a foot of snow. By then it was snowing hard. When we pulled into Lapover there were 18 inches.

The clouds hung low over the canyon, cutting from view Flagstaff Point on the west and Frances Peak on the east. A wind rose from the south, driving the snow before it. Visibility was reduced to 30 yards. The light in Roy's cabin extended the promise of warmth, food, companionship, and music from Roy's mouth organ.

It snowed for two days. Over 18 inches, light and dry as feathers, fell on the hardened crust of a foot and a half of old snow that had been washed by a chinook and then frozen. On the morning of the second day I explored the canyon on snowshoes, heading up the road to Turkey Flat and beyond. It was zero; and at each step the snowshoes sank in deeply.

The Wallowas in the winter are quite different from the Wallowas in summer. In a forest, 7 feet, 15 feet, 20 feet of snow work miracles. Even 3 feet are a revolution, covering most of the down timber and making a broad highway out of a tangled mass of logs and brush. Familiar landmarks disappear. A ravine filled with fescue, the scars of old slides across a mountain, the thin line of the trail swinging back and forth across a steep hillside, a patch of snowbrush, and clumps of willow and alder that mark the transit through a valley in summer—these are hidden from view or transformed. Streams and rivers are shrunk to a fraction, as if barely keeping the pulse of life going until the turbulence of spring.

The game has disappeared. The bears are holed up. The deer have gone to the lower valleys. Elk have moved farther down where some grass can be found and where there are willow, hawthorn, alder, and mountain-mahogany for browsing. Even Lapover at 5500 feet is too high for them. The cougar and coyote have followed this game, for deer and elk are their choice diet.

Wallowa Valley, where the town of Lostine is located, is one of Oregon's most attractive bird areas during midwinter. Even the high Wallowas have a goodly number of winter residents. These include Richardson's grouse, western goshawk, Rocky Mountain pygmy owl, Rocky Mountain hairy woodpecker, three-toed woodpecker, black-headed jay, camp robber, blue jay, Clark's nutcracker, Rocky Mountain pine grosbeak, red crossbill, gray-crowned rosy finch, Montana junco, water ouzel or dipper, Rocky Mountain creeper, Rocky Mountain nuthatch, red-breasted nuthatch, and mountain chickadees. Franklin's grouse and the white-winged crossbill are sometimes present, though less common.

There are also birds that seek out the high Wallowas for their winter home. These are the redpoll and snow bunting that nest on the arctic tundras, and the Bohemian waxwing that nests from British Columbia north to the tree limit in Alaska. Thus one has some company in these remote areas even in wintertime. An occasional rabbit will appear. Pine squirrels and flying squirrels are present. And in the basins the marten make their rounds, traveling long and devious routes for food. But no coyote's cry breaks the stillness of the dawn, no elk crashes through the thicket. A silence has settled on the mountains, deeper than the silence of the desert.

The Wallowas at this time retain only a few memories of summer. The most conspicuous is the snowberry. This is a bush that Lewis and Clark carried back to President Jefferson. Jefferson was enamored with it and on December 8, 1813, wrote Madame de Tesse in Paris: "Lewis's journey across our continent to the Pacific has added a number of new plants to our former stock. Some of them are curious, some ornamental, some useful, and some may by culture be made acceptable to our tables. I have growing, which I destine to you, a very handsome little shrub of the size of a currant bush. Its beauty consists in a great produce of berries of the size of currants, and literally as white as snow, which remain on the bush through the winter, after its leaves have fallen, and make it an object as singular as it is beautiful. We call it the snow-berry bush, no botanical name being yet given to it, but I do not know why we might not call it *Chionicoccos*, or *Kalicoccos*. All Lewis's plants are growing in the garden of Mr. McMahon, a gardener of Philadelphia, to whom I consigned them, and from whom I shall have great pleasure, when peace is restored, in ordering for you any of these or of our other indigenous plants."

The snowberry covers the Wallowa canyons, putting out long roots from which innumerable shoots appear. In early summer it has a flower that can give a pinkish tinge to an entire hillside. Its stems are hollow; and the older, coarser ones make fair pipestems. The Indians so used them. In late fall a white berry shows, pea-sized and snow white. Birds apparently do not touch the berry because of its bitterness. The morning I left Lapover on snowshoes there were snowberries peeping from beneath the snow in protected places under the trees. They were as difficult to see as pearls dropped from a necklace. When I picked one and pressed it between my fingers, it was as tough and nonresilient as a frozen sponge.

Flagstaff Point to the west had buried its nose from view in a low dark cloud floating in from the southwest. Frances Peak, 3500 feet above Lapover on the east, was only the vague outline of a great hulk, like a point of land seen dimly through a mist. In the summer the cliffs below it look like sheer walls of granite. But the powdering of

the snow had brought out thousands of small ledges on the walls—
thin ledges that a rock expert might use as stairs, albeit skimpy ones,
to the top.

There was not a breath of air. There had been no wind for a day;
the snow made a thick, fluffy icing on the evergreen boughs. At
Turkey Flat the Lostine River was a narrow dark thread of a stream.
In the summer it is clear and sparkling, racing with a song in its
throat to join the Wallowa. This winter day it flowed between snowbanks, slow and sluggish and shrunken. It seemed to suffer from
fatigue, barely murmuring down the canyon. Then a water ouzel appeared. He sat midstream on an ice-covered rock and sang his heart
out.

A hundred yards ahead snow fell from a tree. I thought perhaps
some animal had touched its boughs. Then I realized that it must be
the wind, coming in gusty spurts, striking the trees and then veering
off into the sky. It was as if a hand reached from the dark clouds,
causing a shower of impenetrable snow. It blotted everything from
view. I couldn't even see a tree a few feet away.

"Making up into a blizzard," said Roy.

Within the hour the gusts had steadied to a blow. The snow was
gone from the evergreens. In the summer they were supple, bending
in high winds as they played the symphony of the forests; but now
they were frozen sticks.

The wind stung as if it carried sand rather than snow. It swept the
snow into little whirlwinds that danced over the frozen meadows. It
swept the snow from low ridges and piled it against the walls of evergreens in the ravines. There was no quality of mercy or tenderness;
all was harsh and relentless.

As I bent into the storm and shuffled ahead on my snowshoes I
thought how unfriendly mountains can be. In the summer there are
roots to dig, berries to eat, fish to catch. Man can walk or run. He can
climb the ridges and go cross-country. He has freedom of movement.
He can sleep out without real danger even if lost. But in the depths
of winter all is hostile. He may exhaust himself in a few miles. He
may not find shelter or warmth anywhere. There is no assurance of

food except what he has on his back. In a few hours the wind and snow can drop him in his tracks.

These were not unpleasant thoughts, for Roy's cabin, to which I would return before dark, lay behind me only a few miles. I stood only on the edge of the hazards of the woods in winter, so my relatively safe exploration of the snowbound canyon became a bit of adventure.

That evening on my return down the canyon I stopped at our cabin, just above Roy's. I leaned on the rough log gate to the driveway. As I ended a few minutes of daydreaming I realized that something was missing. Something familiar was gone. There was an emptiness about the place. Here on a late summer afternoon I always hear the willow thrush. His nest is below the cabin. His melody floats through the canyon each evening until darkness. When day is done I listen for him. Now he was gone, wintering in South America. Tiny as he is, he left a great emptiness when he departed.

The next morning the sun was bright. The Lostine canyon was brilliant. The rock bulging out of the snow on the canyon walls seemed in contrast to be almost black. Every peak, every hump had deep snow on its shoulders. There were about three feet in the canyon; there were six feet or more on top. The thermometer hovered around zero, and the air was so clear that, as Pat Kane of Double K Ranch would say, "It will shatter if you swing your arm through it." This was a morning of beauty. I put on my snowshoes and headed up the canyon.

As I mushed along in the fluffy snow, I sensed the silence and solitude of the mountains in wintertime. There is no movement, no ripple of life anywhere. On such a morning in a high valley under deep snow man comes closer to God. This is the solitude of all time. Here man has left behind the noise and whir of life. He walks as if he were the first arrival. He finds the inner harmony that comes from communion with the heavens. He can draw strength from the austere, majestic beauty around him.

This was the beginning of winter in the Wallowas. Three feet of snow lay at my cabin. Soon the canyon would be buried under 6 or 8 or 10 feet.

People in the valley below would wake up one morning and find that spring had arrived in a rush. Not so in the high mountains. There spring advances slowly. A few robins and blackbirds return. Fence posts gradually reappear. Occasional patches of bare ground emerge. The Lostine River cuts an ever-widening swath between its snowbanks, as the gentle warmth of a chinook melts them. There will be the creaking and groaning of ice underfoot. Then at night it will freeze hard. The next day the slow grinding process will begin again. The hold of winter on the mountains is not broken in one swift stroke. As Pat Kane once said, "Spring is born slowly and laboriously at Goose Prairie." But when the western tanager appears, the labor is about over.

I choose snowshoes for cross-country travel, partly for ease of travel. Snowshoes, unlike skis, require no special mastery. One walks naturally, with an easy shuffle. Once as a novice I was out with Roy Schaeffer. We had not gone far when my ankles began to ache. He saw that I was lifting the toe of the snowshoe up with each step instead of pushing it forward through the snow in a natural shuffle. That correction eased the ache, and we settled to a steady pace for hours on end.

Snowshoes are easier than skis for climbing. I prefer them for the changeable conditions one gets in long travel—except when the snow is wet and mushy, for then a man can pick up ten or twenty pounds of it with each step and exhaust himself in a few hours. That is when he should hole up and wait for colder weather.

The best snowshoer I knew was Clarence Truitt of Yakima. Clarence traveled the Cascades in summer and winter. For years he headed a Scout troop and introduced scores of boys to the woods. His hikes have probably been unequaled for distance and daring. "You'd never know he was human the way he could walk," Jack Nelson once told me.

Clarence had snowshoed 50 miles in one day in the Cascades. One winter night word came to Yakima that someone at Bumping Lake was ill. Clarence got medicine, rode to Cliffdell below American River, then took to snowshoes. It is 24 miles from Cliffdell to Bumping Lake; he made the round trip in 16¼ hours. Yet travel on either snowshoes or skis can be painfully slow. One day Jack Nelson in wet snow made only two miles from daylight to dark.

Elon, Cragg Gilbert, and I had a comparable experience in the Cascades early in 1949. We were headed for Truitt's cabin on Gold Hill, a few miles off the Chinook Pass road and five or six miles below the summit on the east side of the Cascades. The open slopes of Crown Point, Gold Hill, and Crystal Mountain are rich with the low-bush huckleberry in the summer. There, too, the western black currant and western thimbleberry flourish. In the winter this basin provides as good skiing as one can find anywhere in the Cascades.

The road is usually open to Morse Creek, but on this day it was open only to Lodgepole, about two miles below Morse Creek. We had over four miles to go. There was 14 inches of fresh snow, and it was snowing at the rate of an inch an hour as we left Lodgepole on skis. The snow was a bit on the wet side; breaking trail was therefore not easy. It took us two hours to go the two miles to Morse Creek, even with Cragg, an expert, in the lead.

The trees were loaded. This was not a light skiff of snow; this snow was heavy. The branches of the pine and fir were so weighted they hugged the trunks of the trees, the boughs drooping like wet, folded wings. Only the tamarack, which is deciduous, stood naked and bare.

We were out seven hours and the only sign of life we saw was a pine squirrel. He came down a tree and crossed the trail ahead of us. On each hop he would almost disappear. He would jump out of one snow hole and land in another. In that strenuous way he made a snail's pace across our path.

There was the deep sleepy quiet of the woods in winter, broken only by the shu-e-e-e-e, shu-e-e-e-e, shu-e-e-e-e of the skis gliding through the snow.

At Morse Creek we turned north, left the highway, clambered up a snowbank, and entered the forest. We were in about 12 feet of snow, walking above the blazes on the trees that marked the summer trail. Stands of tightly clustered jack pine looked like low thickets. Tall whitebark pine had shrunk to the size of willow and aspen, and we walked as giants with our heads close to the tops. Occasionally

I could look over the top of a pine as if it were a bush. It was as if we were in a snow field of chaparral.

It was almost dark when we entered the woods at Morse Creek. The snow turned to sleet and then, in turn, to a cold driving rain. The skis of the man out in front sank in about 18 inches, which made breaking trail a punishing task—like walking in deep sticky mud. It took us two hours to go 200 yards, and we were soaked through without and within, from the rain and the perspiration caused by our efforts.

At eight o'clock it was still raining, and we had two more miles to go. We stopped for a consultation. At our present rate it would take us most of the night. We doubted whether we had the energy to go ahead, yet we were three hours from shelter if we turned back.

I remembered Roy's admonition to get under the snow at night. One way is to dig a tunnel into the side of a snowbank, but that would not do tonight because we were wet. We needed a fire. I looked for a snag, recalling how Roy built a fire near one and kept warm in a snow hole. Then I realized that we had neither shovel nor ax. We needed an ax to cut wood; we needed a shovel to dig a hole so that we could follow the fire as it melted its way down. We had taken neither, for Truitt had both at his cabin and we assumed snow conditions would enable us to get there quickly.

I turned to look at the path we had broken. In spite of the snow the woods were so dark I could hardly see our trail even at my feet. There was no invitation from any source—no cabin, no cave, no hollow trunk, no fallen log. Only mute trees were in view, dead stubs of trees buried in snow. I took off my skis. The snow was so thick, soft, and wet that without skis I went in up to my hips on each step. In that way I would not be able to make 200 yards all night long. I would fall in the snow and freeze to death. After floundering a few minutes and exhausting myself I put my skis back on.

An eerie feeling came over me. On every side was danger. I was at last facing the implacable enemies of man, cold and starvation. They pressed in. The trees were ghostly in the misty darkness, their cold boughs stiff fingers of the dead. They formed grotesque figures in the gloom, twisted as with anguish and suffering. They were, indeed, emigrants overtaken by winter and frozen to death. The cold and starvation that overcame them reached out to touch us.

I indulged this fantasy as I stood ready to begin the trek back. When I started up, one ski stuck in the snow, the other went forward, and down I fell. Once down I realized what welcome relief a sleep in snow could be to an exhausted man. The snow had surprising warmth. It extended an invitation to sleep,—attractive, but the most dangerous one that the woods offer.

It took us almost an hour to return to the road and another two hours to return to Lodgepole. We met Truitt and his party coming in on skis. But the heavy snow was too much even for the skiing experts. Each pole picked up a few pounds of snow. The snow balled up on the skis. We floundered for three hours on our return. We got back to our starting point at 11 o'clock at night. We had taken 7 hours to go 4 miles and we were still without shelter. And all this because we had violated one of the first principles Roy had drilled into me: never go into the woods in winter without shovel and ax. There were snags which we could have used to build a fire—if we had had an ax. We could have had the warm comfort of a snow hole—if we had had a shovel.

I did not know until weeks later how wise we were in turning back that night. Disaster had laid in wait for us. The 14 inches of new snow had fallen on old snow. When the new snow on steep slopes became wet it slid on the icy surface that underlay it and roared down the mountainsides in great avalanches. That night three such avalanches swept the Morse Creek trail that led to Truitt's cabin. Each tossed pine and fir trees before it as if they were matches. One missed the cabin by only 100 yards. It started 2000 feet up on the slopes of Crown Point, swept the mountain clean of trees, and spewed thousands of tons of rocks, trees, and snow into the valley. Its swath was 200 yards wide, and the snow it carried was 50 to 60 feet deep.

There were eight feet of snow at Goose Prairie when Elon and I visited it in the winter of 1948. We arrived after dark. Pat Kane, Kay Kershaw, Jack and Kitty Nelson were at Double K. They kept the second-floor lights on or we would never have seen the ranch-house, for the snow was piled high above the first-floor windows. We went in via a ditch through the snow eight feet deep. After dinner we sat by a roaring fire and talked far into the night.

It was raining when we arrived, and the eaves dripped all night; but in the morning it was clear. Old Scab, Buffalo, Baldy, and Nelson Peaks stood clear. Fields of snow lay in the ravines along their sides, and tongues of mist licked at them. But the mist would soon dissolve in a clear blue sky.

The snow at Goose Prairie had packed down in the rain. There were miniature mounds and depressions in its surface from the wind and rain. Only the gables of the cabins at Goose Prairie were visible, for the snow was up to the eaves. Jack Nelson, Elon, and I made a tour of Goose Prairie on snowshoes. It was hard going, for at each step we broke through the light crust.

Under the trees were long dark swaths that looked as though someone had scattered dark ashes through the woods. I asked Jack about them. "Springtails or snow fleas," he said. "They come in millions after a snowstorm. They're not visible on the flat surface of the snow, but they blacken the bottom and edges of a deer track or ski trail." I asked if birds ate them. "They love them," he replied. "Especially the chickadees and rosy finches."

We inspected the cabins that decorate Goose Prairie, those of the Boy Scouts' Camp Fife and others, perhaps a dozen in all. Some of the cabins ran east and west. Jack pointed out why that was dangerous in a country of deep snow.

"In the winter the sun is low in the south," said Jack. "So it melts only the snow on the roof with the southern exposure. The roof with the northern exposure gets no sun. When that happens one roof may be clear and the other have 8 feet of snow on it. That means that tons and tons of snow are all on one side of the cabin. That gives the structure a tremendous thrust." He showed us what he meant. Two cabins had collapsed because of it, and two others had buckled. "Always run a cabin north and south. Then the sun melts the snow evenly on both sides."

My mind went back to our cabin in the Wallowas built by Roy Schaeffer. I realized how wisely Roy had planned, for it too ran north and south, as do all the cabins Roy has ever built in the hills.

On our way up to American River, Elon and I had seen many deer. At the junction of the Tieton and Naches we had seen 50 or more elk. Elk do not ordinarily get down that low, for they do not migrate as far as the deer. But this winter they were down on the open ranges, either because of the severe winter or because of the feed furnished them or both. Some elk, however, were still in the mountains. A herd of 14 had left the ridges and high basins in the fall and descended to Goose Prairie, which lies about 3600 feet. They were still there, 3 bulls and 11 cows. They had pawed the snow for grass until it got too deep. There was some hay fed them at Goose Prairie. But for the most part their diet had been the bark of willow and alder and three mosslike lichens that hung like beards from the boughs of pine and fir trees.

There was a bright yellow lichen (*Litharia vulpina*), often called wolfsbane letharia. It is reported to have been used in the Old World, mixed with other substances, to poison wolves. Hence its name *vulpina*. It was an important dyeplant used both by aboriginal and civilized people prior to the introduction of aniline dyes. Another of the lichens looked like blackish hair. It is *Alectoria fremonitii*, an indigenous lichen of the Western states which was discovered by General John C. Fremont. And a third lichen that the elk were eating was a seagreen hairlike plant called *Alectoria sarmentosa*, a creeping species of wide distribution.

Lichens are one of the earliest forms of life. These species on which the Goose Prairie elk were feeding were members of a family that have been associated with man throughout his long vicissitudes. Llano has reported they were an ancient source of medicine and poisons; they have been used in brewing, distilling, tanning, and dyeing, and have been utilized as raw materials in the perfume and cosmetic industries. The Northwest Indians used at least one species (*Alectoria jubata*) for food. And Llano reports that "The biblical manna of the Israelites appears to have been *Lecanora esculenta* which is still eaten by desert tribes, being mixed with meal to one-third of its weight" (2, *Economic Botany* 15). This lichen, according to Llano, grows in the mountains and is "blown loose into the low-

lands where the thalli pile up in small hummocks in the valley."
And in the subarctic regions certain species of lichens are a main part
of the diet of reindeer and cattle. But the three mosslike lichens
of Goose Prairie seemed to me meager food for elk.

"They haven't had a square meal since November first," said
Jack. And they looked it, for they were gaunt and thin. "The danger
now is the coyote," he added.

"Anything else to bother them here in the winter?" I asked.

"Lynx, bobcat, and bush wolves all winter at Goose Prairie and
Bumping Lake. Not many, however. Worst of all is the coyote."

We walked down to Bumping River, now only a trickle. A water
ouzel was diving into a pool for food. Jack pointed across the river
to a thick stand of willows. "When we get a couple of warm days
in February or March the buds of the willows will come out. Same
is true of alder and cottonwood. Then the elk will go for them and
strip these thickets clean. Elk will walk away from hay for willow
buds."

The elk were up to their shoulders in snow. They ran single file
in trails they had made. They knew the starvation that the mountains offer in the winter. Only the lichens had pulled them through.

In the winter the mountains offer only remnants of their hospitality.
Death stalks man and game when the deep snow comes. The lifeline
is as flimsy as the lichens on the evergreens at Goose Prairie or the
cambium layer under the bark of the bull pine that the Indians
scraped off with a piece of deer bone and ate raw.

There are not many ways of building a campfire in deep snow,
for the fire disappears as the snow melts and man is left on top to
freeze. Clarence Truitt, on his early snowshoe trips in the Cascades,
would often cut green trees and make a platform perhaps six feet
square. On this he would build a small fire. In that way he did not
lose his fire and end up with only a hole in the snow steaming with
smoke. But Roy Schaeffer's snow hole is better.

Crystal Mountain is about four miles from Truitt's cabin at Gold
Hill. It lies 7500 feet high, and is one of the most commanding
views in the Cascades. There is a narrow backbone of mountain

that drops away to the south a mile or more. Steep slopes lie on either side, and when the snow is right they offer exciting ski runs. In the distance Mount Hood punctures the sky with its sharp point. Then come Adams, St. Helens, the Goat Rocks, and Mount Aix. These familiar friends become strangers when a deep snow covers them and the intervening ridges, for the snow wipes out many of the familiar landmarks.

To the north and east are ridges that look like waves of broken glacier ice running to the horizon. Mount Stuart looms on the right. To the west is Rainier, less than ten miles away—so close it seems that one can touch it. The frozen ribbon of White River, running off Rainier, lies immediately below. Little Takhoma and Steamboat Prow—mountains set on the side of Rainier—rise in front. The sheer rock of one of Rainier's most formidable obstacles, Willis Wall, is dark and forbidding against its snowy background. Towering over the whole scene is the massive mountain. Emmons Glacier, the largest on Rainier, is visible its whole length from the summit all the way down to White River. Rainier, deep in snow, is cold, austere, incredibly majestic.

One day in March Elon and I were headed for Crystal Mountain. We had left the car at Morse Creek and walked the two miles to Truitt's cabin, carrying food and supplies. We also bore our snowshoes and skis, for the snow was crusted enough for us to walk on it with ease. The day was overcast, with a feel of snow. There was little sign of life in the woods, nothing except a big bald eagle with a two-foot wingspread that soared along the treetops and lighted at a safe distance on an old snag, watching us until we were out of sight.

There were nine feet of snow on the level at Gold Hill. It had blown in drifts over the cabin, leaving only a suggestion of a mound with a stovepipe sticking out. By the time we reached the cabin the temperature had risen to 41 degrees and there was a slight dripping from the eaves. Near the cabin scatterings of alder poked through the snow. A few warm days had stirred them to life and formed light-green buds at their extremities.

Camp robbers, blue jays, and another small dark-tufted jay that

I did not identify were active about the cabin, searching for bits of food. The Cleaver, a ridge that bounds Morse Creek on the southwest, was blotted out. On the other side the clouds hung low over Gold Hill and Crown Point. But in spite of the haze I could see the line of fracture where whole snow fields had slipped and roared off their slopes.

We stayed at Gold Hill that night. By dusk the temperature had fallen to the twenties and it was snowing. It snowed all night. It was still snowing when we left for Crystal Mountain in the morning. Cragg Gilbert and Bob Strausz joined us. They were on skis; Elon and I wore snowshoes. Each man carried a pack; mine was a trapper Nelson, the others were modified Norwegians. We had a shovel and an ax, light tarps, and sleeping bags, a one-burner gasoline stove, cooking utensils (two pots and a frying pan), dishes, and food.

There were eight or ten inches of fresh powder snow that the wind could pick up as easily as it could dust. The first part of the trip was nearly noiseless, except for the crunch, crunch, crunch, of the snowshoes. The snow-bound valley was deathly still. Snow cut the visibility to a few hundred yards. The basalt cliffs and domes that decorate the Cleaver were hidden. There were two huge mounds on our left that marked old miners' cabins, now buried in snow. This valley is rich in prospector's lore. Here many men, including Tom Fife, had sought gold.

The valley abounds in Alaska yellow cedar (Alaska cypress) with its long delicate leaves. This morning they were snow-dusted, creating a wondrous filigree effect. Then came the wind, gentle at first and finally of blizzard proportions. It whipped the snow into clouds and shook showers from the trees.

It was early afternoon when we came to the head of the Morse Creek basin. Directly above us on the northwest was Crystal Pass; on the southwest was Sourdough Pass, a narrow defile in a knife-edge of basalt. They are low points in the rim of the bowl where Morse Creek rises. We were about 500 feet under Crystal Pass. The growing wind caused us to wonder if it would be wiser to camp below the pass than above it. Cragg and Bob dropped their packs and reconnoitered. They soon came racing down from Crystal Pass, the light snow whirling in clouds from their skis, to report that a blinding blizzard was raging above. We decided to make camp and get under the snow.

We found a snag 12 inches in diameter on the edge of a clump of alpine fir. The snow was at least 15 feet deep. The snag looked like the chimney of an old shack. When we chopped off its top, we had a log about 25 or 30 feet long. The outside wood was wet from snow and rain, but when we split out the core the wood was dry. The snag had collected none of the moisture of the ground in its long decay. We started a fire with small shavings from the core, using what are known as fire flames—a petroleum by-product made by an oil company. They look like small flat cakes of paraffin or beeswax. They burn for about ten minutes, and are quite an asset in wet or wintry weather.

We soon had a good fire burning not far from the trunk of the snag. As it burned the snow melted, and we followed the fire down by shoveling away the snow. As we shoveled, we kept our wood supply with us, since we followed the snag down. Our snow hole was some six feet square. The fire melted about a foot of snow an hour. By the time we went to bed and let the fire go out, we were eight feet down in the snow.

Cooking under such circumstances has special problems. The fire is constantly sinking into the snow, causing pots and pans to tip and food to spill. Even a gasoline stove set in snow is unstable. We lost two pans of water because the heat of the stove melted the snow under it, causing it to tip. Melting snow for water presents several difficulties. If one fills a pan with snow and puts it over the fire, he may ruin the pan, for the first water melted is absorbed by the snow, leaving the bottom of the pan dry. Moreover, the snow, if it is dry, may have as little as five per cent water in it. That was about the content the night we camped below Crystal Pass. Getting enough water for cooking was time-consuming. This was impressed on me because I was thirsty. We had not taken along cans of grapefruit juice, apple juice, or other thirst-quenching liquids; our packs were heavy, so we left them behind. That was a mistake. One perspires heavily on a cross-country snowshoe trip. There usually are no streams where one can quench his thirst. On this March trip we finally resorted to licking snow from the branches of the trees. But snow does not quench thirst, and the melting seemed interminably long.

At last we had soup, made from dried vegetables and meat. We cooked dried beef and made a gravy of flour and dried milk. We made mashed potatoes of dried potatoes. We had bread and butter and cups of hot chocolate. It was a wonderful meal for the snow hole. We ate it in a snowstorm, driven by a bitter cold wind. We huddled close to the fire, and took turns shoveling out the pit.

Cragg and Bob slept in a two-man tent they pitched in a near-by grove. Elon and I dug an alcove into one wall of the snow hole. Here we placed fir boughs. We put a nylon tarp over the boughs and our sleeping bags on the tarp. Pulling the tarp over us, we lay in our alcove as bears would in a hole. About 10 o'clock we let the fire die. Though it stormed all night, we were warm and comfortable.

One has to lie deep in the snow to learn how warm and protective it is. A den in the snow confines the body heat like a blanket or overcoat. It is a snug place, no matter how the wind may howl. One who holes up in the snow understands better the mysteries of woods in the winter. He knows why in severe weather grouse squirm their way under soft snow and lie quiet. He understands why deer bury themselves in drifts, lying a half-day or more with just their heads sticking out. He learns something of the comfort of the bear in hibernation.

As I lay in the snow hole I remembered the evening before in Truitt's cabin. We had to go down icy steps 9 feet to enter it. Once inside I had an experience difficult to describe. I felt closer perhaps than ever before to my friends. We were buried deep in the snow together, sharing the threat of the blizzard. Sleeping in the snow hole was a comparable experience. Lying there in the alcove I felt a new relationship to the wilderness—an affinity even closer than when one lies on the shore of a mountain lake in August or in the heather of a high basin, or on a bed among Indian paintbrush and cinquefoil in a mountain meadow. It was a closer tie than is given by the night music of the treetops under the shoulder of a snow-capped range.

It came to me why this is true. When man holes up in the snow, he returns to earth in a subtle way. He does not return in the manner of a man or a tree or a bird who dies, for then the body is reclaimed by mold and transformed into the dust from which it came. In a deep hollow of the snow, man returns to the womb of the earth to live. Lying in the warm darkness he captures a fleeting sense of the security of that part of his life that existed before his own consciousness. He escapes the reality of the world and lowers the tempo of his own life. He lies relaxed and peaceful, safe in a warm embrace. Death and danger may stalk abroad, but in his retreat there is no risk.

We were up by seven in the morning. The storm was over. The clouds had risen so that we could see Crystal Pass and Sourdough Pass above us. On the crest of the ridges were cornices of snow 20 to 40 feet high, formed by the whipping of the wind. Towering over Sourdough Pass was Sourdough Peak, a jagged blade of rock that commands the ridge.

"How did Sourdough Pass get its name?" I once asked Charles Hussey who in the winter often secludes himself at Gold Hill.

"A long time ago," he said, "a pack train of miners was coming over the pass headed for Gold Hill. A bear frightened the horses. One pack horse started to bolt and the wife of one of the miners shouted, 'Save the sourdough.'"

The clouds hung low over Morse Creek that morning, but we were 6000 feet high and above them. From our altitude they looked like low-hanging fog forming an opaque ceiling over the valley. Far to the southeast was the American Ridge, its hogback sharp against a blue-gray sky, its ledges resplendent with powder snow.

Now the rocky crags of the Cleaver that bounds the Morse Creek basin on the south were in full view. There mountain goats range the year around. That ridge is mounted with basalt formations—knife-like peaks, rounded domes, fluted spires. They often have at their bases cliffs of 200, 300, 500 feet. This morning the peaks and cliffs were coated with snow that seemed to have been driven into the rocks themselves. Only traces of dark basalt could be seen.

Suddenly an avalanche of snow fell from one of the cliffs of the Cleaver a half-mile or so across the basin. It was a white cascade 400 feet high and 50 yards wide. It looked like the white water of a Niagara, even to the mist formed by the finely powdered snow. It was like Niagara except that it was gone in ten seconds. The roar of its passing had what John Muir once described as the "low massy thunder tones of snow avalanches." Again and again it happened: cascades of snow tumbled from cliff after cliff, laying bare the basalt rock and carrying clouds of powdered mist in their wake. Again and again the basin was filled with the deep-throated roar of tons of snow pounding on rocks. A whole mountain shook itself, spraying the valley. Then the basin settled again to the quiet and repose of dead winter.

We had breakfast of soup, oatmeal with butter and dried milk, bacon, bread, and chocolate. As we were washing the dishes, Bob pointed to the top of our snag and said, "Some summer a boy will be riding by this place and look up and see this snag. He'll turn to his father and say, 'Dad, how did that tree over there get chopped off 15 feet above the ground?' And the old man will shake his head and say, 'Don't know, son.' "

Elon chuckled. "They will never hear of Operation Snow Hole or dream there was such a thing."

We put on our snowshoes and skis and shouldered our packs. We were about to start along the mountainside when Cragg spoke up: "Too bad more people don't know about Operation Snow Hole. People in the valley should send their children back in here summer and winter. The young folks should learn how to live dangerously, how to survive in the wilderness on their own. Then they'd be self-reliant and independent. People coddle their children, make them afraid. They forget that the wilderness holds the secrets of survival."

As we left the snow hole and leaned forward under our packs, I looked up at Sourdough Peak. It was being blotted out. A new storm was moving in from the west. The basin would soon be lashed by a biting wind that drove powder snow before it.

Chapter XXI *Klickitat*

ELON, Doug, and I had always planned to climb Mount Adams, but somehow we never got around to it when we were boys. There was a group of alpine specialists in the valley, but we were not part of it. One of the leaders was Elon's older brother, Curtiss. At an early age he, like Clarence Truitt, was testing his heart and lungs against the highest peaks. When we finally climbed Mount Adams (12,307 feet), in August, 1945, Curtiss led the way. He had climbed it first as a boy, and this was his twelfth ascent. He had also scaled Mount Rainier (14,408 feet) seven times. He acquired at an early age an insatiable appetite for the challenging peaks. He climbed all the major ones from Washington to California—Whitney (14,496 feet) once, Shasta (14,162 feet) twice, Lassen (10,496 feet) once, Hood (11,245 feet) five times, St. Helens (9671 feet) five times, Goat Rocks (8201 feet) seven times, Stuart (9470 feet) fifteen times, Glacier Peak (10,436 feet) twice, Shuksan (9038 feet) once, and Baker (10,750 feet) twice. He climbed most of the minor pinnacles within striking distance of Yakima, including Kloochman, Fifes, and Cleman.

Curtiss probably knew the Cascades as intimately as any other man in history, white or Indian. For 27 years he had a scout troop in Yakima sponsored by the Congregational Church. He introduced about 350 boys to the woods, helping them to discover the mysteries of the mountains. When he died the other day from a heart attack, it seemed as though he had expended himself in a brief 54 years so that others might have a fuller life.

He could have spent his week ends in comfort and ease before the fire or at a bridge table in a club, but he chose a harder life. He took every opportunity to lead his troop to the hills. He averaged 30 overnight hikes a year. These trips circled the rim of Yakima Valley, explored all sides of Adams and Rainier, touched on most of the high lakes of the Cascades, tapped the wondrous Goat Rocks region, and followed the ridge of the Cascades from the Columbia on the south to Cady Pass on the north.

He slept on the ground with his scouts. He taught them to build a fire in a wet forest, to chop wood without risk of injury to their feet. He taught them to be unafraid in the dark woods, to go through a forest by the stars and the ridge lines of the mountains. He taught the art of climbing—the synchronizing of lungs and legs; he showed how to assault cliffs and crags. He taught the citizenship of the mountains: clean camps, sanitation, protection of the woods against fire, service to the other chap and consideration of his wants and comforts. The mountains were his training camp for youth.

Doug had been in China for almost 20 years prior to 1941. He had a medical mission at Hofei supported by the Christian Church of Yakima and by a host of his other friends. He came out on the last boat that left Japan for this country prior to Pearl Harbor. For the next four years he practiced medicine in Yakima. He visited Washington, D.C. in May, 1945. We were sitting on my porch as the sun was setting over the hills of Maryland. Talk turned to the Cascades and Mount Adams.

"I suppose you're too soft to climb Mount Adams now," said Doug with a twinkle in his eye. I poked his waistline. "You're the last man who should talk about anybody being soft." Out of an evening of banter came a bargain: We made a date to climb Mount Adams that summer.

Doug picked the first week end after V-J Day. It was the finest week end of the summer, with northwest winds and clear skies. We were to meet at the Maryhill ferry. The banks of the Columbia at Maryhill are barren. Only an occasional willow along the water's edge breaks the immense monotony. On both sides of the river the hills rise abruptly 1000 feet or more, revealing thick layers of lava rock that the Columbia has uncovered in its drive to the sea. Apart from irrigated places, there is nothing but desert life. A Peattie would recognize in these sagebrush plains and canyons, even in

August, the western bee-plant and the golden blazing star. But the bloom of the desert has gone, and there are only sterile remnants of the life that awakens at the touch of spring. There is sage and cheatgrass and some bunchgrass.

It is hot in the sun. The heat of this vast inland empire is dry; it can feel like the blast from a furnace. Of this stretch of country Billy McGuffie once said, "Thae braes are sae lanesome i' the simmer that gin a rabbit gaed through them, he wud hae tae tak his piece wi' him." But the shade of a locust is refreshing in daytime, and the nights are cool.

This is part of the inland area that was covered by sequoias and evergreens some 20 million years ago. Then the clouds of the Pacific dropped their water here and made this land rich and verdant. But the earth buckled and up came the Cascades, shutting out the rain clouds. Gradually desert life took hold; and there it will remain until the Cascades are worn away by wind and frost and rain, and wet ocean winds once more lick this plateau.

This stretch of the Columbia Lewis and Clark found most dreary. There are fish in the river, but no game for miles around. Here they saw the natives using "straw, small willows and southern wood" (sagebrush) for fuel. A cold, raw wind pours down the canyon in winter. That wind turns in the summer, whips across the barren benches on top of the ridges that form the canyon, and picks the dust from fallow wheat land to send it whirling to the east.

Our party met at noon on the Washington side of the Maryhill ferry. We sat in the shade of a locust by an abandoned house and ate lunch. We were gay with expectations. In an hour we were on our way. We went downriver by car to White Salmon. Here we left the semiarid desert behind us, for it is near White Salmon that the eastern slopes begin to catch the drippings from clouds over the Cascades and the rich timber belt begins its reach toward the sea.

At White Salmon we turned north to the Trout Lake guard station of the Forest Service, where we stopped to get a campfire permit. Then we continued north on the Forest Service road to Morrison Creek and Cold Springs, which lay about 6000 feet high on the southern slopes of Adams. The road goes a mile or two beyond Cold

Springs, but we stopped there because it was the last campground with water. Cold Springs has a shelter, a small building with three walls and a roof. We built a fire near the open end and soon had supper ready. We ate extra portions, for this would be our last good meal until we came down the mountain the next evening.

There was excitement in the air, the kind that comes on the evening of a schoolboy's debate, a lawyer's argument before court, or some other adventure. There was talk of crampons, alpenstocks, ice axes, snow glasses, glaciers, snow fields, and mountain peaks up and down the Cascades. We talked of food to eat before and during a climb—and of food not to eat. Doug ran a first-aid station, examining feet, doctoring blisters, applying bandages. We did not sit around the campfire long after supper. We had to be up by 2 A.M. and start climbing by 3 or 3:30 in order to get over the snow fields before the snow got soft and mushy.

We should have slept in comfort, but with darkness came a cold wind. Cold Springs is on a low shoulder of Adams and not far from snow fields. The wind whipped around the edges of our sleeping bags. I slept cold and fitfully, and was wide awake when Curtiss roused the camp at 2 A.M.

Breakfast was frugal. We huddled shivering around a small fire, waiting for water to boil. Tea, cocoa, soup, crackers, and raisins were the breakfast Curtiss had ordered. It was wise to eat light before a climb; then there was less chance of cramps or altitude sickness.

By 3 A.M. we were on our way. Each of us carried chocolate and raisins in a knapsack. Some carried canteens for water; others carried cans of apple juice. The route was northwest on a Forest Service road for a mile or so. The morning star hung against a low shoulder of Mount Adams on our right, as bright and brilliant as any gasoline lamp. It hung so low that it might have been a bright light in a cabin window. It promised a clear morning for the climb and a blue sky at the top.

Curtiss was ahead with a flashlight. By 3:30 we struck a trail that followed a ravine. There was a creek at which we filled canteens. We began to gain altitude steadily. It was a rocky, sandy trail that led into an ancient lava field where benches of the black lava stood solid and unbroken. By 5 o'clock we could see the first snow field ahead. We were now at 7000 feet. The ascent became steeper, and we stopped more frequently for breath. The professional climbers and some of the younger members of our group began to outstrip us: Doug Corpron, Jr. and Ruth Corpron, Curtiss, Cragg, Mark, and Carol Anne Gilbert. They soon left us far behind, taking five hours to our eight for the climb.

Elon, Doug, my son Bill, and I stopped at the edge of the first snow field to study the course. It was 5:30 A.M. and bitter cold, with the wind a gale. The sun was rising, but we could not see it. The snow field we were on was at the bottom of a big bowl. To the east was South Butte, a rugged rampart of Adams that cut off the sunrise. South Butte, a small, disintegrated peak, is a parasitic cone that once was an active volcano.

Ahead was the broad sweep of the mountain. It seemed like a stranger as I first saw it that morning, because the familiar contours of Adams were gone. The last full view had been in the evening of the previous day as we neared camp. Then it towered over us, bumping the sky. Adams Glacier glistened. The black lava rock had a deep bluish tinge. That was the same view, though a more intimate one, that I had enjoyed many times from the Oregon side of the Columbia. Now all was new. Up ahead of us was a snow field broken occasionally by ribs of dark lava rock. It looked like a giant ski run. The high-humped effect of the mountain was gone, for the only top in view was the false top.

There are several routes up Adams. One approaches from the east, climbs Battlement Ridge and goes over the Castle. This is the most difficult and originally was deemed impossible. C. E. Rusk of Yakima, who worked in the land office, headed the group that first climbed the east side. That was in 1921. Clarence Truitt and Clarence Starcher were in the party. Rusk has told the story in his book, *Tales of a Western Mountaineer*. Rusk loved Mount Adams. He explored all its sides, and named most of its glaciers and peaks. When he climbed the east side he went up Rusk Glacier to the bergschrund, where the precipices are 2000 feet high and where the Klickitat Waterfall drops 1000 feet. The Castle is an immense cathedral rock rising 1500 feet out of the eastern slope. Rusk's ashes rest there in a bronze urn which Clarence Truitt and Clarence Starcher carried up the mountain in 1932.

The north-side route, by way of Killen Creek, is hard to get at and little used. But it is perhaps the easiest, for the slope is unbroken and climbing time is from three to six hours. A more difficult route comes up from the west, starting at Trout Lake and crossing Adams Glacier. The Mazama route is the southeast climb from Bird Creek Meadows, going up Mazama Glacier to the point where it joins the trail we took.

Our route led up the south side. Next to the north-side climb it is the easiest, for it has only snow fields, no glaciers. But it is longer, with one great ledge after another to climb over. In some years there is no snow to cross. Then horses could be taken to the top.

We bore right as we crossed the first snow field, hard as ice. Some wore crampons, but hobnails were enough since the slope was gentle. A rib of lava separated the first snow field from the second. As we reached the second, the sun was almost over the mountain's ridge on our right. The wind picked up and blew so hard we had to lean into it. We discovered that we had dressed too lightly. We had not worn woolen underwear, gloves, or mittens. We wore hats instead of caps, and we had no ear muffs. We were soon chilled to the bone. My face burned in the cold wind, and my fingers were numb.

Half-way across the second snow field the sun touched us, but it brought no warmth. To make matters worse, the wind whipped off my hat. It rolled on its brim edge down a snow field that stretched a mile or so off to the east, bouncing crazily as it hit an occasional rock and then continuing its mad way. It rolled on and on until I thought I saw it disappear in the lava field on the far side. I marked the spot, planning to retrieve the hat on our descent. The loss was costly, for the wind did not abate and my ears and face became numb.

We climbed 2000 feet across the two snow fields. Our course had been diagonal to the east. At 9000 feet we reached the saddle. It is a plateau in the high shoulder of the mountain. A steep snow field runs up from the edge of the saddle to the first or false top of the mountain. That snow field is bounded on the east by a hogback of lava rock. Some, including Curtiss and his two sons, Cragg and Mark, climbed the left side of the snow field. Our group went up the hogback formed of huge rocks that had tumbled crazily down the mountain. They often formed spacious rock cairns in which we got the only relief from the wind we were to have all day. We followed this ridge for about an hour, gaining 1000 feet.

At the top of this ridge the course bears west. Here the whole mountainside is made up of pyroclastics—ashes, cinders, pumice, and bombs produced by violent explosions from a volcano. It is a loose formation, as treacherous to traverse as shale. Some of it is spongy in appearance, filled with air holes. Some of the pieces are light, but a fraction of the normal weight of lava rock, and will float when first put in water.

We worked our way west along this slope until we came to the edge of a tongue of snow that stretched from the top of the ridge, some 1000 feet above us, to the first snow field we had crossed. Here we stopped for chocolate, raisins, and apple juice. It was 10 o'clock and we were about 10,500 feet up the mountain. The sun was high.

Sapphire blue lakes tucked away in remote valleys or ravines were the only open spots in the solid green slopes of the Cascades far below. To the east was what we took to be Bench Lake. To the south were nameless other waters of smaller dimension—lakes that as a boy I had heard called spirit lakes, haunted by the gods of rain. To the southwest was Trout Lake, glittering in the sun under the whipping of the wind. To the west was Mount St. Helens with its white, graceful cone.

In front to the south was Mount Hood, pushing up like the edge of a sharp gabled roof. Below us to the left was Little Mount Adams, a conical, isolated peak rising from the southeastern slope of Adams. Like South Butte, it was a parasitic cone that once had spewed lava and pumice. I had seen it first as the sun rose. Far above it, near the upper reaches of Klickitat Glacier, sulfur fumes were rising from crevasses like vapors from some caldron boiling in the vitals of the mountain.

They were perhaps one of the reasons why the Indians never went so high on the mountain as the glaciers. There doubtless were other reasons too: avalanches, blizzards, treacherous footing, absence of game,—and the Tomanowas. These were the spirits and this was their kingdom, a place taboo to man. These spirits were immortal, all-powerful. Man was no match for them. He could neither outwit nor outrun them. Coyote did both, and in so doing became one of man's greatest benefactors; for he brought fire from the mountain and gave it to the Indians.

The procuring of fire (what Kipling called the red flower) from the high Cascades is slightly reminiscent of Prometheus, who stole fire from Olympus and gave it to mankind. Coyote, too, had to steal it, and the gods were angry with him. The fire had been carefully guarded. The Tomanowas had placed it in charge of the Skookum sisters. Stealing it was not easy, for the bare mountainside made it impossible to hide oneself and it was a long way to the valley. Coyote knew the Skookums would outrun him, so he planned to establish relay stations and pass the fire from animal to animal.

Coyote made his way to the pits atop the mountain, where the Skookums guarded the fire day and night. On the change of the guard at dawn, Coyote seized the fire and dashed away. A Skookum at once was hot on his trail. She did indeed catch the tip of his tail in her hand and made it white even to this day. But Coyote reached Wolf and passed the fire to him. And then it was passed to Squirrel, to Chipmunk, to Eagle, and finally to Antelope who waited on the edge of the plains and who sped with it to safety.

Aeschylus presents an infinitely more polished and refined version of the stealing of fire from the heavens than the Indian lore of the Pacific Northwest can provide. But as I watched the boiling sulfurous caverns above Little Mount Adams it seemed to me that Coyote and Prometheus were akin. Their common exploit provided a link between the ancient Greeks and the Pacific Northwest Indians. It is of course not strange that two widely separated cultures would produce stories so similar as those of Coyote and Prometheus. Volcanic mountains have been known throughout the ages, and at times were the source of fire for primitive people. Moreover, from the beginning the heavens have delivered fire to the earth through lightning. It is natural that man should find supernatural forces at work in the skies and in the mountains. Certainly, at one time Mount Adams erupted, blowing off its top, belching smoke and pouring hot molten rock into the valleys. Lava ledges and light pyroclastics that cover its slopes are enduring evidence of an earlier and more violent chapter in its life.

The south hump of Adams, which we were on, was formed by an eruption. Lava flowing from a volcano had built this shoulder. The same happened on all sides of the mountain through parasitic cones still visible: Little Mount Adams, Red Butte, South Butte, and Goat Butte. The Columbia lava flows came in the Miocene some 30,000,000 years ago. Then they were raised and folded with the buckling of the earth's crust to form the Cascades. This was in the late Pliocene, perhaps five or ten million years ago. Then in Pleistocene or glacial time, about two million years ago, came Adams on the upturned edges of this lava. The construction of Mount Adams took a long while. There were long periods of quiet and glaciation, followed by extensions of lava. And so gradually a mountain was built, with fire and heat, over a period of more than a million years. The fires cooled; the construction was done; the process of erosion set in. But the sulfur fumes from the boiling caverns below us proved that Mount Adams was yet growling in its bowels.

The sun had warmed the narrow tongue of snow that lay ahead of us. Earlier in the day when it was frozen the crossing would have been hazardous. One slip and a man might roll down to huge knuckles of lava that dotted the lower edges of the snow field—knuckles large as pianos, though from our altitude they seemed no bigger than walnuts. But now there was no danger, for we sank into snow over our ankles.

A few hundred yards beyond this tongue of snow and to the west, is a knob from which the mountain drops a thousand feet or more.

Here rocks have tumbled from the cliff and rolled 1000 yards or more to ice fields. This was part of the crumbling of Adams. The ice of these fields is grimy in appearance, as glacier ice usually is. Ugly snow seracs and crevasses gave it a wild look, for the seracs were as big as a house, and the yawning crevasses were hundreds of feet deep.

From this cliff's edge we turned north and followed the ridge that leads to the false top of Mount Adams. We were now feeling the full force of the wind; and it was so cold that, in spite of the exertion, my upper legs were as numb as if I had been sitting in a cold exposed place for hours. But the going was easy, for the ridge was covered with sandy pumice that crunched underfoot. It seemed part of an ancient beach that somehow had been raised to the heavens before the waves of the ocean could grind the coarse grains to powder.

Between the false and the real summit is a basin 200 or 300 yards across and 100 or 200 feet below the false top. The brief descent was as welcome as the noon whistle on a hot day in the brickyards. Then came the last 500 feet of the climb. The ascent is abrupt.

Curtiss and his group had gone to the top without stopping. They synchronized their legs and lungs, taking so many breaths to each step, going like motorcars in low gear. In earlier days I had been able to do the same, but it had been 25 years since I had tried it. Doug thought we should take it easy, and we had climbed slowly, resting every ten steps or so. In that way we had done all right.

But the last 500 feet were grueling, as Henry B. Brewer, Methodist farmer missionary and the first white man to climb Mt. Adams, discovered in 1845. The wind was more powerful, and we were facing directly into it. Chitchat and banter were over. This was grim. I climbed the last pitch as if it were a never-ending staircase inside a tower. This was for me as much an ordeal as the last few thousand feet of McKinley (20,300 feet) might be for the young professional. I was generally in good condition but I had not trained for the climb. I did not have the wiry look that goes well with mountaineering. In the worst stretch of the last 500 feet I stopped, breathless and exhausted. I wondered if perhaps I had waited too long to pass this crucial test. Then the words of Homer came back to me, "Be patient now, my soul; thou hast endured still worse than this." And so I lifted my leaden feet and slowly came to the top, 12,307 feet above the sea.

There is a wooden shack on the top of Adams, built years ago by the Forest Service as a lookout. It had been unused for some time. Snow had sifted through the cracks and more than half-filled the cabin. Not far from the lookout are old test holes that some sulfur mining company dug years ago. The mountain is apparently full of sulfur; its fumes are noticeable far down the mountain. The summit deposits seem rich. Who dug the test holes, what engineering problems were confronted, how the problems of cost of production and marketing were thought to be manageable, I do not know. But prospectors had gone clear to the top of Mount Adams in search for riches and there had dug their puny picks into this great giant of the Cascades, leaving their scratches. Steam came from a few vents in the crater, but more conspicuous was the hydrogen sulfide gas escaping through many crevices on the crater's edge.

At the top the mountain seemed a giant cone whose tip had been snipped off by scissors, for the top is almost flat and somewhat circular like the frustum of a cone. It has been estimated that if the sides of the cone were extended they would meet about a thousand feet above the flat summit.

At the summit the wind was a 50-mile gale. We found some protection on the lee side of the lookout. Here on the lookout's south wall was a register box, left by the Mazamas, a famous club of mountaineers. This was August 18, 1945, and 20 people so far had made the climb that year. Three had come in from Seattle over the Adams Glacier. We added our names to the register as eagerly as one adds the name of a new-born child to the family Bible.

We walked to the eastern edge of the table top. Standing on such dizzy points gives some people an urge to plunge into the abyss and sacrifice themselves on the jagged pinnacles below. Those people should stay out of glacier regions. They would find them more frighteningly inviting than all the skyscrapers of the world. But those who like to live dangerously have no such compulsions. They curl their toes tighter, and lean forward the better to see the bottom.

Below was the eerie Klickitat Glacier, tumbling to the east in dis-array, its seracs scattered down its length like huge misshapen ice cubes spilled from a giant's hand. Beyond was the Yakima Indian Reservation and the rich Yakima Valley. Not a cloud was in the sky. The valley lay in the distance against gray sagebrush hills like a rich oasis. Nearer was the serpentine Klickitat winding through green gorges to the Columbia. To the north was the cold hulk of Rainier. A curtain of dark fog hung behind it, so the sweep of the northern reaches of the Cascades was not visible. But the territory in between could be seen in detail. Various lakes were jewels in a dark green tapestry. The largest, Mount Adams Lake, lay at our feet—the lake where three- and four-pound eastern brook come to the dip net as gaily painted with sunset hues as any golden trout I have seen. Farther north were the Goat Rocks silhouetted against the sky, a long broken backbone of rock. Not far from their base were soft edges of the light green meadows of the Klickitat.

As we circled the table top to the north and west, the great ice cliffs of Rusk, Lyman, Lava, Adams, and White Salmon glaciers reached almost to our feet. It seemed as though we were standing on the top edge of a gargantuan cliff of ice that had its roots in deep forests miles below us. These glaciers had the full force of the noon sun on them giving them a dazzling splendor. But it was a splendor that was terrifying too. Man could chop steps with his ice ax and slowly make his way up or across them; but one false step and he would spin to his death in the crevasses that wrinkled their surfaces.

Beyond St. Helens to the southwest hung another fog, so we could not see the Coast Range between the Cascades and the Pacific. But to the south the eye could penetrate at least 500 miles.

We got glimpses of the Columbia, which from our altitude looked like a ribbon of aquamarine rather than the second river of the United States. The dangerous gorge where the emigrants of the 1840's met with disaster now looked like an easy defile through rolling hills. Mount Hood stood clear. Beyond it to the south was Jefferson, named in honor of the President who sent Lewis and Clark on their way to the Pacific. Below it were the Three Sisters, sentinels on the western edge of Bend, Oregon. And way below it was the faint outline of another peak. Clarence Truitt thought it could not have been Shasta, deep in California, that we had seen; but since all other peaks were accounted for, Curtiss and I were convinced it was.

All of these peaks Curtiss had climbed. He spoke of them as things as familiar to him as the lower 40 acres of alfalfa would be to a Cowiche rancher.

I strained my eyes to see my prized Wallowas that reach the edge of Idaho to the east. But they were obscured in a haze of dust particles that in August are whipped up from the wheatlands lying fallow between Arlington, Pendleton, and Spokane. But I could see the verdant Elkhorn or Blue Mountains that skirt Pendleton on the east and run deep into the romantic John Day country in the south. These were the mountains that David Douglas, of fir tree fame, penetrated in 1826 in search of botanical specimens. They are 6000 to 7000 feet high, but this morning they looked like a low-lying blue ridge of New England or Virginia.

It had been my lifelong ambition to reach this spot, and I wanted to stay at the summit several days to study the mountain in its various moods. I would have loved to lie close to the stars on a clear night and see the moon appear over the Wallowas 300 miles to the east. Here storms make up, and lightning waits to be unleashed. Here the sun rises in splendor over orchards and golden fields to the east and sets in glory over the Pacific to the west. Here man would have uninterrupted solitude. There was exultation in my heart, and I felt as if I were entering the presence of some unknown, unseen Power. But the wind drove us from the summit in thirty minutes. With our scant clothing we could not have lived out the day.

Going down was easy. We stuck to the snow as much as we could. It was mushy, good footing for the heels. Curtiss, my son, Bill, and I took a side trip by the snow field where I had lost my hat, and found it in ice water at the edge of the snow. We circled back, dropped below the snow line, reached timber and finally the road that marked the trail's end. We were back at camp at 6 o'clock, making the return trip in about four hours. We soon had a dinner of cantaloupe, chicken, beans, stew, tomatoes, cookies, and watermelon—our first meal in 24 hours.

As we ate Doug told of his climb of Mount Fujiyama in Japan, 12,395 feet high.

"Looks a bit like Mount St. Helens," Doug said. "And it's not any more difficult a climb."

It seems that there are rest stations about every 1000 feet or so on Fujiyama. At each station is a shelter where one can get food and lodging for a few yen. "This morning," Doug added, "when we got above 10,000 feet on Adams, a rest station was the most attractive thing I could think of."

We laughed, and I asked, "So you admit you're pretty soft for the mountains?"

Doug looked at me appraisingly. "Speaking only from a medical point of view, I would say that around 12,000 feet I thought it would take more than a rest station to save you."

Our ascent of Mount Adams was by world competitive standards not difficult. We took a route that avoided glaciers. Mount Adams, in terms of world geography, is one of the minor peaks. Rainier, Shasta, Whitney, and McKinley are all higher. And even those are minor compared with the great peaks of the world, for in the Himalayas of Tibet there are 86 peaks that are over 24,000 feet— three of these over 28,000 feet, six over 27,000, eighteen over 26,000, and Mount Everest reaches 29,141 feet into the heavens. On an ascent of any of those mountains the lowest base camp would probably be no lower than Mount Adams' 12,307 feet. So to the specialists, Mount Adams would be no more than a training ground.

For the average hiker, however, Mount Adams is ideal. There is glacier work if he wants it. The altitude is not a serious problem for one whose heart is sound—in fact altitude is no problem under 10,000 feet for anyone in good physical condition. At 10,000 some people get a slight nausea, but it usually passes. Moreover, the problem of acclimatization from 10,000 to 12,000 feet is not at all serious. Ullman in *Kingdom of Adventure: Everest* tells of those who acclimated themselves above 28,000 feet. The great George Leigh-Mallory was last seen climbing without oxygen within 800 feet of Everest's top. Whether he reached it we will never know, for he was never seen again. But the experience of his group shows how great is the adaptability of the human body to high altitudes.

So the physical experience above 12,000 feet is vastly different from what we experienced on Mount Adams. But as far as one can tell from talks with others and from their chronicles, the spiritual experience is much the same once the glaciers are below you.

That spiritual experience is difficult to describe. It has to do with man's relation to the universe and his Creator. The world on top of Mount Adams is in a real sense a strange and different world from what one ordinarily knows. It is the world as it was millions of years ago. The first impression is that there is no life of any kind. That is not quite correct, for there are traces of lichens at the top. Peattie tells that lichens, traveling on the planetary winds, are to be found higher in the Himalayas than all other plants; they constitute practically the entire plant life on the antarctic continent; they are the first to colonize bare rock (*Flowering Earth*). But at the altitude of Mount Adams man has moved out of the thin rich life zone that encircles the globe. He has left the narrow belt in which he was conceived, where he can get sustenance, grow, and pass life along. Although Mount Adams' top is not hostile to all life, it is hostile to man.

There is a great loneliness about the place. Man was born to gregariousness, to the companionship of trees and grass, of birds and game, as well as the companionship of his kind. There is nothing on the mountain that extends a welcome. No insect, no bird. Not a shrub, bush, or blade of grass to vibrate in the wind. No flower— not even the blush of heather—to suggest immortality, to break the monotony of pumice, sand, and lava. The bleak top of Adams offers no sustenance. It has from the beginning of its time been barren and unproductive. It is waste land; it has no green leaf, the ultimate supplier of heat, shelter, clothing, and food for man.

The feeling that it is no part of man's domain is heightened by the isolation. We were almost a mile above the timber line. The forests below were green splotches. We had left behind the cry of the coyote, the whistle of the bull elk, the screeching of the owl. One could peer long onto the ridges and into the valleys and never see any stirring. Not even a hawk or eagle could be seen soaring above the trees of the ravines along the lower reaches. We had left all familiar sights behind; we were foreigners in a strange place. It was a different world, separate and apart from anything I have known.

A nuclear physicist might think of this lifeless mass of rock in terms of molecular activity and see in it the source of sufficient energy to take drudgery from man's shoulders if wisely used, or to destroy the earth itself if passion rather than reason reigned. But as the Northwest Indians—Yakimas, Cayuses, Walla Wallas, Umatillas, and Chinooks—well knew, this land was beyond the kingdom of man. It was reserved for more powerful forces.

These thoughts tumbled through my mind during the brief thirty minutes we spent on the top of Adams. As I stood in the fierce gale, the first words of the Bible came to my lips: "In the beginning God created the heaven and the earth." This, I thought, is the beginning. Eons ago this planet was hurled into space by some force at least as great as the sun itself. When it cooled there was everywhere—in the valleys, on the ridges, at the highest peaks—nothing but sand, pumice, lava, granite, marble. Inert matter reigned supreme. There was nothing to eat and no plant or animal to eat it. Sunsets made mountain glaciers warm and vibrant, but there was no one to enjoy them. There was no hunting or fishing, no forests, no deer, no fish. There were ugly seracs and dangerous crevasses on the glaciers. Man had not yet appeared, so there was none to tempt death and to achieve and boast.

With this inert matter the Creator fashioned all that lives, moves, breathes. "And the earth brought forth grass, and herb yielding seed after his kind, and the tree yielding fruit, whose seed was in itself after his kind; and God saw that it was good." The Creator brought gas and water together and created the tissue of life. He created the green leaf pigment called chlorophyl to serve as the link between the sun and life and set in motion a force that operates ceaselessly across the world and serves as the basic food factory for every living thing.

"Only when man has done as much," writes Peattie, "may he call himself the equal of a weed" (*Flowering Earth*).

Then the Creator went on and produced an endless diversity of life that is the more amazing and mysterious the better we come to know it. The most exciting of all His creations is man himself. Man has the same amazing diversity as the meadows under Goat Rocks in June. Like the flowers, he has different colors. Like the mountains, he has varying moods. Like the trees of the forests, he has different capacities. Like the coyote and cougar, he has the supreme cunning to hunt and kill in ruthless and predatory ways. Yet, unlike all other forms of life, he has the capacity (as Confucius, Jesus, and Gandhi demonstrated) to be wholly and completely selfless, sacrificing his own existence so that others of his kind may live and find happiness.

One cannot reach the desolate crags that look down on eternal glaciers without deep and strange spiritual experiences. If he ever was a doubter, he will, I think, come down a believer. He will have faith. He will know there is a Creator, a Supreme Being, a God, a Jehovah. He will know it because otherwise the mind cannot comprehend how life could have been created out of the inert matter. When he sees the stuff that was the beginning of life, he will know that it took an omniscient One to sculpture man; to fashion one who can laugh, and cry, and love; to mold out of rock a soul that can aspire to the stars and a heart that can sacrifice all for an idea or a loved one.

When I was climbing Adams, the mountain seemed permanent and indomitable, like the rock of ages. But in my sleeping bag that night, back at Cold Springs, I thought of the temporary nature even of mountains. When Adams was born there were hot lava flows that burned everything they touched and turned forests to cinders. Their heat extended throughout the land. At night the flames from the craters lit up the heavens and threw weird and wondrous colored films against the clouds. Then came explosions that rocked the earth and filled the air with dust that obscured the sun. Ashes and pumice many feet deep were scattered for miles around, like that which last came from St. Helens on November 23, 1842, and fell on The Dalles, Oregon. Then the eruptions became less frequent. The earth cooled. Lichens and all the wonders of botany took hold and blanketed the earth. The wind, frost, rain, snow, and ice started crumbling the mountain.

Erosion works tirelessly. Lava disintegrates to soil. Glaciers carve gashes. Softer rocks are removed. Sharp ridges and ragged crests gradually crumble to build moraines. A center core of hard volcanic rock alone will stand. Then it too will weather, and become a rounded hill. The rounded hill will become a plain. And tens of thousands of years later men will take excursions to find the base of the proud and mighty mountain that folklore tells them stood here in ancient days.

I remembered the erosion of Adams I had seen that day and knew why geologists had called it appalling. Adams was old; it had passed its prime, and like man would some day be leveled.

A slight wind came up and touched the tips of the pine that towered over our camp. The murmur of the trees made it seem that the whole forest was on the move. Indeed, trees do move. Continents have been invaded by flowers, grass, shrubs, and trees. North America has been so invaded three times. The first of these floristic migrations came from Greenland. The second came from the Caribbean in the Cretaceous period some 60 million of years ago. Tropical floras moved northward and eventually covered Oregon and Washington. This was when the Pacific Northwest was subtropical. Then the weather changed and the invaders retreated. Down from the north, probably from Asia, came the third floristic invasion—the pine and fir and redwoods. The Caribbean floras retreated, leaving sturdy remnants behind. The two invaders met. New species were developed and traces of each are found today even in alpine meadows.

And so it is that even mountains and trees move on and a new life takes their place.

I have often thought that the greatest outdoor achievement of all would be to climb Mount Everest. I am not thinking of the achievement of being the first to climb it, though that would add to the adventure. The thrill of accomplishing the well-nigh impossible would be great though a hundred had preceded me. That ambition will never be realized, for the supreme exertions that assault would entail make it an adventure for one in his twenties. When the years were right, I was too involved in other things to conquer any of the giants of the Cascade Range, let alone the Himalayas. But the appetite for it remains, and was only whetted by the adventure of Mount Adams in 1945.

I have often wondered why these glacial peaks beckon men, why they summon them to exhaustion and even to death. Mountain expeditions may serve scientific purposes; but with modern inventions there are easier, less costly ways by which the ends of science can be served. Men do not often climb these peaks just as stunts, though they do on occasion. I knew a man who made a wager he could climb Rainier, and then in order to collect his bet hired two guides —one to pull and the other to push him to the top. In that way he made the last 4000 feet.

As we climbed Mount Adams I remembered the story of Clarence Truitt and his experience. Clarence wanted above all else to join the first Byrd expedition to the Antarctic. He applied and found he would be required to submit evidence of his outdoor stamina. So he and Clarence Starcher and Quinn A. Blackburn put their heads together and planned a crucial test. They would climb Hood, St. Helens, Adams, Goat Rocks, and Rainier in nine days.

Truitt and Starcher drove from Yakima to Hood and climbed the north side from Cloud Cap Inn. They hiked down the south side to Government Camp, where their car was waiting, then they drove to Spirit Lake at the foot of St. Helens where Blackburn met them. That took one day. There they turned over the car to a friend and went the rest of the way on foot. The second day the three of them climbed St. Helens and were back at its base at 3 o'clock that after-noon. It is 40 miles cross-country between St. Helens and Adams, wild and broken country made up of a series of parallel ridges around 4000 feet high. When a climber gets on one knifelike ridge, he must drop 3000 or 4000 feet to the valley and climb another ridge just like it. These ridges are known in the West as niggerheads because of the black heads of basalt that decorate them. Clarence and his companion started across this rough country at 3 o'clock, and traveled until 10 that night. They were up again at 2 A.M. and continued until 10 the third night. At that time they were near the timber line of Adams on its north side.

The morning of the fourth day they followed the north side of Adams to the top, went down the same side, and headed for Goat Rocks.

"Got mixed up in the fog and went 15 miles out of our way that day," Clarence told me.

The fifth day they climbed Gilbert Peak and slept that night somewhere in the wilderness to the west. The sixth day they climbed Rainier over Kautz Glacier, then thought to be an impossible ascent. They got to its top at 7 P.M., were back at Camp Muir at midnight, and down to Paradise Inn at 2 A.M.

"Did you get a good night's sleep?" I asked.

"After a fashion," Clarence answered. "Tried to sleep in beds in a tent but the wind whipped the sidewalls so hard we couldn't sleep. We went outside and made out on the ground."

Blackburn left the party at Ohanapecosh Hot Springs and returned to Seattle.

Early the eighth day the two Clarences pushed through the rough wilderness to the east, up and down the ridges, and came out at Bumping Lake on the ninth day.

All they had to eat for these nine days were peanuts, raisins, wheat, and a few fish they caught. They had no dishes, or salt and pepper. They had no bedrolls. They carried long underwear in their haversacks and put it on at night.

"Why didn't you go with Byrd to the Antarctic?" I asked.

"Blackburn went," replied Clarence. And even after twenty years there was disappointment in his voice as he added: "But family matters developed so I couldn't go. Starcher couldn't go either."

A desire for a stunt does not sustain men through long ordeals such as Clarence Truitt endured. Nor is mountaineering merely another form of physical culture. It involves more than legs and lungs. It is not exercise; it is adventure. When Mallory, who perished on Everest, was asked why he wanted to climb it, he answered, "Because it is there." And in commenting on an unsuccessful assault of its peak he said, "Have we vanquished an enemy? None but ourselves."

When I climbed Mount Adams I think I found the answer to the question of why men stake everything to reach these peaks, yet obtain no visible reward for their exhaustion. It came to me when I almost failed on the last steep pitch of Adams and was pushed on by Homer's words. Man's greatest experience—the one that brings supreme exultation—is spiritual, not physical. It is the catching of some vision of the universe and translating it into a poem or work of art, into a Sermon on the Mount, into a Gettysburg Address, into a mathematical formula that unlocks the doors of atomic energy. This is a drive that develops early in life. Boys have it. The lad who picks up an arrowhead in the woods has established his first vivid and dramatic contact with history. It was the hand of a redman, now dead for centuries perhaps, that found this stone of agate or obsidian and fashioned from it a jagged-edged knife point to drop a rabbit or deer. Having received it from the redman, this boy walks for a moment by the redman's side in a long, silent, swinging stride. And he even may discover that he, a mere boy, can stalk a deer and by soft tread and quick thinking match the wits of one of the smartest of all animals.

The same experience comes in a host of other discoveries along the mountain trail: how to put one's heart and lungs and legs into low gear for mastery of a mountainside; how to rub sticks together to make fire; how to fashion lures to deceive trout or to construct traps for chipmunks; what mushrooms are edible; what differences mark the species of trees and grasses. These are discoveries that bring as strange a thrill to a boy as test-tube discoveries bring to a biochemist. In adult life the same kind of experiences can be seen in Thoreau's *Walden* and in Peattie's *The Road of the Naturalist* and *Almanac for Moderns*. They can indeed be seen in every laboratory where scales of ignorance are being removed and new tissues of knowledge revealed. The satisfaction is the same.

The climbing of the high peaks of the world falls in that category. The excitement is not the view to be seen, the flirtation with danger, or the communion with the universe that the high peaks afford. These play a part, but they are usually secondary. The challenge is in the discovery of the outermost limits of one's own endurance.

Sound heart and lungs are not enough for mastery of the peaks. It takes the power of the spirit too, a resolve and determination that knows no limit even when the feet are too heavy to lift. It is spirit against matter, the power of the soul to drive the legs above fatigue and to push an exhausted body without whimper. It is more than what we call guts. It is the positive force that requires a man to go forward even when every muscle rebels. It is man against the mountain—finite man against the universe.

In these moments man discovers himself: what the limits of his endurance are, how far the spirit will enable him to go. Then he discovers the power of his soul to carry him on.

When he wins, there comes an exquisite moment, a feeling that anything is possible. There comes a sense of austerity, a feeling of peace. All the tensions are gone. Man stands powerful and unconquered atop the world. He has destroyed nothing to get there, except the doubts and fears that sought to prevent him from discovering his true worth.

If there is failure, no bitterness follows. His respect for the mountain increases. He has not failed; he has only discovered the limits of his own strength and the power of the universe. If there has been no niggardly effort, no compromise on his part, there is no room for regret. He stands proud and erect, not broken or sad. He has found a force greater than himself. It is a master whom he admires and respects. When he is beaten by his fellow man, dark hatred may grow in his heart. When he is beaten by the mountain, he bows to it.

This is a spiritual experience that is difficult to describe. But I am sure it is not peculiar to just a few of us. I find the same thought running through much of the literature on mountaineering: James Ramsey Ullman, R. L. G. Irving, Frank S. Smythe, Sir Francis Younghusband, T. Howard Somervell, Clarence King, George Leigh-Mallory, Those who do no more than enjoy the glories of the high peaks from the valleys will perhaps have difficulty in understanding the experience of which I speak. But by the same token, man does not learn about fly-fishing merely by practicing his casting in a pool in the city park.

Chapter XXII   *Kloochman*

KLOOCHMAN ROCK stands on the southern side of the Tieton Basin in the Cascades. It is an oval-shaped lava rock, running lengthwise northwest by southeast, a half-mile or more. It rises 2000 feet above the basin. The first third of its elevation is gained through gentle slopes of pine and fir. Next are a few hundred yards of tumbled rock. Then there is the cliff rising to the sky, 1200 feet or more—straight as the Washington Monument and over twice as high.

Kloochman is a rock of many moods. I remember it at sunset from the top of Hogback Mountain, 15 or 20 miles to the west. Then it was the most commanding view in the vast expanse of the Tieton. It glistened in the spotlight of the low-lying sun like a primordial monster with skin of burnished armor. Its humped back bristled to the sky; its snout was buried in deep brush. I recall Kloochman on an overcast day from Blue Slide Lookout on Darling Mountain, which lies to the southwest. Then it was a tumbled mass of dreary rock with no charm or challenge. Looking up from the base of the towering wall, I have felt insignificant and fragile beyond words. At such a time Kloochman has represented a power and force too great for man. I also have stood under the cliffs at sunrise, when every crack and crevice in Kloochman's eastern wall has been visible. There is nothing forbidding about the rock at such a time. When in that mood, it has seemed to extend a friendly invitation to mount its ramparts.

Kloochman is an Indian name for woman. And those who see it first from the north or east might not think the name to be wholly inappropriate. The northwest end of the rock has been eroded by wind and frost and rain so as to leave naked two gnarled and chewed teats pointing to the sky. That fact may have deeper significance than

314

we know. The Indian legend has it that Kloochman is a woman turned to stone. There was a chief of the Yakimas known as Meow-wah. He was peaceful and noted for his wisdom and virtue. He was a bachelor. The wiles of beautiful Indian maidens were lost on him. His people decided an effort should be made to have him wed. So they chose the four loveliest girls from all the tribes and sent them to him from the north, south, east, and west, bearing gifts. Meow-wah heard of the plan and consulted Coyote. When the four beauties came near, Coyote turned them all into stone. The Indian maiden who came from the south was turned into Kloochman or Woman Rock. Coyote, to make the job complete, turned Meow-wah into the mountain now called Goose Egg.

I climbed Kloochman in the summer of 1948. My climb was a leisurely one. There are vast rock fields at the base of the towering cliffs—rock fields fringed with willow, Douglas maple, creambush, currant, and serviceberry. And occasionally the edges of these fields are decorated with dark green splotches of the prostrate juniper. I worked my way through these shrubs as I skirted the base of the rock and finally found on the east an easy incline leading to the top. Almost all the way up I found patches of a dwarf pentstemon, dark purple and lightly scented. It grew along the wall wherever there was a handful of dirt. The delicacy of the flower atoned for the coarse and ragged basalt that in some violent upthrust formed this old sentinel of Tieton Basin.

There were fleecy clouds in the west. All else was clear. At my feet lay the milky Tieton Reservoir, stretching for miles behind the concrete dam between Westfall Rocks and Goose Egg. Around the reservoir were ancient landmarks that I had known intimately as a boy. To the northwest were Russell Ridge and Boot Jack Rock. Behind Boot Jack was the valley of Indian Creek that leads up to Blankenship Meadows and Tumac. To the west were Big Peak, Round, and Hogback. To the southwest were Bear, Darling, and Short and Dirty Ridge. These formed a semicircle around the reservoir.

Behind me to the east were Chimney Peaks, looking in the late sun like cones of miniature volcanoes.

As I sat on top of Kloochman that afternoon, I relived an earlier ascent of my youth—far from being so leisurely and peaceful.

It was in 1913 when Doug was 19 and I was not quite 15 that the two of us made this climb of Kloochman. Walter Kohagen, Doug, and I were camped in the Tieton Basin at a soda spring. The basin was then in large part a vast rich bottomland. We were traveling light, one blanket each. The night, I recall, was so bitter cold that we took turns refueling the campfire so that we could keep our backs warm enough to sleep. We rose at the first show of dawn, and cooked frying-pan bread and trout for breakfast. We had not planned to climb Kloochman, but somehow the challenge came to us as the sun touched her crest.

After breakfast we started circling the rock. There are fairly easy routes up Kloochman, but we shunned them. When we came to the southeast face (the one that never has been conquered, I believe) we chose it. Walter decided not to make the climb, but to wait at the base of the cliff for Doug and me. The July day was warm and cloudless. Doug led. The beginning was easy. For 100 feet or so we found ledges six to twelve inches wide we could follow to the left or right. Some ledges ran up the rock ten feet or more at a gentle grade. Others were merely steps to another ledge higher up. Thus by hugging the wall we could either ease ourselves upward or hoist ourselves from one ledge to another.

When we were about 100 feet up the wall, the ledges became narrower and footwork more precarious. Doug suggested we take off our shoes. This we did, tying them behind us on our belts. In stocking feet we wormed up the wall, clinging like flies to the dark rock. The pace was slow. We gingerly tested each toehold and fingerhold for loose rock before putting our weight on it. At times we had to inch along sidewise, our stomachs pressed tightly against the rock, in order to gain a point where we could reach the ledge above us. If we got on a ledge that turned out to be a cul-de-sac, the much more dangerous task of going down the rock wall would confront us. Hence we picked our route with care and weighed the advantages of several choices which frequently were given us. At times we could not climb easily from one ledge to another. The one above might be a foot or so high. Then we would have to reach it with one knee, slowly bring the other knee up, and then, delicately balancing on both knees on the upper ledge, come slowly to our feet by pressing close to the wall and getting such purchase with our fingers as the lava rock permitted.

In that tortuous way we made perhaps 600 feet in two hours. It was late forenoon when we stopped to appraise our situation. We were in serious trouble. We had reached the feared cul-de-sac. The two- or three-inch ledge on which we stood ended. There seemed none above us within Doug's reach. I was longer-legged than Doug; so perhaps I could have reached some ledge with my fingers if I were ahead. But it was impossible to change positions on the wall. Doug was ahead and there he must stay. The problem was to find a way to get him up.

Feeling along the wall, Doug discovered a tiny groove into which he could press the tips of the fingers of his left hand. It might help him maintain balance as his weight began to shift from the lower ledge to the upper one. But there was within reach not even a lip of rock for his right hand. Just out of reach, however, was a substantial crevice, one that would hold several men. How could Doug reach it? I could not boost him, for my own balance was insecure. Clearly, Doug would have to jump to reach it—and he would have but one jump. Since he was standing on a ledge only a few inches wide, he could not expect to jump for his handhold, miss it, and land safely. A slip meant he would go hurtling down some 600 feet onto the rocks. After much discussion and indecision, Doug decided to take the chance and go up.

He asked me to do him a favor: If he failed and fell, I might still make it, since I was longer-legged; would I give certain messages to his family in that event? I nodded.

"Then listen carefully. Try to remember my exact words," he told me. "Tell Mother that I love her dearly. Tell her I think she is the most wonderful person in the world. Tell her not to worry—that I did not suffer, that God willed it so. Tell Sister that I have been a mean little devil but I had no malice towards her. Tell her I love her too —that some day I wanted to marry a girl as wholesome and cheery and good as she.

"Tell Dad I was brave and died unafraid. Tell him about our climb in full detail. Tell Dad I have always been very proud of him, that some day I had planned to be a doctor too. Tell him I lived a clean life, that I never did anything to make him ashamed. . . . Tell Mother, Sister, and Dad I prayed for them."

Every word burned into me. My heart was sick, my lips quivered. I pressed my face against the rock so Doug could not see. I wept.

All was silent. A pebble fell from the ledge on which I squeezed. I counted seconds before it hit 600 feet below with a faint, faraway tinkling sound. Would Doug drop through the same space? Would I follow? When you fall 600 feet do you die before you hit the bottom? Closing my eyes, I asked God to help Doug up the wall.

In a second Doug said in a cheery voice, "Well, here goes."

A false bravado took hold of us. I said he could do it. He said he would. He wiped first one hand then the other on his trousers. He placed both palms against the wall, bent his knees slowly, paused a split second, and jumped straight up. It was not much of a jump— only six inches or so. But that jump by one pressed against a cliff 600 feet in the air had daredevil proportions. I held my breath; my heart pounded. The suspense was over.

Doug made the jump, and in a second was hanging by two hands from a strong, wide ledge. There was no toehold; he would have to hoist himself by his arms alone. He did just that. His body went slowly up as if pulled by some unseen winch. Soon he had the weight of his body above the ledge and was resting on the palms of his hands. He then put his left knee on the ledge, rolled over on his side, and chuckled as he said, "Nothing to it."

A greater disappointment followed. Doug's exploration of the ledge showed he was in a final cul-de-sac. There was no way up.

There was not even a higher ledge he could reach by jumping. We were now faced with the nightmare of going down the sheer rock wall. We could not go down frontwards because the ledges were too narrow and the wall too steep. We needed our toes, not our heels, on the rock; and we needed to have our stomachs pressed tightly against it. Then we could perhaps feel our way. But as every rock expert knows, descent of a cliff without ropes is often much more difficult than ascent.

That difficulty was impressed on us by the first move. Doug had to leave the ledge he had reached by jumping. He dared not slide blindly to the skimpy ledge he had just left. I must help him. I must move up the wall and stand closer to him. Though I could not possibly hold his weight, I must exert sufficient pressure to slow up his descent and to direct his toe onto the narrow ledge from which he had just jumped.

I was hanging to the rock like a fly, twelve feet or more to Doug's left. I inched my way toward him, first dropping to a lower ledge and then climbing to a higher one, using such toeholds as the rock afforded and edging my way crabwise.

When I reached him I said, "Now I'll help."

Doug lowered himself and hung by his fingers full length. His feet were about six inches above the ledge from which he had jumped. He was now my responsibility. If he dropped without aid or direction he was gone. He could not catch and hold to the scanty ledge. I had little space for maneuvering. The surface on which I stood was not more than three inches wide. My left hand fortunately found an overhead crevice that gave a solid anchor in case my feet slipped.

I placed my right hand in the small of Doug's back and pressed upward with all my might. "Now you can come," I said.

He let go gently, and the full weight of his body came against my arm. My arm trembled under the tension. My left hand hung onto the crack in the rock like a grappling hook. My stomach pressed against the wall as if to find mucilage in its pores. My toes dug in as I threw in every ounce of strength.

Down Doug came—a full inch. I couldn't help glancing down and seeing the rocks 600 feet below.

Down Doug moved another inch, then a third. My left hand seemed paralyzed. The muscles of my toes were aching. My right arm shook. I could not hold much longer.

Down came Doug a fourth inch. I thought he was headed for destruction. His feet would miss the only toehold within reach. I could not possibly hold him. He would plunge to his death because my arm was not strong enough to hold him. The messages he had given me for his family raced through my mind. And I saw myself, sick and ashamed, standing before them, testifying to my own inadequacy, repeating his last words.

"Steady, Doug. The ledge is a foot to your right." He pawed the wall with the toes of his foot, searching.

"I can't find it. Don't let go."

The crisis was on us. Even if I had been safely anchored, my cramped position would have kept me from helping him much more. I felt helpless. In a few seconds I would reach the physical breaking point and Doug would go hurtling off the cliff. I did not see how I could keep him from slipping and yet maintain my own balance.

I will never know how I did it. But I tapped some reserve and directed his right foot onto the ledge from which he had earlier jumped. I did it by standing for a moment on my left foot alone and then using my right leg as a rod to guide his right foot to the ledge his swinging feet had missed.

His toes grabbed the ledge as if they were the talons of a bird. My right leg swung back to my perch.

"Are you OK?" I asked.

"Yes," said Doug. "Good work."

My right arm fell from him, numb and useless. I shook from exhaustion and for the first time noticed that my face was wet with perspiration. We stood against the rock in silence for several minutes, relaxing and regaining our composure.

Doug said: "Let's throw our shoes down. It will be easier going."

So we untied them from our belts and dropped them to Walter
Kohagen, who was waiting at the rock field below us.

Our descent was painfully slow but uneventful. We went down
backwards, weaving a strange pattern across the face of the cliff as
we moved from one side to the other. It was perhaps midafternoon
when we reached the bottom, retrieved our shoes, and started around
the other side of the rock. We left the southeast wall unconquered.

But, being young, we were determined to climb the rock. So once
more we started to circle. When we came to the northwest wall,
we selected it as our route.

Here, too, is a cliff rising 1000 feet like some unfinished pyramid.
But close examination shows numerous toe- and fingerholds that
make the start at least fairly easy. So we set out with our shoes on.

Again it was fairly easy going for a hundred feet or so, when Doug,
who was ahead, came to a ledge to which he could not step. On later
climbs we would send the longer-legged chap ahead. And on other
occasions Doug himself has used a rope to traverse this spot. But
this day success of the climb depended at this point on Doug's short
legs alone. The ledge to which he must move was up to his hips.
There were few fingerholds overhead, and none firm enough to carry
his whole weight. Only a few tiny cracks were within reach to serve
as purchase for him. But Doug would not give up.

He hitched up his trousers, and grasped a tiny groove of rock with
the tips of the fingers of his left hand, pressing his right hand flat
against the smooth rock wall as if it had magical sticking power.
Slowly he lifted his left knee until it was slightly over the ledge above
him. To do so he had to stand tiptoe on his right foot. Pulling with
his left hand, he brought his right knee up. Doug was now on both
knees on the upper ledge. If he could find good purchase overhead
for his hands, he was safe. His hands explored the wall above him.
He moved them slowly over most of it without finding a hold. Then
he reached straight above his head and cried out, "This is our lucky
day."

He had found strong rough edges of rock, and on this quickly
pulled himself up. His hands were on a ledge a foot wide. He lay

down on it on his stomach and grasped my outstretched hand. The pull of his strong arm against the drop of 100 feet or more was as comforting an experience as any I can recall. In a jiffy I was at his side. We pounded each other on the shoulders and laughed.

My own most serious trouble was yet to come. For a while Doug and I were separated. I worked laterally along a ledge to the south, found easier going, and in a short time was 200 feet or more up the rock wall. I was above Doug, 25 feet or so, and 50 feet to his right. We had been extremely careful to test each toe- and finger-hold before putting our trust in it. Kloochman is full of treacherous rock. We often discovered thin ledges that crumbled under pressure and showered handfuls of rock and dust down below. Perhaps I was careless; but whatever the cause, the thin ledge on which I was standing gave way.

As I felt it slip, I grabbed for a hold above me. The crevasse I seized was solid. But there I was, hanging by my hands 200 feet in the air, my feet pawing the rock. To make matters worse, my camera had swung between me and the cliff when I slipped. It was a crude and clumsy instrument, a box type that I carried on a leather strap across my shoulders. Its hulk was actually pushing me from the cliff. I twisted in an endeavor to get rid of it, but it was firmly lodged between me and the wall.

I yelled to Doug for help. He at once started edging toward me. It seemed hours, though it was probably not over a few minutes. He shouted, "Hang on, I'll be there."

Hang on I did. My fingers ached beyond description. They were frozen to the rock. My exertion in pawing with my feet had added to the fatigue. The ache of my fingers extended to my wrists and then along my arms. I stopped thrashing around and hung like a sack, motionless. Every second seemed a minute, every minute an hour. I did not see how I could possibly hold.

I would slip, I thought, slip to sure death. I could not look down because of my position. But in my mind's eye I saw in sharp outline the jagged rocks that seemed to pull me toward them. The camera kept pushing my fingers from the ledge. I felt them move. They began to give way before the pull of a force too great for flesh to resist.

Fright grew in me. The idea of hanging helpless 200 feet above the abyss brought panic. I cried out to Doug but the words caught in my dry throat. I was like one in a nightmare who struggles to shout —who is then seized with a fear that promises to destroy him.

Then there flashed through my mind a family scene. Mother was sitting in the living room talking to me, telling me what a wonderful man Father was. She told me of his last illness and his death. She told me of his departure from Cleveland, Washington to Portland, Oregon for what proved to be a fatal operation. His last words to her were: "If I die it will be glory. If I live, it will be grace."

The panic passed. The memory of those words restored reason. Glory to die? I could not understand why it would be glory to die. It would be glory to live. But as Father said, it might take grace to live, grace from One more powerful than either Doug or I.

And so again that day I prayed. I asked God to save my life, to save me from destruction on this rock wall. I asked God to make my fingers strong, to give me strength to hang on. I asked God to give me courage, to make me unafraid. I asked God to give me guts, to give me power to do the impossible.

My fingers were as numb as flesh that is full of novocaine. They seemed detached from me, as if they belonged to someone else. My wrists, my shoulders, cried out for respite from the pain. It would be such welcome relief if they could be released from the weight that was on them.

Hang on? You can't hang on. You are a weakling. The weaklings die in the woods.

Weakling? I'll show you. How long must I hang on? All day? OK, all day then. I'll hang on, I'll hang on. O God, dear God, help me hang on!

I felt someone pushing my left foot upwards. It was Doug. As if through a dream his voice was saying, "Your feet are 18 inches below your toehold." Doug found those toeholds for my feet.

I felt my shoes resting in solid cracks. I pulled myself up and leaned on my elbows on the ledge to which my hands had been glued. I flexed my fingers and bent my wrists to bring life back.

Doug came up abreast of me and said, "We're even Stephen now."

"Even Stephen?"

"Today each of us has saved the other's life."

It was shortly above the point where Doug saved my life that we discovered a classic path up Kloochman. It is a three-sided chimney chute, a few feet wide, that leads almost to the top. There are several such chutes on Kloochman. In later years Cragg Gilbert and Louis Ulrich went up Devil's Chimney on the northeast face in a seven-hour nerve-wracking climb with ropes. Clarence Truitt and many others have gone up the chimney chute that Doug and I discovered. Then as now this chute was filled with loose rock that had to be cleared away. To negotiate the chute we took off our shoes and tied them to our belts. We climbed the chute in stocking feet, pressing our hands and feet against the opposing walls as we kept our backs to the abyss below us. This day we went up the chute with ease, stopping every eight feet or so to measure our progress.

The sun was setting when we reached the top. We were gay and buoyant. We talked about the glories of the scene in front of us. We bragged a bit about our skill in rock work—how we must be part mountain goat to have reached the top. We shouted and hallooed to the empty meadows far below us.

On Kloochman Rock that July afternoon both Doug and I valued life more because death had passed so close. It was wonderful to be alive, breathing, using our muscles, shouting, seeing.

We stayed briefly at the top. We went down as we came up, in stocking feet. We raced against darkness, propelled by the thought of spending the night on Kloochman's treacherous wall.

It was deep dusk when we rejoined Walter on the rock fields at the base. We put on our shoes and hurried on. We entered the woods at double-quick time, seeking the trail that led toward the South Fork of the Tieton. We saw the trail from the edge of a clearing as a faint, light streak in a pitch-black night. We had two ways of keeping on it. We had no matches or torch or flashlight. But we could feel the edges with our feet. And we could search out the strip of night sky over the path.

We finally decided that it would take too long to follow the trail to camp in this groping way. We'd take a short cut to Westfall Rocks, whose formless shape we could see against the sky. We took to the brush on our right, and kept our hands out in front to ward off boughs and branches. We crossed a marshy bog where we went in up to our knees. We came to soft earth where we went in up to our hips.

There were animals in the brush. We could hear them in the thickets, disturbed by our approach, and going out ahead of us. Thinking they might be bear, we paused to listen. "Cattle," said Doug.

We reached the Tieton River, which we knew could not be forded in many places in that stretch. So we took off our pants, shoes, and shirts and rolled them in bundles which we held on our heads. We waded out into the dark, cold, swift river, Doug in the lead. We had by accident picked one of the few good fords in the Tieton. We were never in water over our waists.

Then we dressed and located the road leading back to camp. As we started along it Doug said: "You know, Bill, there is power in prayer."

That night I prayed again. I knelt on a bed of white fir boughs beside the embers of a campfire and thanked God for saving Doug's life and mine, for giving us the strength to save each other.

When I climbed Kloochman in 1948, my steps were more cautious and measured than they had been in 1913. There was less dash, less abandon in this adult ascent. I took my ease, feeling my way with care. But the memories of the earlier trip were still fresh in my mind as if it had happened only the previous week instead of thirty-five years ago.

As I climbed, I realized how conservative man became in his physical endeavors as he passed his thirties. I was not thinking of wind or stamina, for mine were both good. I was thinking of the subtle forces that control the reflexes. It struck home why only young men make good fighter pilots—how it is that age fast takes the daredevil out of man. There was a thrill in this adult climb, but the reckless, carefree attitude of the earlier day had gone.

Yet I relived the experience of 1913. Places, as well as smells and shapes and sounds, can be symbols of fear and terror. He who, after long years of absence, revisits a place associated with sadness or guilt or suffering is likely to relive for a moment the sensations he experienced there. The forces at work are subtle; and unless he is aware of their influences, he may be painfully disturbed or upset. Unless he recognizes the part these imponderables play in human emotions, he may indeed be seized with a new discomfiture greater than the one that seized him earlier at the selfsame place.

The day I climbed Kloochman as a man, all the sensations of the earlier trip returned to me. There was the trembling excitement of the start. Doug's messages to his family raced once more through my mind, as if he had just uttered them. I saw Doug make his jump up the side of the cliff while he was 600 feet in the air. I saw him hanging on the ledge, doomed to die. I felt the weight of his body against my arm. I felt myself slipping slowly from the rock to destruction. It seemed once more that demons were pulling at my feet with a power too great for flesh and blood to resist. Once again little vestiges of the old fear passed through me.

Those, however, were fleeting sensations. When I came to the top a sense of calm came over me, a deep peace, the feeling a man has when he is with the woman he loves. And with the calm came pride.

Kloochman was in my very heart. Here we had accomplished the impossible. We had survived terrible ordeals on her sheer walls. We had faced death down; and because of our encounter with it, we had come to value life the more. On these dark walls in 1913 I had first communed with God. Here I had felt the presence of a Mighty Force, infinitely beyond man. Here I had known the strength of unseen hands helping me along ledges.

I sat on the top of the rock looking to the west. The sun was dipping. The milky waters of the Tieton Reservoir hid forever from the eyes of man the gorgeous McAllister Meadows where we used to camp. Beyond was the wild panorama of the Tieton—cliffs, snowy peaks, hillsides of evergreen as soft in the late sun as the folds of a velvet gown, jagged fingers of rocks, jumbled ridges. It is the country that Doug and I have long loved. It is where Doug once said he wanted his ashes scattered. There was not a breath of wind. There was a deep and profound quiet. The only life in sight was a hawk, the slow-flying mouser type. But he uttered no sound as he caught mysterious currents of air and glided away to some resting place on Short and Dirty Ridge to the southwest.

I wondered if Kloochman had been a testing ground for other lads. I wondered if others had met on her walls the challenge of life and death. I knew now what a boy could not know, that fear of death was the compound of all other fears. I knew that long years ago I had begun to shed on Kloochman's walls the great, overpowering fear.

Kloochman became that day a symbol of adversity and challenge— of the forces that have drawn from man his greatest spiritual and physical achievements.

Voltaire said that "History is the sound of heavy boots going upstairs and the rustle of satin slippers coming down." This country fortunately is still in the "heavy boots" stage of history. That is a stage of a nation's life that is often marked by the tramp of the boots of armies bent on conquest. It is usually evidenced by robust attitudes. But those attitudes can be expressed in ways less destructive than war. The growth of society, as Arnold Toynbee shows, is the successful response to challenge. The challenge may be the existence of some form of slavery, the poverty of a desert, the rigors of mountains, or a war. When the challenge is met and the goal achieved, there is a tremendous impetus for growth. A powerful energizing force is let loose that produces men and ideas that are dynamic.

This country is in that stage of growth. It is not bent on military conquest as were most of the countries which have sent armies across continents and oceans. In the realm of physical forces this nation has its true bent on the conquest of angry rivers, unproductive wastelands, erosion, the atom. In the realm of human relations it is bent on conquest of poverty and disease, high prices and scarcity, industrial injustice, racial prejudices, and the virus of political ideologies that would corrode and destroy the values of Western civilization.

These are powerful challenges. The fact that many of them are subtle and invisible makes them no less potent. A prejudice can be as ominous and threatening as a man with a bayonet. The issues that challenge this generation call for bold and daring action. They demand men who live dangerously—men who place adventure ahead of security, men who would trade the comfort of today for the chance of scaling a new peak of progress tomorrow. That activity demands men who fear neither men nor ideas. For it is only when fear is cast out that the full creative energies are unleashed. Then one is unhampered by hesitation and indecision. One's energies are not diverted to the making of some futile or hideous sacrifice at the altar of a sick ego.

When man knows how to live dangerously, he is not afraid to die. When he is not afraid to die, he is, strangely, free to live. When he is free to live, he can become bold, courageous, reliant. There are many ways to learn how to live dangerously. Men of the plains have had the experience in the trackless blizzards that sweep in from the north. Those who go out in boats from Gloucester have known it in another form. The mountains that traverse this country offer still a different way, and one that for many is the most exciting of all. The mountains can be reached in all seasons. They offer a fighting challenge to heart, soul, and mind, both in summer and winter. If throughout time the youth of the nation accept the challenge the mountains offer, they will help keep alive in our people the spirit of adventure. That spirit is a measure of the vitality of both nations and men. A people who climb the ridges and sleep under the stars in high mountain meadows, who enter the forest and scale the peaks, who explore glaciers and walk ridges buried deep in snow—these people will give their country some of the indomitable spirit of the mountains.

A light wind came up from the northwest. The sun slipped behind the jaggedness of Hogback Mountain far to the west. I started down

Kloochman so as to have the treacherous ledges behind and above me before darkness. I had not gone far when the evening star appeared. By the time I cleared the brush below the rock fields, this would be my only sure guide to the road where I had left my car.

I stood in the silence of the gathering night, charting my course by it. Then the words my father had spoken came back: "If I die it will be glory. If I live, it will be grace."

That was his evening star—a faith in a power greater than man. That was the faith of our fathers—a belief in a God who controlled man and the universe. It manifested itself in different ways to different people. It was written by scholars and learned men into dozens of different creeds. There were sects and schisms and religious disputes. But riding high above all such secular controversies was the faith in One who was the Creator, the Giver of Life, the Omnipotent.

Man's age-long effort has been to be free. Throughout time he has struggled against some form of tyranny that would enslave his mind or his body. So far in this century three epidemics of it have been let loose in the world.

We can keep our freedom through the increasing crises of history only if we are self-reliant enough to be free. We cannot become self-reliant if our dominant desire is to be safe and secure; under that influence we could never face and overcome the adversities of this competitive age. We will be self-reliant only if we have a real appetite for independence.

Dollars, guns, and all the wondrous products of science and the machine will not be enough: "This night thy soul shall be required of thee."

We need a faith—the faith of our fathers. We need a faith that dedicates us to something bigger and more important than ourselves or our possessions. We need a faith to which we commit our lives. We need a faith for which it would be glory to die. Only if we have such a faith are we free to live.

I dropped off the cliff, cleared the rocks below, and entered the dark woods.

Glossary

Ahtanum. A tributary of the Yakima coming in from the west; a ridge of hills; a town; the name of a small tribe amalgamated with the Yakimas. Its Indian meaning is "a stream which salmon ascend" or "the creek by the long mountain."

alpenstock. An iron-pointed staff used in mountain climbing.

andesite. A dark-grayish rock, containing plagioclase with augite, hornblende, and hypersthene.

Astor. The Astor party reached the mouth of the Columbia by ship on March 22, 1811 and built a settlement which they called Astoria. In February, 1812 the Astor overland party headed by Wilson Price Hunt arrived there. See Washington Irving, *Astoria.*

basalt. A dark gray or black igneous rock, containing plagioclase and augite. See Russell, *Volcanoes of North America;* Mendenhall, "Shorter Contributions to General Geology, 1925" (U.S. Geological Survey, 1926); "Water Supply and Irrigation Papers," H. Doc. No. 53, 57th Cong., 1st Session; "Water Supply and Irrigation Papers," No. 4 (U.S. Geological Survey, 1897).

bergschrund. The crevasse or series of crevasses at the upper end of a glacier, where the glacier breaks away from snow fields.

Bitterroot Mountains. A range in Montana named for the bitterroot or rock rose (*Lewisia rediviva*) which bears the name of the senior member of the famous expedition. The word *rediviva* means "that lives again." Roots that have lain for years in an herbarium will indeed grow again. The Bitterroot Valley and the Bitterroot National Forest were also named in its honor.

Blue Lake. A lake in the Wallowas where the snow when compressed has a bluish tinge. The same is true of the moss, etc., in the lake.

Blue Mountains. A range of mountains in eastern Oregon and eastern Washington that rises at its highest point over 9000 feet. It was so named because of its azure appearance.

Boise. The capital of Idaho. Its name originated in 1834 by a party of French Canadians. They had traversed the Idaho desert where there was no tree for a hundred miles or so. They camped on the mesa overlooking the site of the city of Boise and seeing below them a river lined with poplars and cottonwoods they exclaimed "Voyez les bois!"

Bonneville. Capt. Benjamin L. E. Bonneville led an expedition of over 100 men into the Oregon territory in 1832-35. Washington Irving recorded it in *The Adventures of Captain Bonneville.* Bonneville wintered one year on the Salmon River, which is on the Idaho side of the Snake River.

Borah, William E. He was elected to the United States Senate from Idaho in 1907, after being defeated for the office in 1903.

Bridger, Jim. In 1822 he formed a fur-trapping expedition that went to the headwaters of the Missouri. He was in the fur business for the next 20 years. He established a way-station, Fort Bridger, Wyoming, on the Oregon trail in 1843. He also served for years in the government service as a scout.

Bumble. A lake in the Wallowas near Cheval and bearing the childhood nickname of William O. Douglas, Jr. It was so named because he carried eastern brook trout to it and planted them there.

Bumping. We-not-put Wah-tum was the Indian name. The early maps show it as Plenham and then as Tannum. L. V. McWhorter, famous authority on the Yakimas, got the story of the naming of Bumping Lake and Bumping River from David Longmire, one of the first early settlers. McWhorter told it to Jack Nelson as follows: A few old-timers were camped on the lower reaches of the stream that flows out of the lake. At that point the wild and rugged surface of the river was startlingly perceptible as it came tumbling down from a higher plane than where they were standing. One of them commented on the broken character of the water and how it seemed to be "bumping" along.

Cascades. The range that extends from Canada, through Washington and Oregon, and into California to the gap south of Lassen Peak. David Douglas was apparently the first to use the name. The Wilkes Expedition in 1841 charted the mountains as the Cascade Range.

Cheval. The name of a lake in the Wallowas. It was so named as a result of a hilarious story Gabrielson told Lewis Carpenter of the Forest Service one night when they were camped there. The story concerned the difficulty an American doughboy had in France in talking to a Frenchman about a horse.

Coast Range. A low range of hills running from Washington to California between the Cascades and the Pacific Ocean.

Columbia River. It was also called the Oregon by Jonathan Carver in 1766-67. Capt. Robert Gray called it the Columbia after his ship. He crossed its bar on May 11, 1792. The Indians called it Shoca-tilcum (Chocka-lilum) meaning "water friend" or "friendly water."

Cowiche. (Tquiwitass) a ridge of hills; a creek flowing into the Naches; the valley through which the creek runs; a town. It means "foot log crossing."

cows. A generic term for roots of various species of *Lomatium.* Lewis and Clark first noticed them in eastern Washington on May 4, 1806. Clark called it "a white meley root which is very fine in soup after being dried and pounded." The plants of *Lomatium* are highly palatable to sheep and cattle.

crampons. Metal clamps that are laced on shoes to increase footing on snow and ice.

Cretaceous. A period of geologic time in the Mesozoic era.

crevasse. A fissure in a glacier formed when the ice passes over irregularities in a valley or on a mountain slope so as to produce a tension on the upper surface of the ice, causing it to crack.

Deschutes. A river, county, and town. Its derivation was French, "river of the falls." Lewis and Clark called it "Clark's river."

Diamond. A lake in the Wallowas so named because it was stocked with trout by a sheepherder of that name.

Douglas, David. A British botanist who visited the Pacific Northwest in 1830 and again in 1832 and 1833, making a botanical field research. He reached as far east as the Blue Mountains of eastern Washington and Oregon. Most of his field research was in the Cascades south of the Columbia. As a result of his research he introduced 215 plants. See Harvey, *Douglas of the Fir.*

Eagle Cap. The peak in the center of the Wallowas, so named because when this range was called in early years the Eagle Mountains it was supposed to top all other elevations. It is 9675 feet high.

Eocene. A subdivision of the Tertiary period and dating about 53,000,000 years ago.

Glacial. See Pleistocene.

Grande Ronde. A valley in eastern Oregon and the river that drains it. The river is a tributary of the Imnaha. The valley and river got their name from the fact that the valley is a large, rounded one hemmed in by hills. The river was called the Welleweah by Lewis and Clark.

granitic rock. The granitic rock of the Wallowas is quartz diorite and granodiorite, composed of sodic andesite, quartz, biotite, muscovite, augite, ilmenite, mica, hornblende, orthoclase, titanite.

Hart Mountain. A mountain in southern Oregon. It has been variously spelled as Hartz, Hart, or Heart. Henry and Johnnie Wilson ran cattle in this region in the 1880's. Their brand was a heart. Stanley Jewett's research shows that the name "Heart" was thus given to the ranch and various points in the vicinity. Usage has changed the spelling.

Hawkins Pass. A pass in the Wallowas named for Albert Hawkins, an enthusiastic mountaineer and one who deeply loved the Wallowas. He was on the staff of the Portland Oregonian for years and died May 8, 1930.

Hell's Canyon. A gorge on the Snake which is the deepest on the continent—7900 feet. It begins 90 miles south of Lewiston, Idaho, and ends at Johnson's Bar. The drop of the Snake in Hell's Canyon is 12½ feet per mile. See Bailey, *Hell's Canyon*.

Hobo Lake. A lake in the Wallowas so named because Bob Bowman found an unknown hobo camped there. It is one of the highest lakes in the Wallowas, lying at 8300 feet.

Hoh. The name of a river rising on Mount Olympus of the Olympic Range and flowing west into the Pacific. It was the name of a band of Quillayute Indians.

Huckleberries. There are no true huckleberries in the Cascades or Wallowas. They are species of a genus (*Vaccinium*) of blueberries. The chief species are the dwarf blueberry (*V. cespitosum*), the big whortleberry (*V. membranaceum*), and the grouse whortleberry (*V. scoparium*).

Idaho. From a Nez Perce word Ee-da-how meaning "light on the mountains."

Imnaha. A river and a town. The river, a tributary of the Snake, was called Innahar by Lewis and Clark. Its Indian meaning was "the land ruled over by a chief called Imna."

John Day. A town and river in eastern Oregon named for John Day, a Virginia backwoodsman, who was a member of the Astor overland party.

John Henry. A lake in the Wallowas named for John Henry Wilson who worked a mine near by.

Johnson, Hiram. He was elected Governor of California in 1910, ran with Theodore Roosevelt on the Bull Moose ticket in 1912, re-elected Governor in 1914, and elected to the United States Senate in 1917.

Chief Joseph. Famous chief of the Nez Perce tribe whose ancestral home was the Wallowa Mountains. These Indians wintered on the Imnaha. The story of Chief Joseph has been told by Chester A. Fee in *Chief Joseph: a Biography of a Great Indian* (1936) and Helen A. Howard in *War Chief Joseph* (1941).

Kautz Glacier. A glacier on Mount Rainier named for Lt. X. V. Kautz who tried to climb Rainier in 1857, who lost his hat and 14 pounds of weight in the process, and did not recover for many weeks.

king salmon or chinook salmon is the most prized of Pacific Coast salmon.

Kittitas. The valley north of Yakima, a county, and a town. Its Indian meaning was "place of white chalk" or "clay gravel valley."

Klickitat. The name of an Indian tribe, the Indian name for a mountain (Mount Adams), a river which flows into the Columbia, a county, glacier, and pass. Its Indian meaning is "galloping horse" or sometimes "beyond."

La Grande. A leading city of eastern Oregon located in the famous Grande Ronde Valley.

Lapover. The name of Roy Schaeffer's place on the Lostine River. It was so named when Bob Bowman owned the property. He had working for him a chap who came from a town in Arkansas that lapped over into Texas. The man talked about the lapover so much that Bob Bowman decided it should be the name of the man's new home in the Wallowas. Cf. McArthur, *Oregon Geographic Names.* There is also a Lapover Lake in the Wallowas.

Lewis and Clark. This expedition, promoted by Thomas Jefferson and authorized by Congress, was headed by Capt. Meriwether Lewis and Capt. William Clark. There were 45 in the party that left St. Louis on May 14, 1804. They reached the mouth of the Columbia River on November 18, 1805, where they wintered. They started east on March 23, 1806 and reached St. Louis September 23, 1806. Only one man died on the trip and he in the early stages of it. They described in their journals around 500 biological specimens which were almost equally divided between the botanical and the zoological. They found many new species in each group, some of whom were named after them. The story of the expedition has been told in prose that is close to poetry by Peattie in *Forward the Nation.* Their discoveries are carefully catalogued by Criswell in *Lewis and Clark: Linguistic Pioneers.* And see Coues, *Lewis and Clark Expedition,* particularly Vol. 3.

Lewis Lake. The pleistocene lake that lay on the Great Plain of the Columbia. It was named by Lt. T. W. Symons for Capt. Meriwether Lewis.

lichen. "Find a symbiosis in which the partners have become indeed united, indissoluble, two organisms made one flesh having a form and a life history peculiar to their combined self, and you have come upon the creation of life in a new biologic dimension. You have come to the lichens. Those minutely forested maps painted upon the boulders in my cactus garden, those waving beards that hang upon the live-oaks in the valley ranges, are dual plants; half of any lichen is an alga, commonly a Blue-Green such as one sees living free on the north side of trees in a wet wood, occasionally a true Green, rarely and astonishingly a Red. The other partner is a fungus, usually one of the cup fungi; hence the tiny colored elf-cups so common in the fruiting of a lichen. . . . The alga, in the lichen form, does the green business, the photosynthesis; the fungus provides capital of water, preventing the other from drying out." Peattie, *Flowering Earth.*

Lostine. A river and a town. It was named by an early settler for Lostine, Kansas.

Malheur. A river, lake, and county in Oregon. The river sometimes disappears underground into huge rock caverns. In one of these caverns, French trappers of the Hudson Bay Company once hid their supplies. Peter Skene Ogden wrote in his *Journals* that the river was called "unfortunate" because of "goods and furs, hid here, discovered and stolen by the natives."

Matterhorn. A rugged peak in the Wallowas which was named after the one in the Swiss Alps. It is 10,004 feet high.

Minam. A town, lake, river, and meadow. The river flows into the Wallowa at the town which is shortly above where the Wallowa flows into the Grande Ronde. It derived from an Indian word E-mi-ne-wah meaning a valley where a plant that the Indians used for food grew.

Miocene. A subdivision of the Tertiary period and dating about 33,000,000 years ago.

Moraine. A rock debris carried by glacial ice. When it gathers on the sides of the glacier, it is called a lateral moraine. When it gathers at the bottom of the glacier, it is called a terminal moraine.

Naches. A river flowing into the Yakima from the west; the name of a town located on that river; a pass over the Cascades; and a gap. In Indian language it means "one water" or "good or pure water" or "a big flow of water."

Nelson pack. The frame is principally composed of two parallel pieces of wood that run lengthwise of the body and is covered with canvas forming a large pocket.

Norwegian pack. An oblong-shaped pack on a light metal frame so designed as to place the weight just above the hips.

pack basket. A strong reed basket with shoulder straps.

parasitic cones. Volcanoes that develop on the sides of older volcanoes.

Pasco. A town in Washington on the Columbia near the mouth of the Snake. Its meaning is probably "flattest and hottest place."

Pendleton. A town in Oregon, famous for for its annual Round-up. It was named for George Hunt Pendleton, democratic candidate for President in 1864.

Pinchot, Gifford. Chief of the Forest Service 1898 to 1910; Governor of Pennsylvania 1923 to 1927 and from 1931 to 1935.

Pleistocene. This is the glacial period of geologic time, dating back about 1,700,000 years.

Pliocene. A subdivision of the Tertiary period and dating about 15,000,-000 years ago.

Prosser. A town in the Lower Yakima Valley named for William F. Prosser, an early homesteader.

pyroclastic rock. This is rock that has been broken up by volcanic processes. It may be a molten lava or rock that has been hurled from volcanoes. The latter includes dustlike particles known as volcanic ash, coarser fragments called cinders, and rounded fragments called volcanic bombs.

Quillayute. A river rising in the Olympic Range and flowing west into the Pacific. It was the name of an Indian tribe.

Quinault. A river rising in the Olympic Range and flowing west into the Pacific. It was the name of an Indian tribe.

rosin. The sap of conifers, which becomes firm and brittle after long exposure to the air.

rucksack. A light, canvas bag with shoulder straps and outside pockets.

run. A path or trail made by deer, elk, antelope, or goats.

Sacajawea. A peak in the Wallowas named after the famous woman of the Shoshones who was a guide to Lewis and Clark. It is 10,033 feet high.

Selah. A valley to the northwest of Yakima; also the gap to the north of the town of Yakima. Its Indian meaning was "still water" or "smooth water" or "water that moves slowly."

seracs. Blocks into which a glacier breaks on steep slopes.

Siskiyou Mountains. They are part of the Klamath Mountains that lie between the Coast Range and the Cascades in southwestern Oregon and northwestern California. Its Indian meaning was "a bob-tailed horse." The range took its name from the loss of a bob-tailed horse there in 1828 by an officer of the Hudson Bay Company during a snowstorm.

Snake. A winding, serpentine river that rises in Wyoming and flows into the Columbia near Pasco, Washington. It was called by early Canadian voyageurs the accursed, mad river. It was called Lewis River by Lewis and Clark. It was named after the Snake Indians (Shoshones).

snowbrush (Ceanothus velutinus). Discovered and named botanically by David Douglas (the eponym of the Pacific Northwest's most important tree, the Douglas fir) on high hills near the headwaters of the Columbia in what is now Stevens County, Washington. Douglas introduced it into the British Isles. It's a large genus, McMinn having classified 55 species. It is not a conserver of water. Copeland has shown that at an altitude of a mile in the Sierra it gives off water at a rate representing a loss of two feet per unit of leaf area during the active season.

Steamboat. A lake in the Wallowas, so named because a small island in the lake is shaped like a steamboat.

Steens Mountain. This mountain in southeast Oregon was named for Major Enoch Steens who drove a band of Snake Indians over it in 1860.

Tertiary. A period of geologic time in the Cenozoic era. It was in the age of mammals and embraces the Eocene, Oligocene, Miocene, and Pliocene.

Tieton. A river that is a tributary of the Naches; a town, basin, peak, and storage dam and reservoir. Its Indian meaning was "little river" or "milky water."

Tombstone. A lake in the Wallowas so named because a granite shaft stands at one end of it. See McArthur, *Oregon Geographic Names.*

Toppenish. A town in the Lower Yakima Valley; an Indian agency. Its Indian meaning was people of the trail coming from the foot of the hill or land coming down or sloping.

Umatilla. An Indian tribe; a town in Oregon; a river. In Indian language it meant "gathering of the sand." It is also said to mean "lots of rocks." In the Lewis and Clark Journals it is spelled Youmalolam.

Union Gap. The gap to the south of the town of Yakima; a town. In Indian language it is *Pahotecute* meaning "putting two heads together."

Volcanic Ash. See Pyroclastic Rock.

Waiilatpu. The site of the mission established by Marcus Whitman. It is near Walla Walla, Washington. Its Indian meaning was "the place of rye grass."

Walla Walla. The name of an Indian tribe; a river; a valley; a city in Washington. In Indian language Walla meant "running water." Repetition of a word diminutized it. So Walla Walla meant "a small rapid river." The "Wallah-Wallah" Indians were the kindliest that Lewis and Clark met on their expedition.

Wallowa. A county, town, and river. Its Indian meaning was "fish trap."

Wallowa Mountains. These mountains lie in the northeast corner of Oregon close to the Idaho and Washington lines. They are roughly in the form of a wagon wheel, Eagle Cap being the hub and the various ridges running to it as spokes. They are often referred to as the Blue Mountains but are in fact separate from them.

Wapato. A town in the Lower Yakima Valley, an irrigation project, a diversion dam, and canal. Its Indian meaning was "potato," a tuber the size of a small egg. The Indians would often roast it in coals and, as Lewis and Clark noted, eat it skin and all. Ben Hur Lampman in *The Coming of the Pond Fishes* gives the best account of it. The ponds of the Pacific Northwest used to contain "great water gardens of Wapato" with their arrow-shaped leaves. But the carp, which were introduced into the west side ponds, have grubbed most of it out and there is little left now. The Indian squaws gathered the Wapato by wading in the water and loosening the tubers with their feet. The tubers, when loosened, floated to the surface. The squaws kept a canoe alongside into which they placed the tubers. Lampman says that "when boiled, the tuber is starchy and palatable, having a flavor somewhat like that of green corn."

Wenas. A town, a valley, a tributary of the Yakima flowing in from the northwest. Its Indian meaning was "coming in" or "last camping." The creek was first charted by Capt. George B. McClellan in 1853.

Whitman, Marcus. A medical missionary from New York who with his wife, Narcissa Prentiss, founded in 1836 a mission at Waiilatpu in the Walla Walla Valley. They were murdered by Cayuse Indians in 1847.

Wilson Basin. A meadow in the Wallowas named for John Henry Wilson who worked a mine on its eastern edge.

Yakima. The name of a valley, river, peak, city, county in Washington, and an Indian tribe.

In the early chronicles the name was sometimes spelled Yookooman, Eyakama, Yacamah, or Yakama. There is uncertainty as to the meaning of the name. It has been translated as lake water, black bear, people of the narrow river, runaway, big belly, growing family, tribe expansion. The last two were endorsed by L. V. McWhorter, adopted member of the tribe and their doughty champion through the years. His translation signifies that the Yakimas were a loose confederation of many tribes, or perhaps more accurately, the product of many mergers.

But Professor Lyman in his History of the Yakima Valley suggests that the word is derived from Neaneeya-keema which means "we meet and part" or "neutrality." The origin of the word, he suggests, was the result of a meeting at Union Gap of the Spokanes, a neighboring tribe to the east, and the Yakimas. The Yakima River was called the Tapetett or Tapteel when Lewis and Clark came through the Columbia River basin in 1805. And Professor Lyman suggests that that was the original name of the tribe, the word Yakima being of fairly recent origin, though in use when the first settlers arrived.

The first white men to see the Yakimas were Lewis and Clark in 1805. They met the branch of the Yakimas called the Chimnapum who lived near the mouth of the river. Their Journals relate that those Indians "live in a State of comparitive happiness"; the men take a greater share of the work burden of the squaws than is common among Indians and are "content with one wife." They also "respect the aged with veneration." Lewis and Clark described their lodges: They were 15 to 60 feet in length supported by six-foot poles and covered with large mats made of rushes. At the top of the walls are spaces 12 to 15 inches wide left for admission of light and the escape of smoke from the fires that are built in the middle of the house. Clark noted that the roofs "are nearly flat, which proves to me that rains are not common in the open Countrey."